THE wallFLOWER
YAMATONADESHIKO SHICHIHENGE

Volume 32

Tomoko Hayakawa

Translated and adapted by
Christine Dashiell

Lettered by
Sara Linsley

KC KODANSHA COMICS

Contents

WALLFLOWER'S BEAUTIFUL (?) CAST OF CHARACTERS

SUNAKO IS A DARK LONER WHO LOVES HORROR MOVIES. WHEN HER AUNT, THE LANDLADY OF A BOARDING HOUSE, LEAVES TOWN WITH HER BOYFRIEND, SUNAKO IS FORCED TO LIVE WITH FOUR HANDSOME GUYS. SUNAKO'S AUNT MAKES A DEAL WITH THE BOYS, WHICH CAUSES NOTHING BUT HEADACHES FOR SUNAKO: "MAKE SUNAKO INTO A LADY, AND YOU CAN LIVE RENT-FREE FOR THREE YEARS."

BUT THE ROAD TO BECOMING A LADY ISN'T EASY, AS SHE SEEMS TO BE BARRELING DOWN THE OTHER DIRECTION!

IN THE LAST VOLUME, SUNAKO LENT A HELPING HAND TO KYŌHEI AFTER HE'D BEEN TURNED INTO AN ICE MAN, AND THE BOND BETWEEN THE TWO DEEPENED... ♡

OR SO IT SEEMED! ONLY THEIR FEELINGS OF FRIENDSHIP DEEPENED, BUT THEY'RE MAKING AS LITTLE PROGRESS AS EVER IN THE ROMANCE DEPARTMENT.

THESE BEAUTIFUL BOYS ARE HOPING TO TURN THEIR "FRIEND" INTO A "LADY," BUT THINGS DON'T LOOK PROMISING AT ALL!

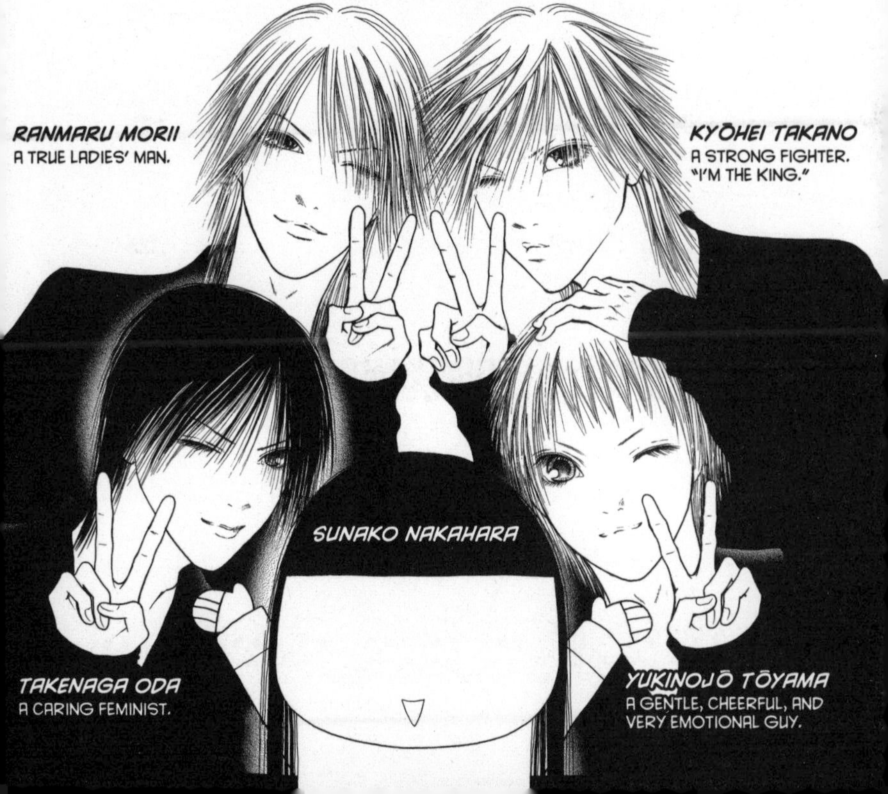
RANMARU MORII
A TRUE LADIES' MAN.
KYŌHEI TAKANO
A STRONG FIGHTER. "I'M THE KING."
SUNAKO NAKAHARA
TAKENAGA ODA
A CARING FEMINIST.
YUKINOJŌ TŌYAMA
A GENTLE, CHEERFUL, AND VERY EMOTIONAL GUY.

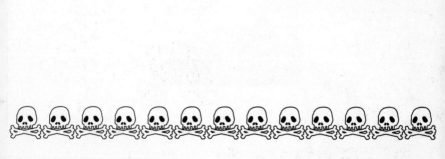

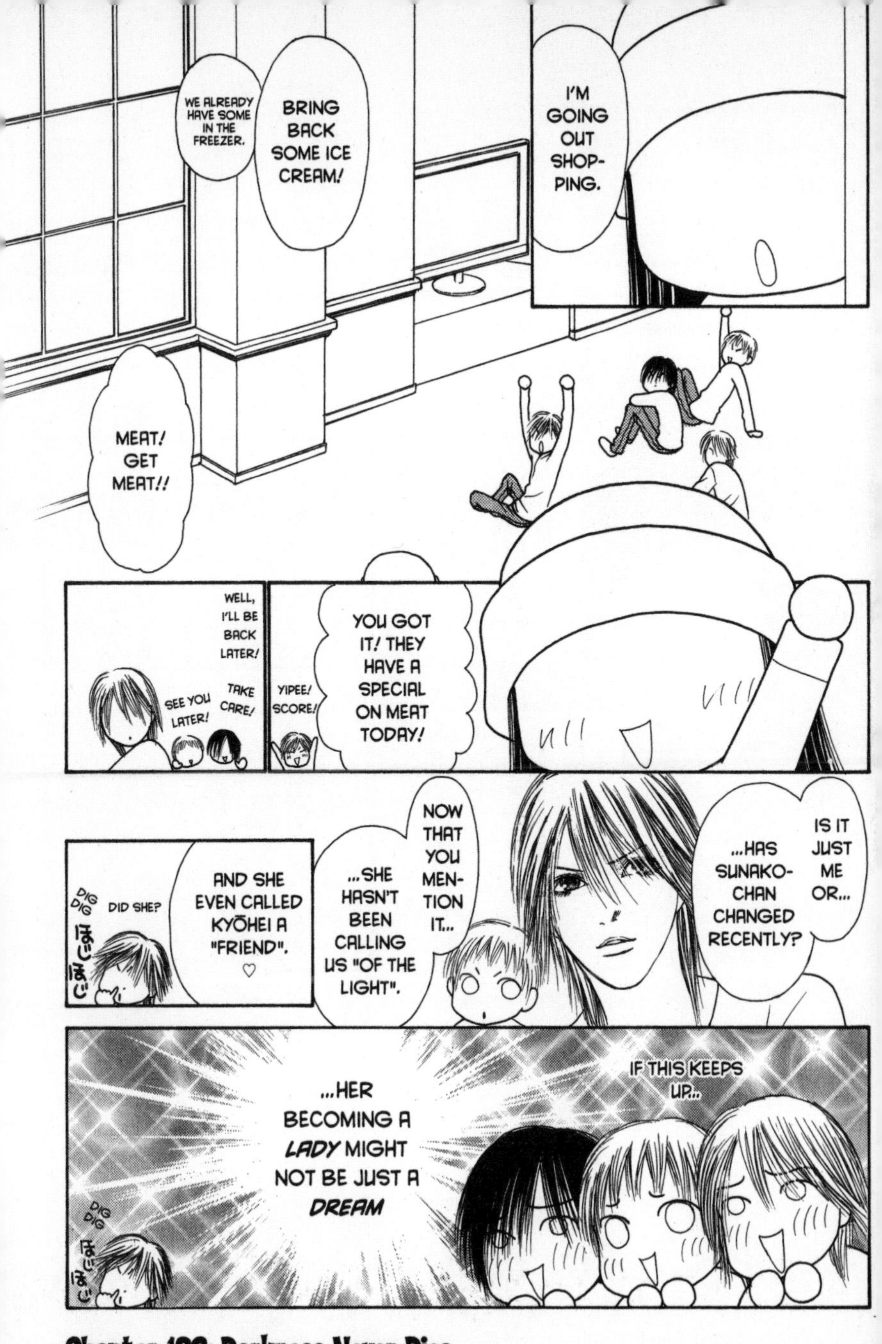
I'M GOING OUT SHOP-PING.
BRING BACK SOME ICE CREAM!
WE ALREADY HAVE SOME IN THE FREEZER.
MEAT! GET MEAT!!
YOU GOT IT! THEY HAVE A SPECIAL ON MEAT TODAY!
YIPEE! SCORE!
WELL, I'LL BE BACK LATER!
TAKE CARE!
SEE YOU LATER!
IS IT JUST ME OR...
...HAS SUNAKO-CHAN CHANGED RECENTLY?
NOW THAT YOU MEN-TION IT...
...SHE HASN'T BEEN CALLING US "OF THE LIGHT".
AND SHE EVEN CALLED KYŌHEI A "FRIEND". ♡
DID SHE?
DIG DIG
ほじほじ
IF THIS KEEPS UP...
...HER BECOMING A LADY MIGHT NOT BE JUST A DREAM
DIG DIG
ほじほじ

Chapter 128: Darkness Never Dies

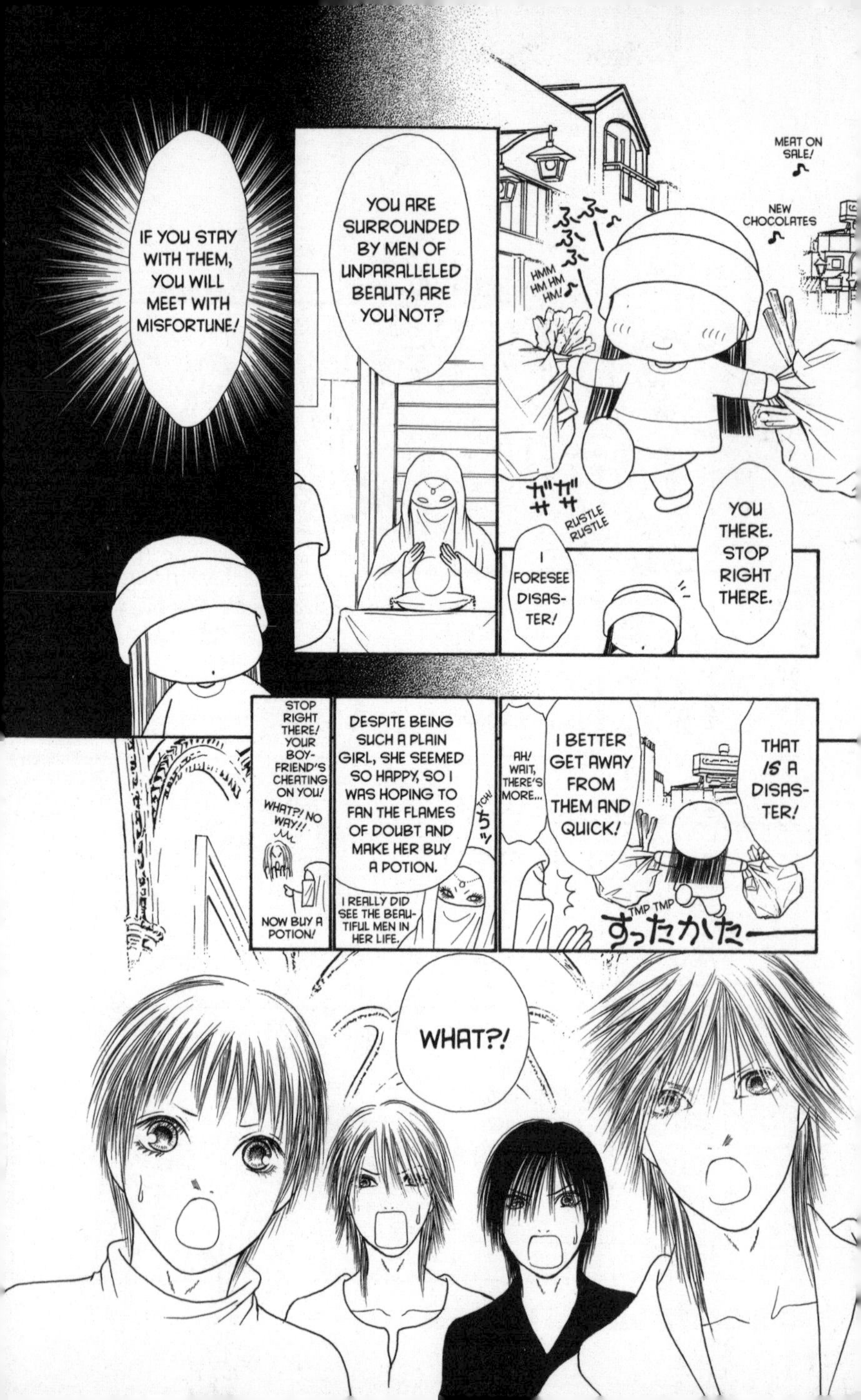

MEAT ON SALE! ♪
NEW CHOCOLATES ♪
ふ～ふ～ふ～ふ～♪
HMM HM HM HM! ♪
ガサガサ
RUSTLE RUSTLE
YOU THERE. STOP RIGHT THERE.
I FORESEE DISASTER!
YOU ARE SURROUNDED BY MEN OF UNPARALLELED BEAUTY, ARE YOU NOT?
IF YOU STAY WITH THEM, YOU WILL MEET WITH MISFORTUNE!
THAT *IS* A DISASTER!
I BETTER GET AWAY FROM THEM AND QUICK!
AH! WAIT, THERE'S MORE...
すったかたー
TMP TMP
DESPITE BEING SUCH A PLAIN GIRL, SHE SEEMED SO HAPPY, SO I WAS HOPING TO FAN THE FLAMES OF DOUBT AND MAKE HER BUY A POTION.
ちッ
TCH!
I REALLY DID SEE THE BEAUTIFUL MEN IN HER LIFE.
STOP RIGHT THERE! YOUR BOYFRIEND'S CHEATING ON YOU!
WHAT?! NO WAY!!
NOW BUY A POTION!
WHAT?!

Chapter 128: Darkness Never Dies

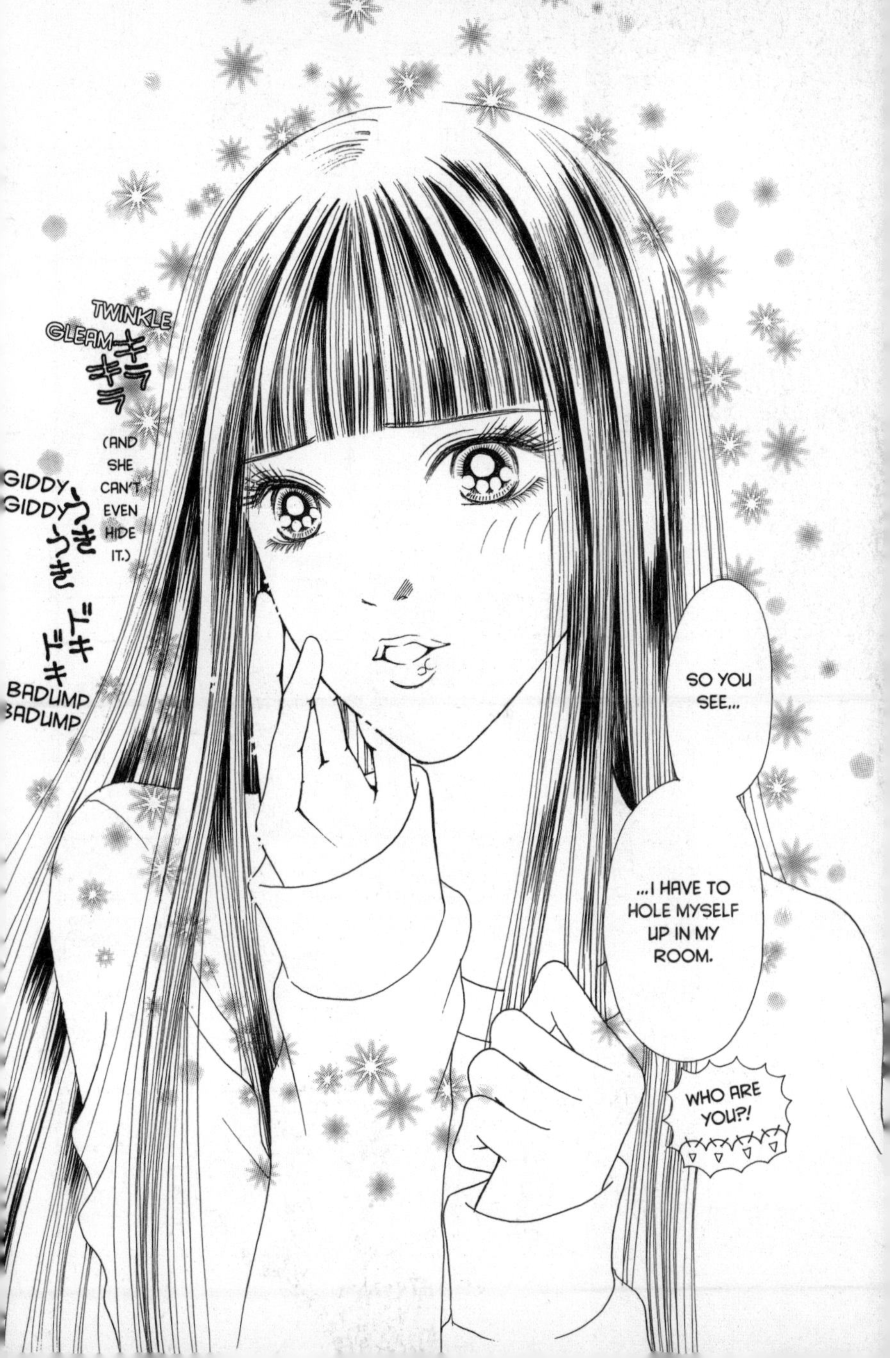

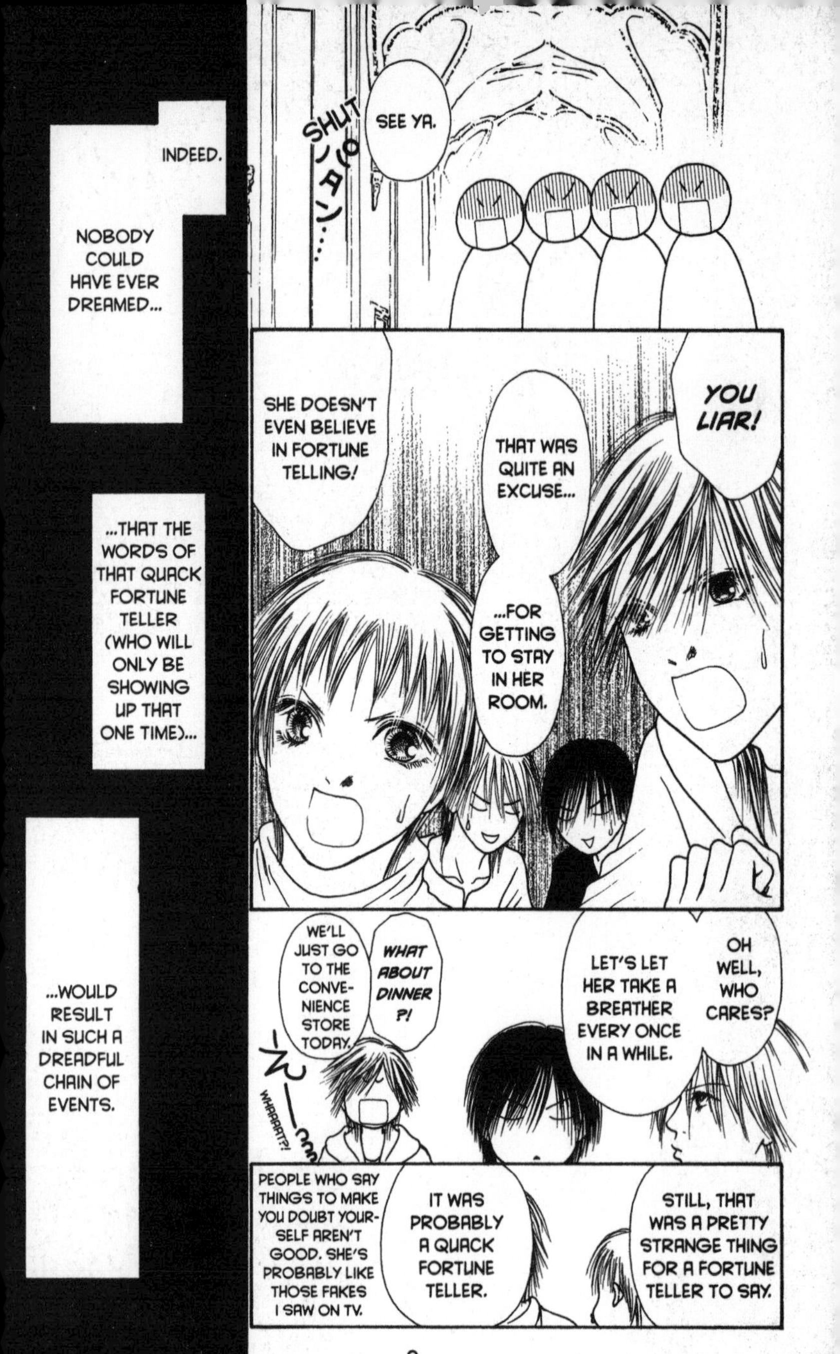
SEE YA.
SHUT
バタン…
YOU LIAR!
THAT WAS QUITE AN EXCUSE...
...FOR GETTING TO STAY IN HER ROOM.
SHE DOESN'T EVEN BELIEVE IN FORTUNE TELLING!
OH WELL, WHO CARES?
LET'S LET HER TAKE A BREATHER EVERY ONCE IN A WHILE.
WHAT ABOUT DINNER?!
WE'LL JUST GO TO THE CONVENIENCE STORE TODAY.
WHAAAAT?!
STILL, THAT WAS A PRETTY STRANGE THING FOR A FORTUNE TELLER TO SAY.
IT WAS PROBABLY A QUACK FORTUNE TELLER.
PEOPLE WHO SAY THINGS TO MAKE YOU DOUBT YOURSELF AREN'T GOOD. SHE'S PROBABLY LIKE THOSE FAKES I SAW ON TV.
INDEED.
NOBODY COULD HAVE EVER DREAMED...
...THAT THE WORDS OF THAT QUACK FORTUNE TELLER (WHO WILL ONLY BE SHOWING UP THAT ONE TIME)...
...WOULD RESULT IN SUCH A DREADFUL CHAIN OF EVENTS.

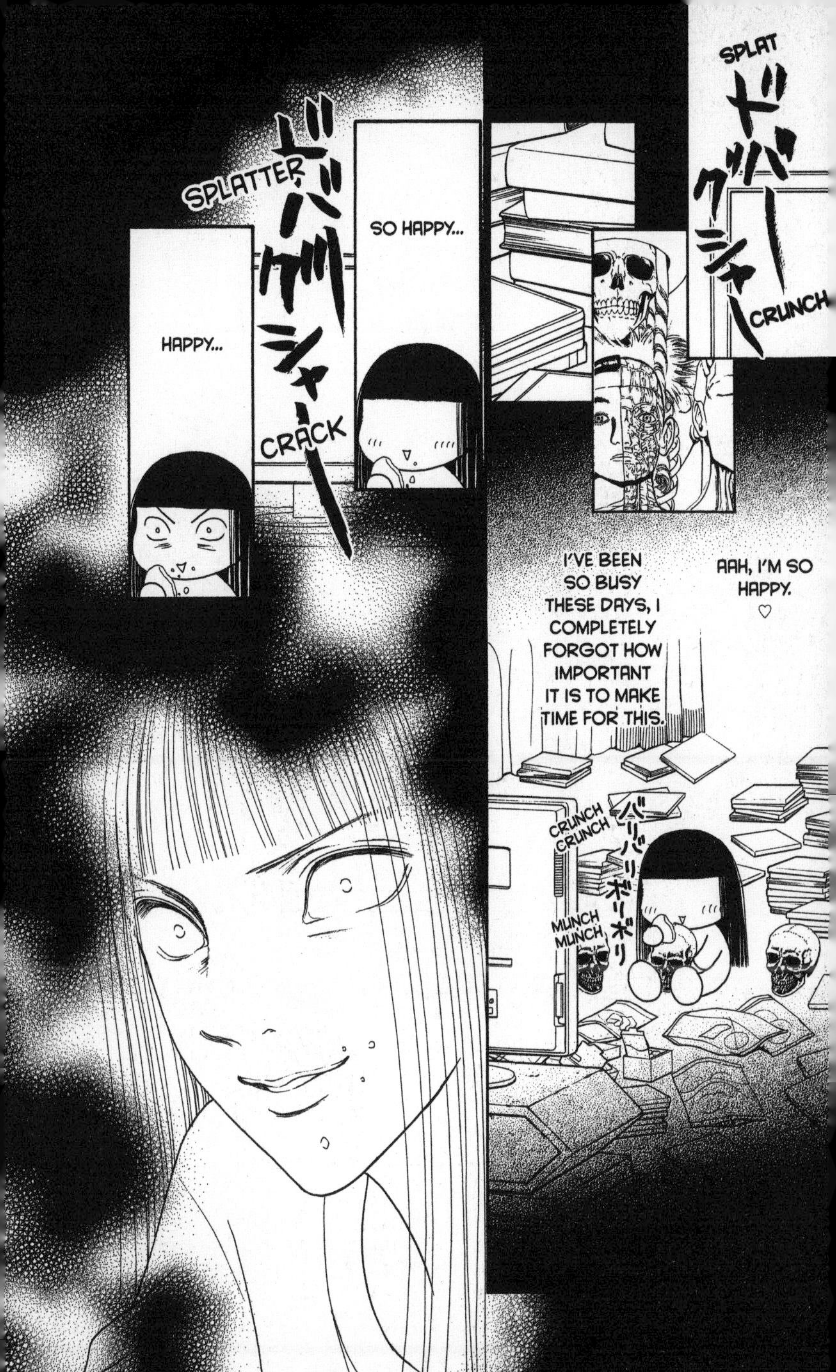
SPLAT
ドバーグシャー
CRUNCH
SO HAPPY...
SPLATTER
ズバグシャー
CRACK
HAPPY...
AAH, I'M SO HAPPY. ♡
I'VE BEEN SO BUSY THESE DAYS, I COMPLETELY FORGOT HOW IMPORTANT IT IS TO MAKE TIME FOR THIS.
CRUNCH CRUNCH
バリバリ
MUNCH MUNCH
ボリボリ

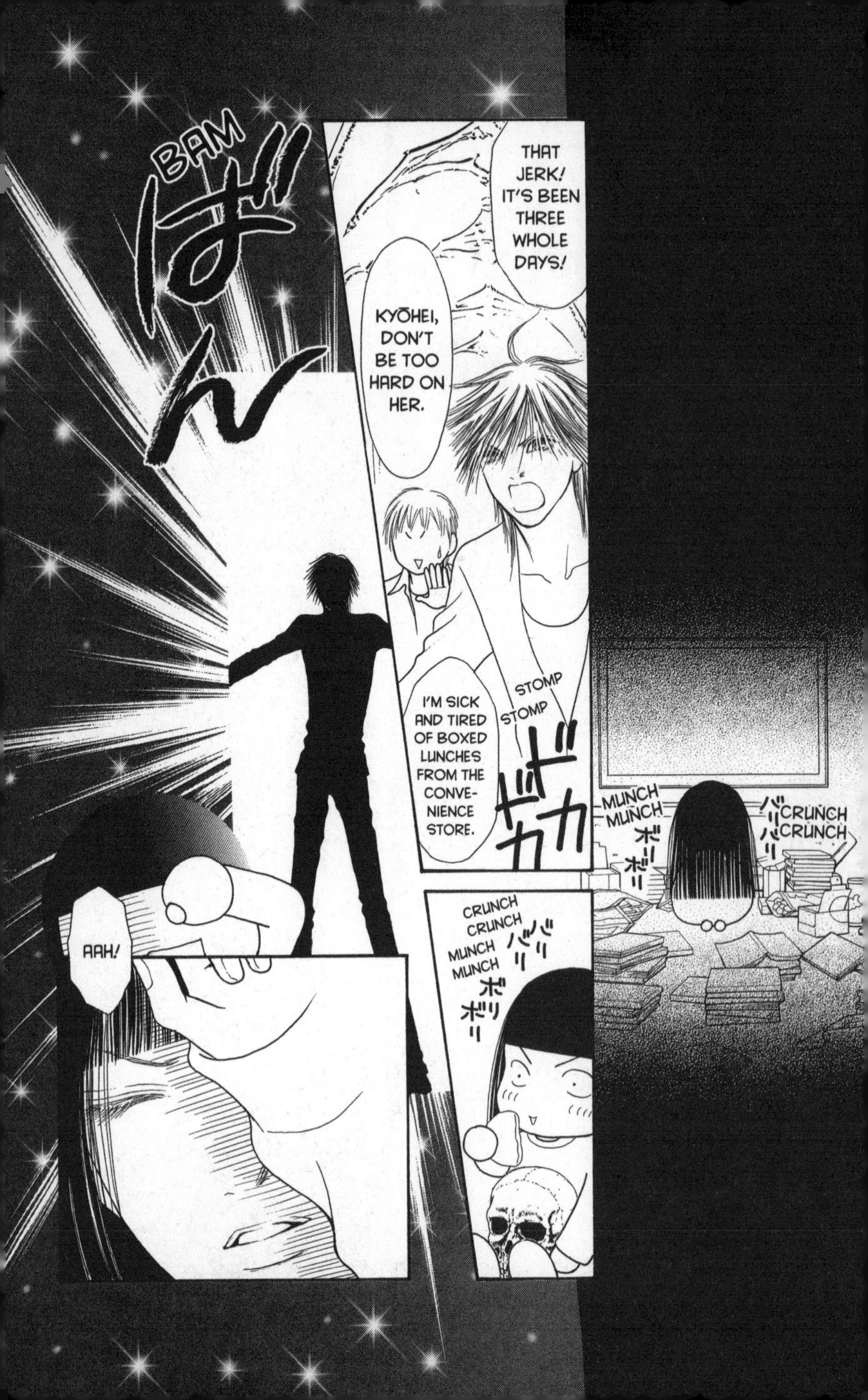
バリバリ
CRUNCH CRUNCH
ボリボリ
MUNCH MUNCH
THAT JERK! IT'S BEEN THREE WHOLE DAYS!
KYŌHEI, DON'T BE TOO HARD ON HER.
I'M SICK AND TIRED OF BOXED LUNCHES FROM THE CONVE-NIENCE STORE.
STOMP STOMP
ドカドカ
CRUNCH CRUNCH
バリバリ
MUNCH MUNCH
ボリボリ
ばん
BAM
AAH!

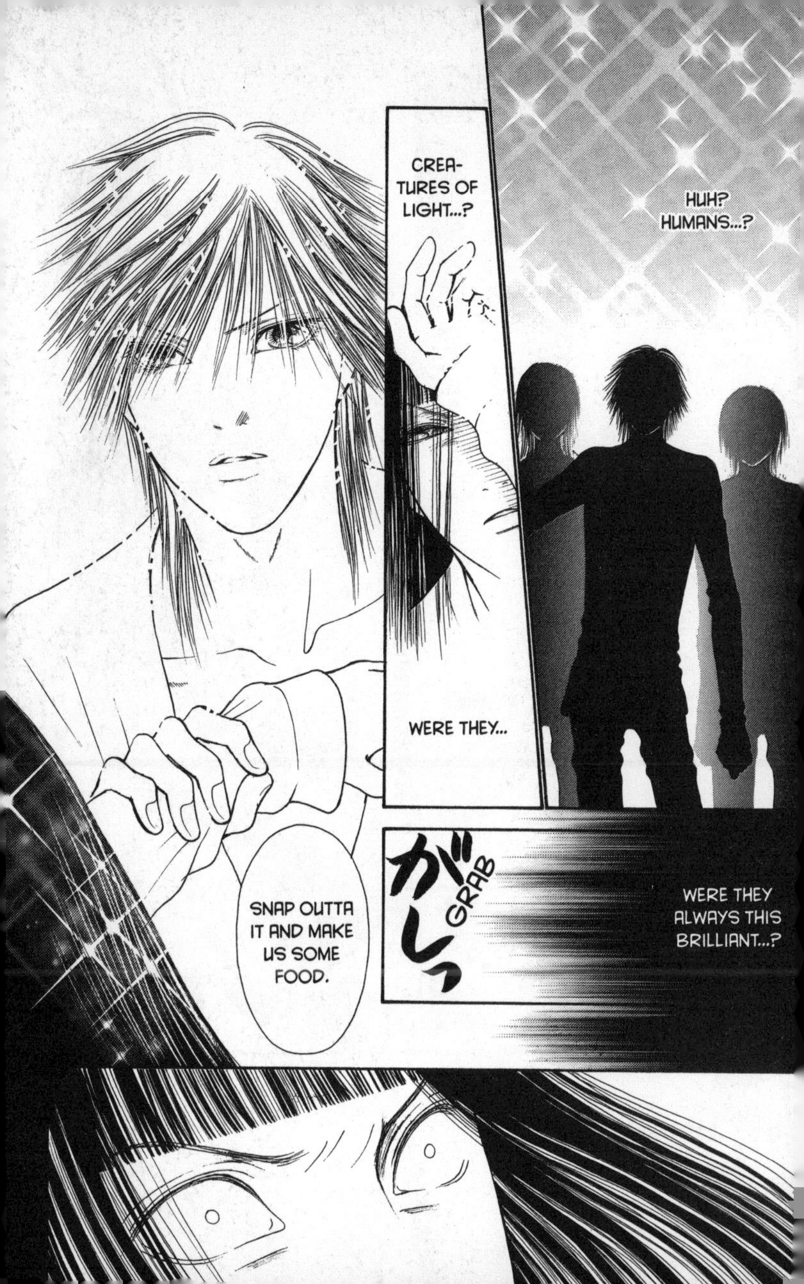
HUH? HUMANS...?
CREATURES OF LIGHT...?
WERE THEY...
WERE THEY ALWAYS THIS BRILLIANT...?
がしっ GRAB
SNAP OUTTA IT AND MAKE US SOME FOOD.

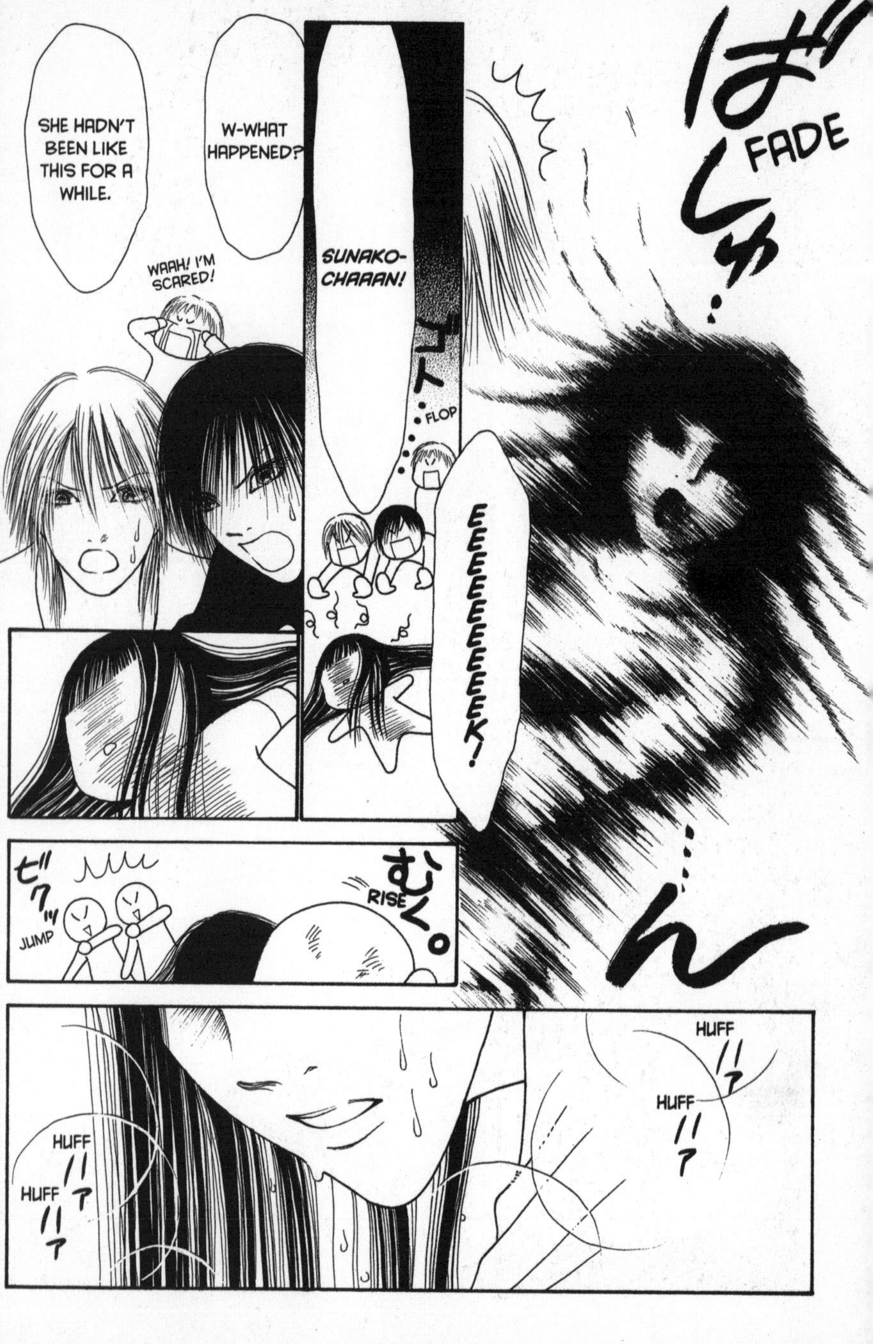
ばしゅ…
FADE
…ん
SUNAKO-CHAAAN!
ゴト…
FLOP
EEEEEEEEEEK!
W-WHAT HAPPENED?
SHE HADN'T BEEN LIKE THIS FOR A WHILE.
WAAH! I'M SCARED!
むく。
RISE
ビクッ
JUMP
HUFF
ハア
HUFF
ハア
HUFF
ハア
HUFF
ハア

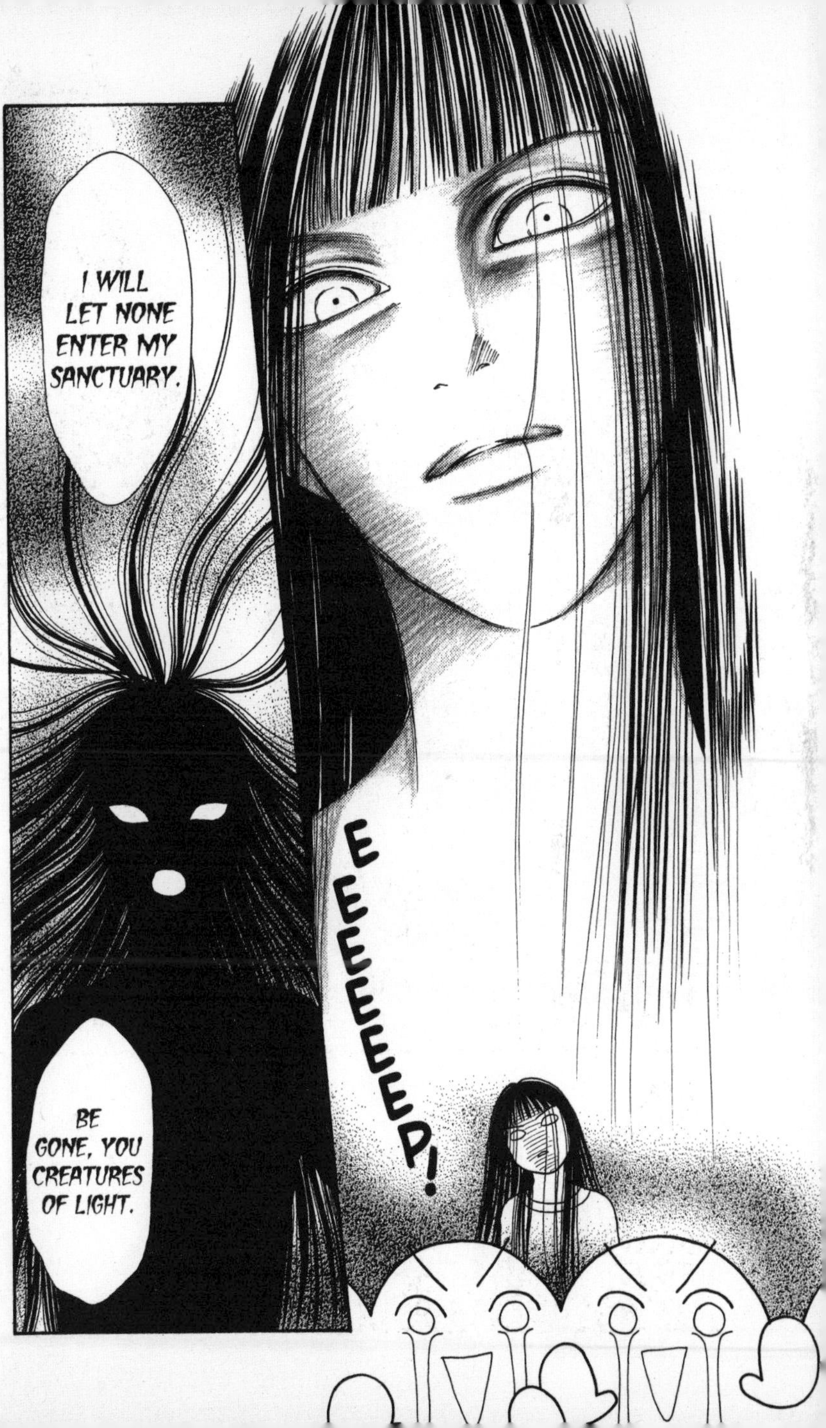
I WILL LET NONE ENTER MY SANCTUARY.
EEEEEEP!
BE GONE, YOU CREATURES OF LIGHT.

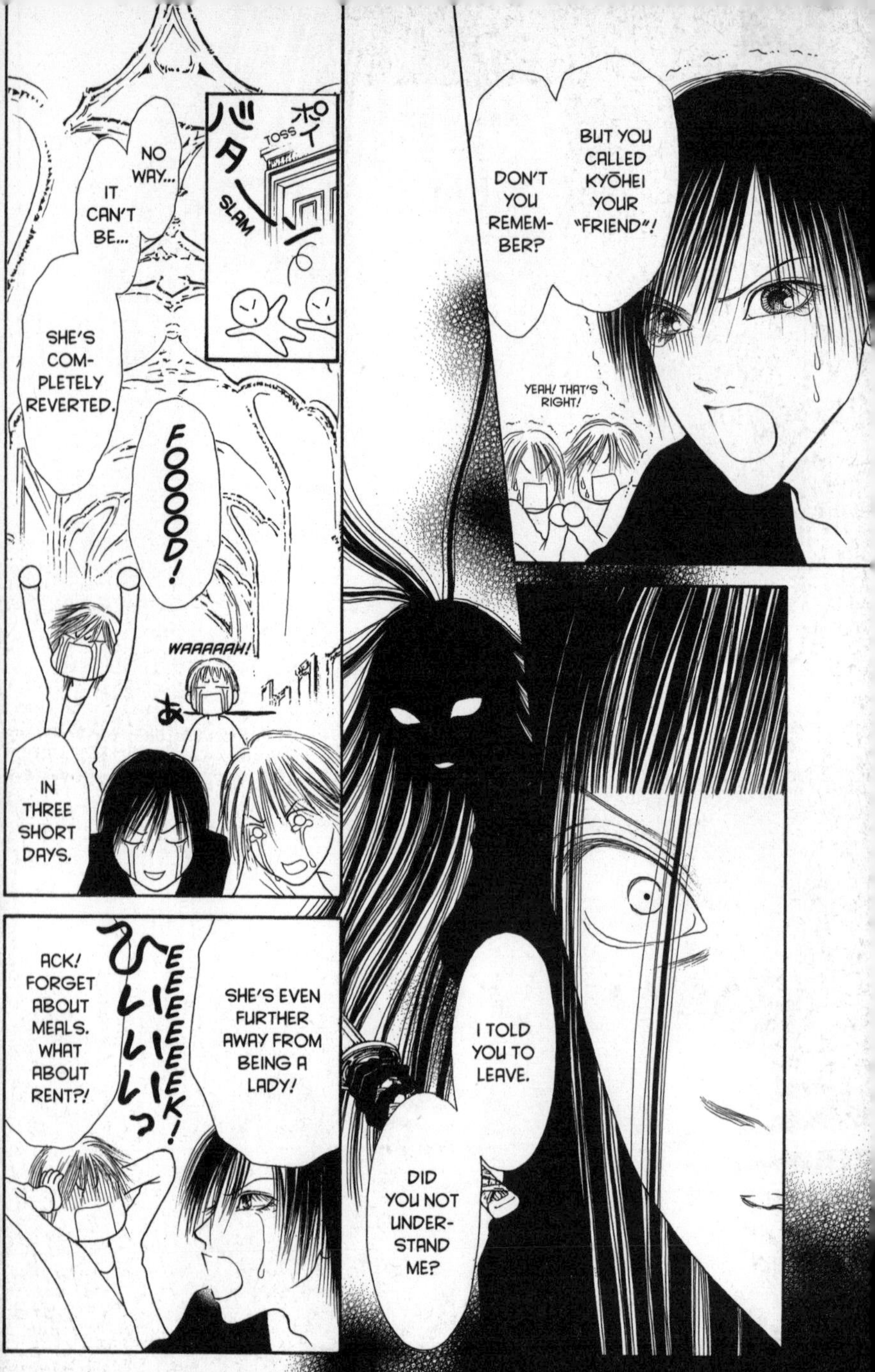
BUT YOU CALLED KYŌHEI YOUR "FRIEND"!
DON'T YOU REMEMBER?
YEAH! THAT'S RIGHT!
I TOLD YOU TO LEAVE.
DID YOU NOT UNDERSTAND ME?
ポイ
TOSS
バタン
SLAM
NO WAY... IT CAN'T BE...
SHE'S COMPLETELY REVERTED.
FOOOOOD!
WAAAAAH!
あ
IN THREE SHORT DAYS.
SHE'S EVEN FURTHER AWAY FROM BEING A LADY!
EEEEEEEK!
ひぃぃぃっ
ACK! FORGET ABOUT MEALS. WHAT ABOUT RENT?!

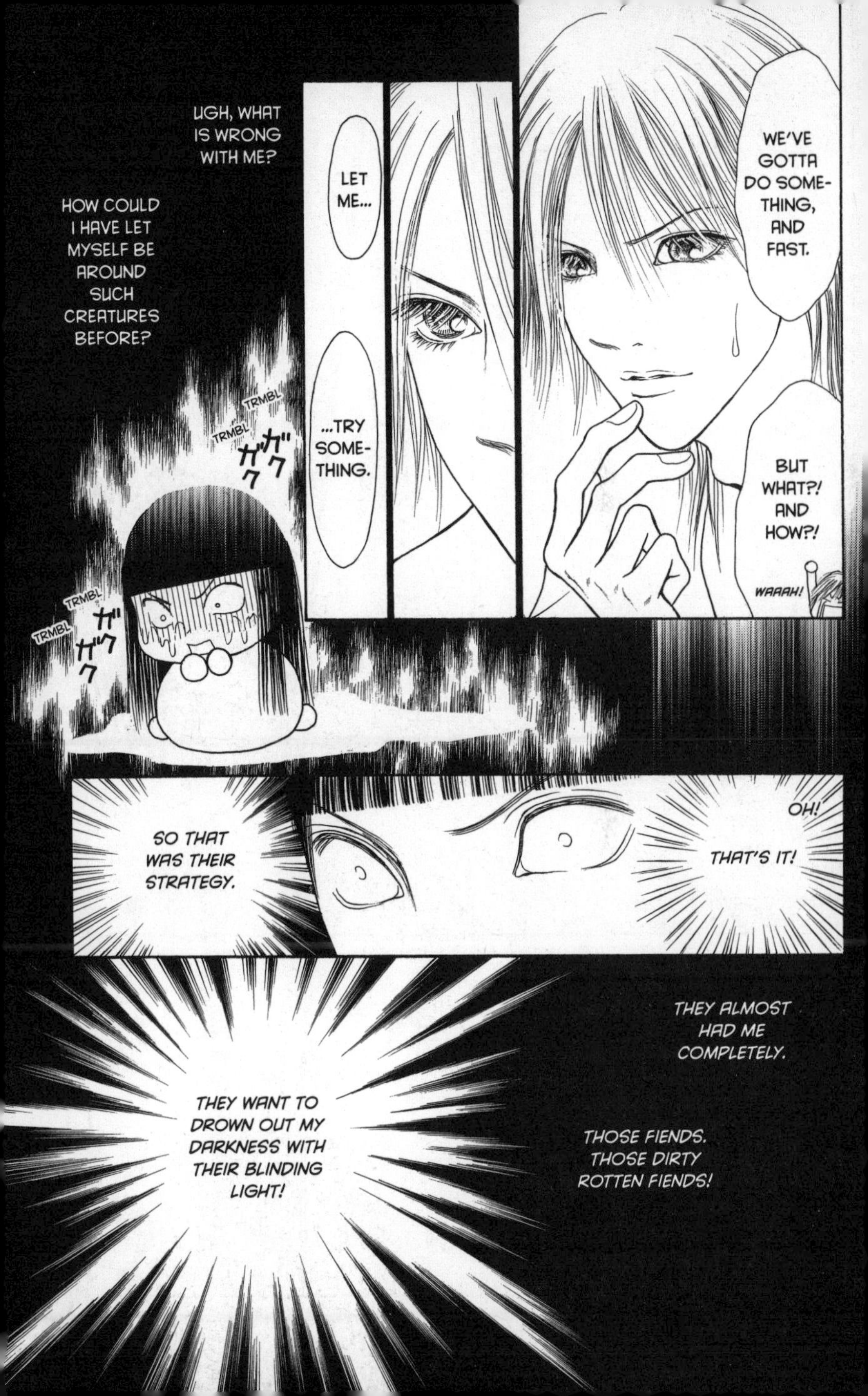

WE'VE GOTTA DO SOME-THING, AND FAST.
BUT WHAT?! AND HOW?!
WAAAH!
LET ME...
...TRY SOME-THING.
UGH, WHAT IS WRONG WITH ME?
HOW COULD I HAVE LET MYSELF BE AROUND SUCH CREATURES BEFORE?
TRMBL TRMBL
ガクガク
TRMBL TRMBL
ガクガク
OH!
THAT'S IT!
SO THAT WAS THEIR STRATEGY.
THEY ALMOST HAD ME COMPLETELY.
THOSE FIENDS. THOSE DIRTY ROTTEN FIENDS!
THEY WANT TO DROWN OUT MY DARKNESS WITH THEIR BLINDING LIGHT!

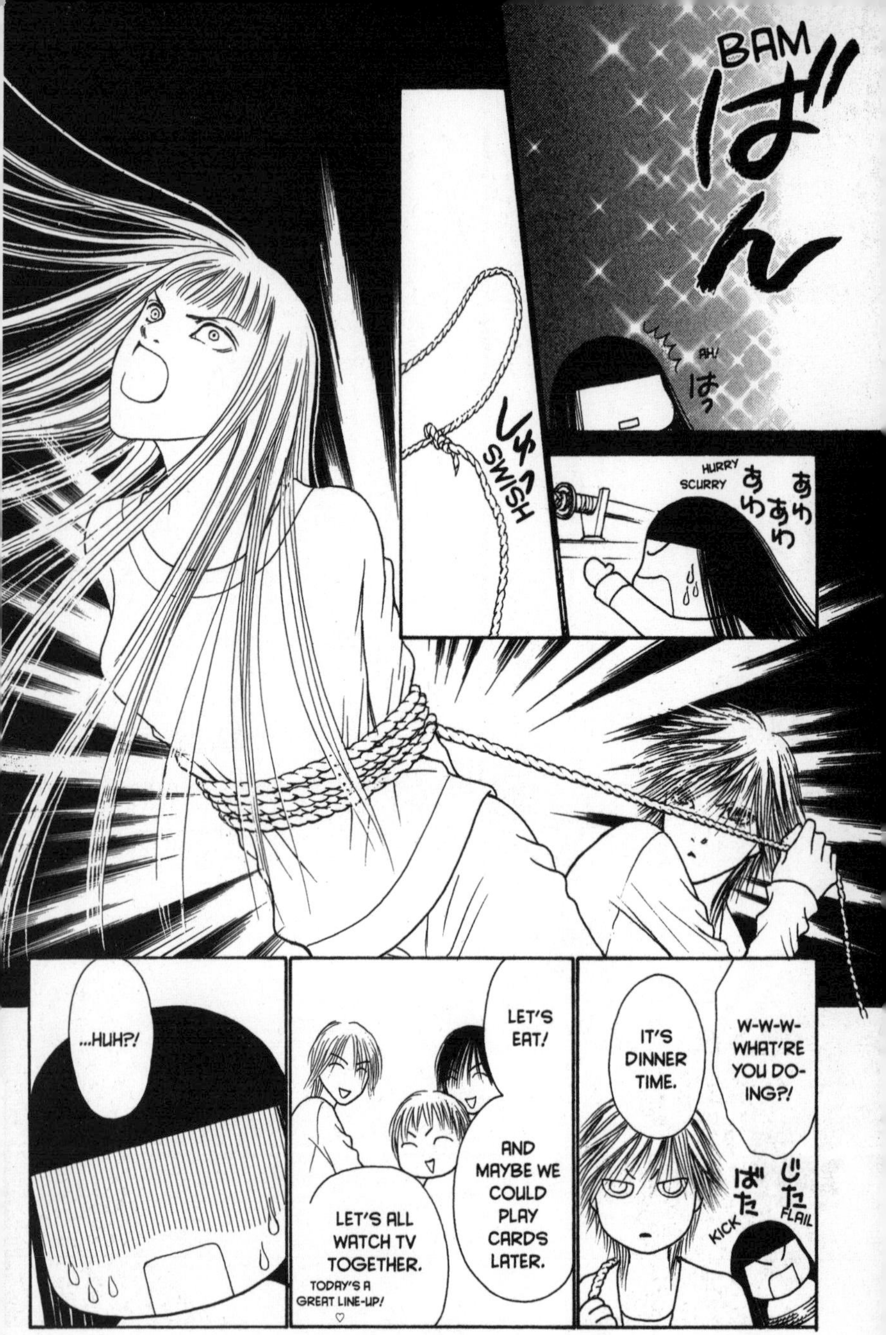

BAM
ばん
AH!
はっ
HURRY SCURRY
あわあわ
しゅっ
SWISH
W-W-W-WHAT'RE YOU DOING?!
IT'S DINNER TIME.
じた FLAIL
ばた KICK
LET'S EAT!
AND MAYBE WE COULD PLAY CARDS LATER.
LET'S ALL WATCH TV TOGETHER.
TODAY'S A GREAT LINE-UP! ♡
...HUH?!

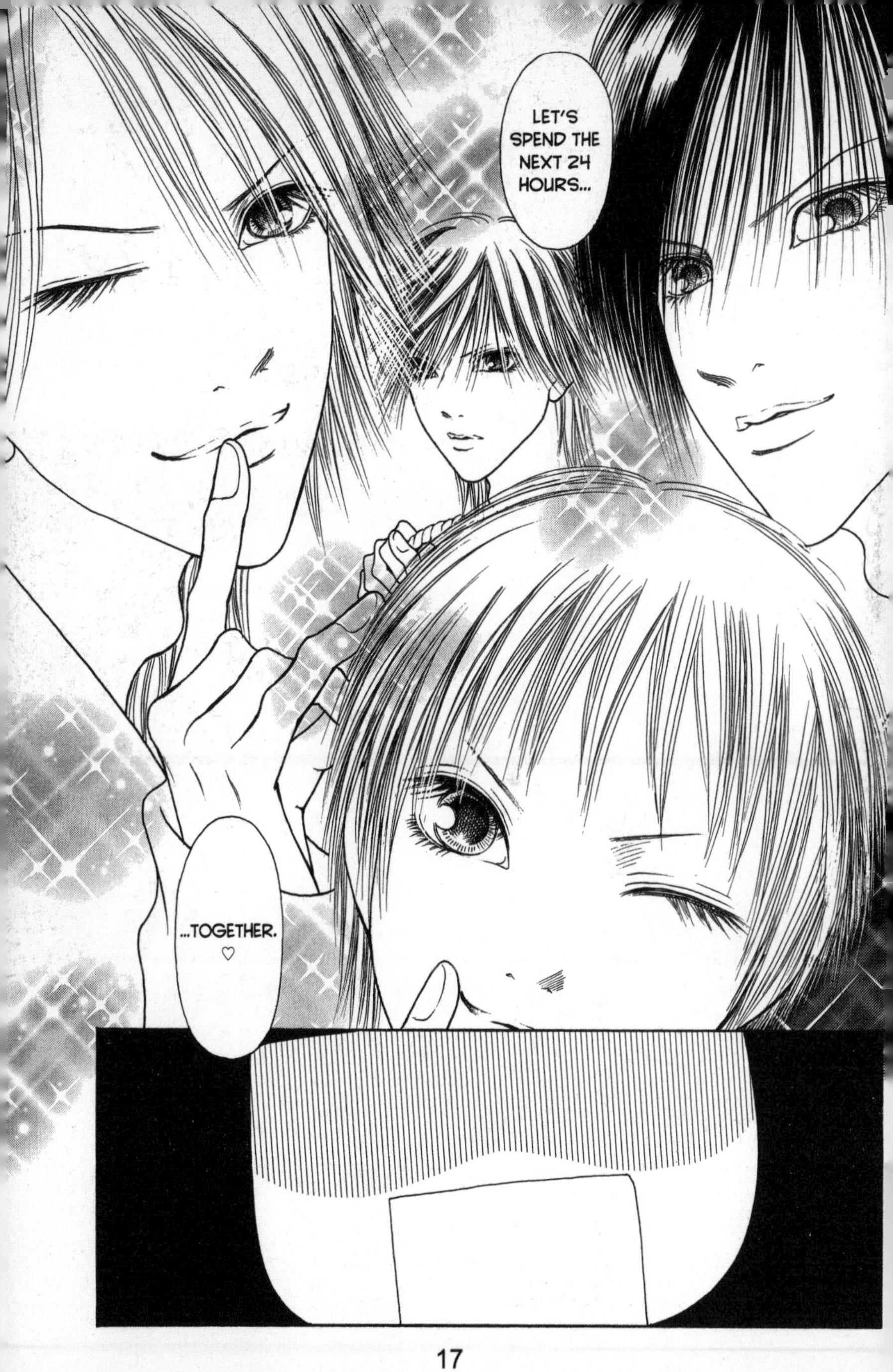

LET'S SPEND THE NEXT 24 HOURS...
...TOGETHER. ♡

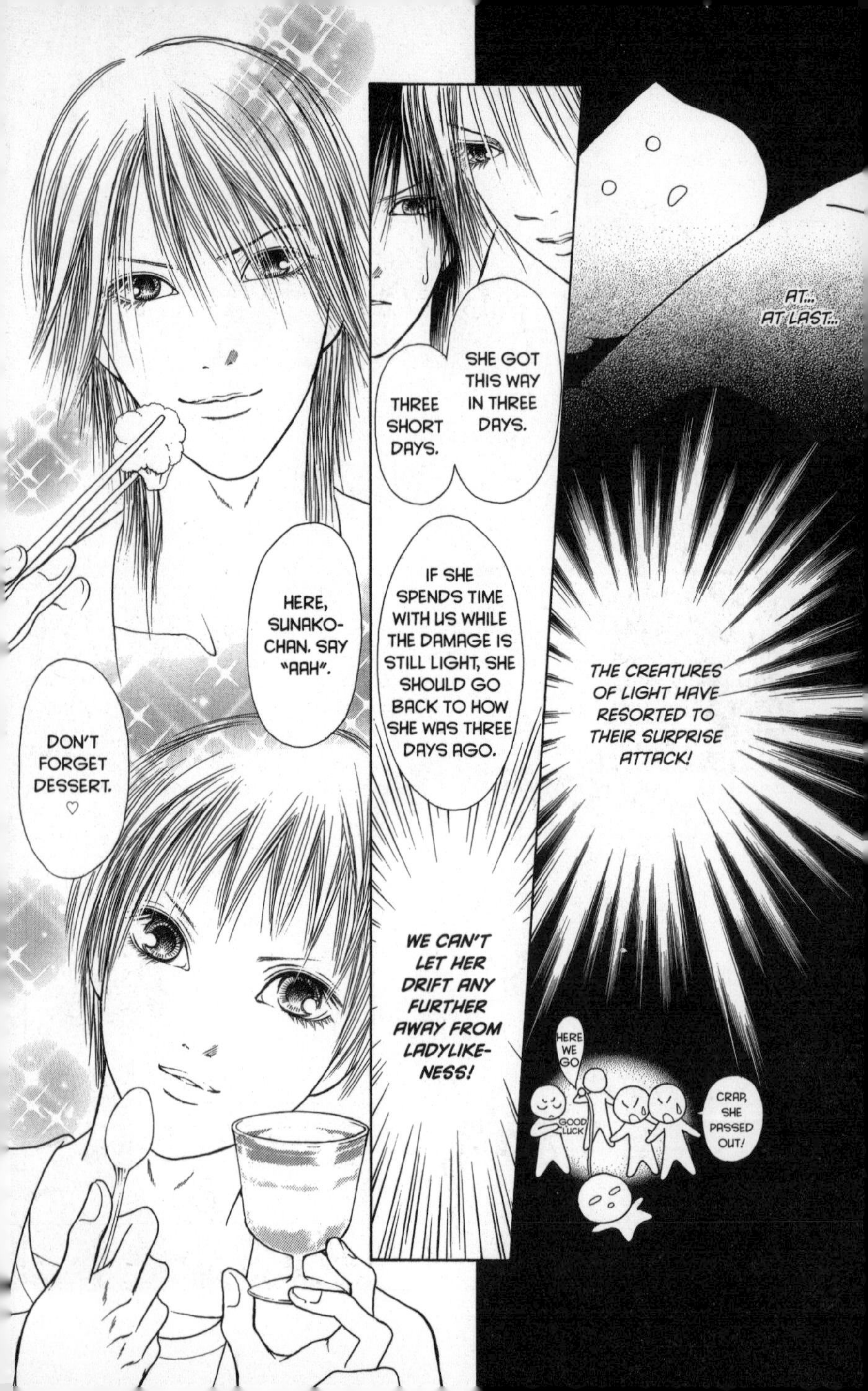
AT... AT LAST...
THE CREATURES OF LIGHT HAVE RESORTED TO THEIR SURPRISE ATTACK!
CRAP, SHE PASSED OUT!
HERE WE GO
GOOD LUCK
SHE GOT THIS WAY IN THREE DAYS.
THREE SHORT DAYS.
IF SHE SPENDS TIME WITH US WHILE THE DAMAGE IS STILL LIGHT, SHE SHOULD GO BACK TO HOW SHE WAS THREE DAYS AGO.
WE CAN'T LET HER DRIFT ANY FURTHER AWAY FROM LADYLIKE-NESS!
HERE, SUNAKO-CHAN. SAY "AAH".
DON'T FORGET DESSERT. ♡

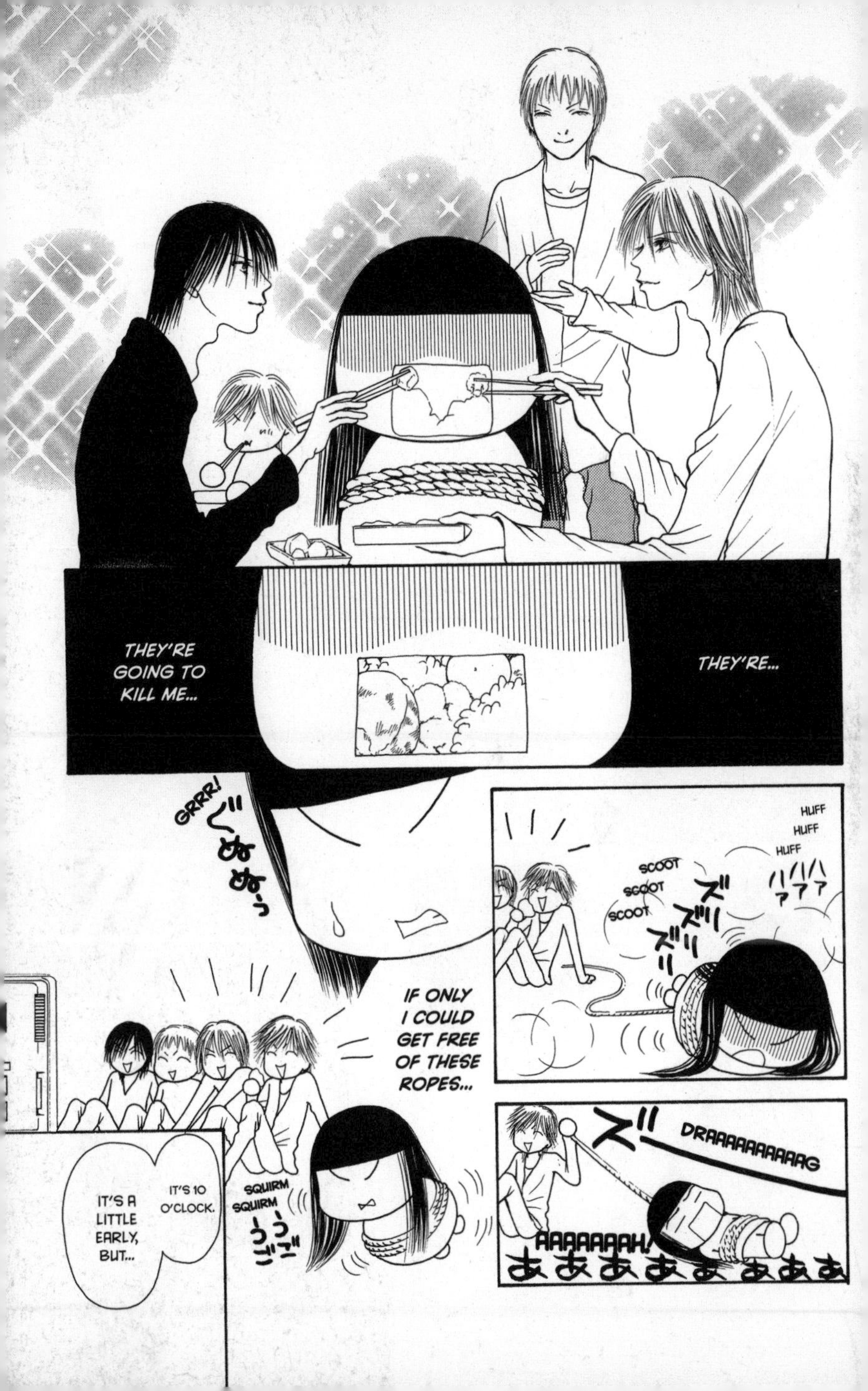
THEY'RE...
THEY'RE GOING TO KILL ME...
HUFF
HUFF
HUFF
ハァハァハァ
SCOOT
SCOOT
SCOOT
ズリズリズリ
ズ
DRAAAAAAAAAAG
AAAAAAAAH!
あああああああ
GRRR!
ぐぬぬぬっ
IF ONLY I COULD GET FREE OF THESE ROPES...
SQUIRM
SQUIRM
うごうご
IT'S 10 O'CLOCK.
IT'S A LITTLE EARLY, BUT...

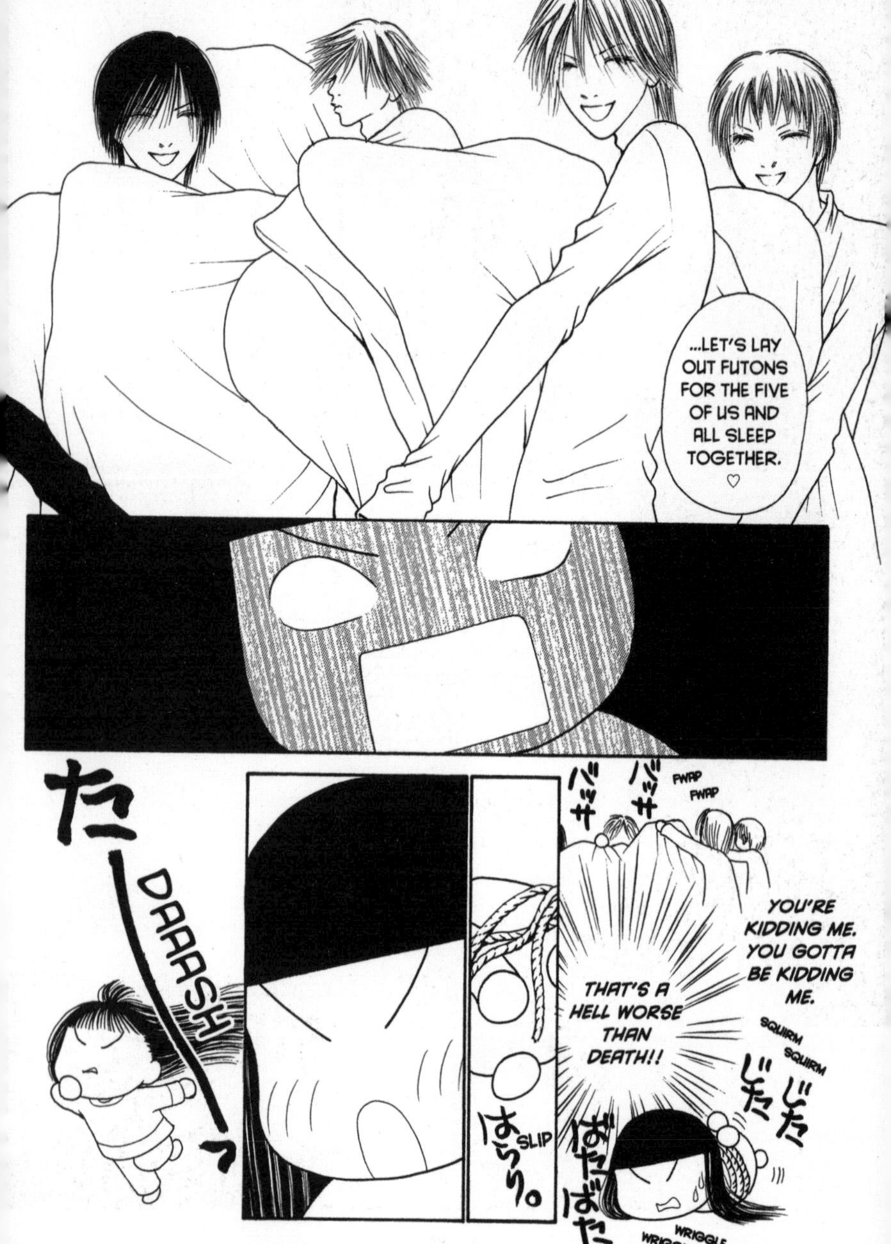
...LET'S LAY OUT FUTONS FOR THE FIVE OF US AND ALL SLEEP TOGETHER. ♡
バッサ バッサ
FWAP FWAP
YOU'RE KIDDING ME. YOU GOTTA BE KIDDING ME.
THAT'S A HELL WORSE THAN DEATH!!
じたじた
SQUIRM SQUIRM
ばたばた
WRIGGLE WRIGGLE
はらり。
SLIP
たーっ
DAAASH

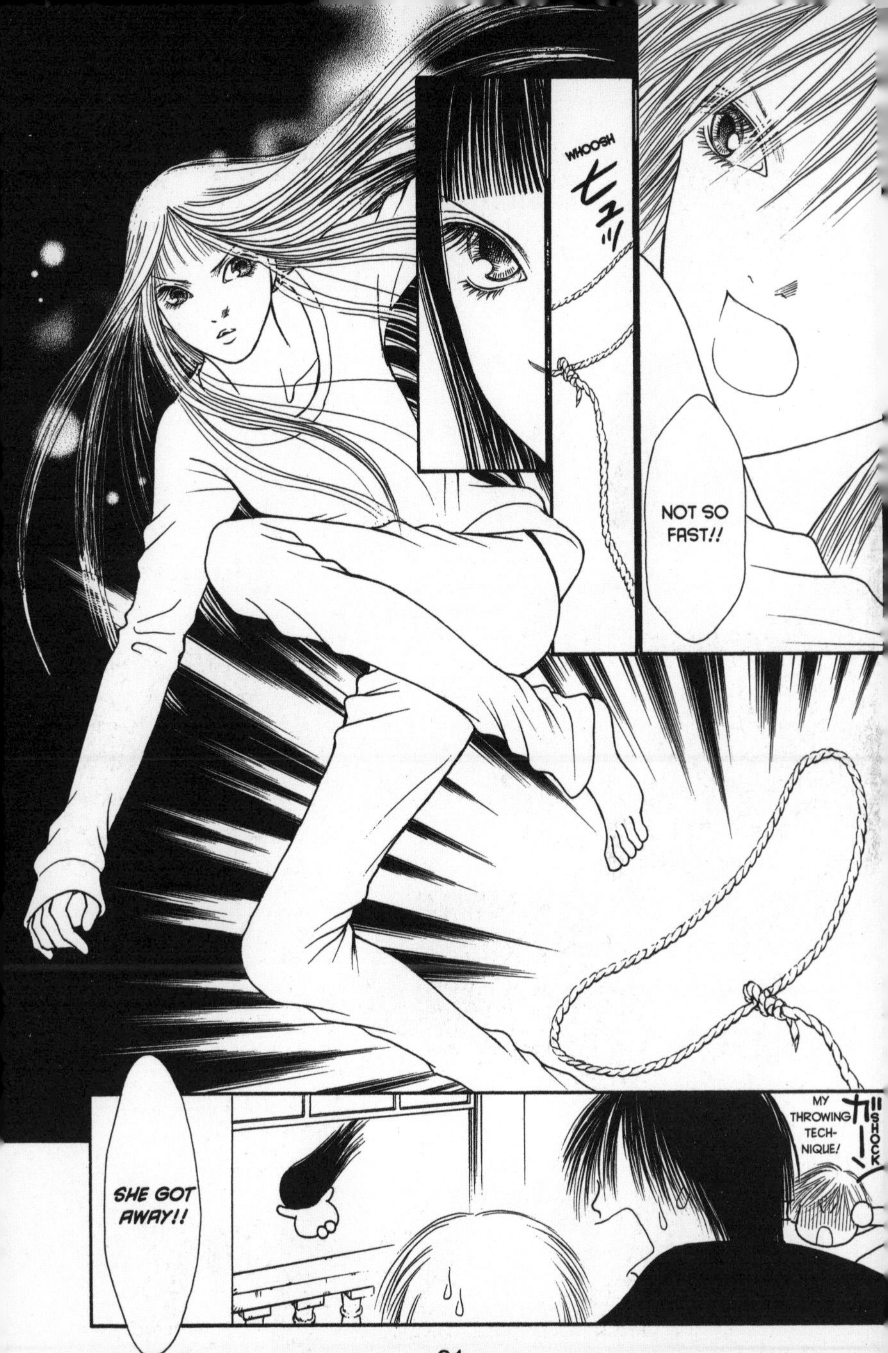
NOT SO FAST!!
WHOOSH
ヒュッ
MY THROWING TECHNIQUE!
SHOCK
SHE GOT AWAY!!

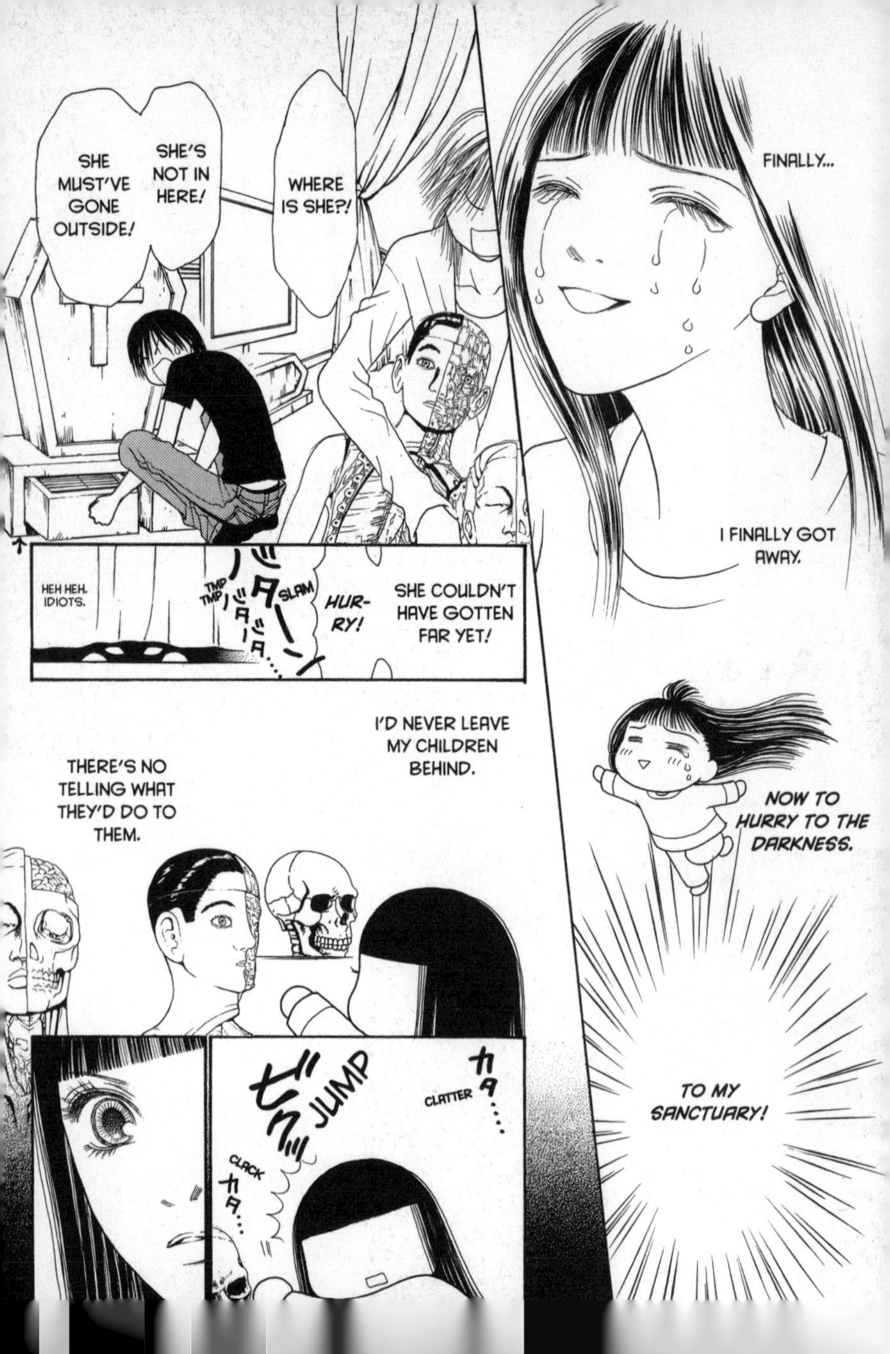
FINALLY...
I FINALLY GOT AWAY.
NOW TO HURRY TO THE DARKNESS.
TO MY SANCTUARY!
WHERE IS SHE?!
SHE'S NOT IN HERE!
SHE MUST'VE GONE OUTSIDE!
SHE COULDN'T HAVE GOTTEN FAR YET!
HUR-RY!
SLAM
TMP TMP
HEH HEH. IDIOTS.
I'D NEVER LEAVE MY CHILDREN BEHIND.
THERE'S NO TELLING WHAT THEY'D DO TO THEM.
CLATTER
JUMP
CLACK

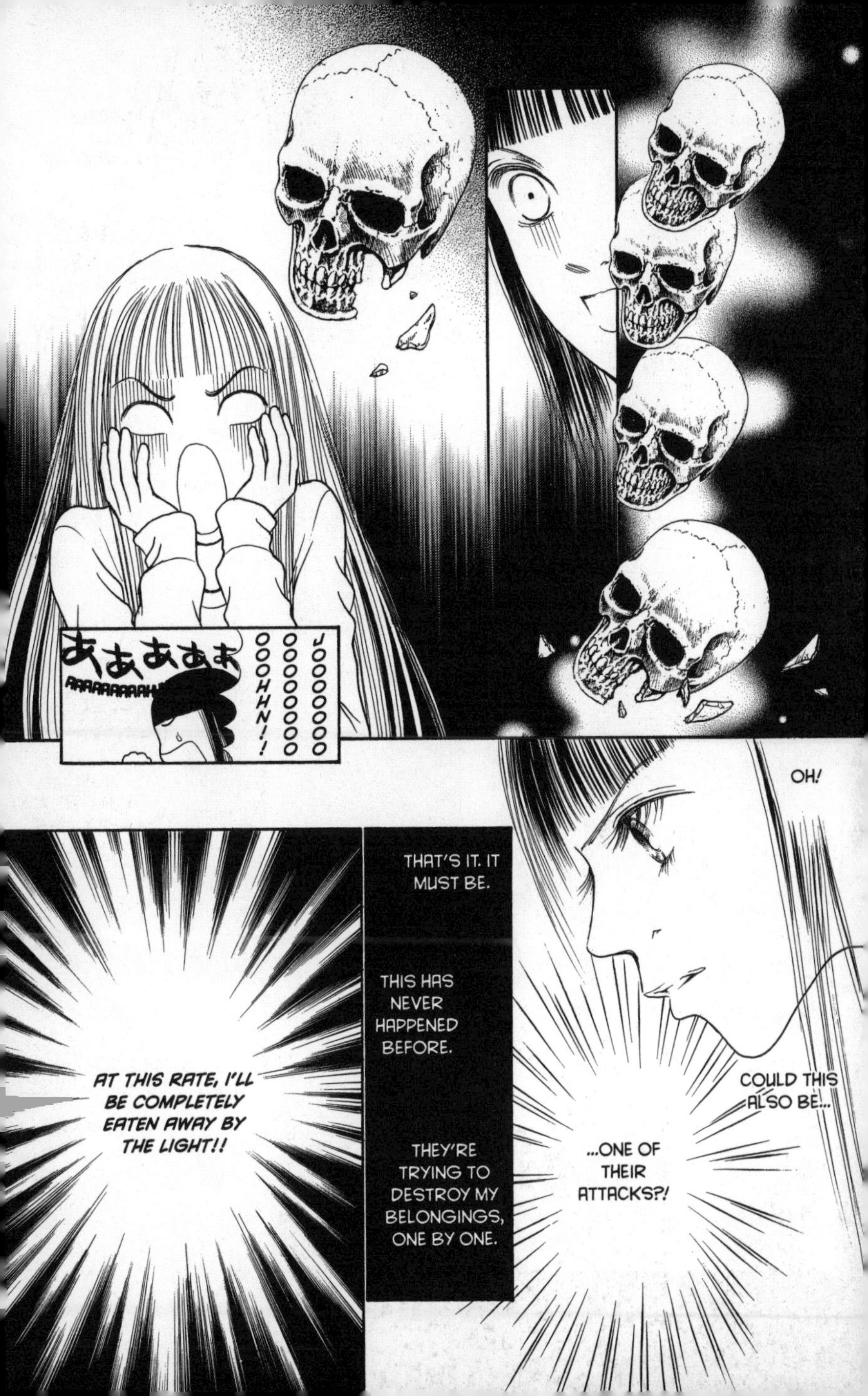
JOOOOOOOOOOOOOOOOOOOHHN!!
あああああ
AAAAAAAAH
OH!
COULD THIS ALSO BE...
...ONE OF THEIR ATTACKS?!
THAT'S IT. IT MUST BE.
THIS HAS NEVER HAPPENED BEFORE.
THEY'RE TRYING TO DESTROY MY BELONGINGS, ONE BY ONE.
AT THIS RATE, I'LL BE COMPLETELY EATEN AWAY BY THE LIGHT!!

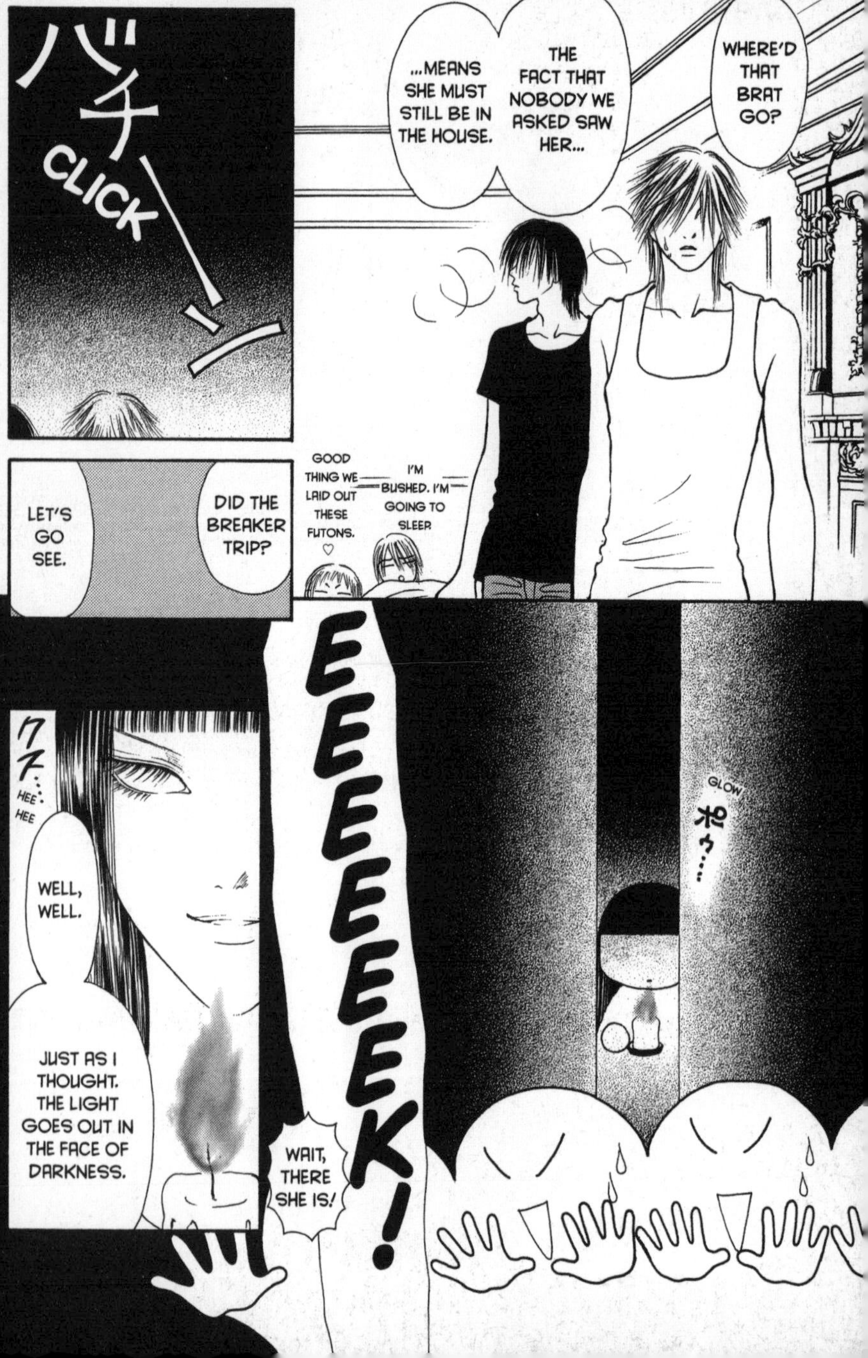
WHERE'D THAT BRAT GO?
THE FACT THAT NOBODY WE ASKED SAW HER...
...MEANS SHE MUST STILL BE IN THE HOUSE.
I'M BUSHED. I'M GOING TO SLEEP.
GOOD THING WE LAID OUT THESE FUTONS. ♡
バチーン
CLICK
DID THE BREAKER TRIP?
LET'S GO SEE.
GLOW
ポウ…
EEEEEEEK!
WAIT, THERE SHE IS!
クフ…
HEE HEE
WELL, WELL.
JUST AS I THOUGHT. THE LIGHT GOES OUT IN THE FACE OF DARKNESS.

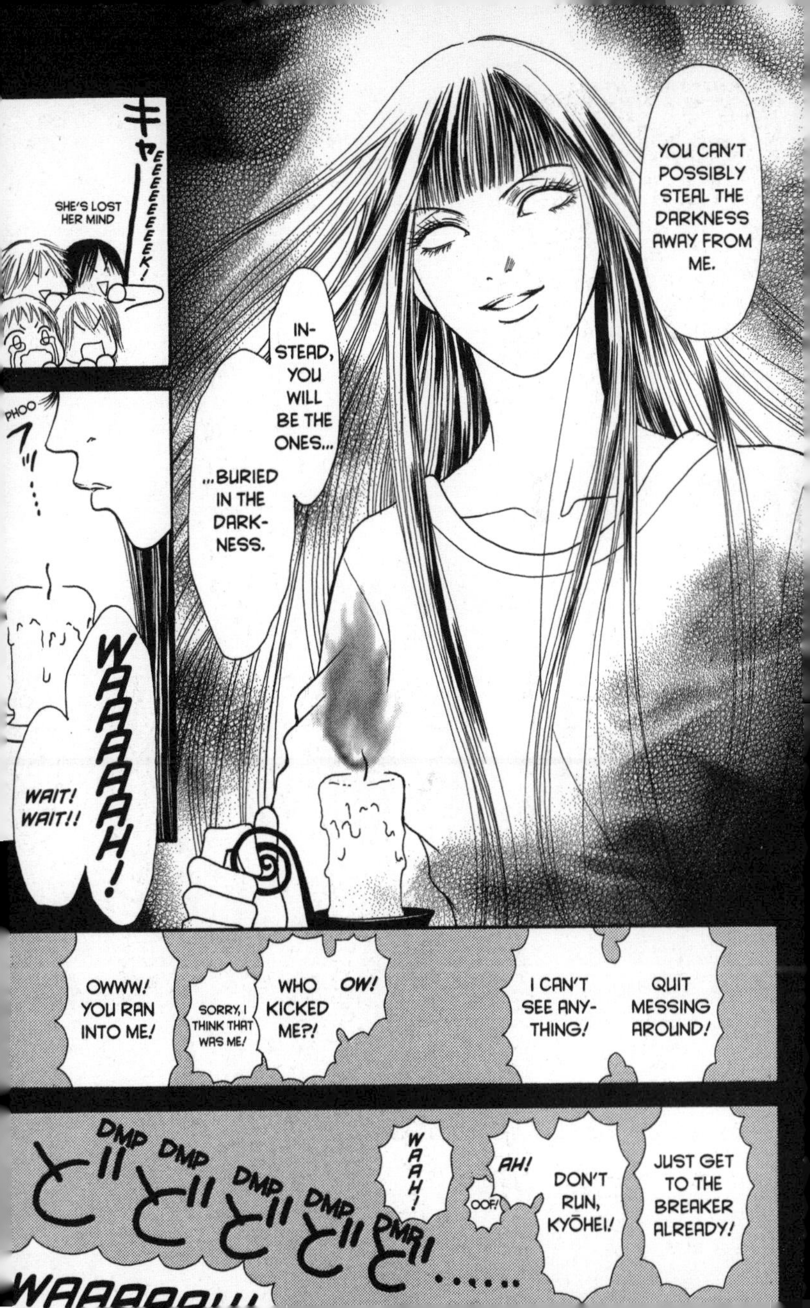

YOU CAN'T POSSIBLY STEAL THE DARKNESS AWAY FROM ME.
IN-STEAD, YOU WILL BE THE ONES...
...BURIED IN THE DARKNESS.
キャEEEEEEEEEK!
SHE'S LOST HER MIND
PHOO
フッ...
WAAAAAAH!
WAIT! WAIT!!
QUIT MESSING AROUND!
I CAN'T SEE ANY-THING!
OW!
WHO KICKED ME?!
SORRY, I THINK THAT WAS ME!
OWWW! YOU RAN INTO ME!
JUST GET TO THE BREAKER ALREADY!
DON'T RUN, KYŌHEI!
AH!
OOF!
WAAH!
DMP DMP DMP DMP DMP
ど" ど" ど" ど" ど"......

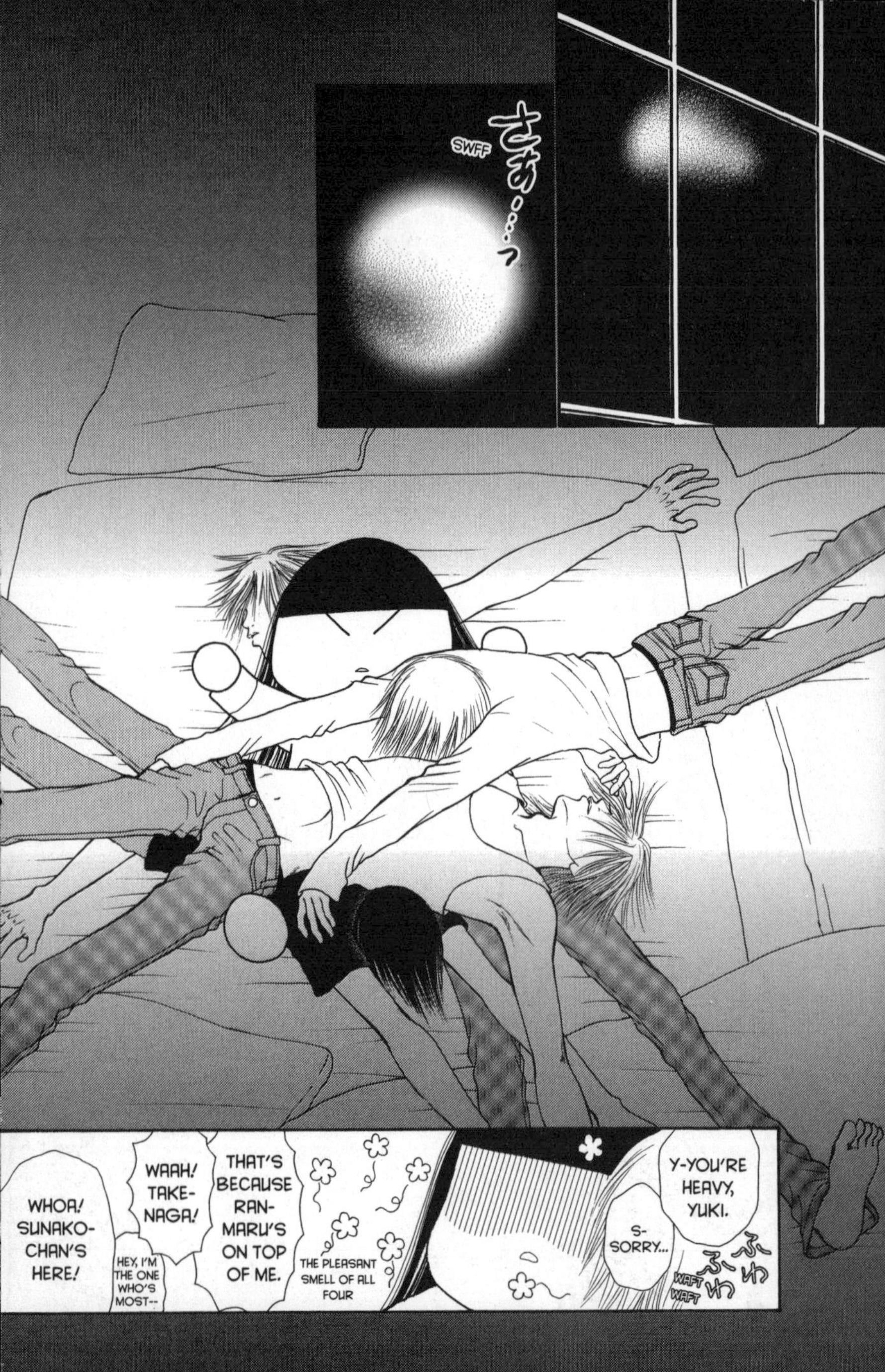
さあ…っ
SWFF
ふわ ふわ
WAFT WAFT
Y-YOU'RE HEAVY, YUKI.
S-SORRY...
THE PLEASANT SMELL OF ALL FOUR
THAT'S BECAUSE RAN-MARU'S ON TOP OF ME.
WAAH! TAKE-NAGA!
HEY, I'M THE ONE WHO'S MOST--
WHOA! SUNAKO-CHAN'S HERE!

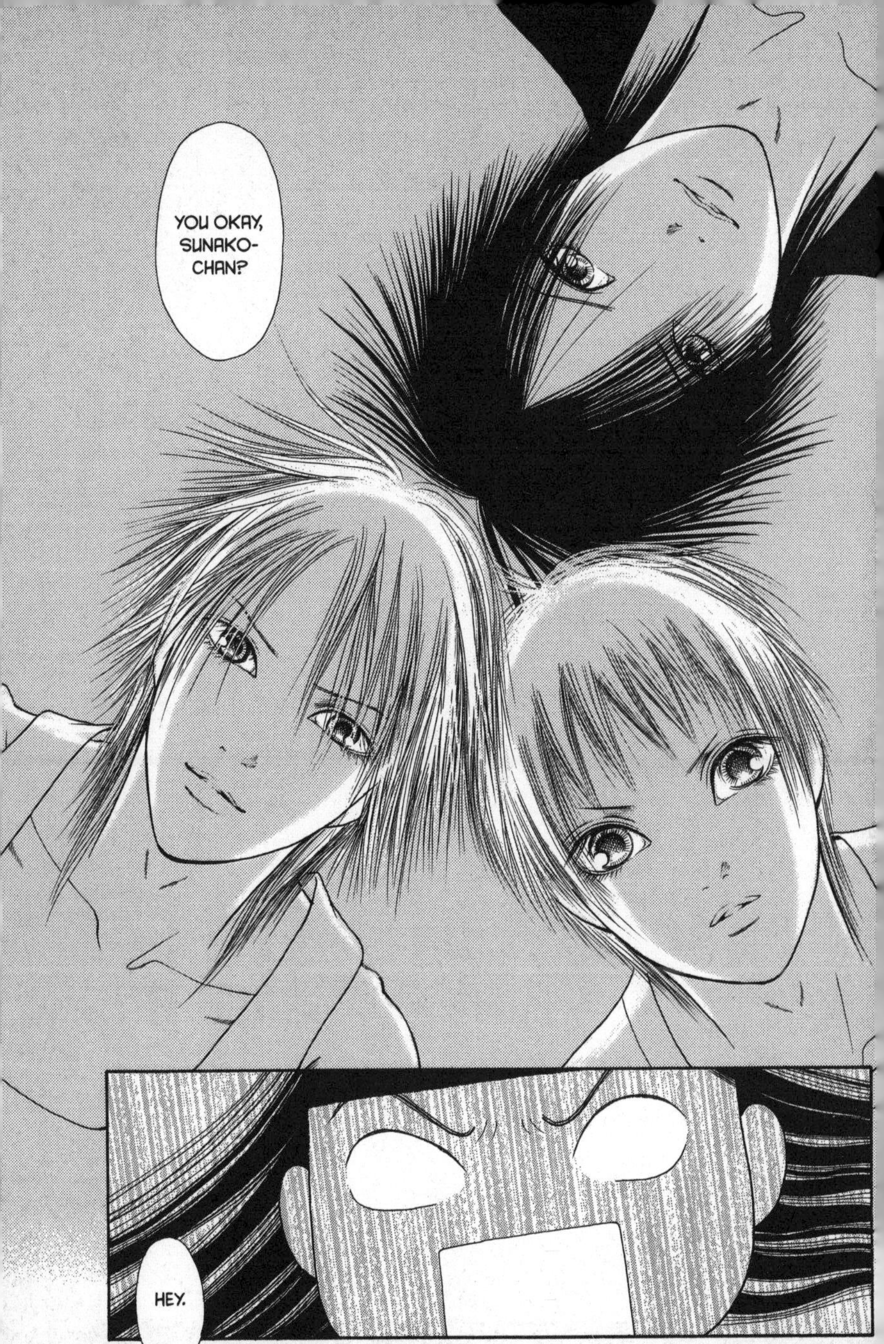
YOU OKAY, SUNAKO-CHAN?
HEY.

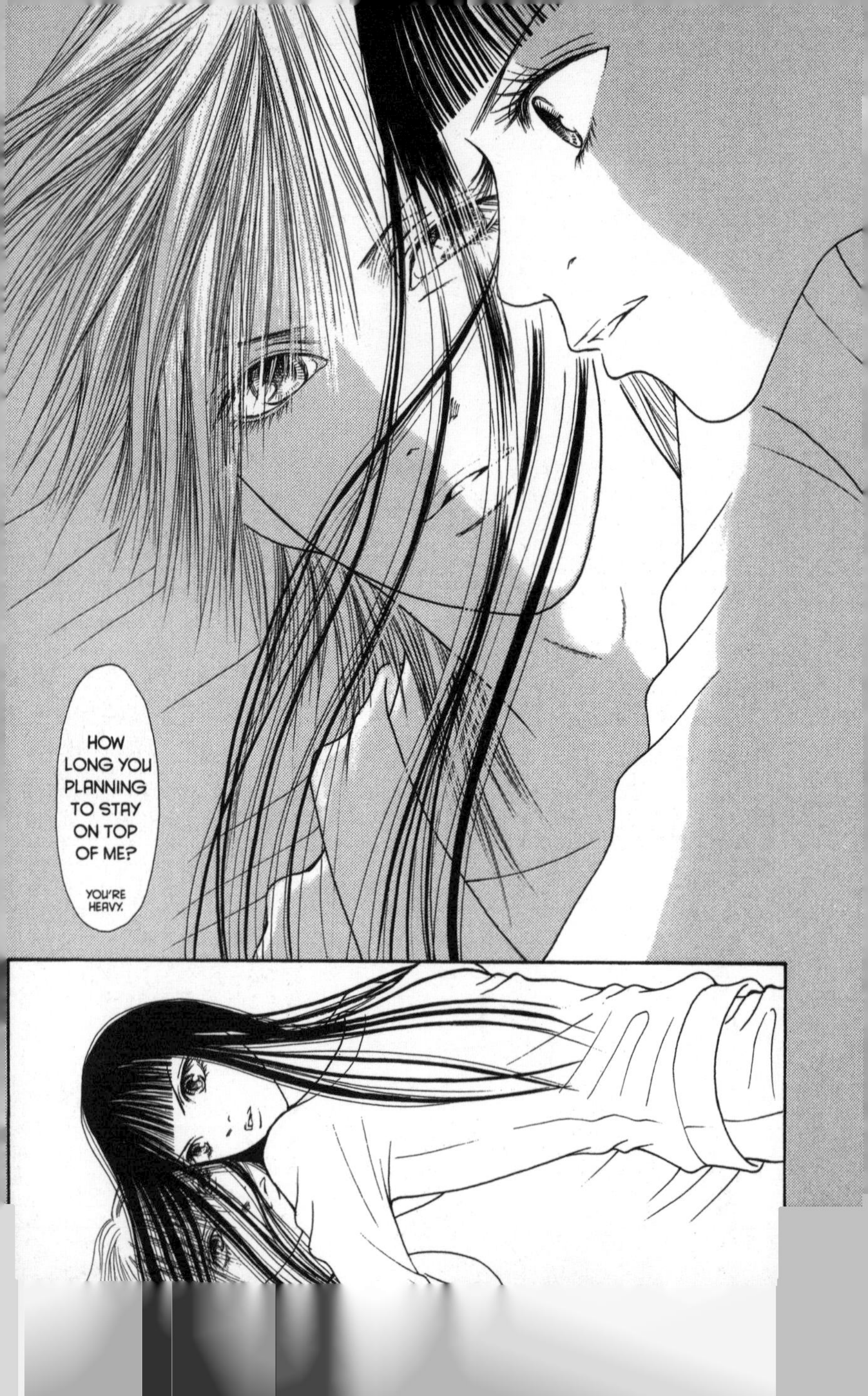
HOW LONG YOU PLANNING TO STAY ON TOP OF ME?
YOU'RE HEAVY.

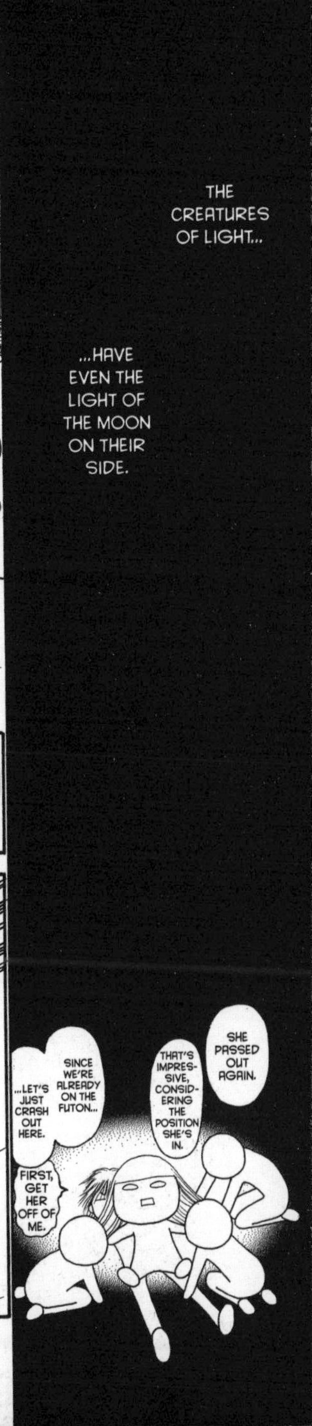
THE CREATURES OF LIGHT...
...HAVE EVEN THE LIGHT OF THE MOON ON THEIR SIDE.
SHE PASSED OUT AGAIN.
THAT'S IMPRESSIVE, CONSIDERING THE POSITION SHE'S IN.
SINCE WE'RE ALREADY ON THE FUTON...
...LET'S JUST CRASH OUT HERE.
FIRST, GET HER OFF OF ME.

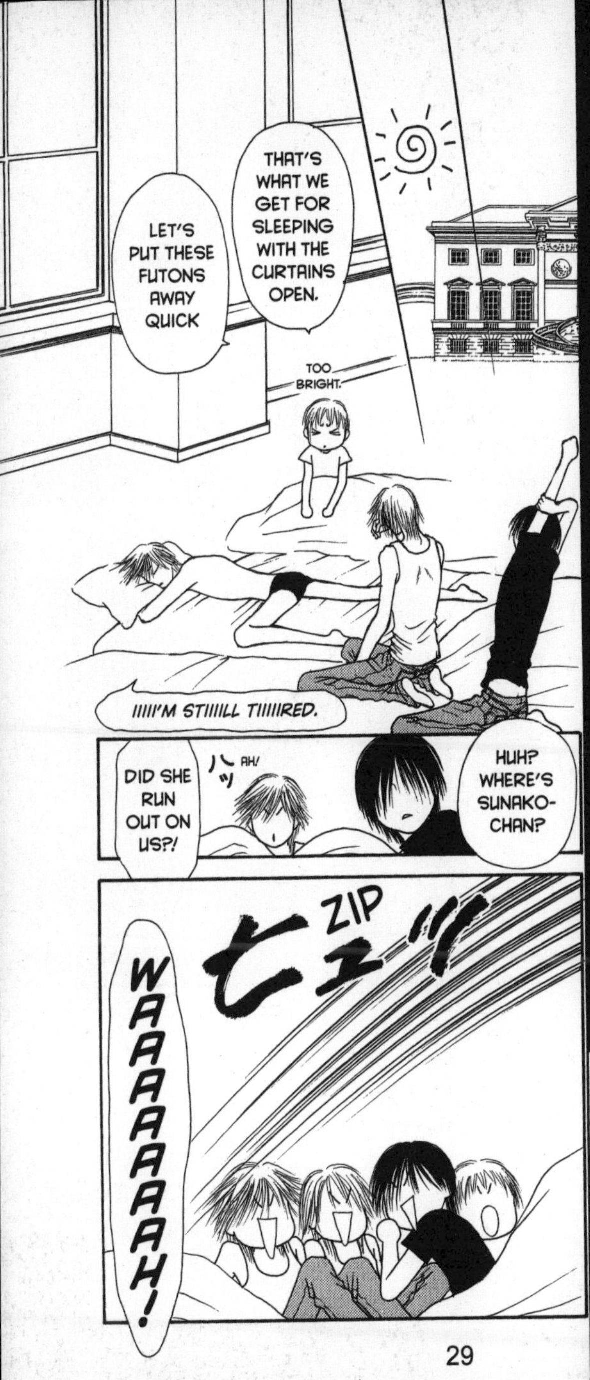
THAT'S WHAT WE GET FOR SLEEPING WITH THE CURTAINS OPEN.
LET'S PUT THESE FUTONS AWAY QUICK
TOO BRIGHT.
IIIII'M STIIIILL TIIIIRED.
HUH? WHERE'S SUNAKO-CHAN?
ハッ AH!
DID SHE RUN OUT ON US?!
ピューッ ZIP
WAAAAAAAAAAH!

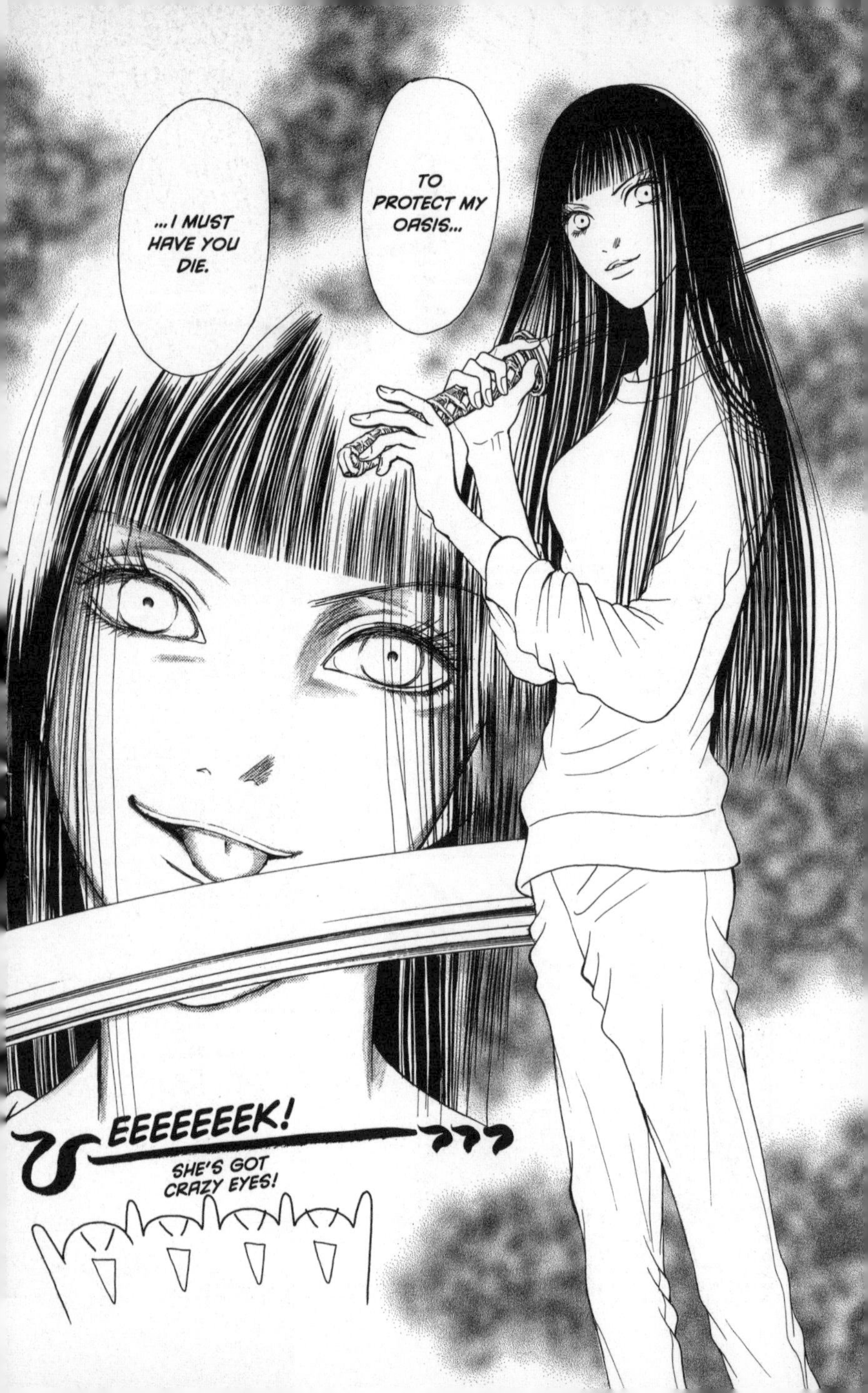
TO PROTECT MY OASIS...
...I MUST HAVE YOU DIE.
EEEEEEEK!
SHE'S GOT CRAZY EYES!

Welcome to Malletts Creek
Branch
You checked out the following
items:

1. The Wallflower 32
   Barcode:
   31621211260704 Due:
   9/28/2018
2. The wallflower 31
   Barcode:
   31621211052682 Due:
   9/28/2018

You were helped by Library

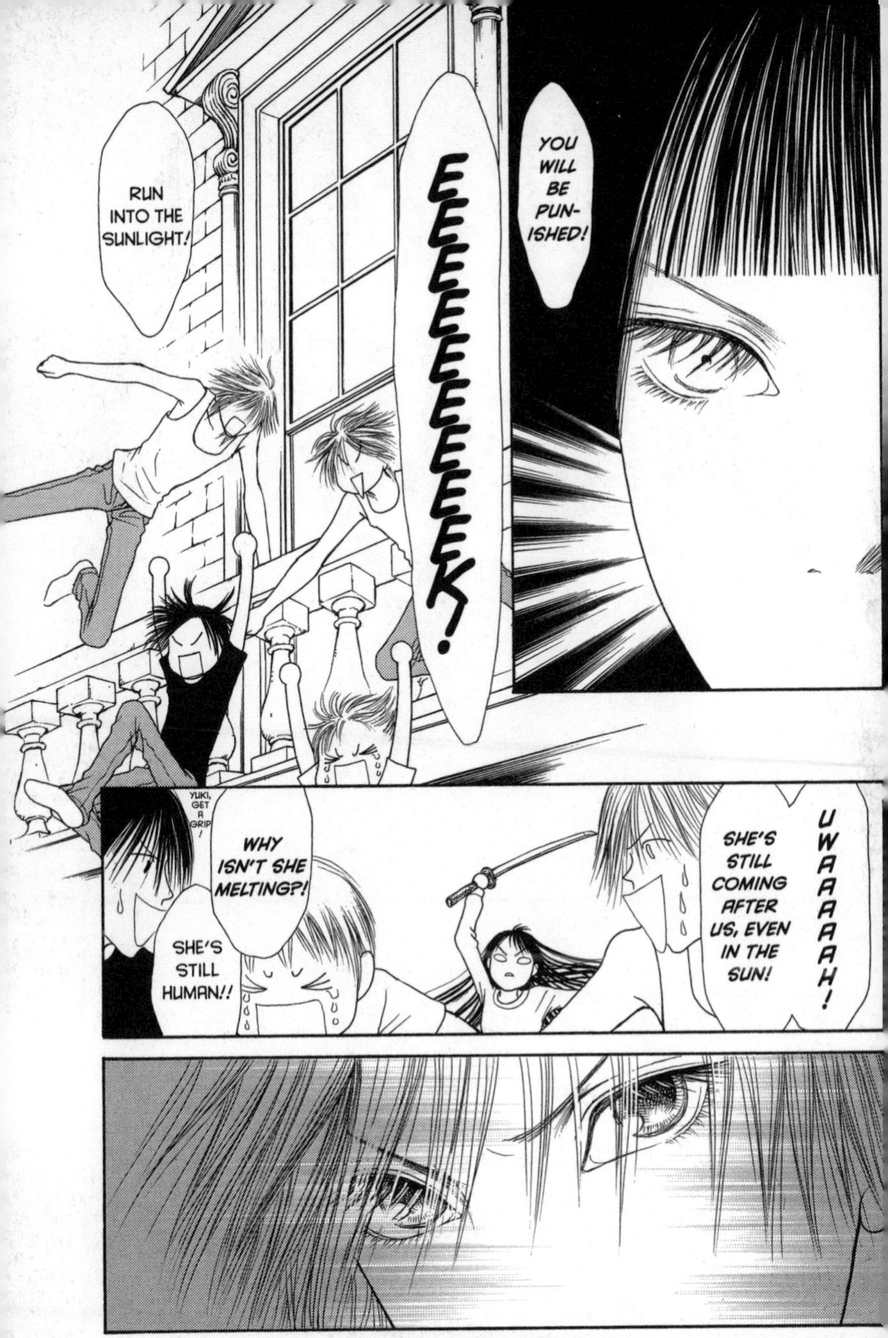
YOU WILL BE PUN-ISHED!
EEEEEEEEEEEEEK!
RUN INTO THE SUNLIGHT!
UWAAAAAAH!
SHE'S STILL COMING AFTER US, EVEN IN THE SUN!
WHY ISN'T SHE MELTING?!
YUKI, GET A GRIP!
SHE'S STILL HUMAN!!

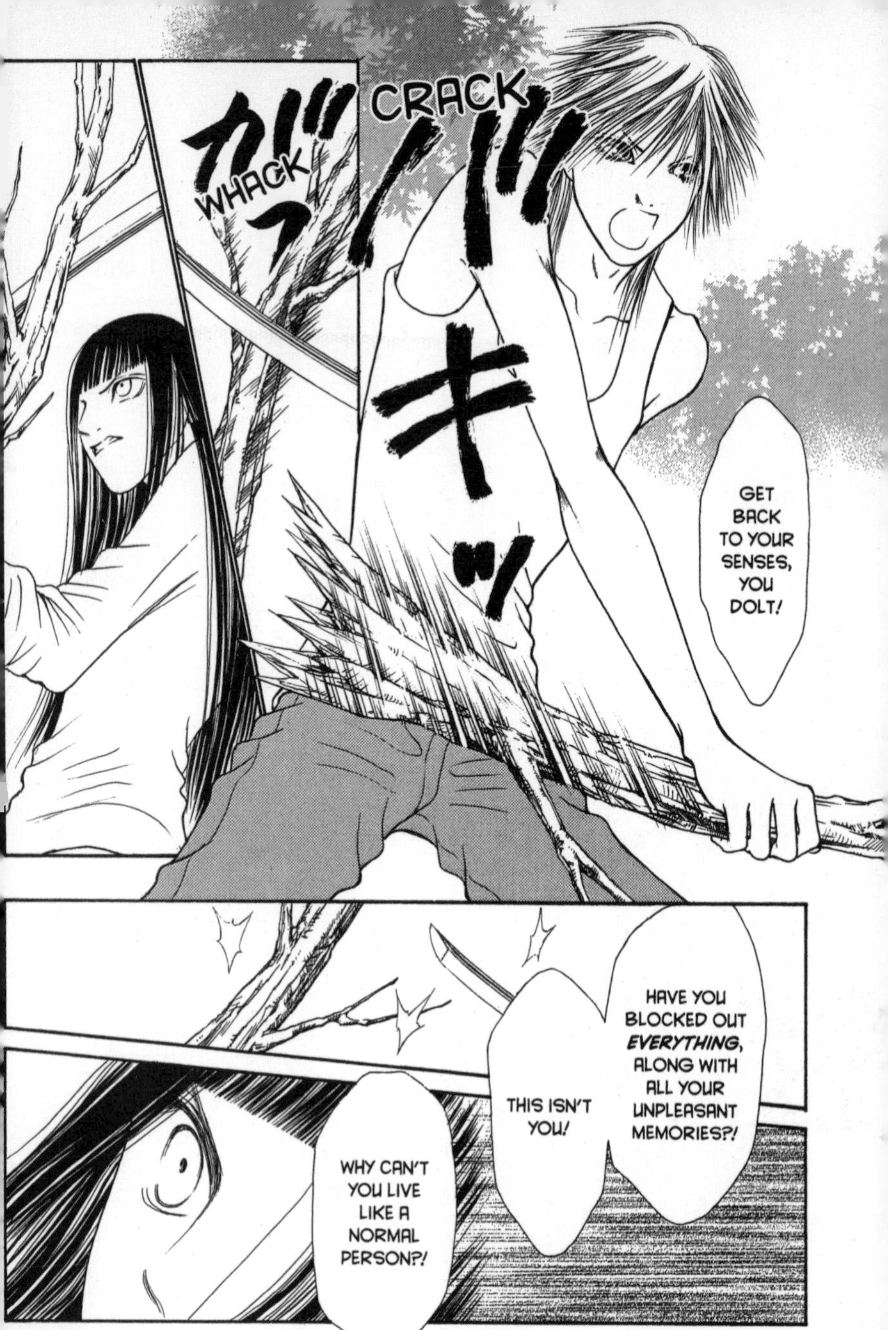
CRACK
WHACK
GET BACK TO YOUR SENSES, YOU DOLT!
HAVE YOU BLOCKED OUT *EVERYTHING*, ALONG WITH ALL YOUR UNPLEASANT MEMORIES?!
THIS ISN'T YOU!
WHY CAN'T YOU LIVE LIKE A NORMAL PERSON?!

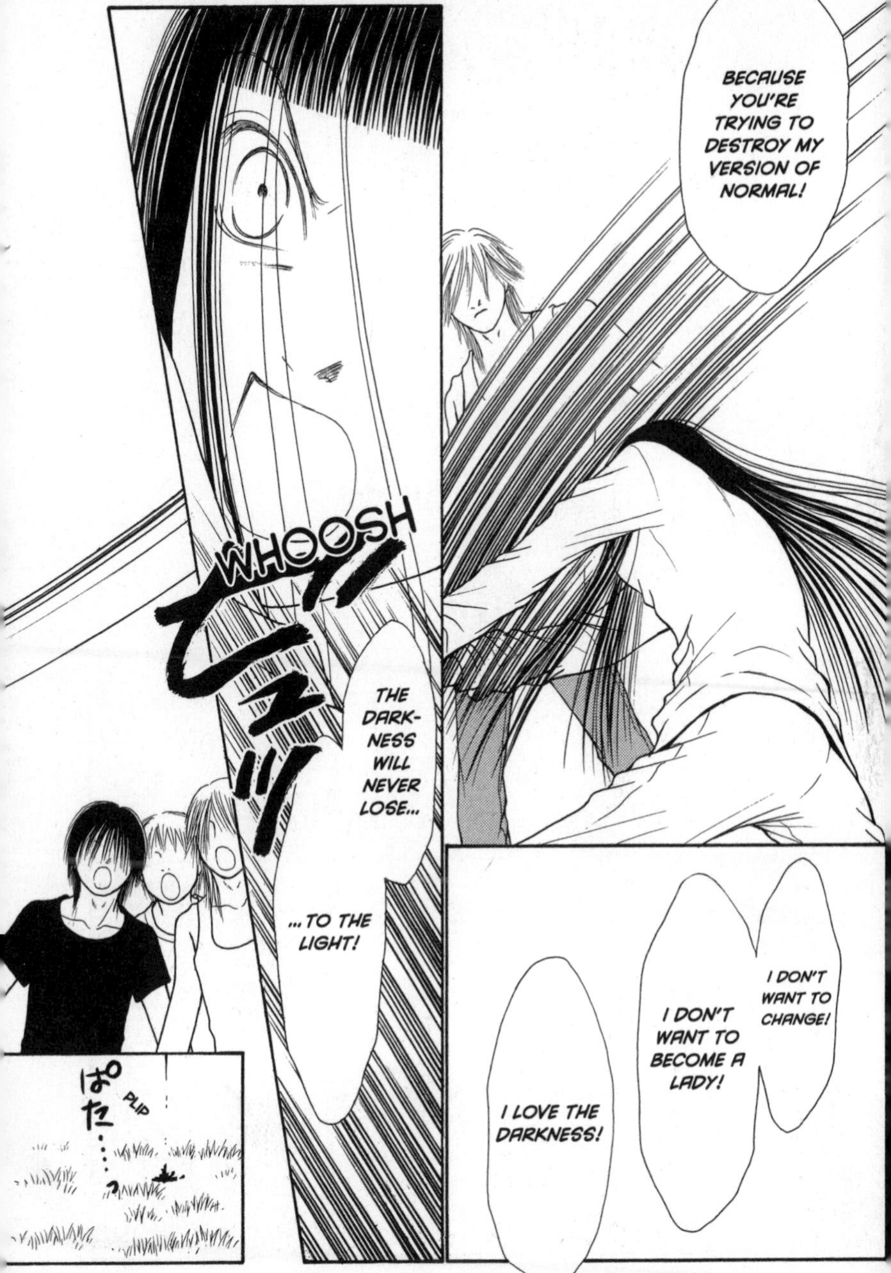
BECAUSE YOU'RE TRYING TO DESTROY MY VERSION OF NORMAL!
WHOOSH
THE DARKNESS WILL NEVER LOSE...
...TO THE LIGHT!
PLIP
I DON'T WANT TO CHANGE!
I DON'T WANT TO BECOME A LADY!
I LOVE THE DARKNESS!

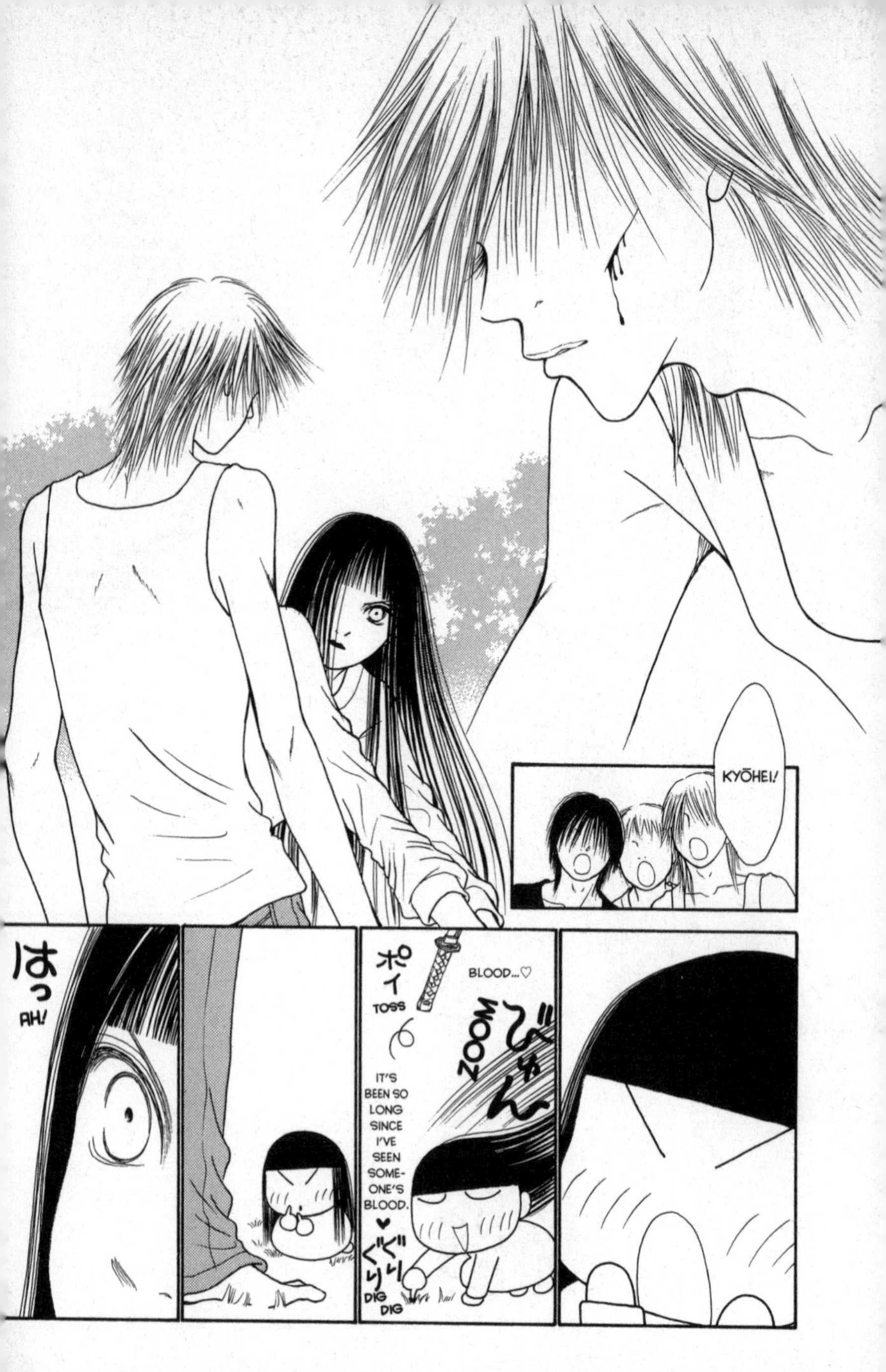
KYŌHEI!
びゅん
ZOOM
BLOOD...♡
ポイ
TOSS
IT'S BEEN SO LONG SINCE I'VE SEEN SOME-ONE'S BLOOD.♥
ぐりぐり
DIG DIG
はっ
AH!

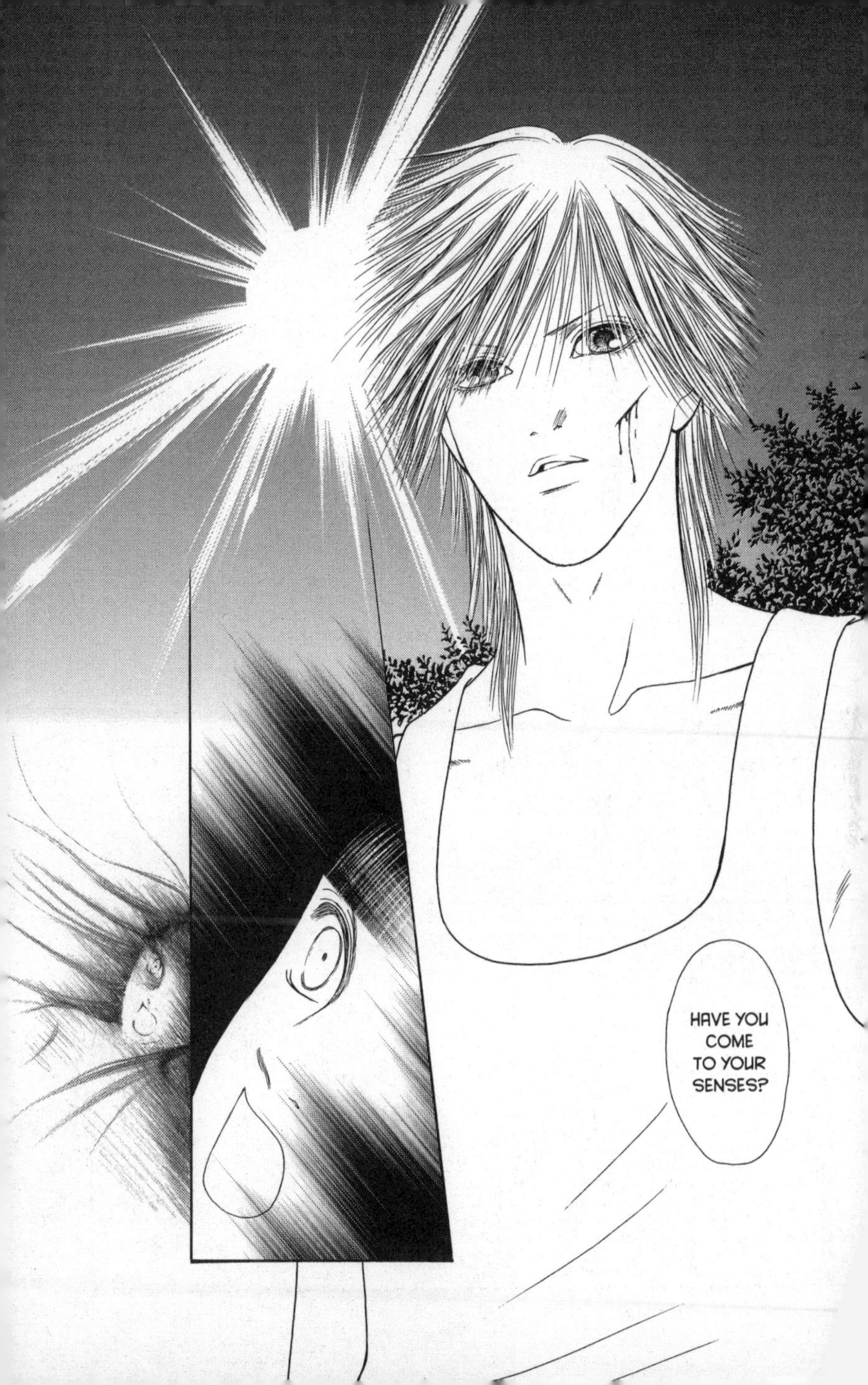
HAVE YOU COME TO YOUR SENSES?

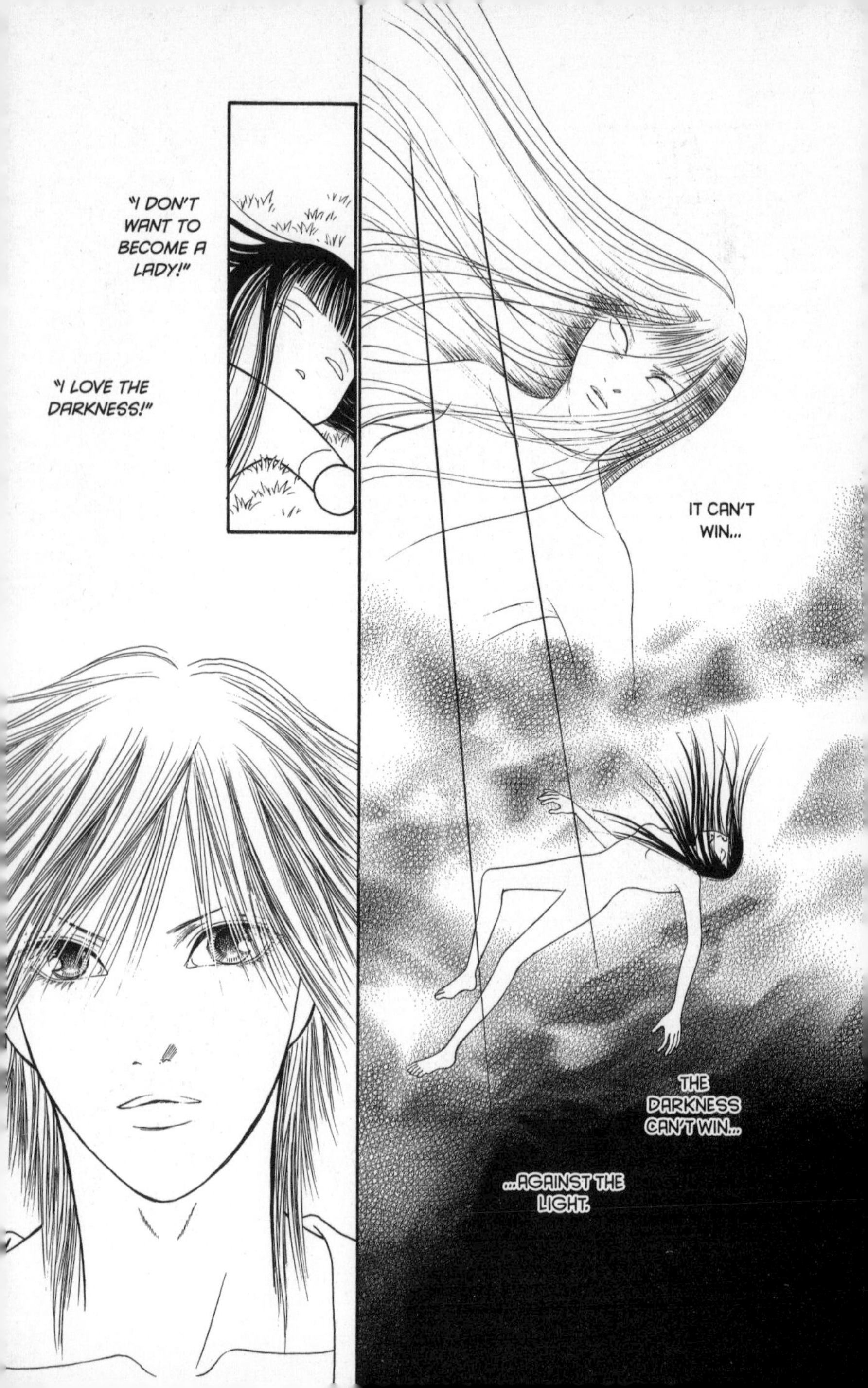
IT CAN'T WIN...
THE DARKNESS CAN'T WIN...
...AGAINST THE LIGHT.
"I DON'T WANT TO BECOME A LADY!"
"I LOVE THE DARKNESS!"

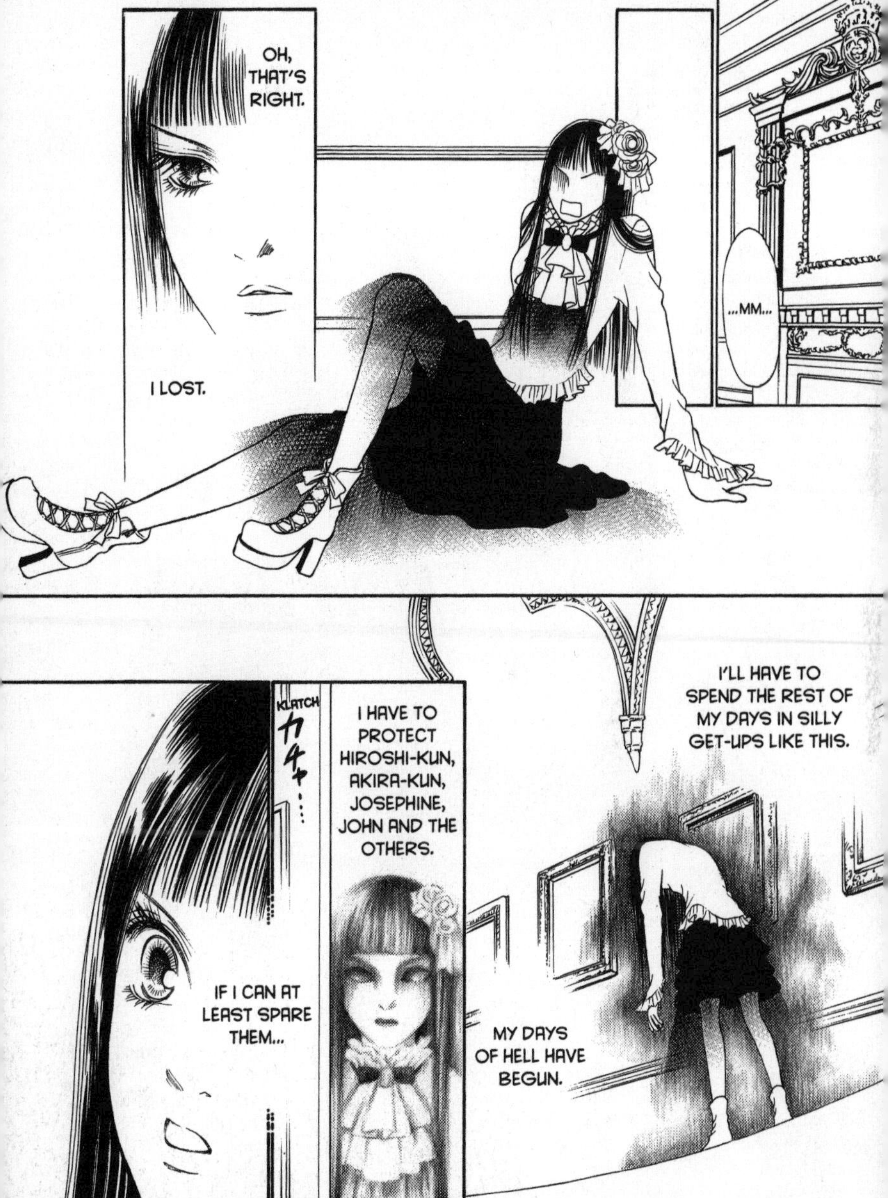
...MM...
OH, THAT'S RIGHT.
I LOST.
I'LL HAVE TO SPEND THE REST OF MY DAYS IN SILLY GET-UPS LIKE THIS.
MY DAYS OF HELL HAVE BEGUN.
I HAVE TO PROTECT HIROSHI-KUN, AKIRA-KUN, JOSEPHINE, JOHN AND THE OTHERS.
KLATCH
カチャ....
IF I CAN AT LEAST SPARE THEM...

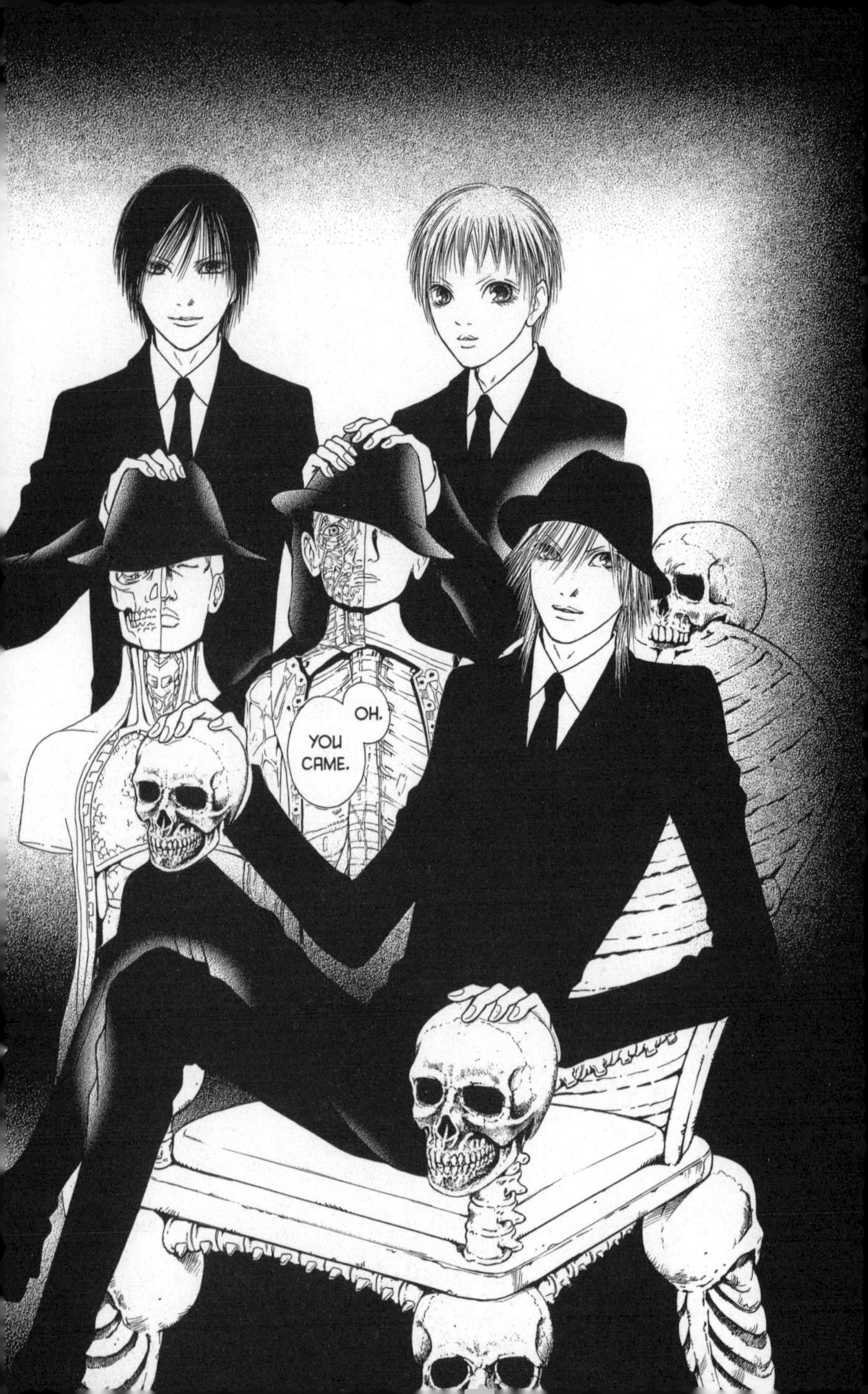
OH. YOU CAME.

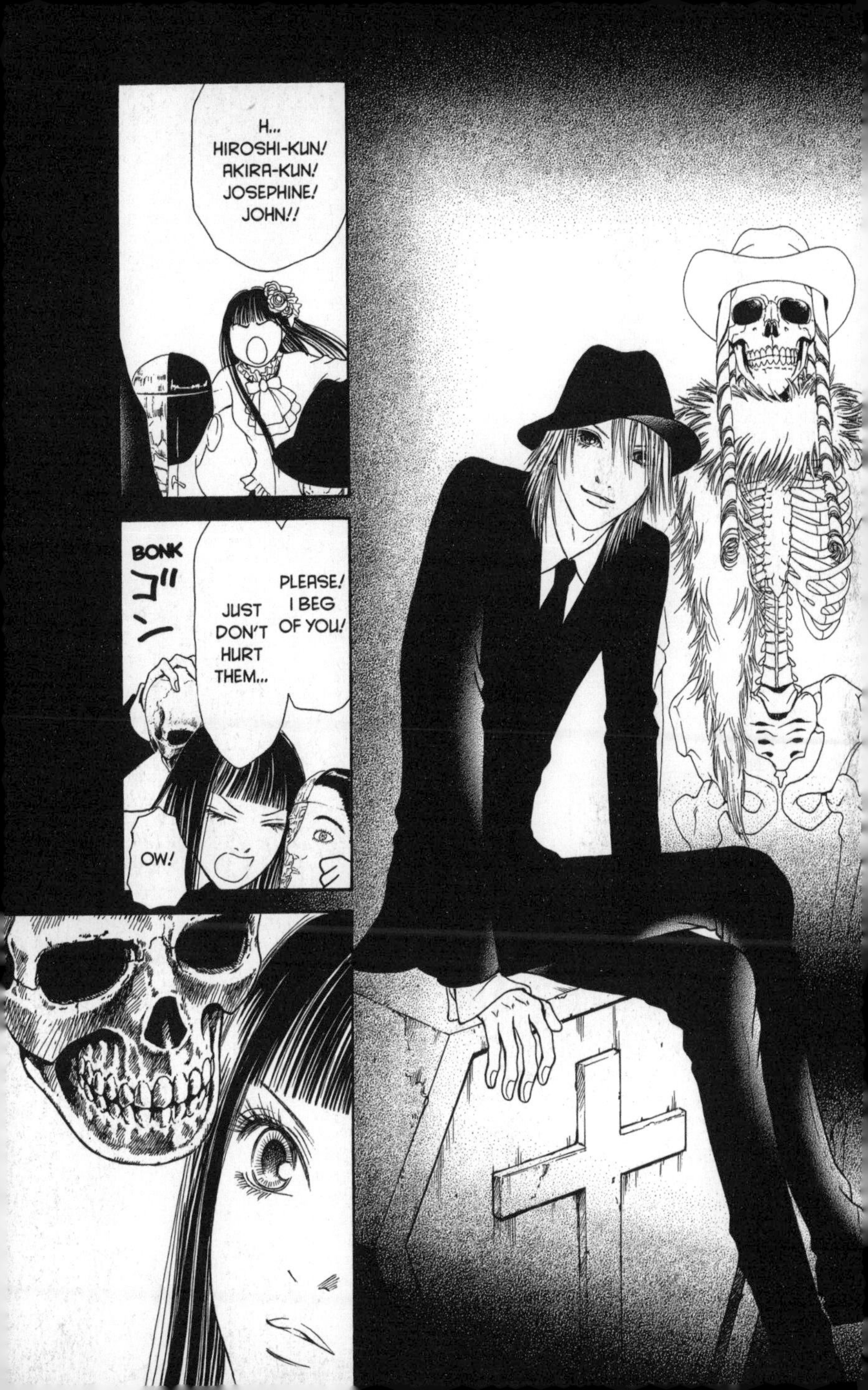
H... HIROSHI-KUN! AKIRA-KUN! JOSEPHINE! JOHN!!
PLEASE! I BEG OF YOU!
JUST DON'T HURT THEM...
BONK
ゴン
OW!

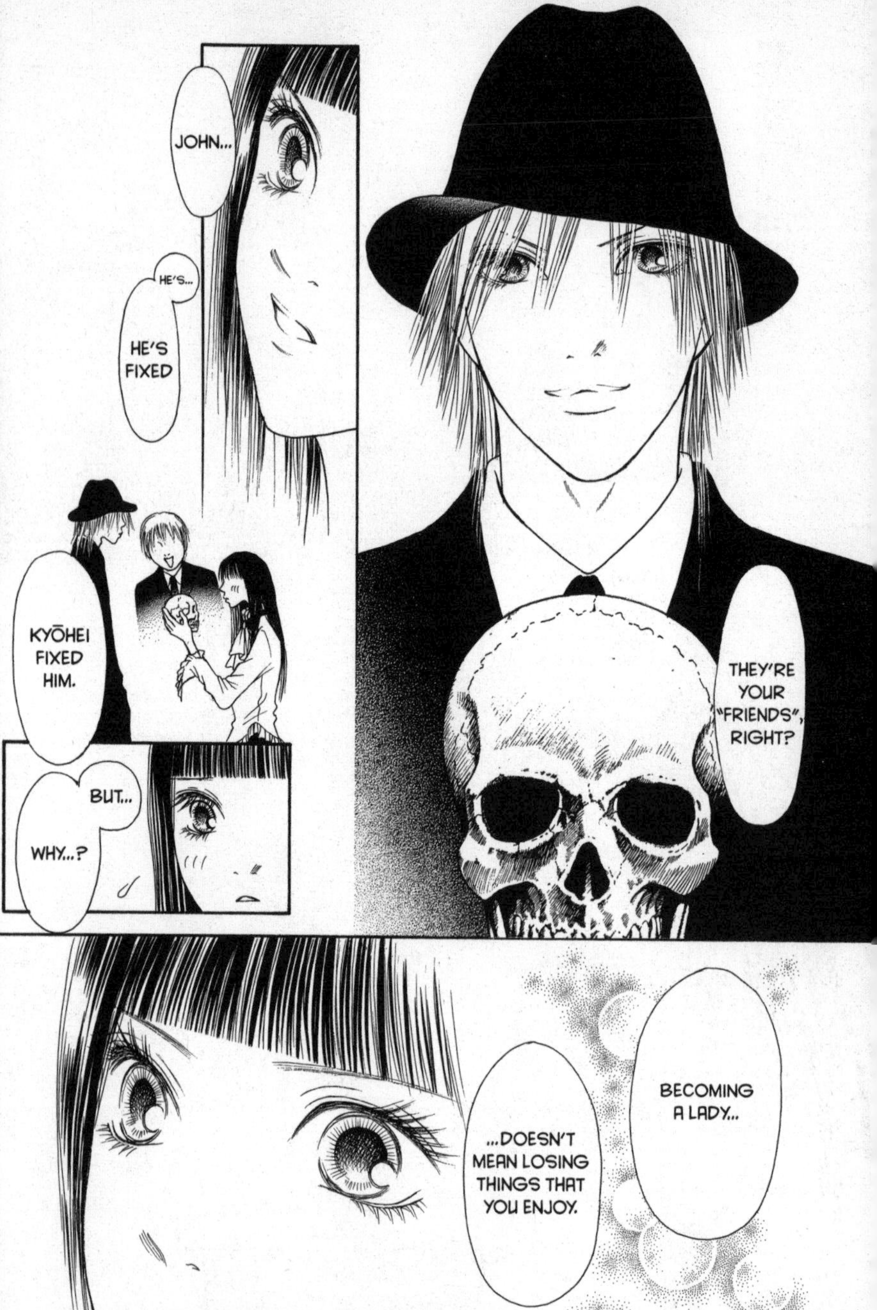
THEY'RE YOUR "FRIENDS", RIGHT?
JOHN...
HE'S...
HE'S FIXED
KYŌHEI FIXED HIM.
BUT...
WHY...?
BECOMING A LADY...
...DOESN'T MEAN LOSING THINGS THAT YOU ENJOY.

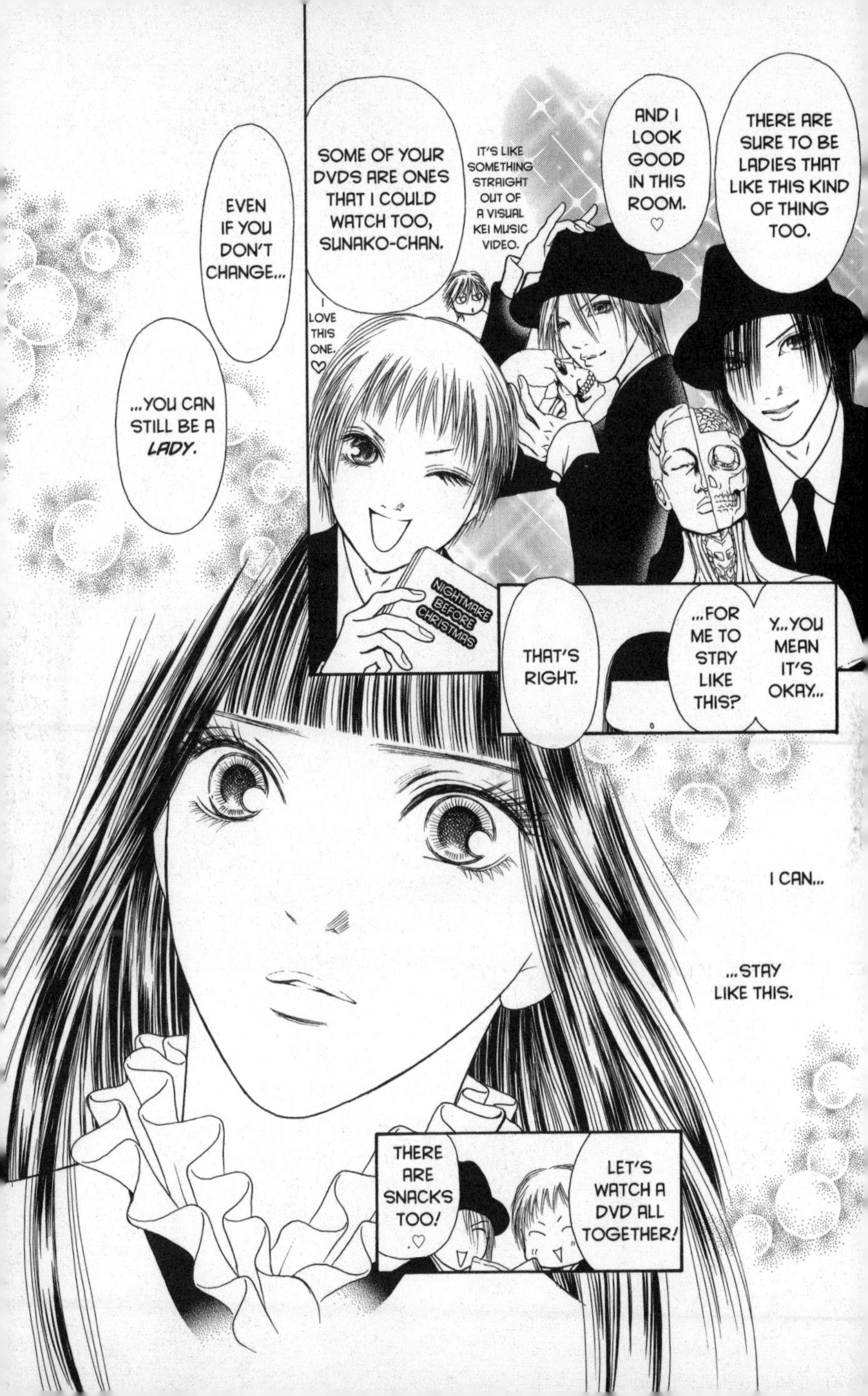
THERE ARE SURE TO BE LADIES THAT LIKE THIS KIND OF THING TOO.
AND I LOOK GOOD IN THIS ROOM. ♡
IT'S LIKE SOMETHING STRAIGHT OUT OF A VISUAL KEI MUSIC VIDEO.
SOME OF YOUR DVDS ARE ONES THAT I COULD WATCH TOO, SUNAKO-CHAN.
I LOVE THIS ONE. ♡
NIGHTMARE BEFORE CHRISTMAS
EVEN IF YOU DON'T CHANGE...
...YOU CAN STILL BE A *LADY*.
Y...YOU MEAN IT'S OKAY...
...FOR ME TO STAY LIKE THIS?
THAT'S RIGHT.
I CAN...
...STAY LIKE THIS.
LET'S WATCH A DVD ALL TOGETHER!
THERE ARE SNACKS TOO! ♡

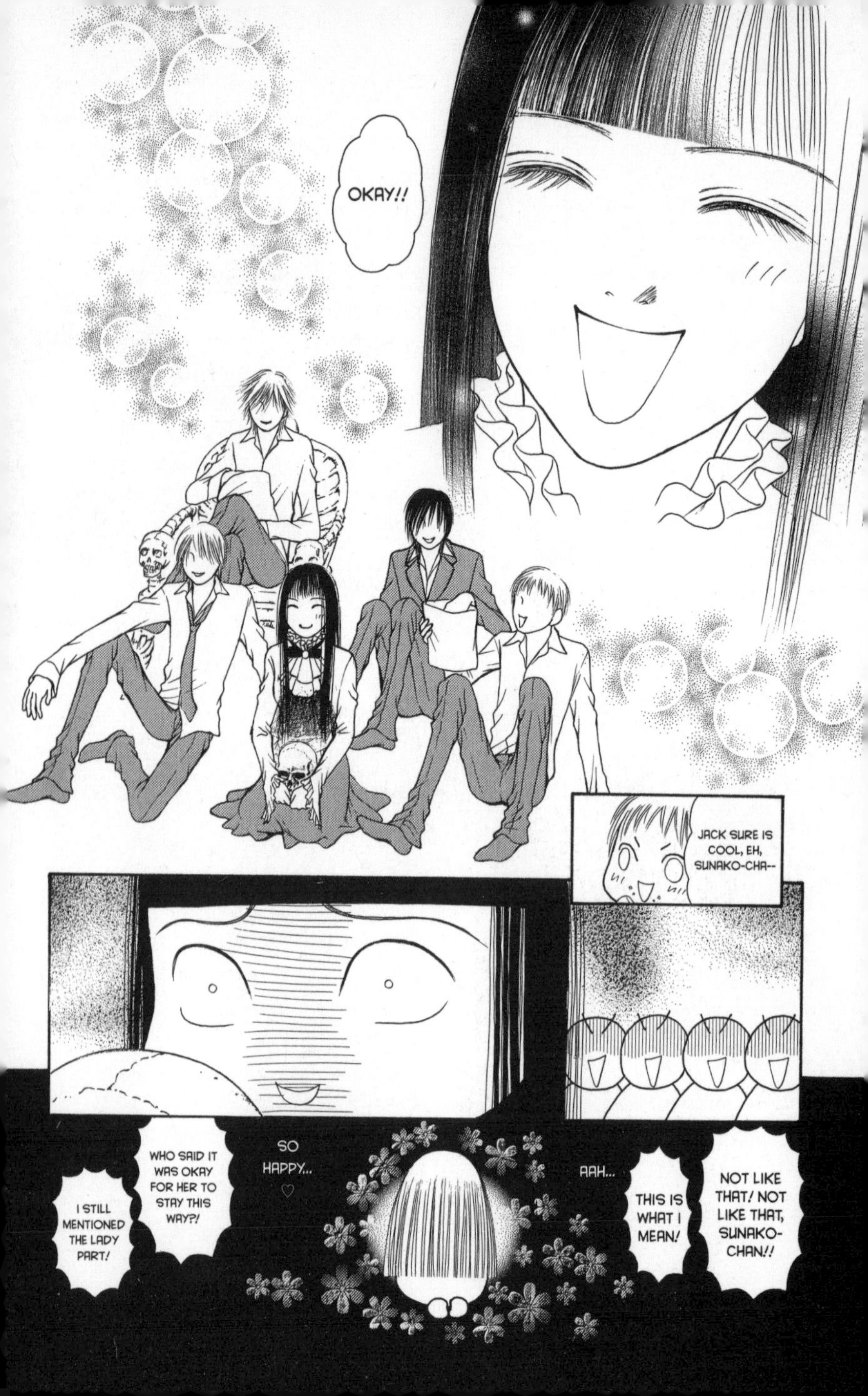
OKAY!!
JACK SURE IS COOL, EH, SUNAKO-CHA--
NOT LIKE THAT! NOT LIKE THAT, SUNAKO-CHAN!!
THIS IS WHAT I MEAN!
AAH...
SO HAPPY... ♡
WHO SAID IT WAS OKAY FOR HER TO STAY THIS WAY?!
I STILL MENTIONED THE LADY PART!

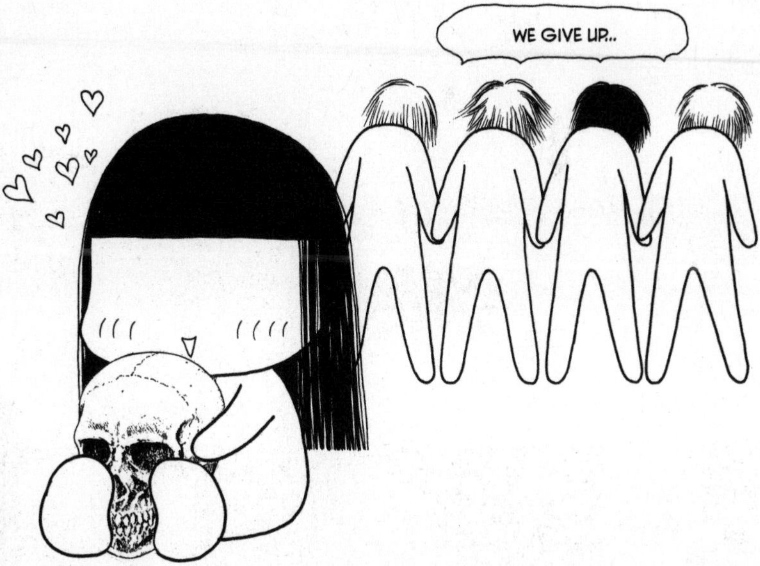
WE GIVE UP...

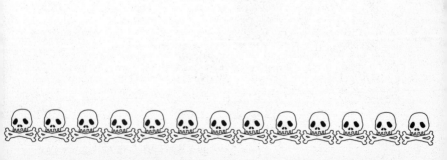

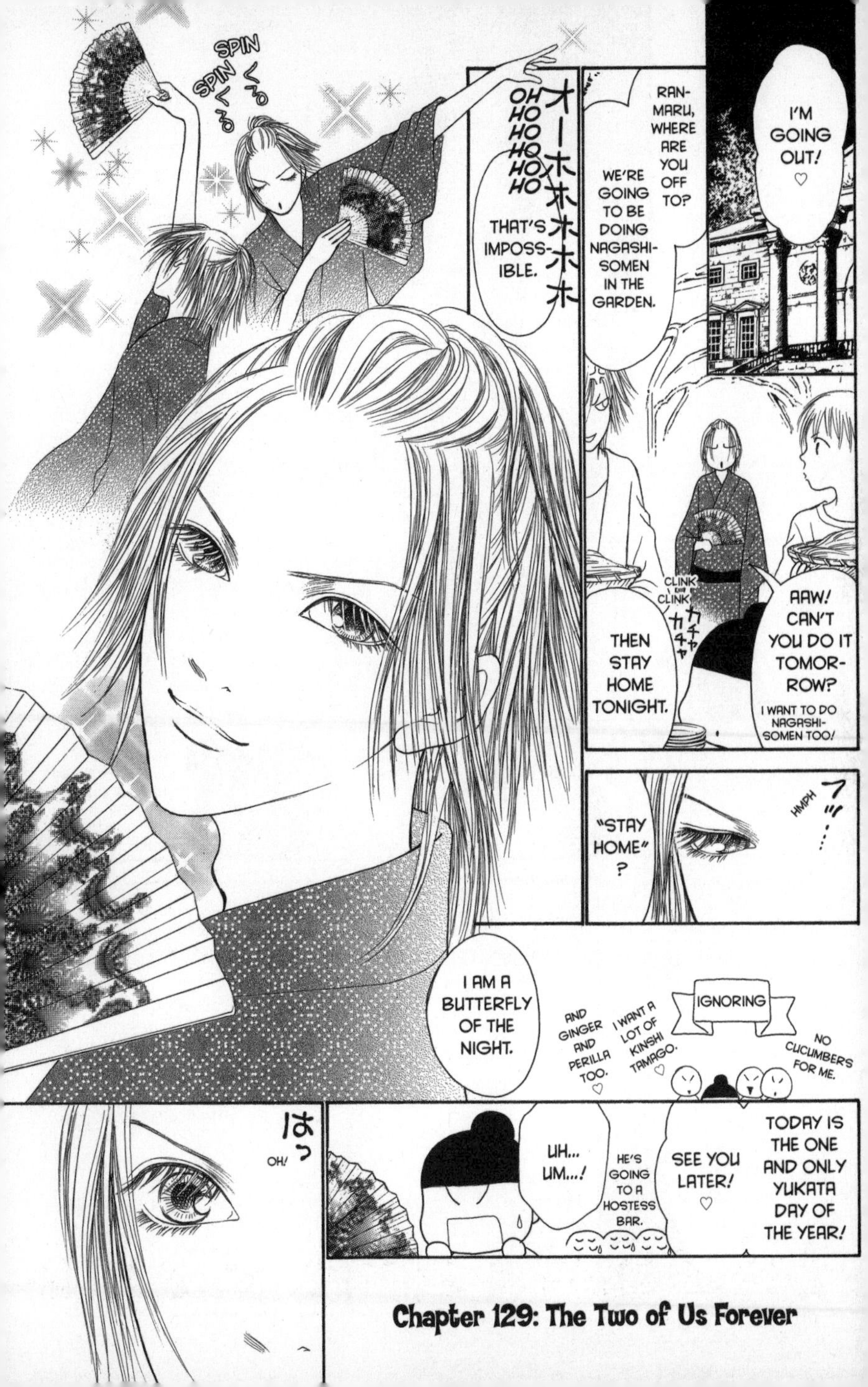
I'M GOING OUT! ♡
RAN-MARU, WHERE ARE YOU OFF TO?
WE'RE GOING TO BE DOING NAGASHI-SOMEN IN THE GARDEN.
AAW! CAN'T YOU DO IT TOMORROW?
I WANT TO DO NAGASHI-SOMEN TOO!
カチャカチャ
CLINK CLINK
THEN STAY HOME TONIGHT.
オーホホホホホ
OH HO HO HO HO HO HO
THAT'S IMPOSS-IBLE.
HMPH
"STAY HOME"?
くるくる
SPIN SPIN
I AM A BUTTERFLY OF THE NIGHT.
IGNORING
NO CUCUMBERS FOR ME.
I WANT A LOT OF KINSHI TAMAGO. ♡
AND GINGER AND PERILLA TOO. ♡
TODAY IS THE ONE AND ONLY YUKATA DAY OF THE YEAR!
SEE YOU LATER! ♡
HE'S GOING TO A HOSTESS BAR.
UH... UM...!
はっ
OH!

Chapter 129: The Two of Us Forever

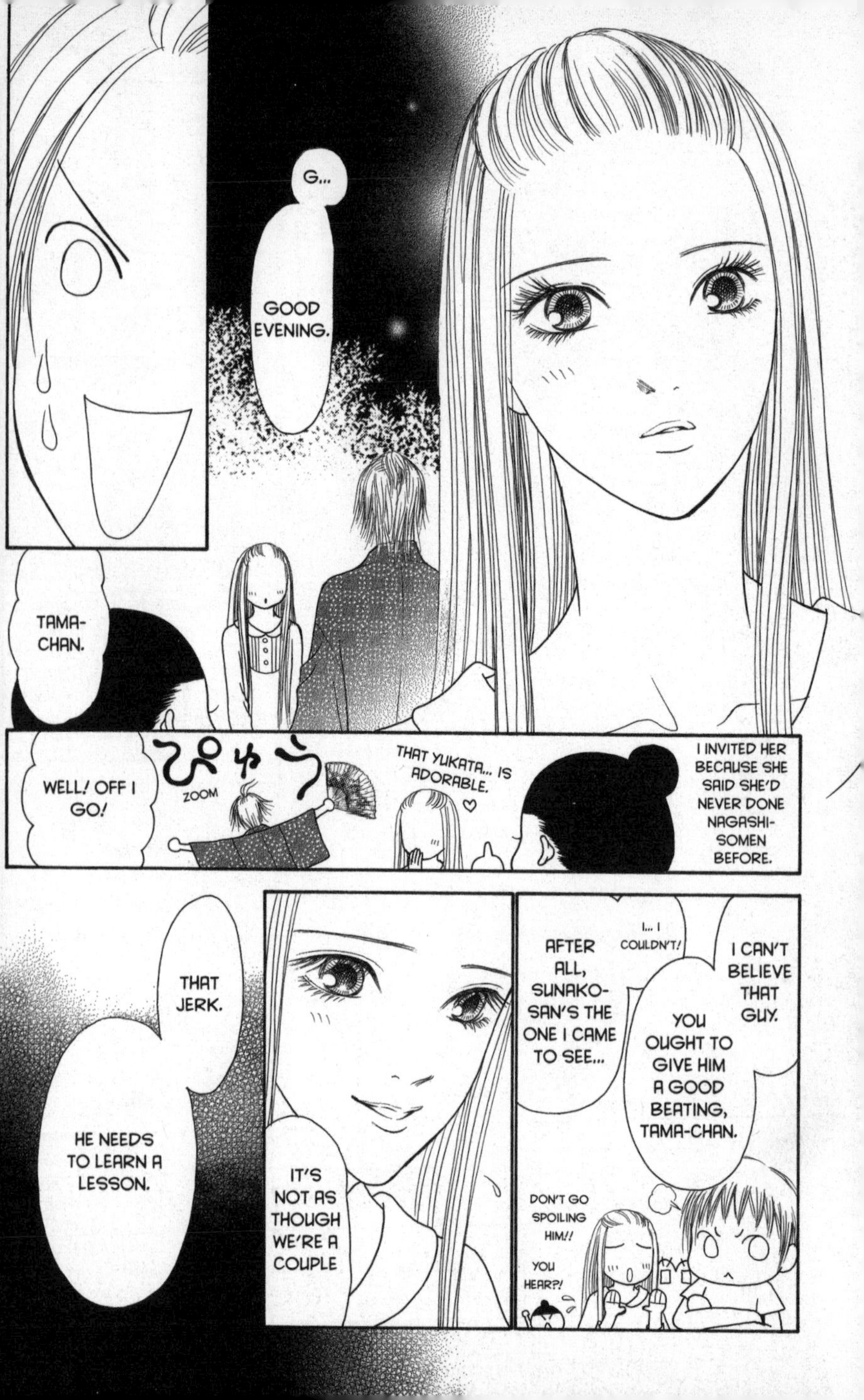
G...
GOOD EVENING.
TAMA-CHAN.
I INVITED HER BECAUSE SHE SAID SHE'D NEVER DONE NAGASHI-SOMEN BEFORE.
THAT YUKATA... IS ADORABLE. ♡
ぴゅう
ZOOM
WELL! OFF I GO!
I CAN'T BELIEVE THAT GUY.
I... I COULDN'T!
AFTER ALL, SUNAKO-SAN'S THE ONE I CAME TO SEE...
YOU OUGHT TO GIVE HIM A GOOD BEATING, TAMA-CHAN.
DON'T GO SPOILING HIM!!
YOU HEAR?!
IT'S NOT AS THOUGH WE'RE A COUPLE
THAT JERK.
HE NEEDS TO LEARN A LESSON.

Chapter 129. The Two of Us Forever

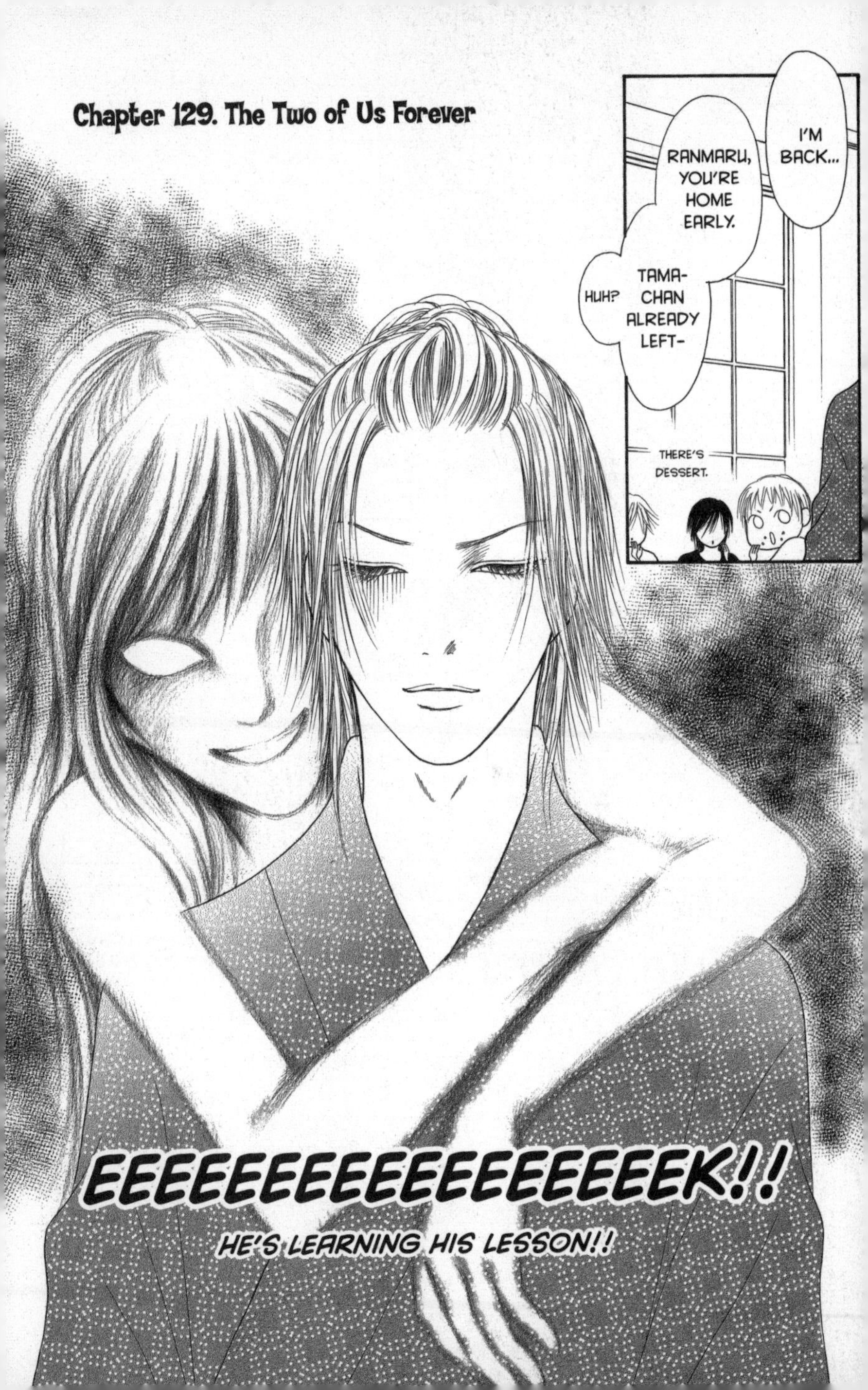
I'M BACK...
RANMARU, YOU'RE HOME EARLY.
TAMA-CHAN ALREADY LEFT-
HUH?
THERE'S DESSERT.
EEEEEEEEEEEEEEEEEK!!
HE'S LEARNING HIS LESSON!!

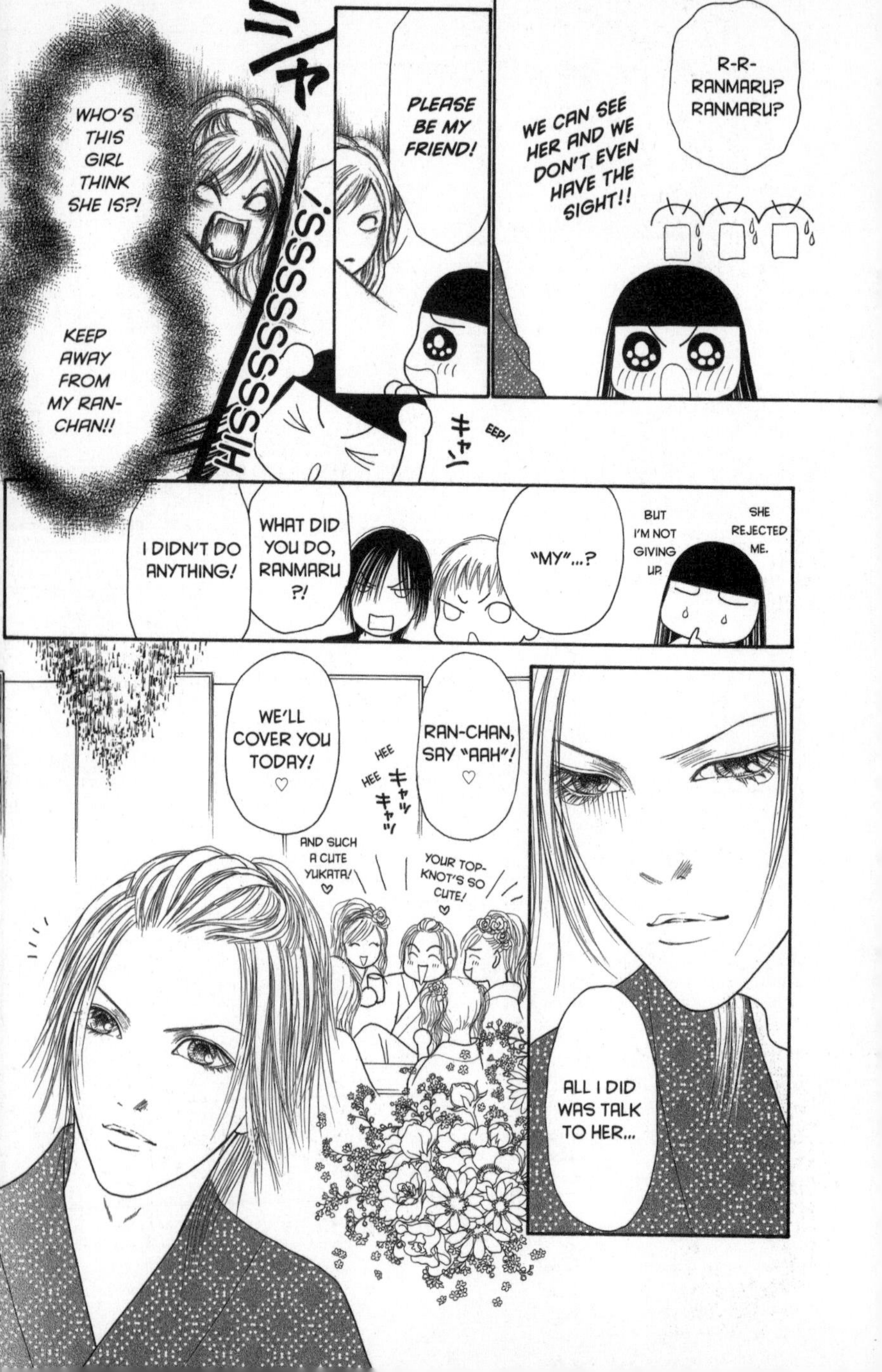
R-R-RANMARU? RANMARU?
WE CAN SEE HER AND WE DON'T EVEN HAVE THE SIGHT!!
PLEASE BE MY FRIEND!
シャ
WHO'S THIS GIRL THINK SHE IS?!
KEEP AWAY FROM MY RAN-CHAN!!
HISSSSSSSSS!
キャン
EEP!
SHE REJECTED ME.
BUT I'M NOT GIVING UP.
"MY"...?
WHAT DID YOU DO, RANMARU?!
I DIDN'T DO ANYTHING!
ALL I DID WAS TALK TO HER...
RAN-CHAN, SAY "AAH"! ♡
WE'LL COVER YOU TODAY! ♡
HEE HEE
キャッキャッ
YOUR TOP-KNOT'S SO CUTE! ♡
AND SUCH A CUTE YUKATA! ♡

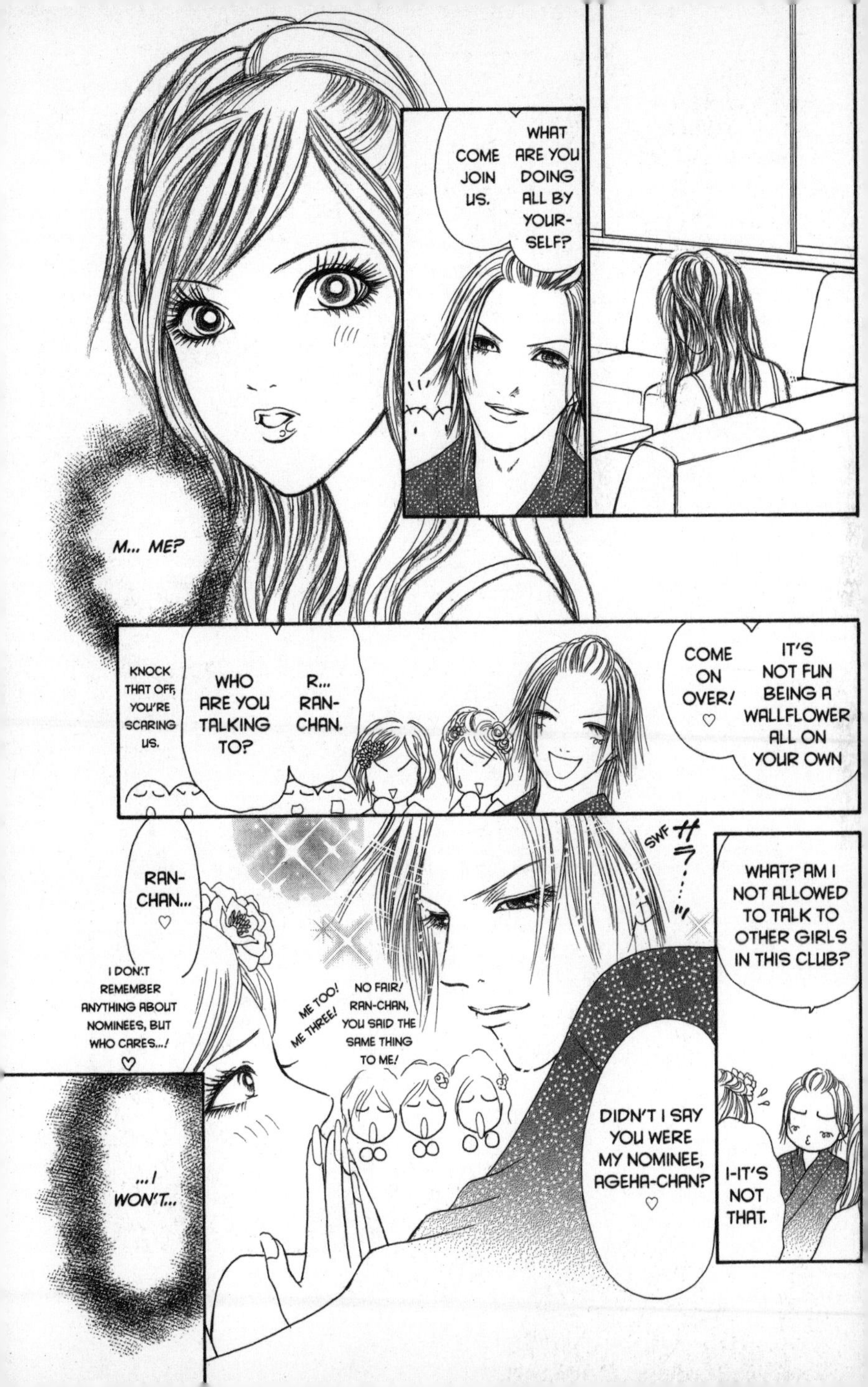
WHAT ARE YOU DOING ALL BY YOURSELF?
COME JOIN US.
M... ME?
IT'S NOT FUN BEING A WALLFLOWER ALL ON YOUR OWN
COME ON OVER! ♡
R... RAN-CHAN.
WHO ARE YOU TALKING TO?
KNOCK THAT OFF, YOU'RE SCARING US.
WHAT? AM I NOT ALLOWED TO TALK TO OTHER GIRLS IN THIS CLUB?
I-IT'S NOT THAT.
SWF
DIDN'T I SAY YOU WERE MY NOMINEE, AGEHA-CHAN? ♡
NO FAIR! RAN-CHAN, YOU SAID THE SAME THING TO ME!
ME TOO! ME THREE!
RAN-CHAN... ♡
I DON'T REMEMBER ANYTHING ABOUT NOMINEES, BUT WHO CARES...! ♡
...I WON'T...

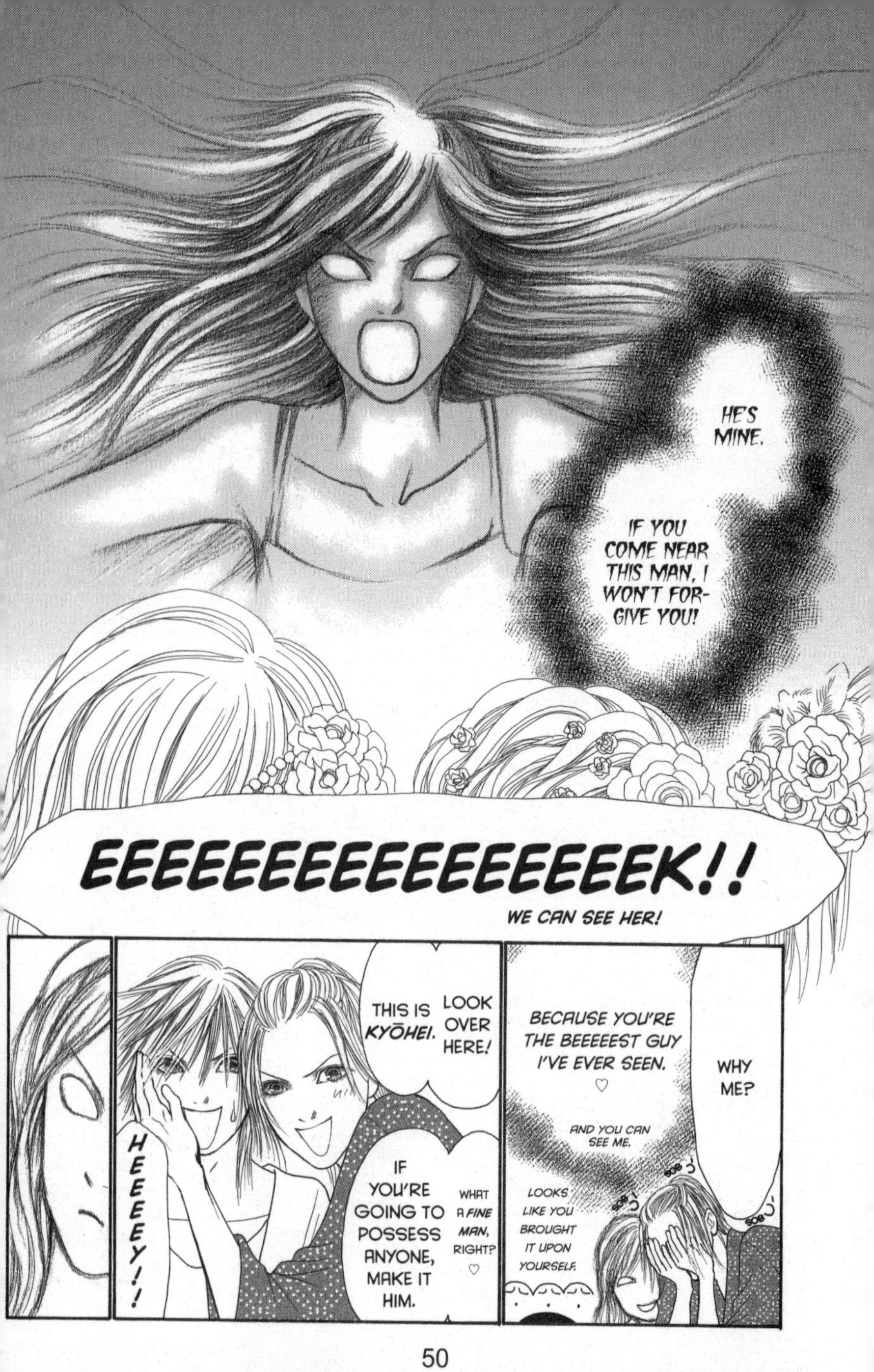
HE'S MINE.
IF YOU COME NEAR THIS MAN, I WON'T FOR-GIVE YOU!
EEEEEEEEEEEEEEEK!!
WE CAN SEE HER!
WHY ME?
BECAUSE YOU'RE THE BEEEEEST GUY I'VE EVER SEEN. ♡
AND YOU CAN SEE ME.
SOB
SOB
SOB
LOOKS LIKE YOU BROUGHT IT UPON YOURSELF.
LOOK OVER HERE!
THIS IS KYŌHEI.
WHAT A FINE MAN, RIGHT? ♡
IF YOU'RE GOING TO POSSESS ANYONE, MAKE IT HIM.
HEEEEEY!!

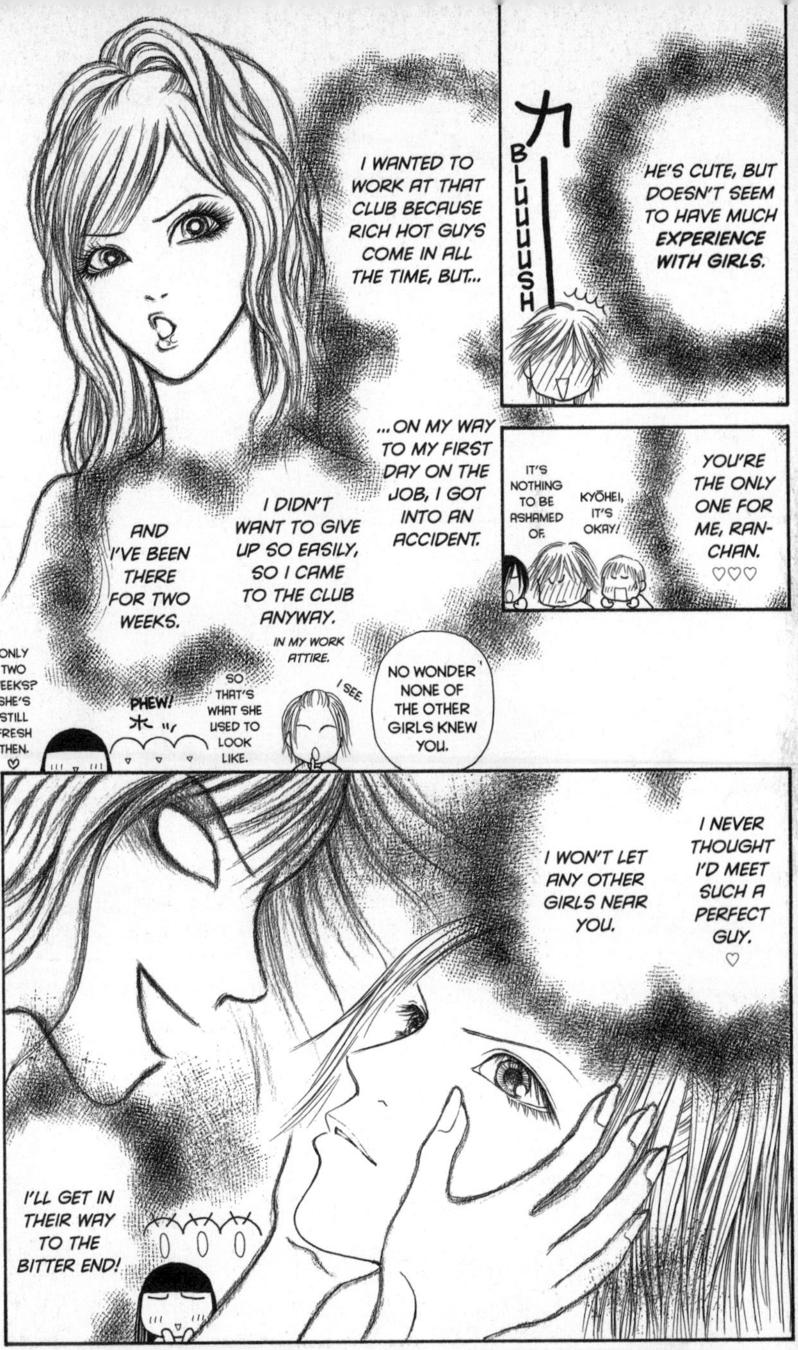
カ
BLUUUUSH
HE'S CUTE, BUT DOESN'T SEEM TO HAVE MUCH EXPERIENCE WITH GIRLS.
YOU'RE THE ONLY ONE FOR ME, RAN-CHAN. ♡♡♡
KYŌHEI, IT'S OKAY!
IT'S NOTHING TO BE ASHAMED OF.
I WANTED TO WORK AT THAT CLUB BECAUSE RICH HOT GUYS COME IN ALL THE TIME, BUT...
...ON MY WAY TO MY FIRST DAY ON THE JOB, I GOT INTO AN ACCIDENT.
I DIDN'T WANT TO GIVE UP SO EASILY, SO I CAME TO THE CLUB ANYWAY.
AND I'VE BEEN THERE FOR TWO WEEKS.
NO WONDER NONE OF THE OTHER GIRLS KNEW YOU.
I SEE.
IN MY WORK ATTIRE.
SO THAT'S WHAT SHE USED TO LOOK LIKE.
PHEW!
ホッ
ONLY TWO WEEKS? SHE'S STILL FRESH THEN. ♡
I NEVER THOUGHT I'D MEET SUCH A PERFECT GUY. ♡
I WON'T LET ANY OTHER GIRLS NEAR YOU.
I'LL GET IN THEIR WAY TO THE BITTER END!

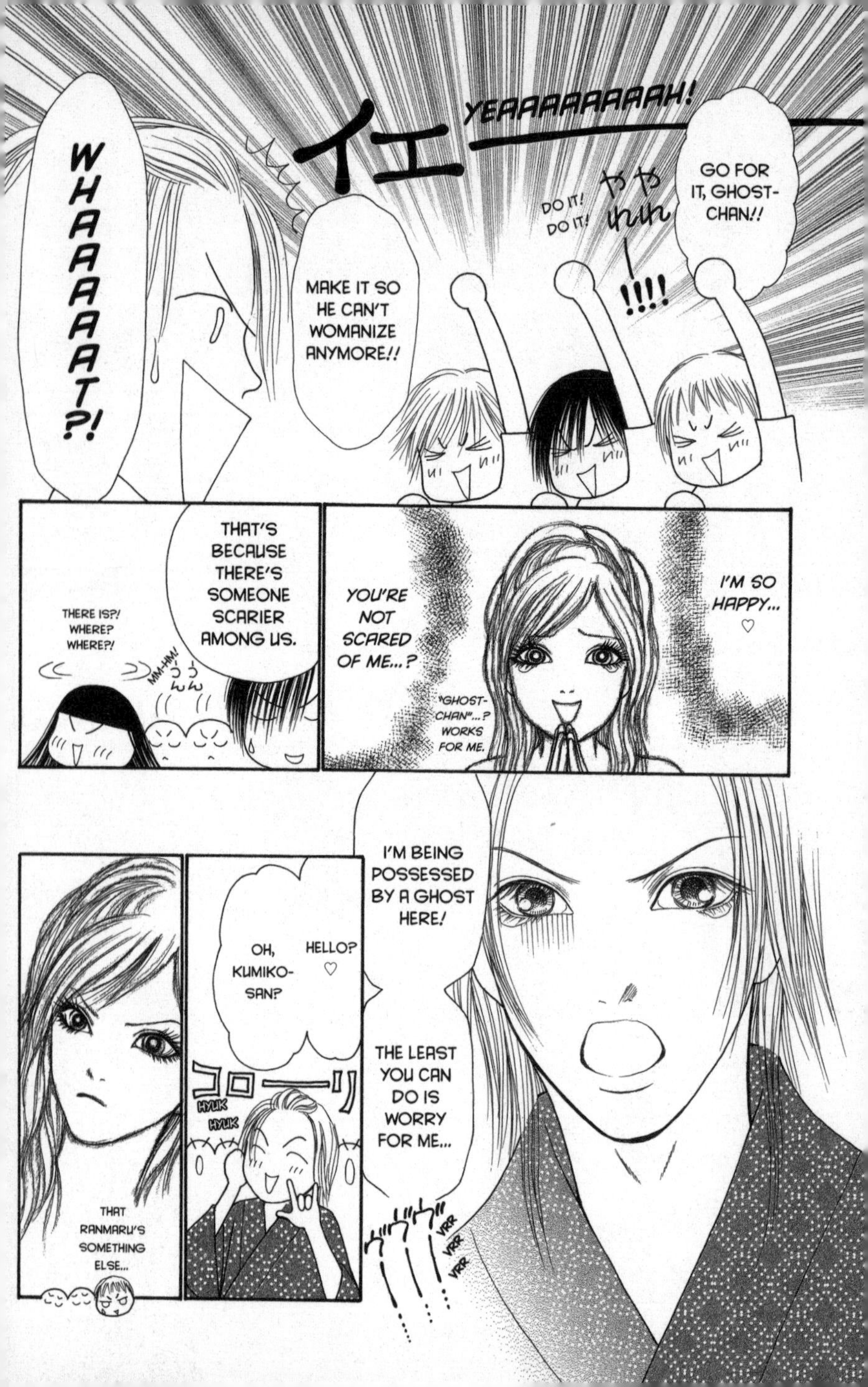

イエー
YEAAAAAAAAH!
GO FOR IT, GHOST-CHAN!!
やれやれー!!!!
DO IT! DO IT!
MAKE IT SO HE CAN'T WOMANIZE ANYMORE!!
WHAAAAAAAT?!
I'M SO HAPPY... ♡
YOU'RE NOT SCARED OF ME...?
"GHOST-CHAN"...? WORKS FOR ME.
THAT'S BECAUSE THERE'S SOMEONE SCARIER AMONG US.
うんうん
MM-HM!
THERE IS?! WHERE? WHERE?!
I'M BEING POSSESSED BY A GHOST HERE!
THE LEAST YOU CAN DO IS WORRY FOR ME...
ヴヴヴ
VRR VRR VRR
HELLO? ♡
OH, KUMIKO-SAN?
コローリ
HYUK HYUK
THAT RANMARU'S SOMETHING ELSE...

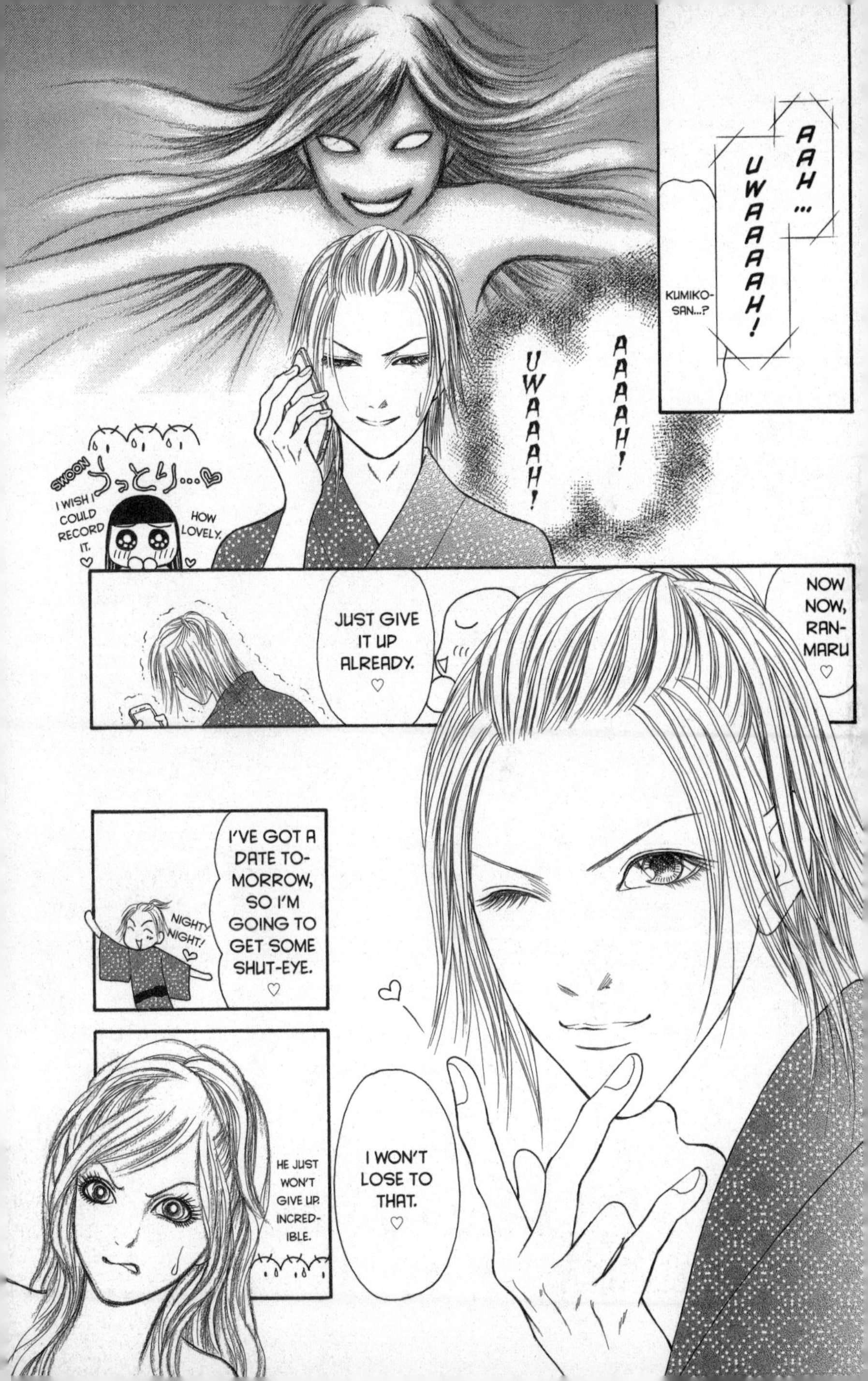
AAH... UWAAAAAH!
KUMIKO-SAN...?
AAAAAH!
UWAAAAH!
SWOON うっとり…♡
HOW LOVELY.
I WISH I COULD RECORD IT. ♡
NOW NOW, RAN-MARU ♡
JUST GIVE IT UP ALREADY. ♡
I WON'T LOSE TO THAT. ♡
I'VE GOT A DATE TO-MORROW, SO I'M GOING TO GET SOME SHUT-EYE. ♡
NIGHTY NIGHT! ♡
HE JUST WON'T GIVE UP. INCREDIBLE.

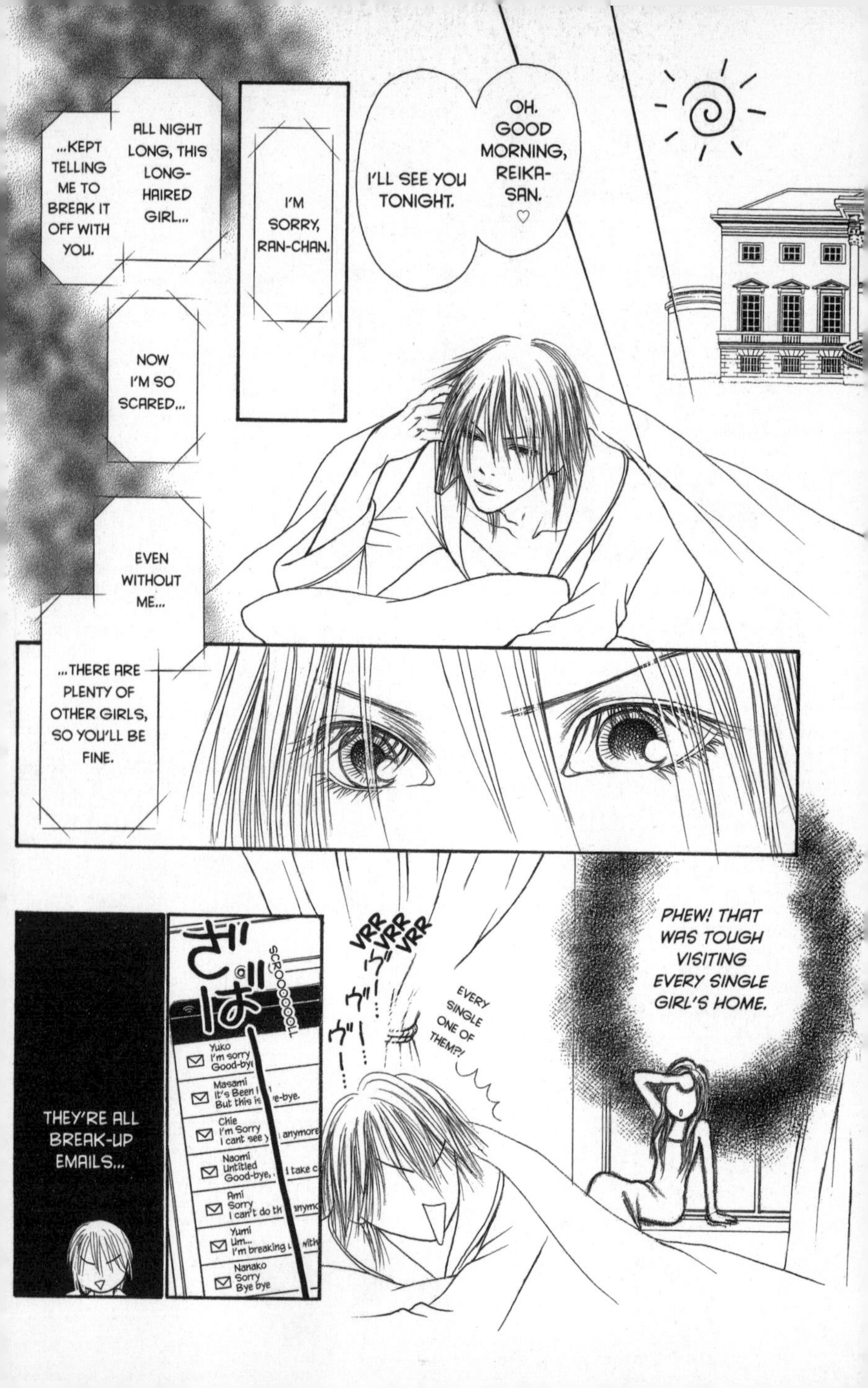

OH. GOOD MORNING, REIKA-SAN. ♡
I'LL SEE YOU TONIGHT.
I'M SORRY, RAN-CHAN.
ALL NIGHT LONG, THIS LONG-HAIRED GIRL...
...KEPT TELLING ME TO BREAK IT OFF WITH YOU.
NOW I'M SO SCARED...
EVEN WITHOUT ME...
...THERE ARE PLENTY OF OTHER GIRLS, SO YOU'LL BE FINE.
PHEW! THAT WAS TOUGH VISITING EVERY SINGLE GIRL'S HOME.
EVERY SINGLE ONE OF THEM?!
VRR VRR VRR
ヴー… ヴー… ヴー…
SCROOOOOOLL
Yuko I'm sorry Good-bye
Masami It's Been But this is ye-bye.
Chie I'm Sorry I cant see y anymore
Naomi Untitled Good-bye, take c
Ami Sorry I can't do th anymo
Yumi Um... I'm breaking with
Nanako Sorry Bye bye
THEY'RE ALL BREAK-UP EMAILS...

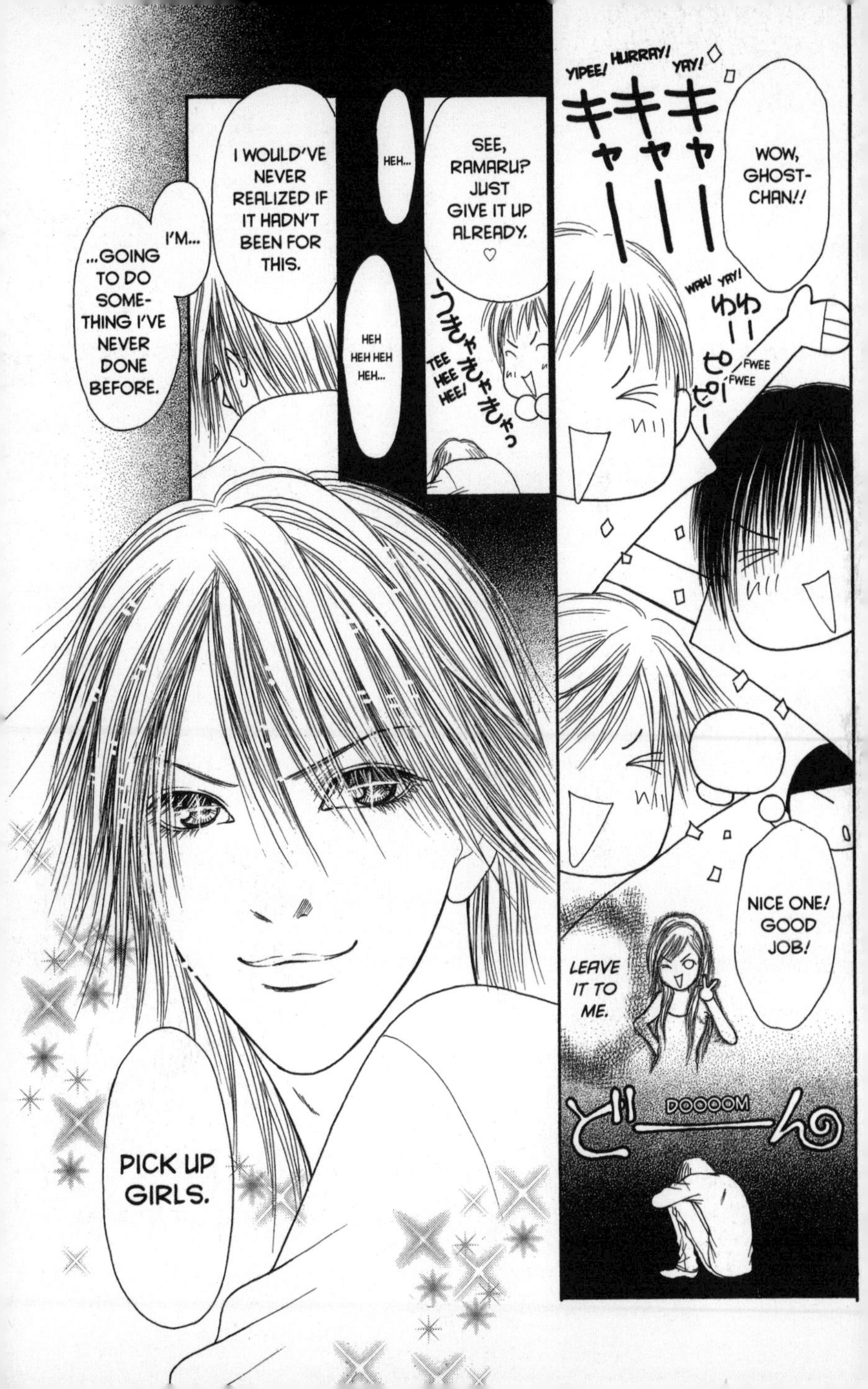
WOW, GHOST-CHAN!!
YAY!
HURRAY!
YIPEE!
キャー キャー キャー
WAH! YAY!
わーわー
FWEE FWEE
ぴーぴー
NICE ONE! GOOD JOB!
LEAVE IT TO ME.
DOOOOM
どーん
SEE, RAMARU? JUST GIVE IT UP ALREADY. ♡
TEE HEE HEE!
うきゃきゃきゃっ
HEH...
HEH HEH HEH HEH...
I WOULD'VE NEVER REALIZED IF IT HADN'T BEEN FOR THIS.
I'M...
...GOING TO DO SOME-THING I'VE NEVER DONE BEFORE.
PICK UP GIRLS.

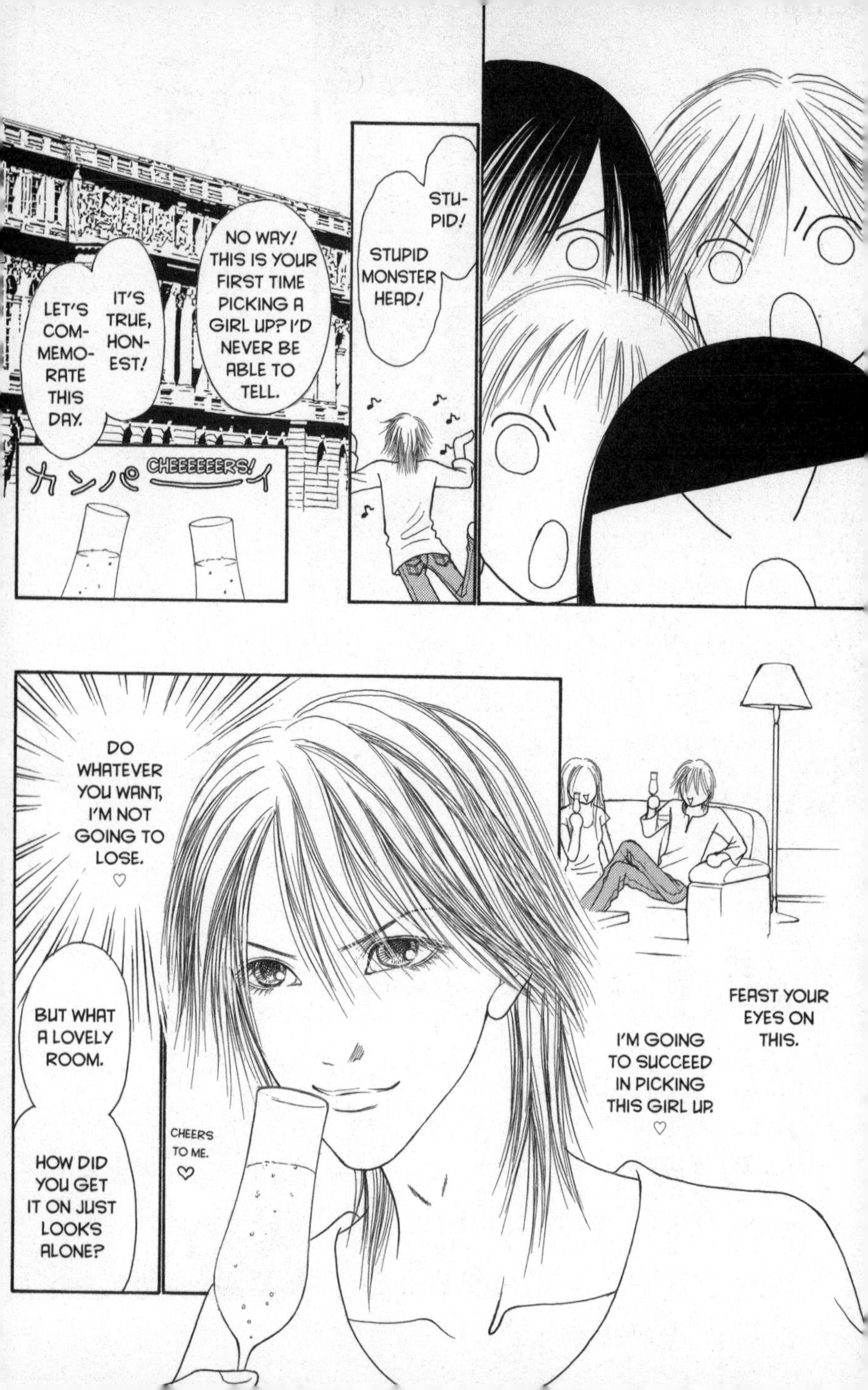
STU-PID!
STUPID MONSTER HEAD!
NO WAY! THIS IS YOUR FIRST TIME PICKING A GIRL UP? I'D NEVER BE ABLE TO TELL.
IT'S TRUE, HONEST!
LET'S COMMEMORATE THIS DAY.
カンパーイ
CHEEEEEEERS!
FEAST YOUR EYES ON THIS.
I'M GOING TO SUCCEED IN PICKING THIS GIRL UP. ♡
DO WHATEVER YOU WANT, I'M NOT GOING TO LOSE. ♡
CHEERS TO ME. ♡
BUT WHAT A LOVELY ROOM.
HOW DID YOU GET IT ON JUST LOOKS ALONE?

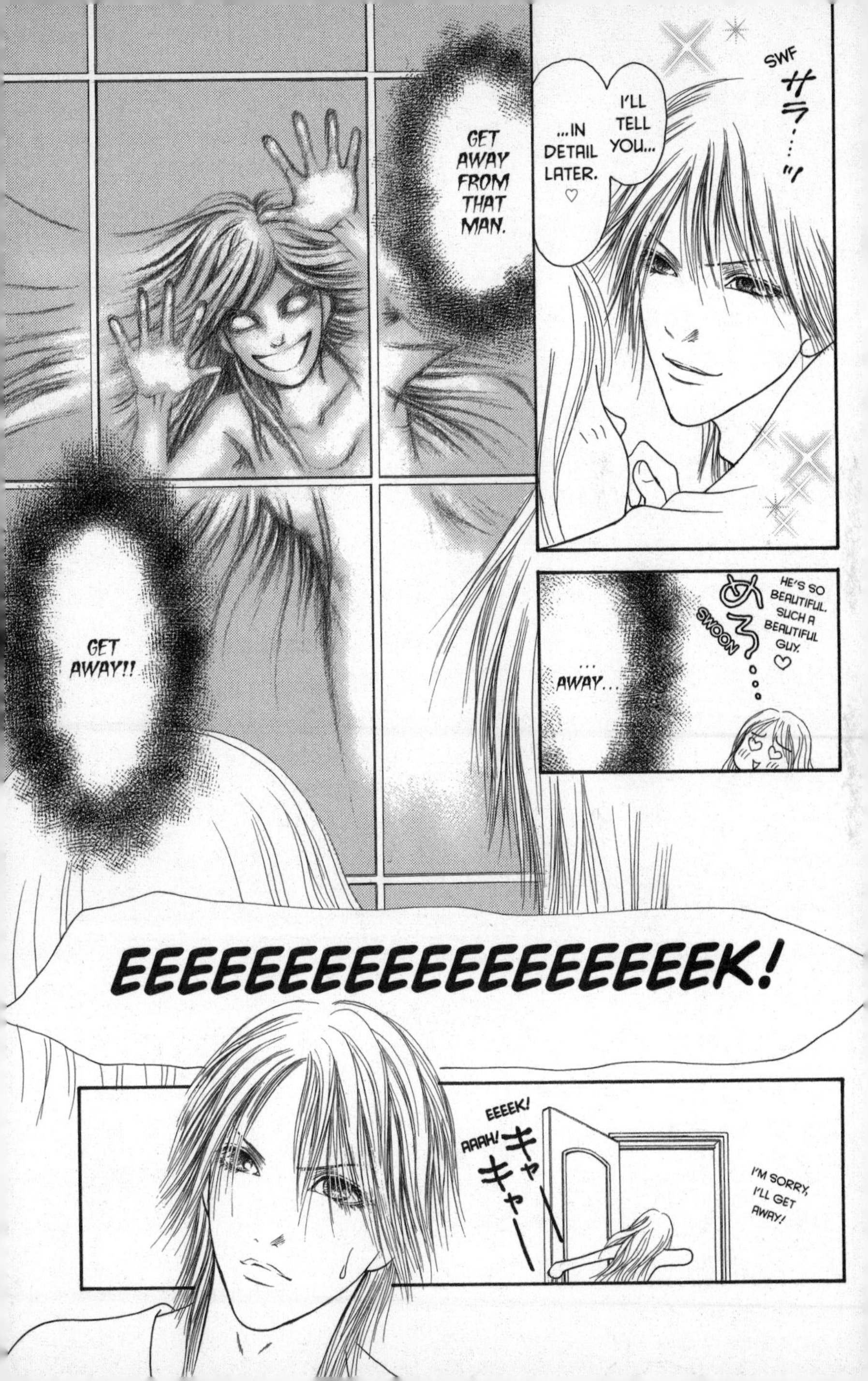
SWF
サラ…!
I'LL TELL YOU...
...IN DETAIL LATER. ♡
HE'S SO BEAUTIFUL. SUCH A BEAUTIFUL GUY. ♡
SWOON
めろ
... AWAY...
GET AWAY FROM THAT MAN.
GET AWAY!!
EEEEEEEEEEEEEEEEEEEEEEK!
I'M SORRY, I'LL GET AWAY!
EEEEK!
キャー
AAAH!
キャー

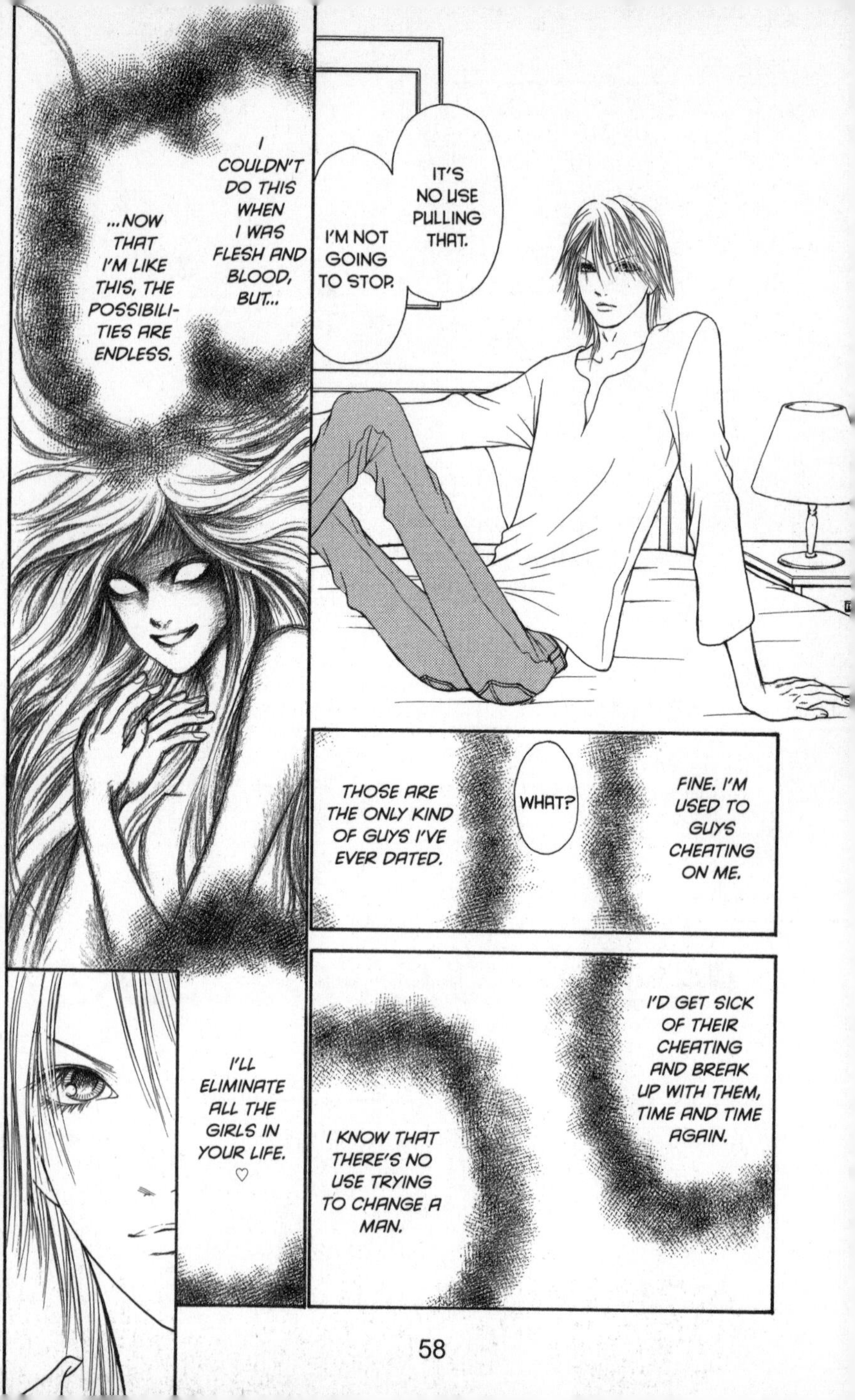
IT'S NO USE PULLING THAT.
I'M NOT GOING TO STOP.
I COULDN'T DO THIS WHEN I WAS FLESH AND BLOOD, BUT...
...NOW THAT I'M LIKE THIS, THE POSSIBILITIES ARE ENDLESS.
I'LL ELIMINATE ALL THE GIRLS IN YOUR LIFE. ♡
FINE. I'M USED TO GUYS CHEATING ON ME.
WHAT?
THOSE ARE THE ONLY KIND OF GUYS I'VE EVER DATED.
I'D GET SICK OF THEIR CHEATING AND BREAK UP WITH THEM, TIME AND TIME AGAIN.
I KNOW THAT THERE'S NO USE TRYING TO CHANGE A MAN.

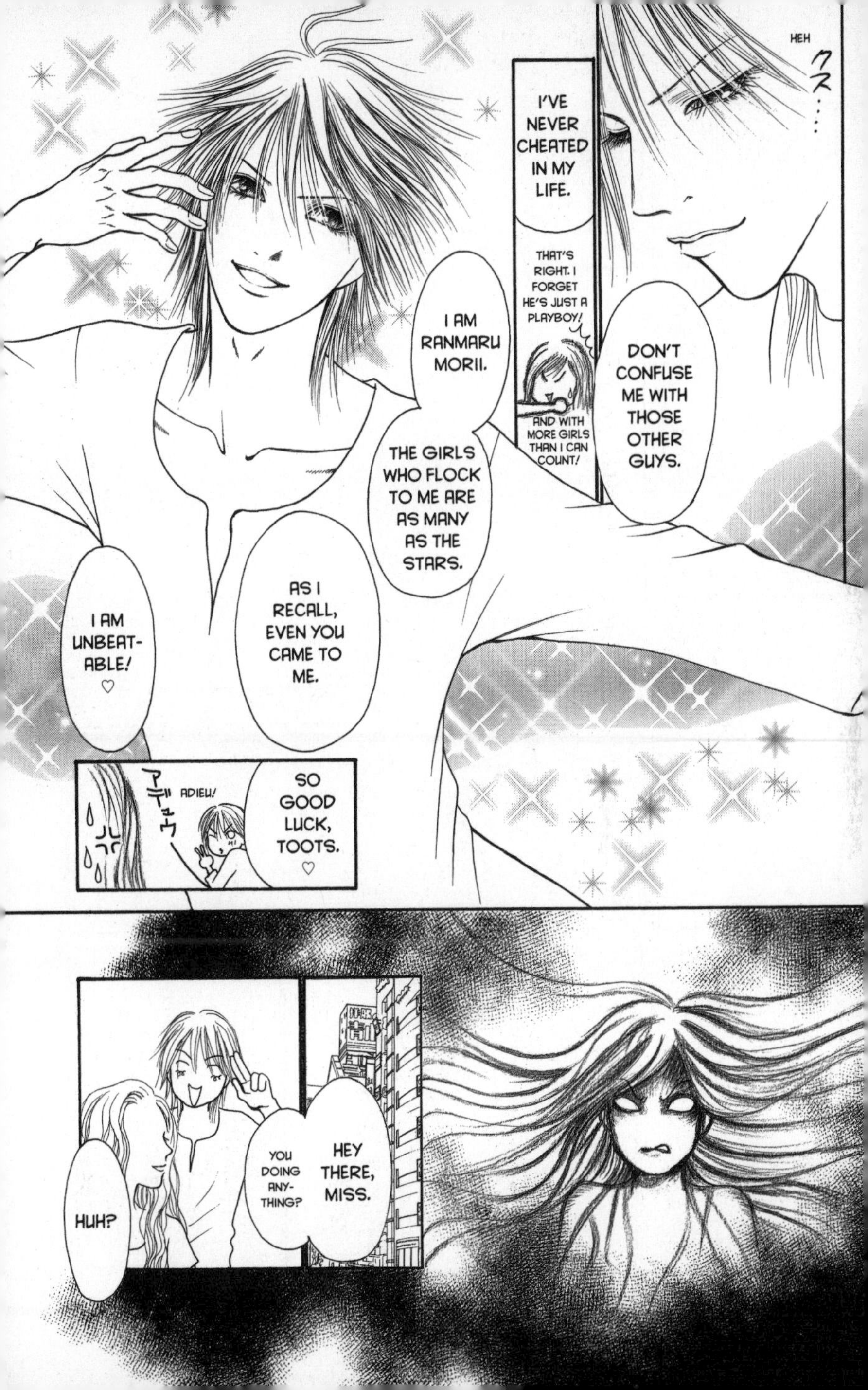

HEH
クス…
I'VE NEVER CHEATED IN MY LIFE.
DON'T CONFUSE ME WITH THOSE OTHER GUYS.
THAT'S RIGHT. I FORGET HE'S JUST A PLAYBOY!
AND WITH MORE GIRLS THAN I CAN COUNT!
I AM RANMARU MORII.
THE GIRLS WHO FLOCK TO ME ARE AS MANY AS THE STARS.
AS I RECALL, EVEN YOU CAME TO ME.
I AM UNBEAT-ABLE! ♡
SO GOOD LUCK, TOOTS. ♡
ADIEU!
HEY THERE, MISS.
YOU DOING ANY-THING?
HUH?

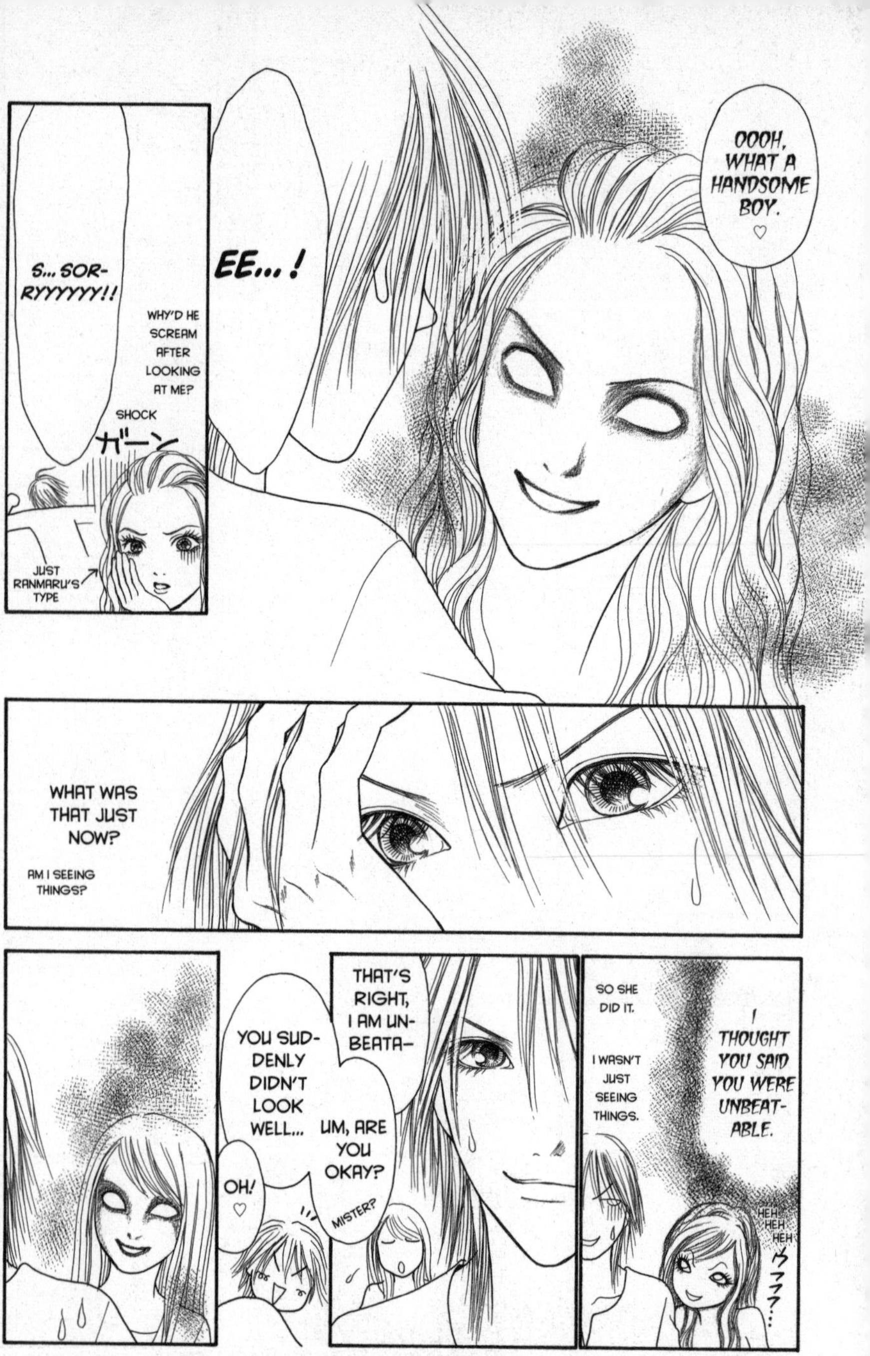
OOOH, WHAT A HANDSOME BOY. ♡
EE...!
S... SOR-RYYYYYY!!
WHY'D HE SCREAM AFTER LOOKING AT ME?
SHOCK
ガーン
JUST RANMARU'S TYPE
WHAT WAS THAT JUST NOW?
AM I SEEING THINGS?
I THOUGHT YOU SAID YOU WERE UNBEAT-ABLE.
SO SHE DID IT.
I WASN'T JUST SEEING THINGS.
HEH HEH HEH
ウフフフ...
THAT'S RIGHT, I AM UN-BEATA-
UM, ARE YOU OKAY?
MISTER?
YOU SUD-DENLY DIDN'T LOOK WELL...
OH! ♡

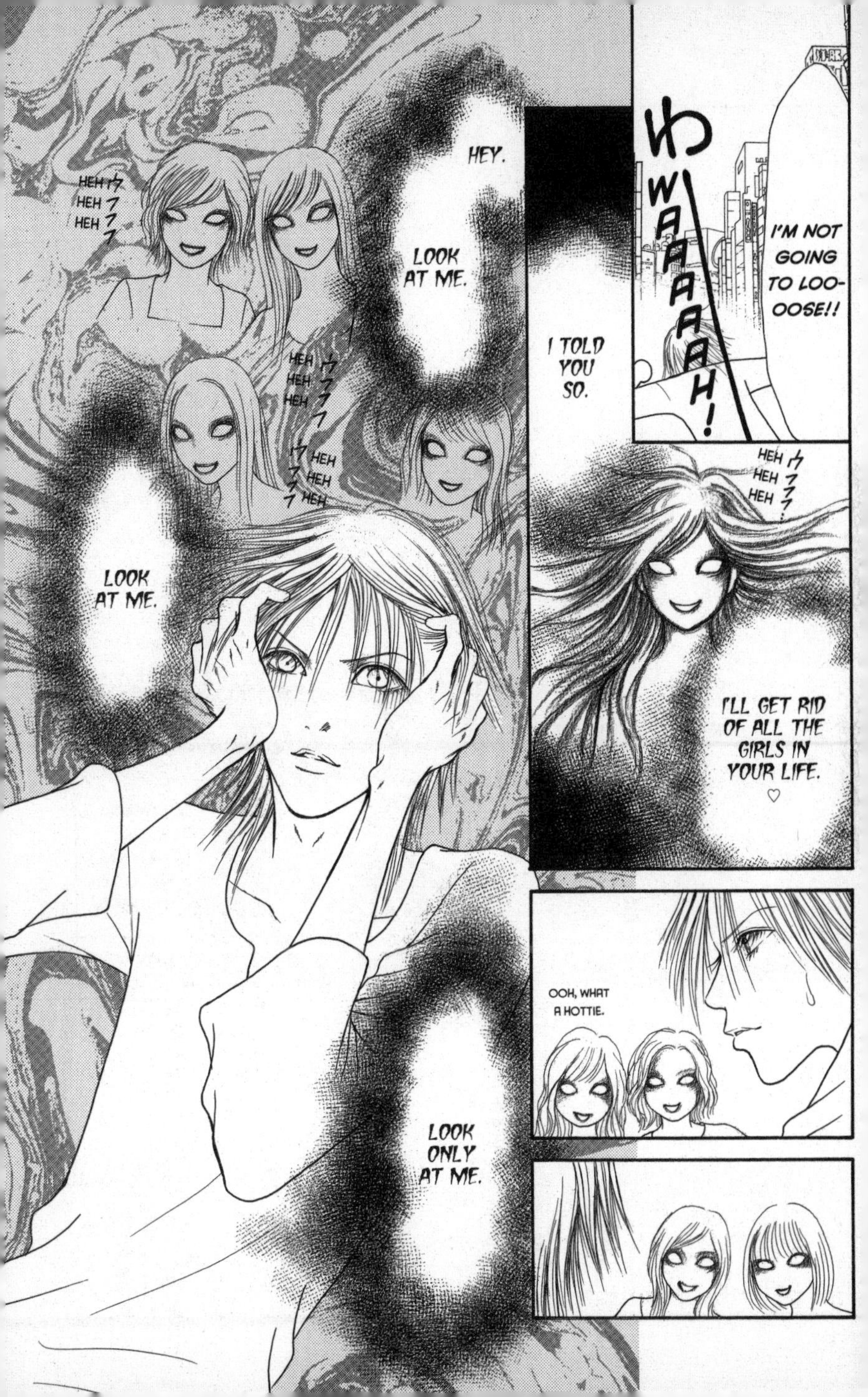

わ
WAAAAAH!
I'M NOT GOING TO LOO-OOSE!!
HEH HEH HEH ウフフ
I'LL GET RID OF ALL THE GIRLS IN YOUR LIFE. ♡
OOH, WHAT A HOTTIE.
HEY.
LOOK AT ME.
I TOLD YOU SO.
HEH HEH HEH ウフフ
HEH HEH HEH ウフフ
HEH HEH HEH ウフフ
LOOK AT ME.
LOOK ONLY AT ME.

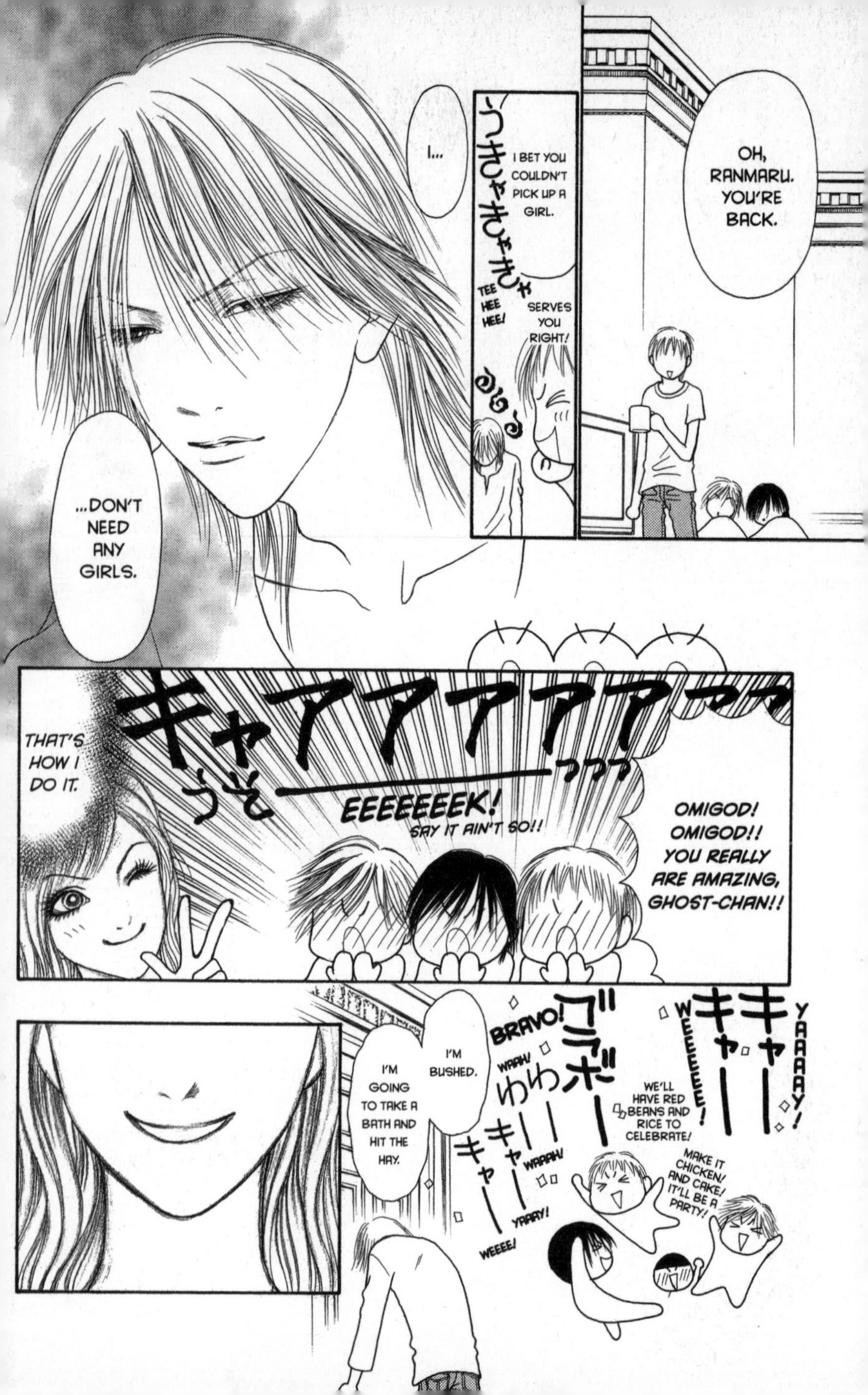
OH, RANMARU. YOU'RE BACK.
うきゃきゃきゃ
I BET YOU COULDN'T PICK UP A GIRL.
TEE HEE HEE!
SERVES YOU RIGHT!
I...
...DON'T NEED ANY GIRLS.
キャアアアアアー
うそ――
EEEEEEEK!
SAY IT AIN'T SO!!
OMIGOD! OMIGOD!! YOU REALLY ARE AMAZING, GHOST-CHAN!!
THAT'S HOW I DO IT.
キャーキャー
YAAAAAY!
WEEEEEE!
ブラボー
BRAVO!
わわー
WAAH!
WE'LL HAVE RED BEANS AND RICE TO CELEBRATE!
MAKE IT CHICKEN! AND CAKE! IT'LL BE A PARTY!
キャーキャー
WAAAH!
YAAAY!
WEEEE!
I'M BUSHED.
I'M GOING TO TAKE A BATH AND HIT THE HAY.

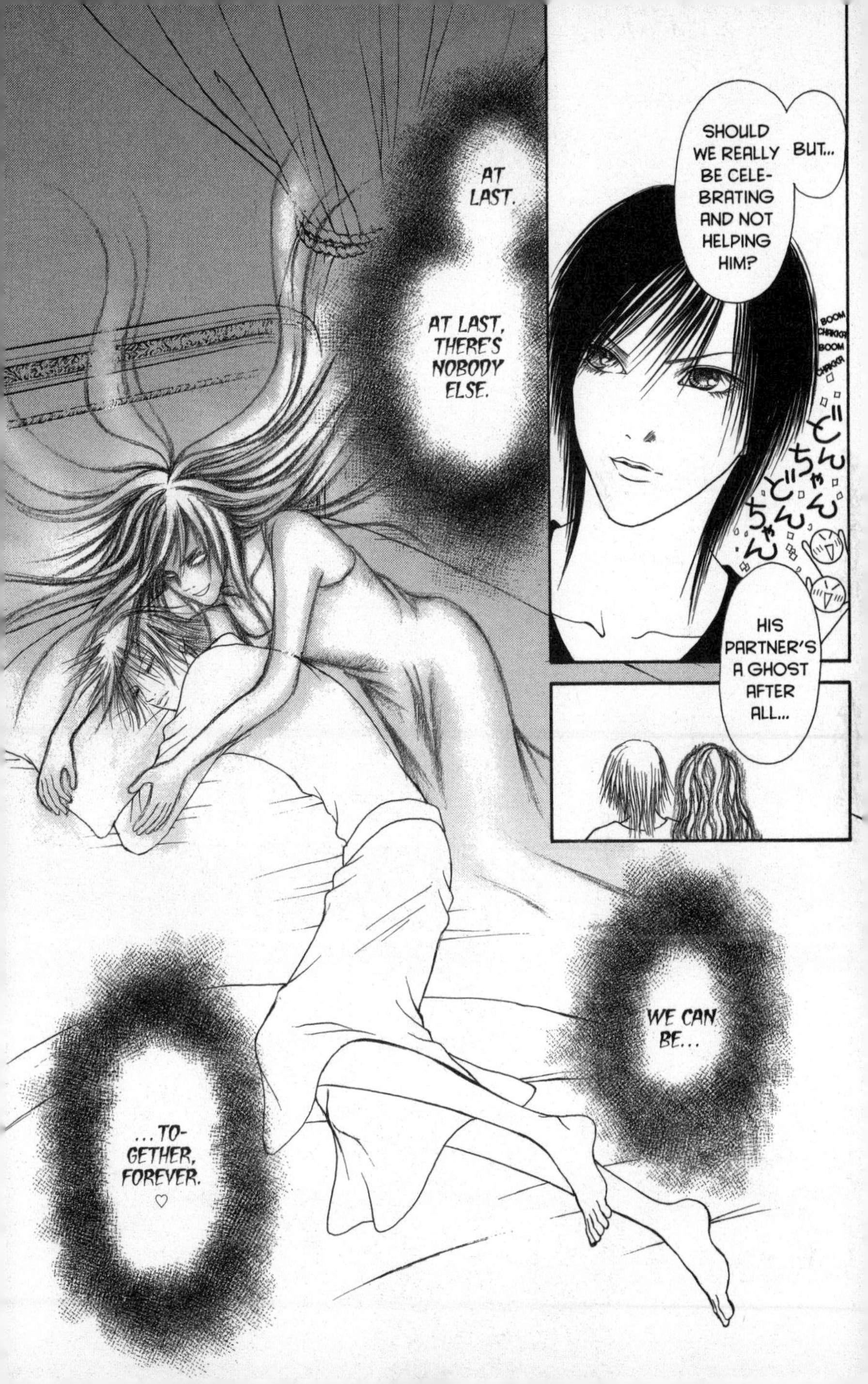
BUT...
SHOULD WE REALLY BE CELEBRATING AND NOT HELPING HIM?
BOOM CHAKKA BOOM CHAKKA
どんちゃんどんちゃん
HIS PARTNER'S A GHOST AFTER ALL...
AT LAST.
AT LAST, THERE'S NOBODY ELSE.
WE CAN BE...
...TOGETHER, FOREVER. ♡

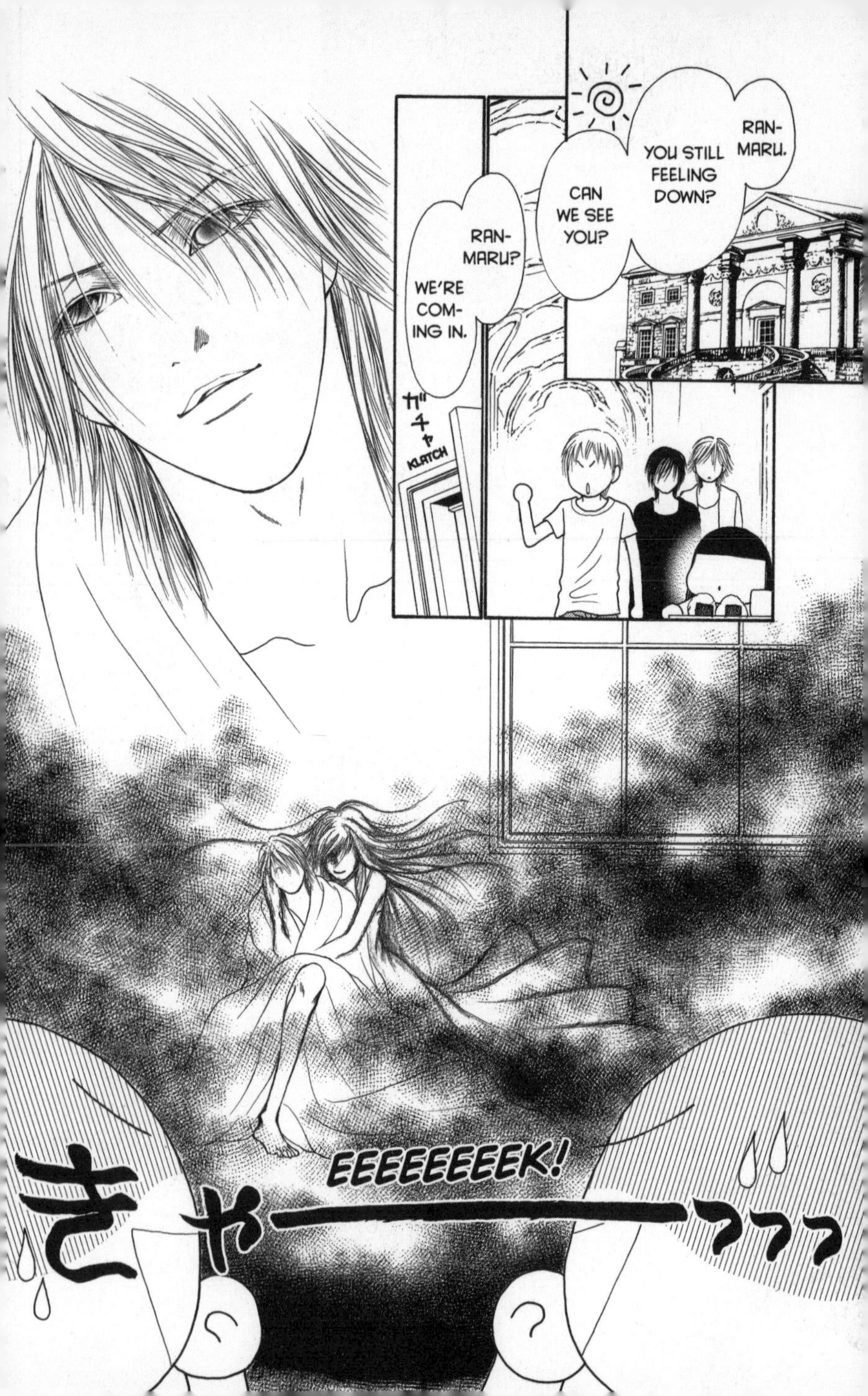
RAN-MARU.
YOU STILL FEELING DOWN?
CAN WE SEE YOU?
RAN-MARU?
WE'RE COM-ING IN.
ガチャ
KLATCH
EEEEEEEEEK!
きゃーーーーーっっっ

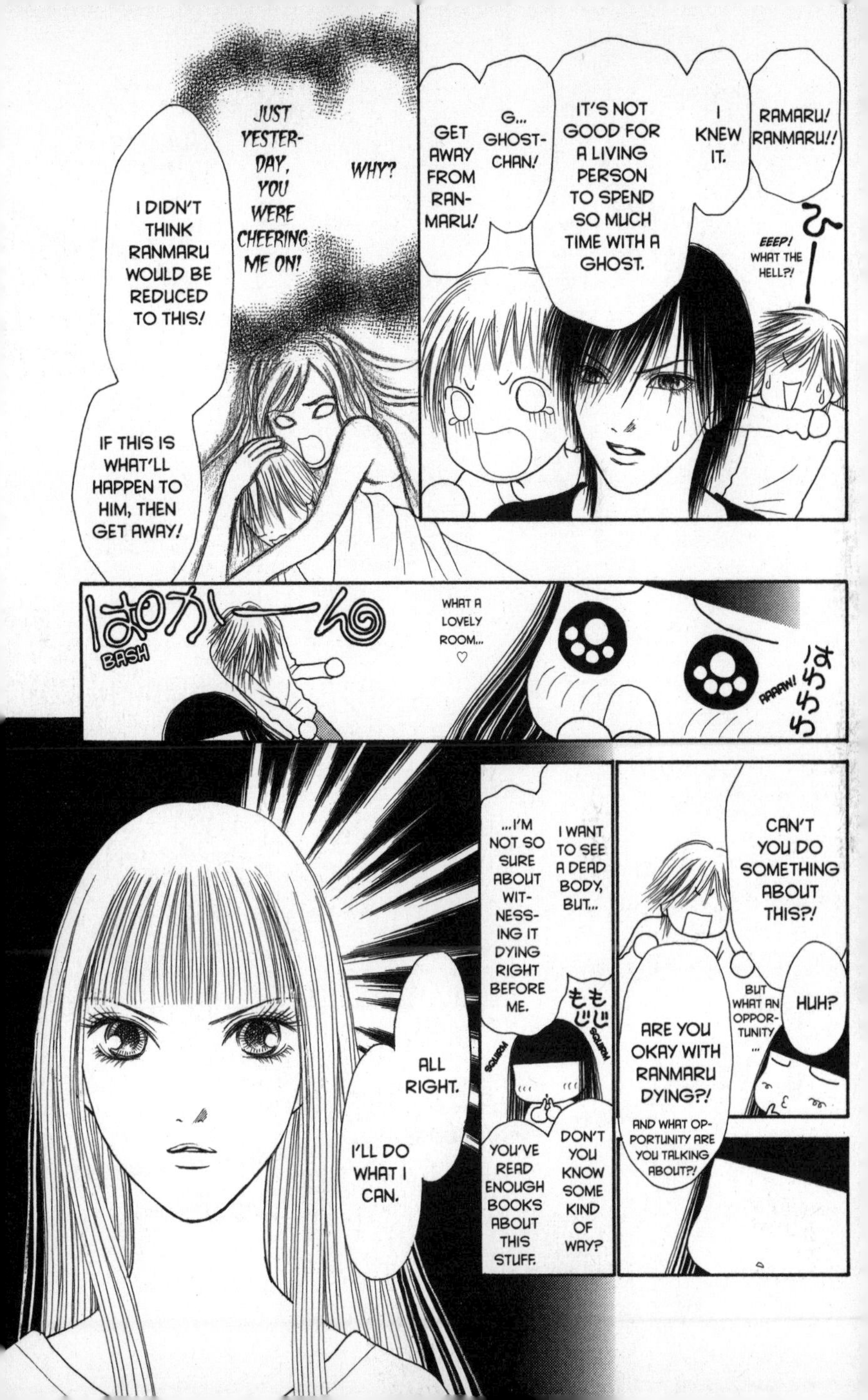
RAMARU! RANMARU!!
ひー
EEEP! WHAT THE HELL?!
I KNEW IT.
IT'S NOT GOOD FOR A LIVING PERSON TO SPEND SO MUCH TIME WITH A GHOST.
G... GHOST-CHAN!
GET AWAY FROM RAN-MARU!
WHY?
JUST YESTER-DAY, YOU WERE CHEERING ME ON!
I DIDN'T THINK RANMARU WOULD BE REDUCED TO THIS!
IF THIS IS WHAT'LL HAPPEN TO HIM, THEN GET AWAY!
RAAAW!
WHAT A LOVELY ROOM... ♡
BASH
CAN'T YOU DO SOMETHING ABOUT THIS?!
HUH?
BUT WHAT AN OPPOR-TUNITY...
ARE YOU OKAY WITH RANMARU DYING?!
AND WHAT OP-PORTUNITY ARE YOU TALKING ABOUT?!
I WANT TO SEE A DEAD BODY, BUT...
...I'M NOT SO SURE ABOUT WIT-NESS-ING IT DYING RIGHT BEFORE ME.
もじもじ
SQUIRM
SQUIRM
DON'T YOU KNOW SOME KIND OF WAY?
YOU'VE READ ENOUGH BOOKS ABOUT THIS STUFF.
ALL RIGHT.
I'LL DO WHAT I CAN.

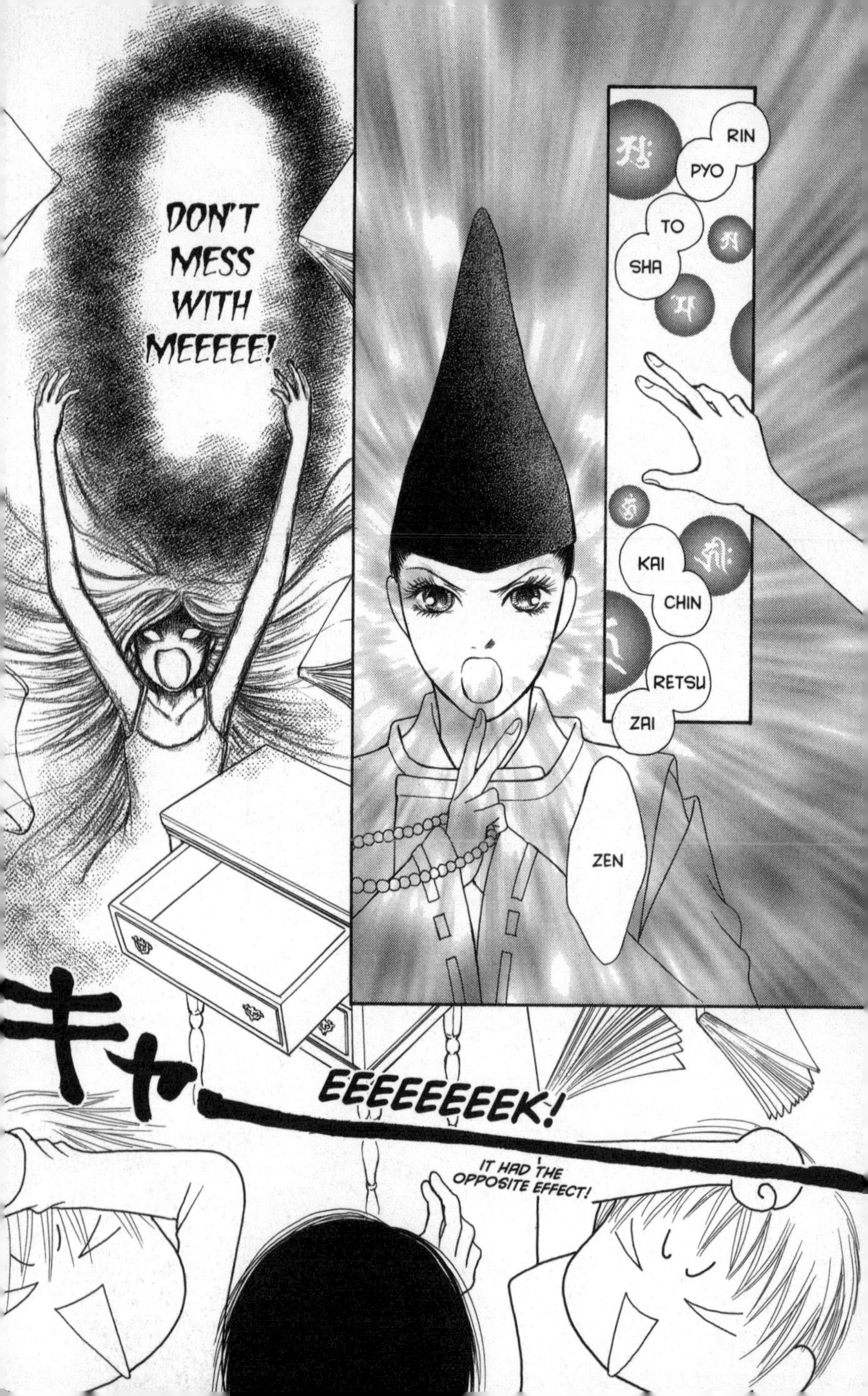
RIN
PYO
TO
SHA
KAI
CHIN
RETSU
ZAI
ZEN
DON'T MESS WITH MEEEEE!
キャー
EEEEEEEEEK!
IT HAD THE OPPOSITE EFFECT!

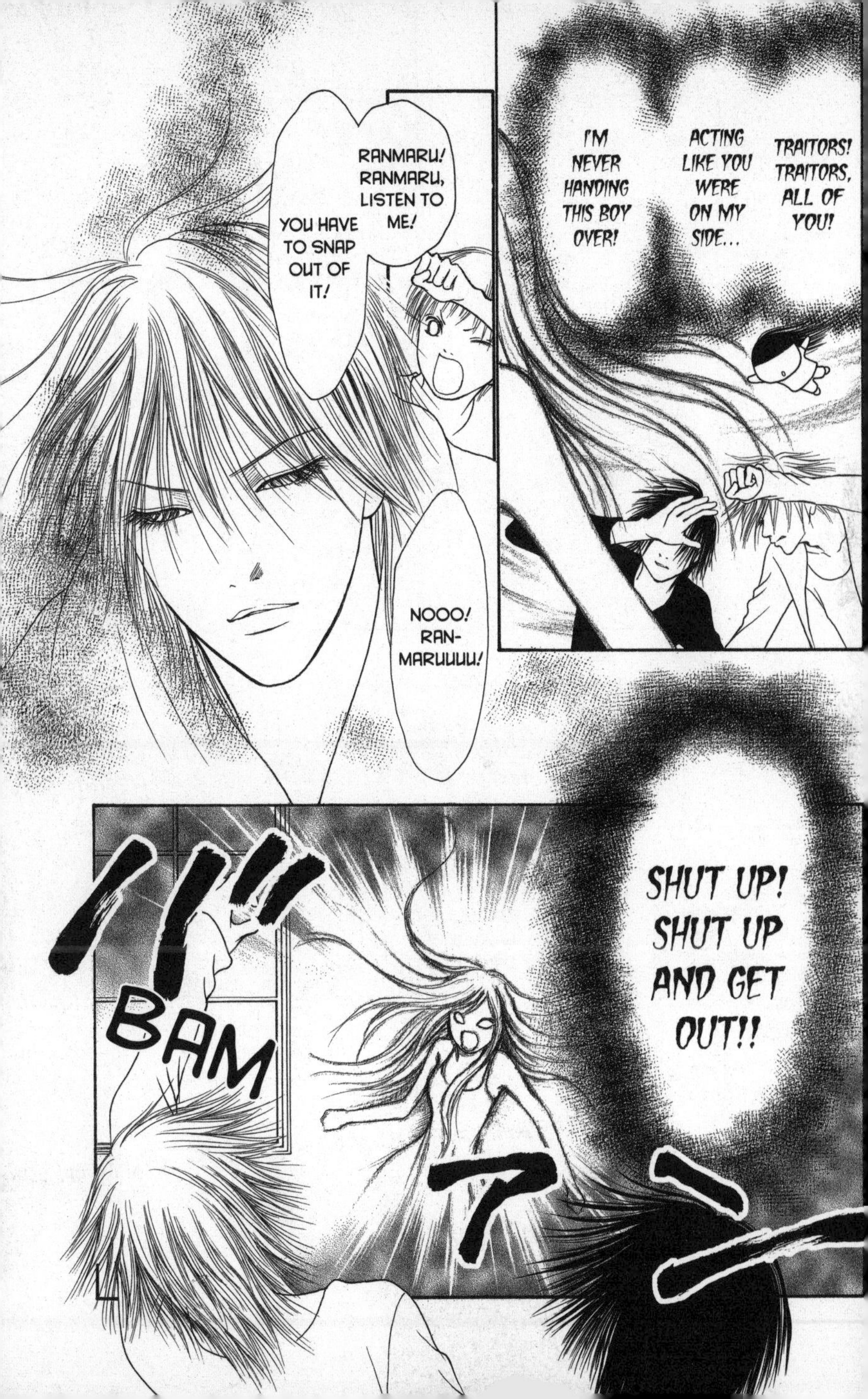

TRAITORS! TRAITORS, ALL OF YOU!
ACTING LIKE YOU WERE ON MY SIDE...
I'M NEVER HANDING THIS BOY OVER!
RANMARU! RANMARU, LISTEN TO ME!
YOU HAVE TO SNAP OUT OF IT!
NOOO! RAN-MARUUUU!
SHUT UP! SHUT UP AND GET OUT!!
BAM

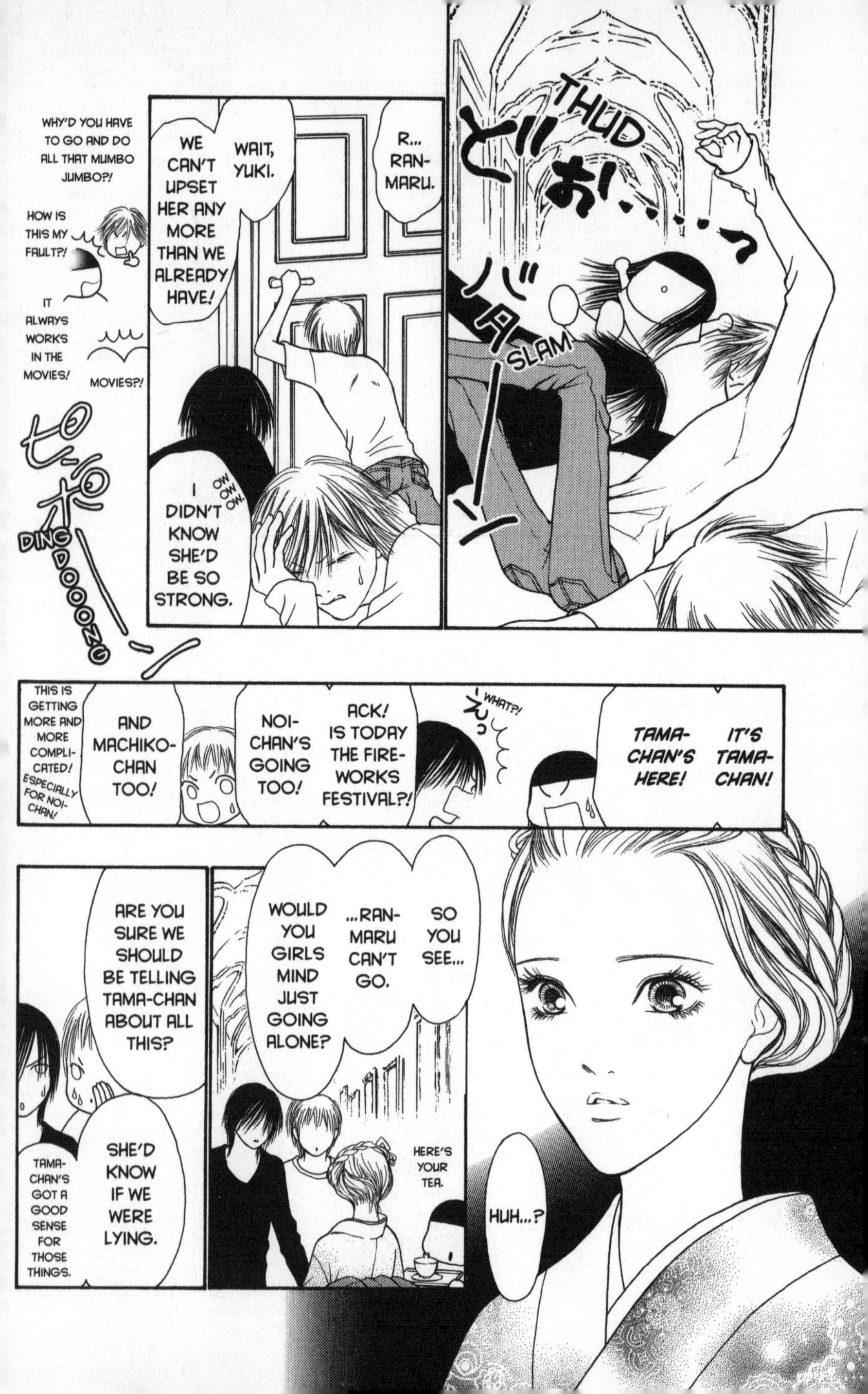
THUD
SLAM
R... RAN-MARU.
WAIT, YUKI.
WE CAN'T UPSET HER ANY MORE THAN WE ALREADY HAVE!
OW OW OW.
I DIDN'T KNOW SHE'D BE SO STRONG.
WHY'D YOU HAVE TO GO AND DO ALL THAT MUMBO JUMBO?!
HOW IS THIS MY FAULT?!
IT ALWAYS WORKS IN THE MOVIES!
MOVIES?!
DING DOOOONG
IT'S TAMA-CHAN!
TAMA-CHAN'S HERE!
WHAT?!
ACK! IS TODAY THE FIRE-WORKS FESTIVAL?!
NOI-CHAN'S GOING TOO!
AND MACHIKO-CHAN TOO!
THIS IS GETTING MORE AND MORE COMPLICATED! ESPECIALLY FOR NOI-CHAN!
HUH...?
SO YOU SEE...
...RAN-MARU CAN'T GO.
WOULD YOU GIRLS MIND JUST GOING ALONE?
HERE'S YOUR TEA.
ARE YOU SURE WE SHOULD BE TELLING TAMA-CHAN ABOUT ALL THIS?
SHE'D KNOW IF WE WERE LYING.
TAMA-CHAN'S GOT A GOOD SENSE FOR THOSE THINGS.

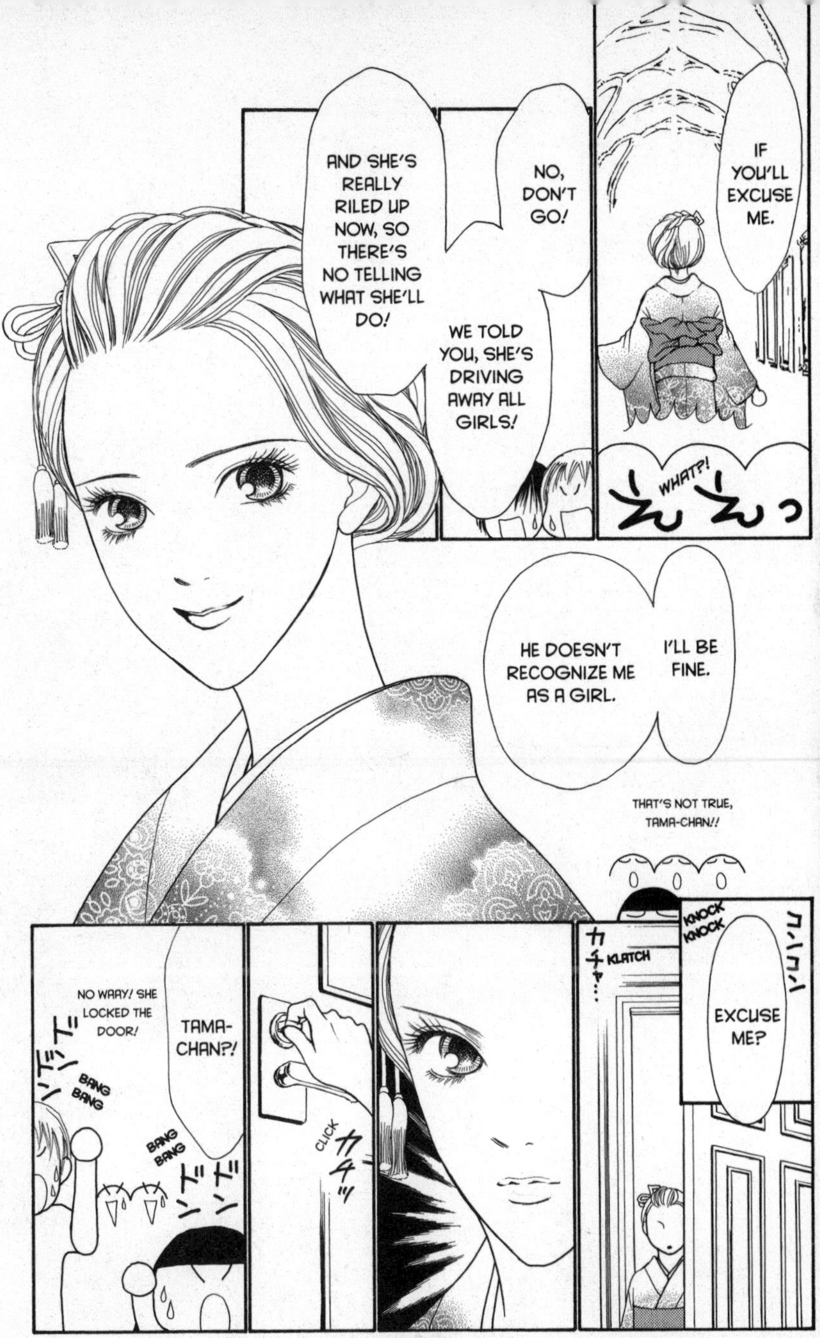
IF YOU'LL EXCUSE ME.
WHAT?!
NO, DON'T GO!
WE TOLD YOU, SHE'S DRIVING AWAY ALL GIRLS!
AND SHE'S REALLY RILED UP NOW, SO THERE'S NO TELLING WHAT SHE'LL DO!
I'LL BE FINE.
HE DOESN'T RECOGNIZE ME AS A GIRL.
THAT'S NOT TRUE, TAMA-CHAN!!
KNOCK KNOCK
EXCUSE ME?
KLATCH
CLICK
TAMA-CHAN?!
NO WAAY! SHE LOCKED THE DOOR!
BANG BANG
BANG BANG

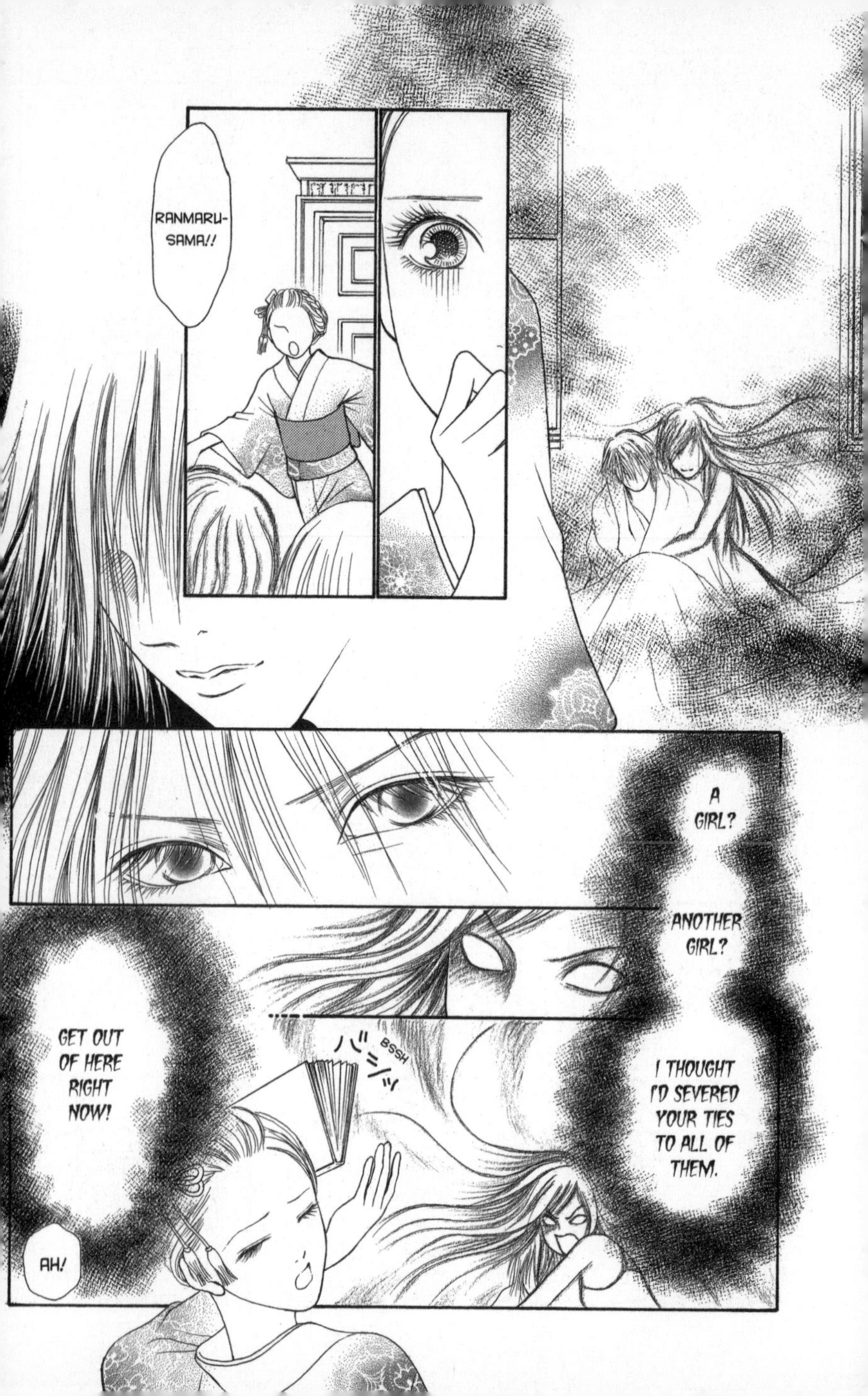
RANMARU-SAMA!!
A GIRL?
ANOTHER GIRL?
I THOUGHT I'D SEVERED YOUR TIES TO ALL OF THEM.
バシッ BSSH
GET OUT OF HERE RIGHT NOW!
AH!

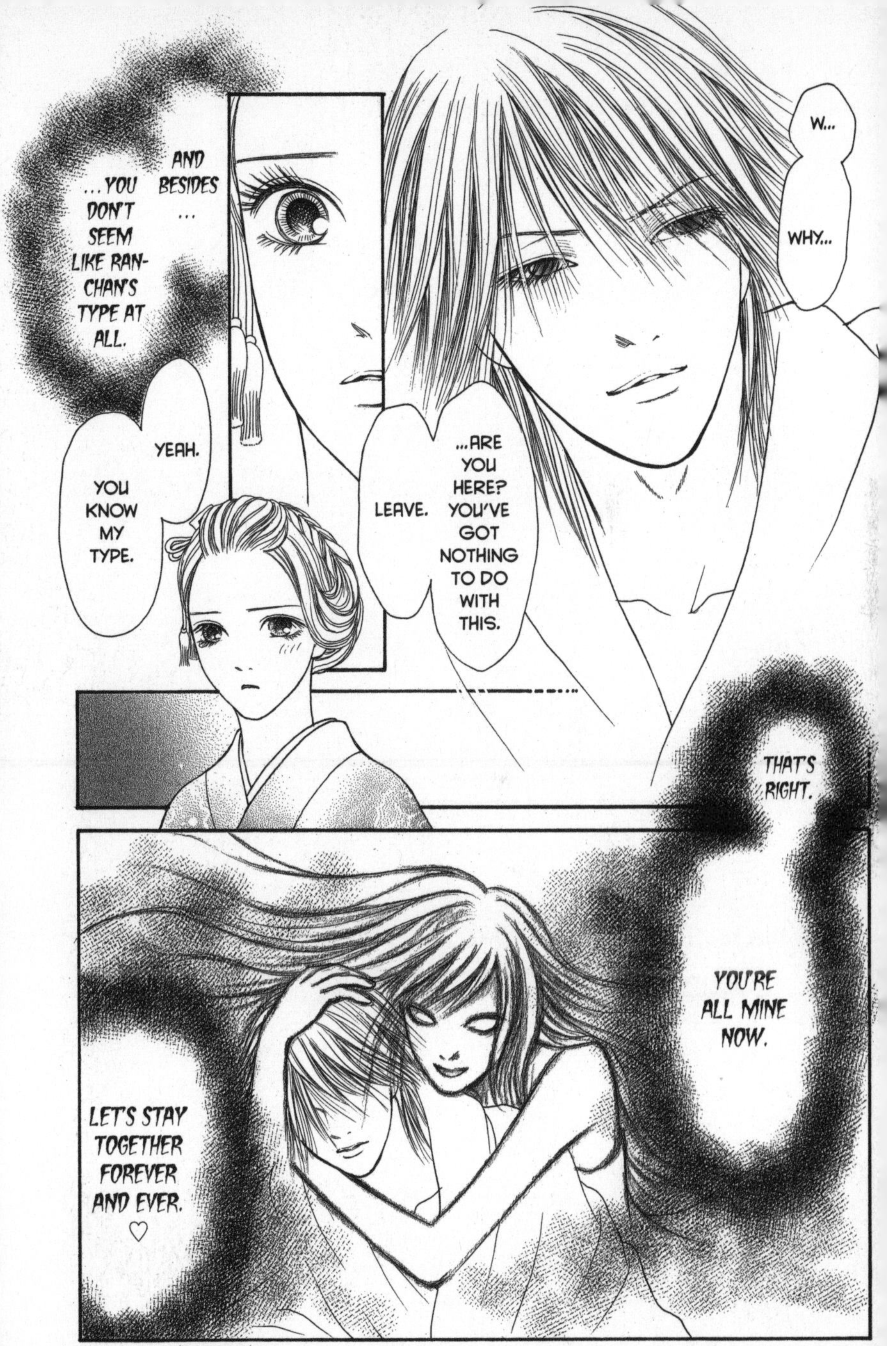
W...
WHY...
...ARE YOU HERE? YOU'VE GOT NOTHING TO DO WITH THIS.
LEAVE.
AND BESIDES...
...YOU DON'T SEEM LIKE RAN-CHAN'S TYPE AT ALL.
YEAH.
YOU KNOW MY TYPE.
THAT'S RIGHT.
YOU'RE ALL MINE NOW.
LET'S STAY TOGETHER FOREVER AND EVER. ♡

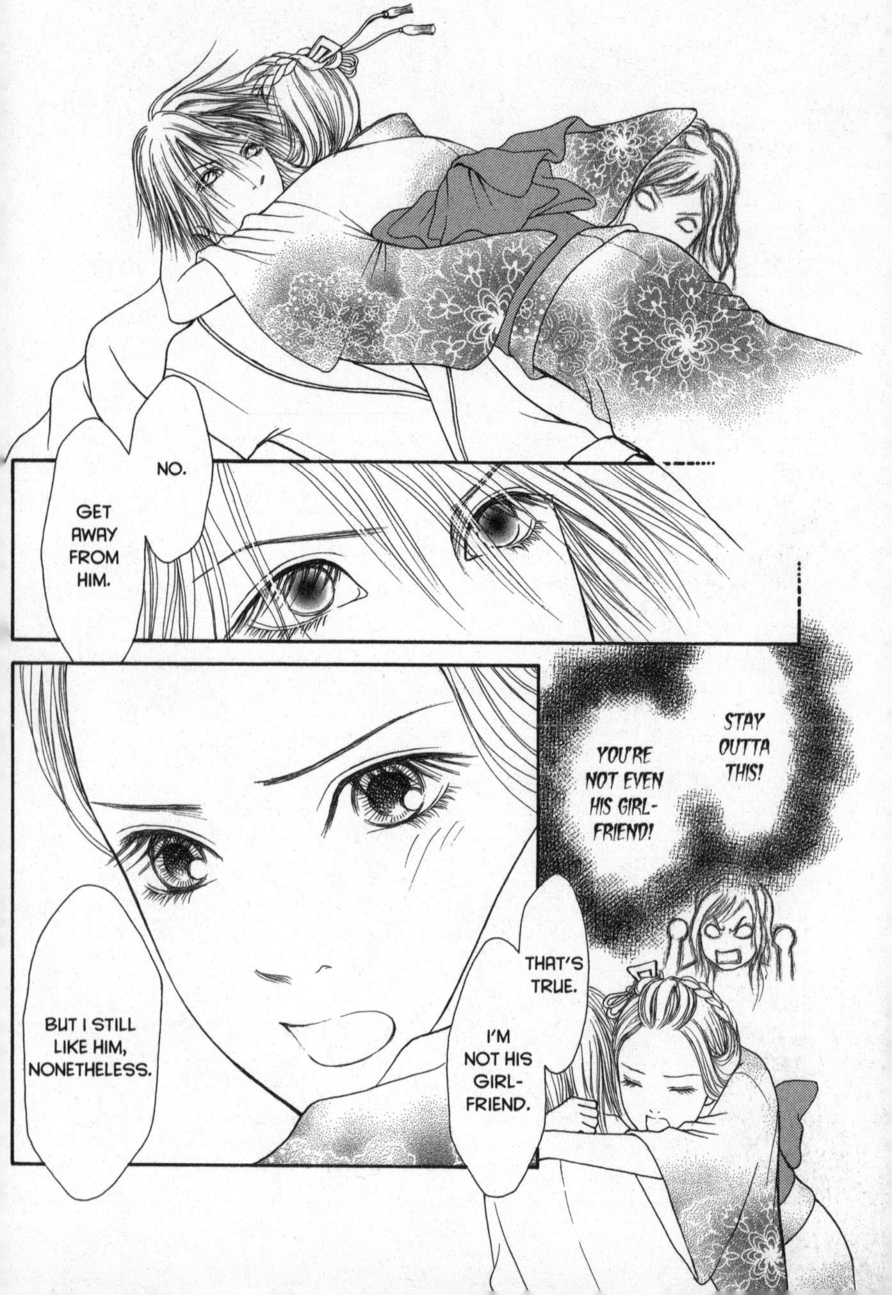
NO.
GET AWAY FROM HIM.
STAY OUTTA THIS!
YOU'RE NOT EVEN HIS GIRL-FRIEND!
THAT'S TRUE.
I'M NOT HIS GIRL-FRIEND.
BUT I STILL LIKE HIM, NONETHELESS.

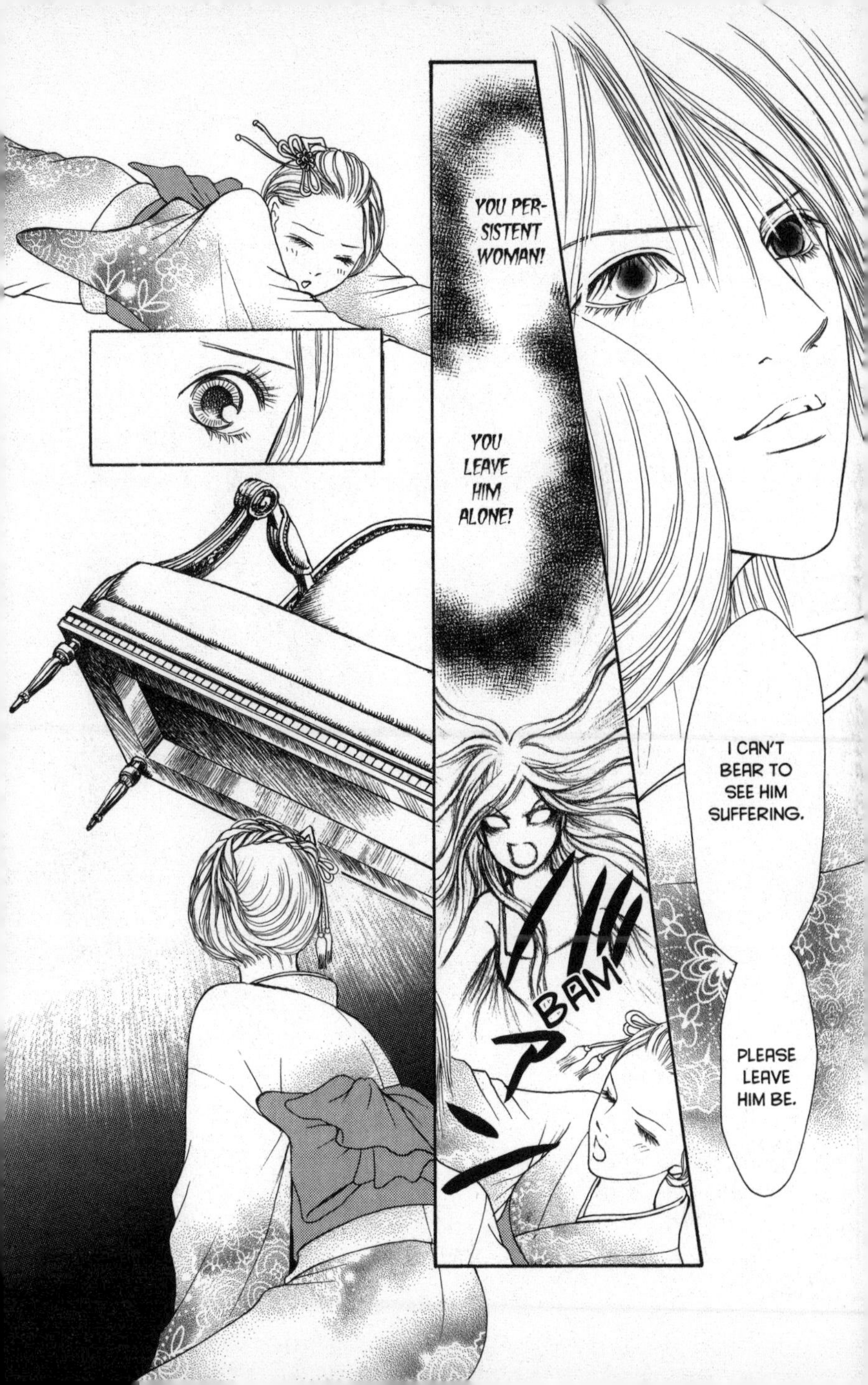
I CAN'T BEAR TO SEE HIM SUFFERING.
PLEASE LEAVE HIM BE.
YOU PERSISTENT WOMAN!
YOU LEAVE HIM ALONE!
BAM

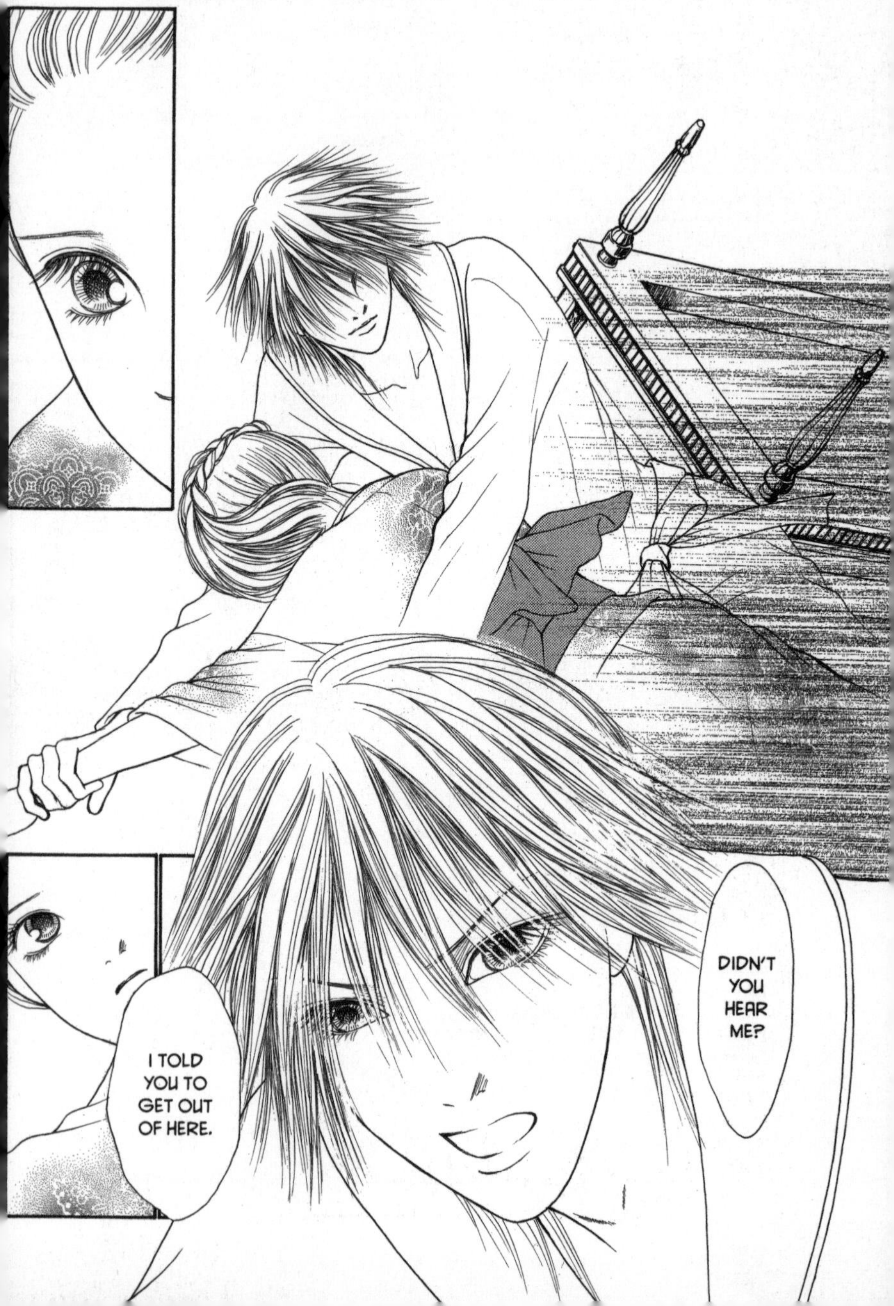
DIDN'T YOU HEAR ME?
I TOLD YOU TO GET OUT OF HERE.

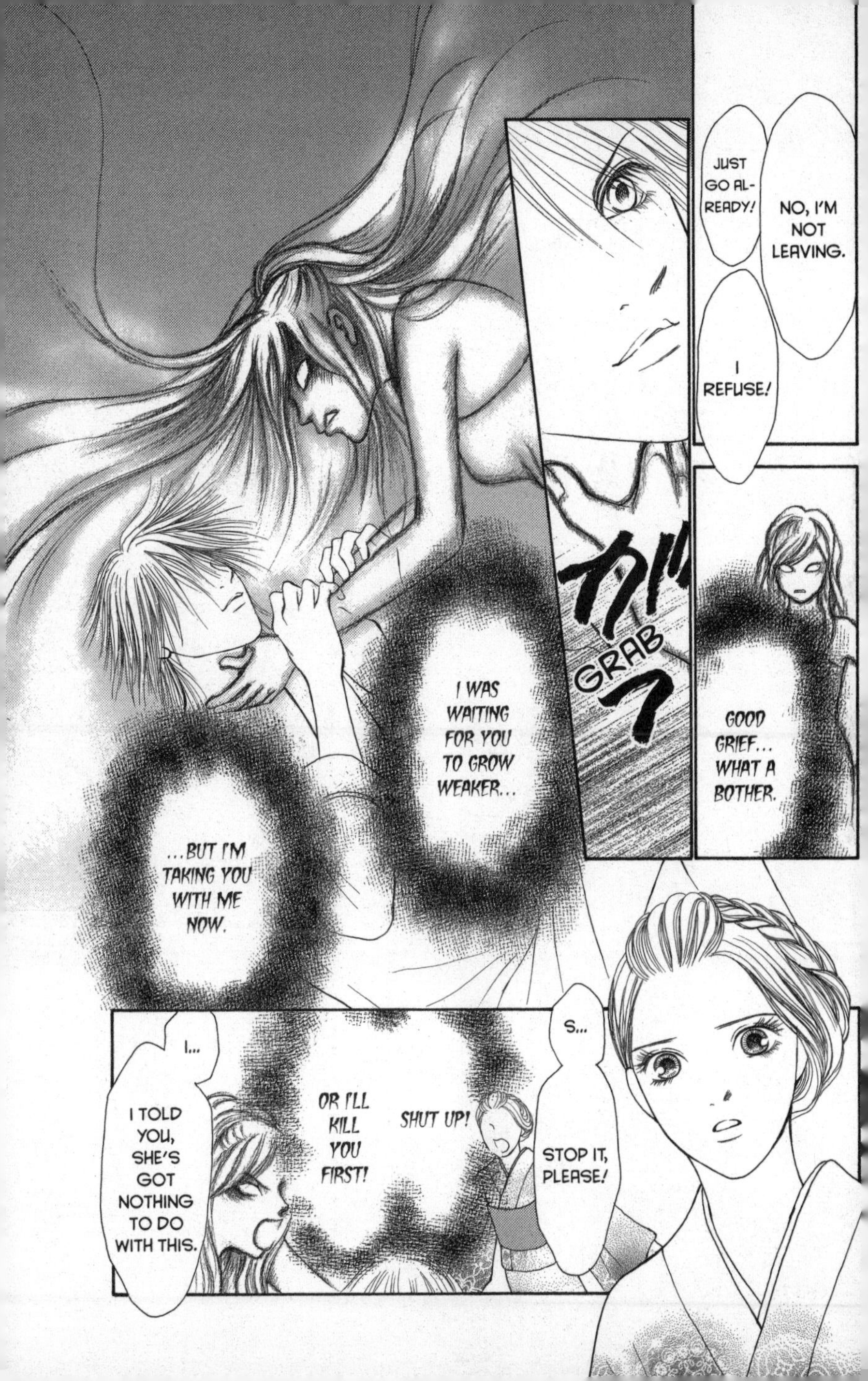
NO, I'M NOT LEAVING.
JUST GO AL-READY!
I REFUSE!
GOOD GRIEF... WHAT A BOTHER.
GRAB
I WAS WAITING FOR YOU TO GROW WEAKER...
...BUT I'M TAKING YOU WITH ME NOW.
S...
STOP IT, PLEASE!
SHUT UP!
OR I'LL KILL YOU FIRST!
I...
I TOLD YOU, SHE'S GOT NOTHING TO DO WITH THIS.

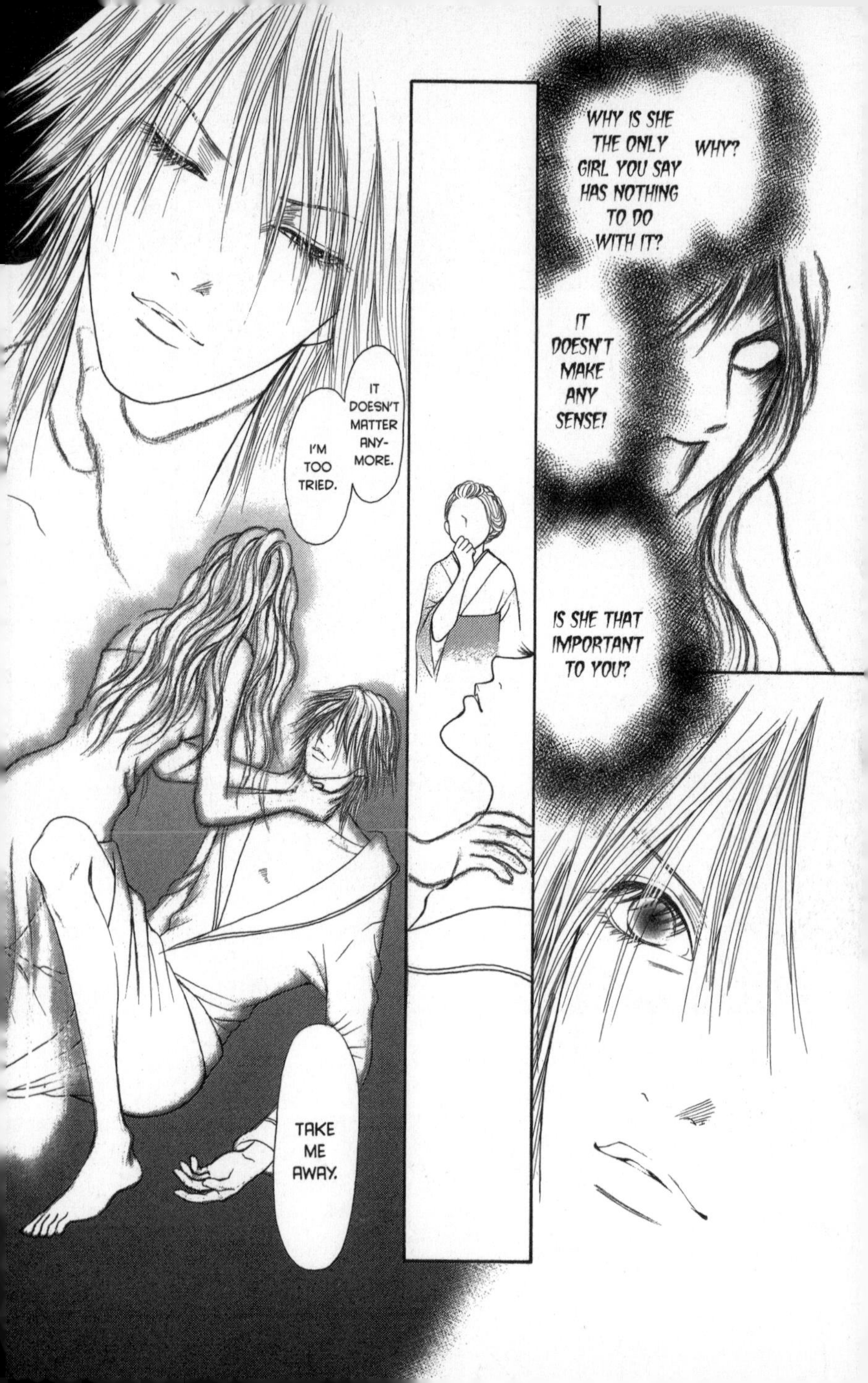
WHY?
WHY IS SHE THE ONLY GIRL YOU SAY HAS NOTHING TO DO WITH IT?
IT DOESN'T MAKE ANY SENSE!
IS SHE THAT IMPORTANT TO YOU?
IT DOESN'T MATTER ANY-MORE.
I'M TOO TRIED.
TAKE ME AWAY.

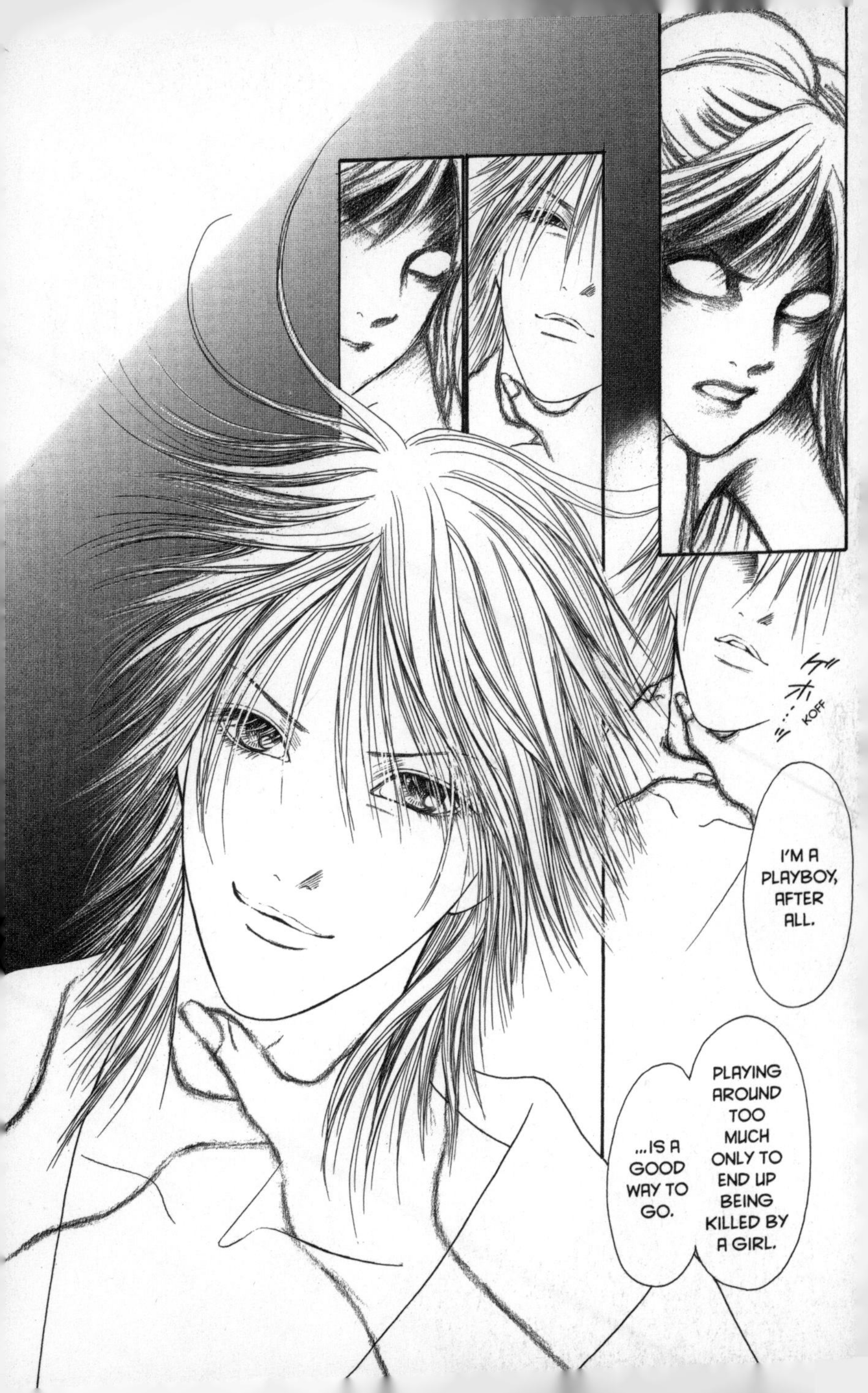
ゲホ…ッ
KOFF
I'M A PLAYBOY, AFTER ALL.
PLAYING AROUND TOO MUCH ONLY TO END UP BEING KILLED BY A GIRL.
...IS A GOOD WAY TO GO.

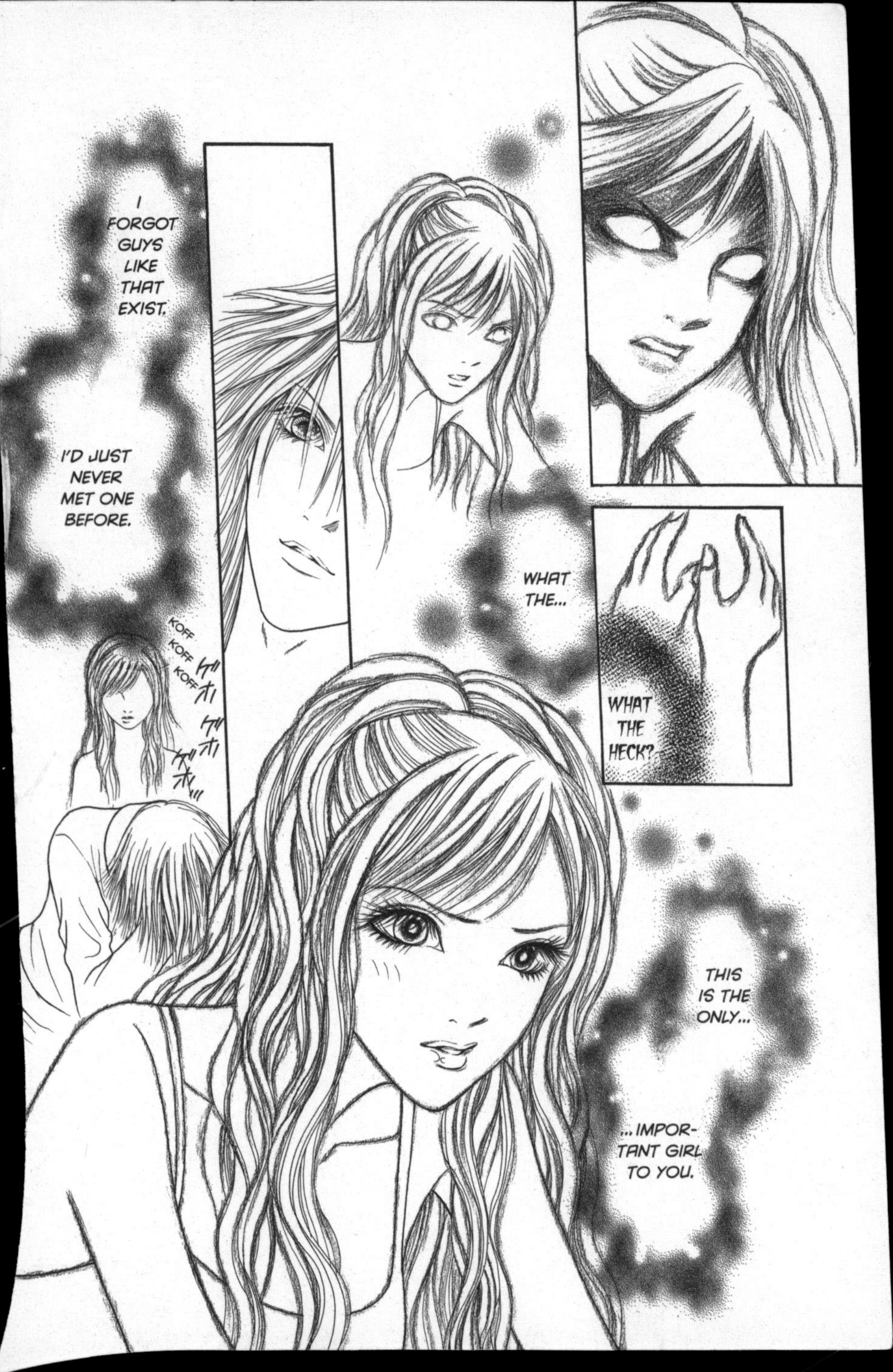
WHAT THE...
WHAT THE HECK?
I FORGOT GUYS LIKE THAT EXIST.
I'D JUST NEVER MET ONE BEFORE.
KOFF KOFF KOFF
THIS IS THE ONLY...
...IMPORTANT GIRL TO YOU.

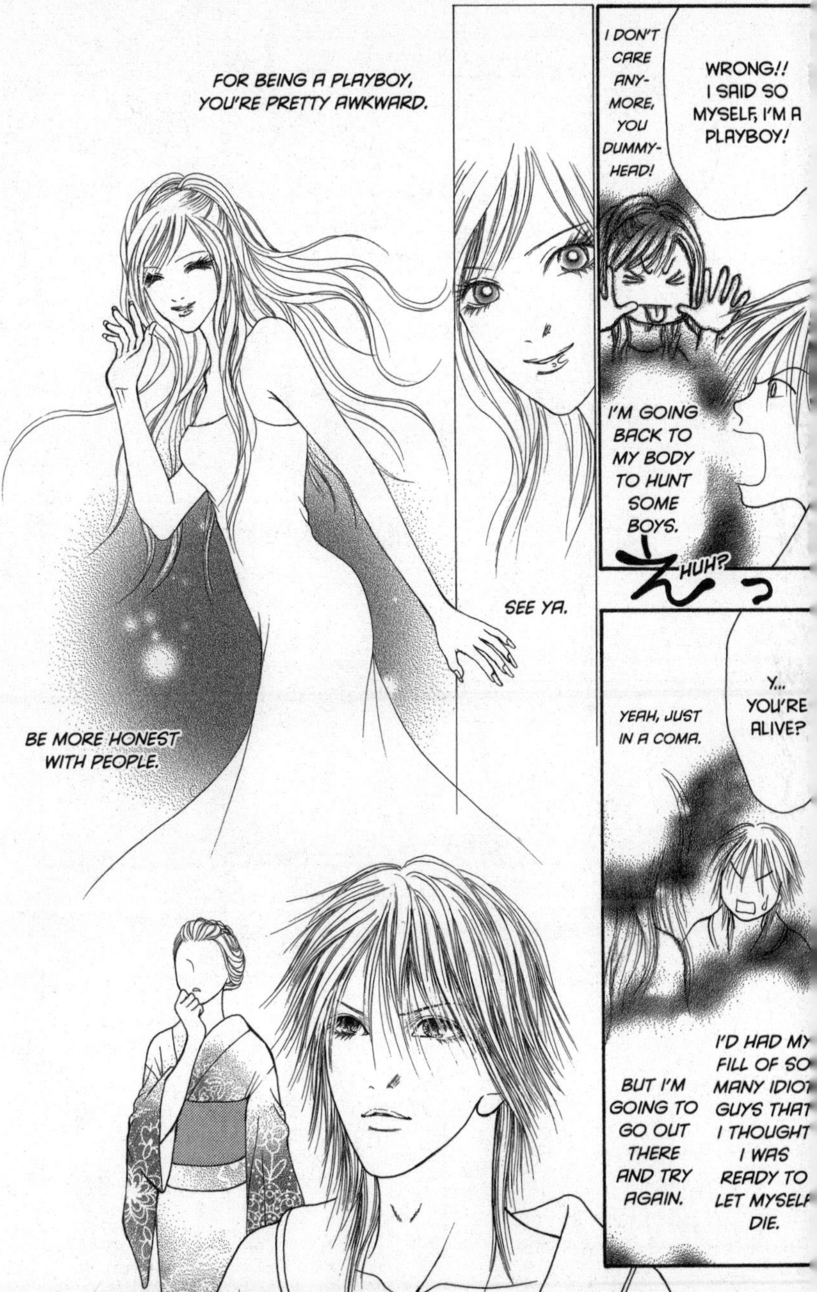

WRONG!! I SAID SO MYSELF, I'M A PLAYBOY!
I DON'T CARE ANYMORE, YOU DUMMY-HEAD!
I'M GOING BACK TO MY BODY TO HUNT SOME BOYS.
HUH?
Y... YOU'RE ALIVE?
YEAH, JUST IN A COMA.
I'D HAD MY FILL OF SO MANY IDIOT GUYS THAT I THOUGHT I WAS READY TO LET MYSELF DIE.
BUT I'M GOING TO GO OUT THERE AND TRY AGAIN.
SEE YA.
FOR BEING A PLAYBOY, YOU'RE PRETTY AWKWARD.
BE MORE HONEST WITH PEOPLE.

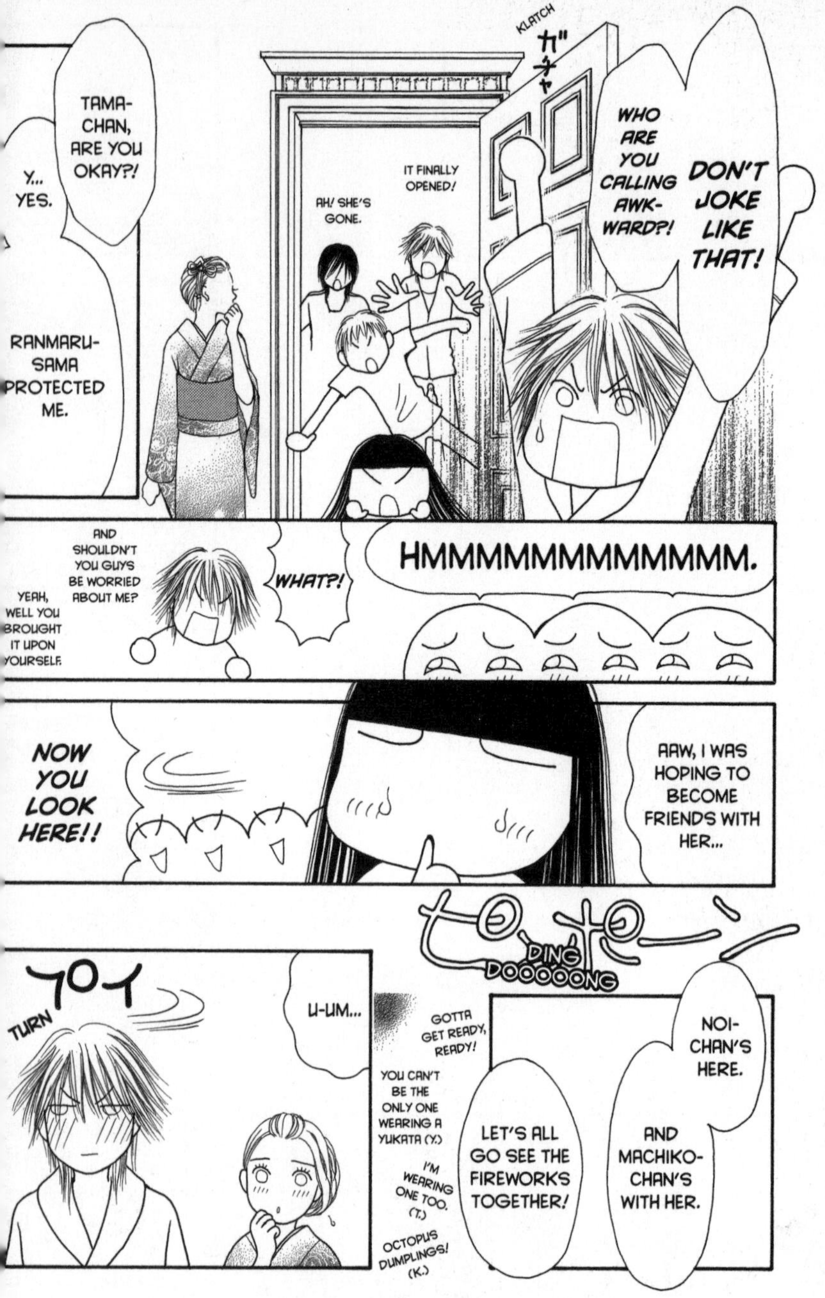
DON'T JOKE LIKE THAT!
WHO ARE YOU CALLING AWK-WARD?!
ガチャ
KLATCH
IT FINALLY OPENED!
AH! SHE'S GONE.
TAMA-CHAN, ARE YOU OKAY?!
Y... YES.
RANMARU-SAMA PROTECTED ME.
HMMMMMMMMMMMM.
WHAT?!
AND SHOULDN'T YOU GUYS BE WORRIED ABOUT ME?
YEAH, WELL YOU BROUGHT IT UPON YOURSELF.
AAW, I WAS HOPING TO BECOME FRIENDS WITH HER...
NOW YOU LOOK HERE!!
ピンポーン
DING DOOOOOONG
NOI-CHAN'S HERE.
AND MACHIKO-CHAN'S WITH HER.
LET'S ALL GO SEE THE FIREWORKS TOGETHER!
GOTTA GET READY, READY!
YOU CAN'T BE THE ONLY ONE WEARING A YUKATA (Y.)
I'M WEARING ONE TOO. (T.)
OCTOPUS DUMPLINGS! (K.)
U-UM...
フイ
TURN

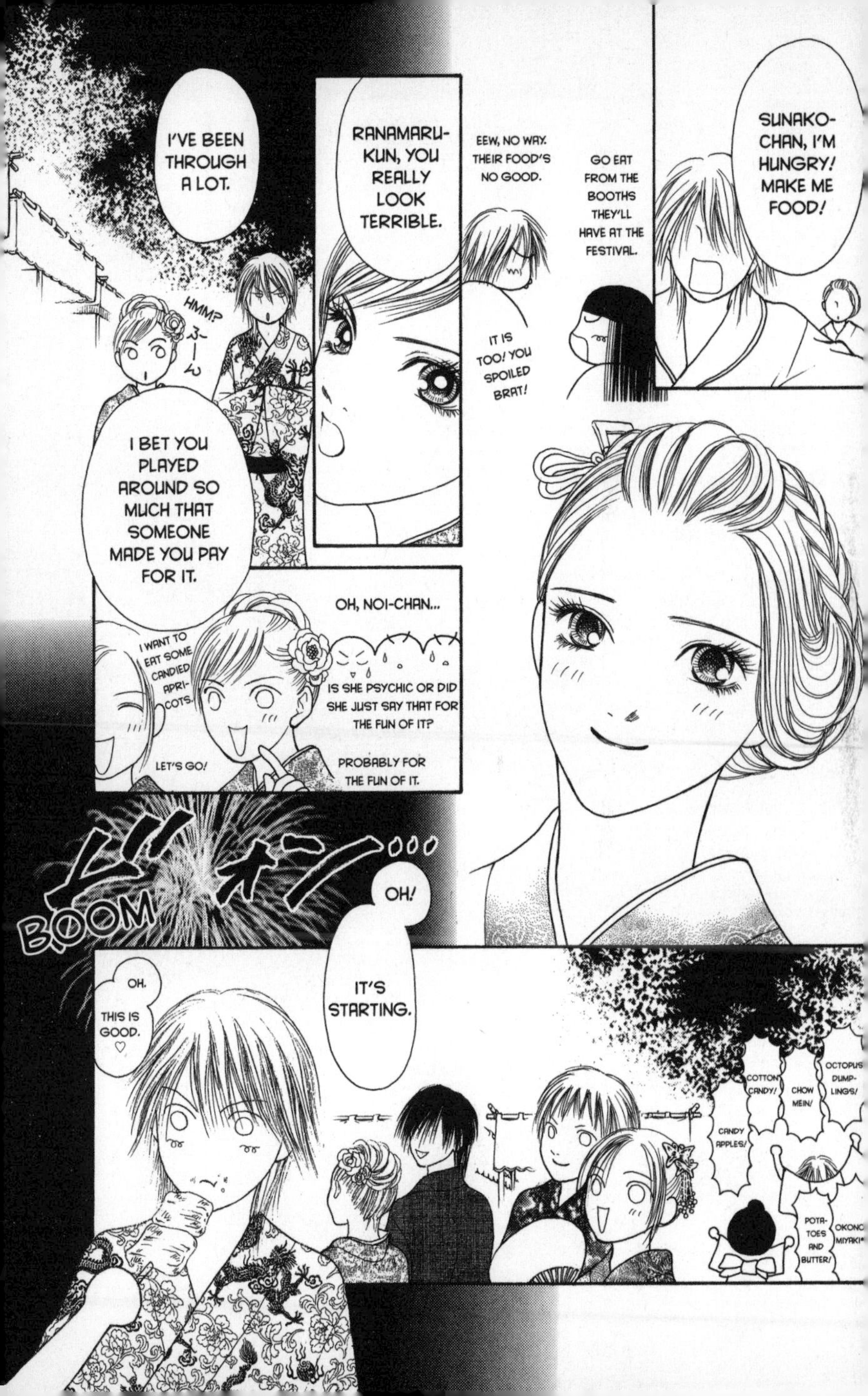
SUNAKO-CHAN, I'M HUNGRY! MAKE ME FOOD!
GO EAT FROM THE BOOTHS THEY'LL HAVE AT THE FESTIVAL.
EEW, NO WAY. THEIR FOOD'S NO GOOD.
IT IS TOO! YOU SPOILED BRAT!
RANAMARU-KUN, YOU REALLY LOOK TERRIBLE.
I'VE BEEN THROUGH A LOT.
HMM? ふーん
I BET YOU PLAYED AROUND SO MUCH THAT SOMEONE MADE YOU PAY FOR IT.
OH, NOI-CHAN...
IS SHE PSYCHIC OR DID SHE JUST SAY THAT FOR THE FUN OF IT?
PROBABLY FOR THE FUN OF IT.
I WANT TO EAT SOME CANDIED APRICOTS.
LET'S GO!
BOOM
OH!
IT'S STARTING.
OCTOPUS DUMPLINGS!
CHOW MEIN!
COTTON CANDY!
CANDY APPLES!
OKONOMIYAKI*
POTATOES AND BUTTER!
OH. THIS IS GOOD. ♡

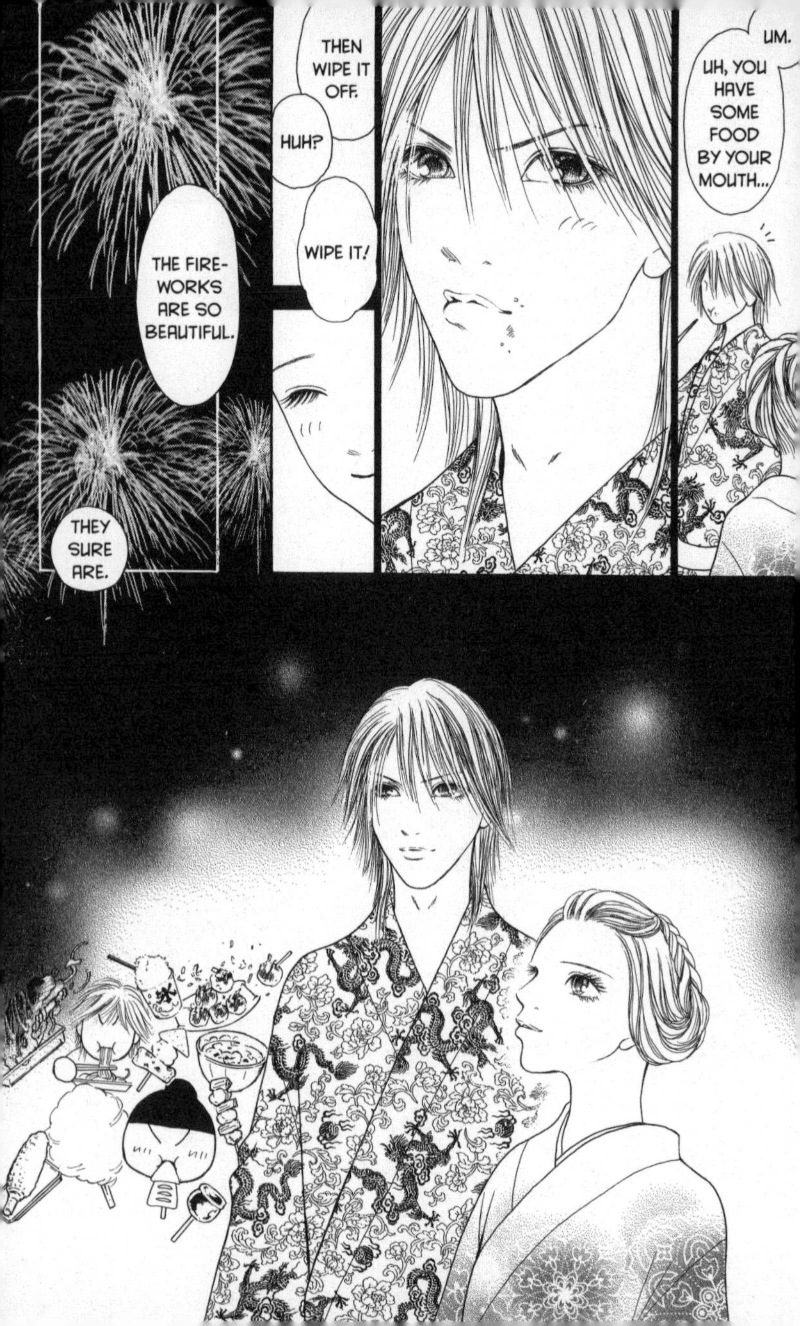
UM.
UH, YOU HAVE SOME FOOD BY YOUR MOUTH...
THEN WIPE IT OFF.
HUH?
WIPE IT!
THE FIRE-WORKS ARE SO BEAUTIFUL.
THEY SURE ARE.

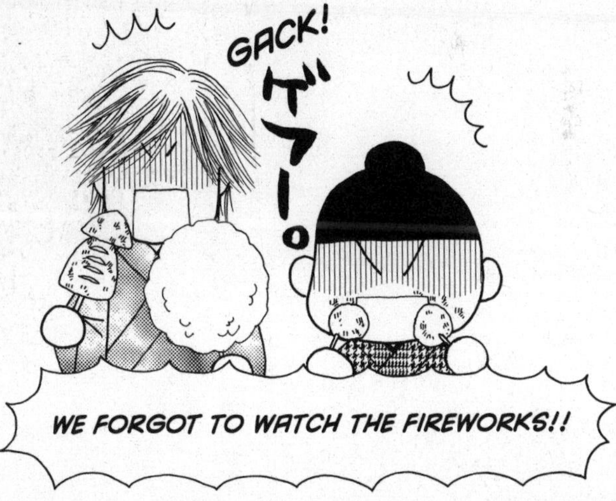
GACK!
ゲアー。
WE FORGOT TO WATCH THE FIREWORKS!!

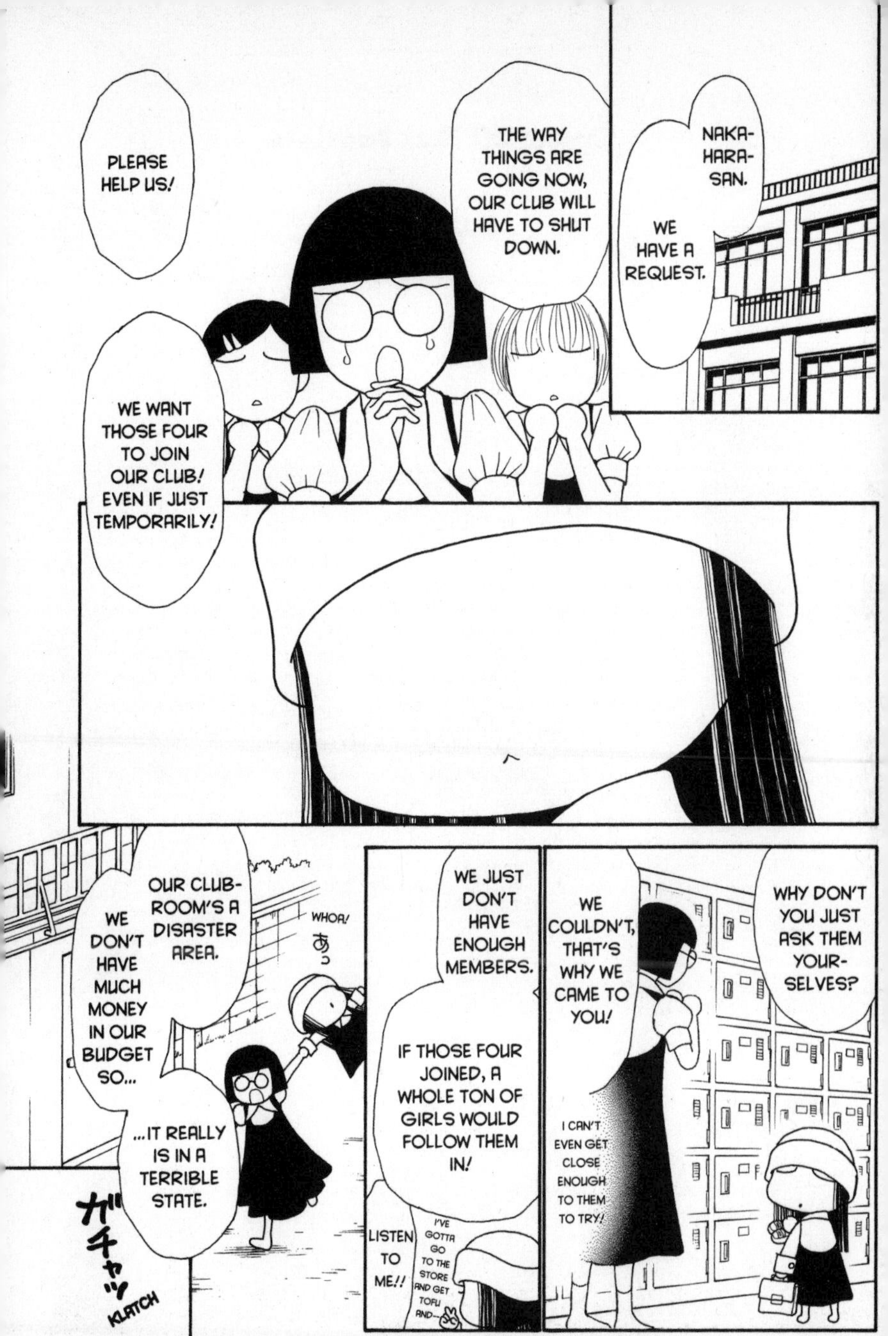
NAKA-HARA-SAN.
WE HAVE A REQUEST.
THE WAY THINGS ARE GOING NOW, OUR CLUB WILL HAVE TO SHUT DOWN.
PLEASE HELP US!
WE WANT THOSE FOUR TO JOIN OUR CLUB! EVEN IF JUST TEMPORARILY!
WHY DON'T YOU JUST ASK THEM YOUR-SELVES?
WE COULDN'T, THAT'S WHY WE CAME TO YOU!
I CAN'T EVEN GET CLOSE ENOUGH TO THEM TO TRY!
WE JUST DON'T HAVE ENOUGH MEMBERS.
IF THOSE FOUR JOINED, A WHOLE TON OF GIRLS WOULD FOLLOW THEM IN!
I'VE GOTTA GO TO THE STORE AND GET TOFU AND—
LISTEN TO ME!!
OUR CLUB-ROOM'S A DISASTER AREA.
WE DON'T HAVE MUCH MONEY IN OUR BUDGET SO...
WHOA! あっ
...IT REALLY IS IN A TERRIBLE STATE.
ガチャッ KLATCH

Chapter 130. Black Swan Lake

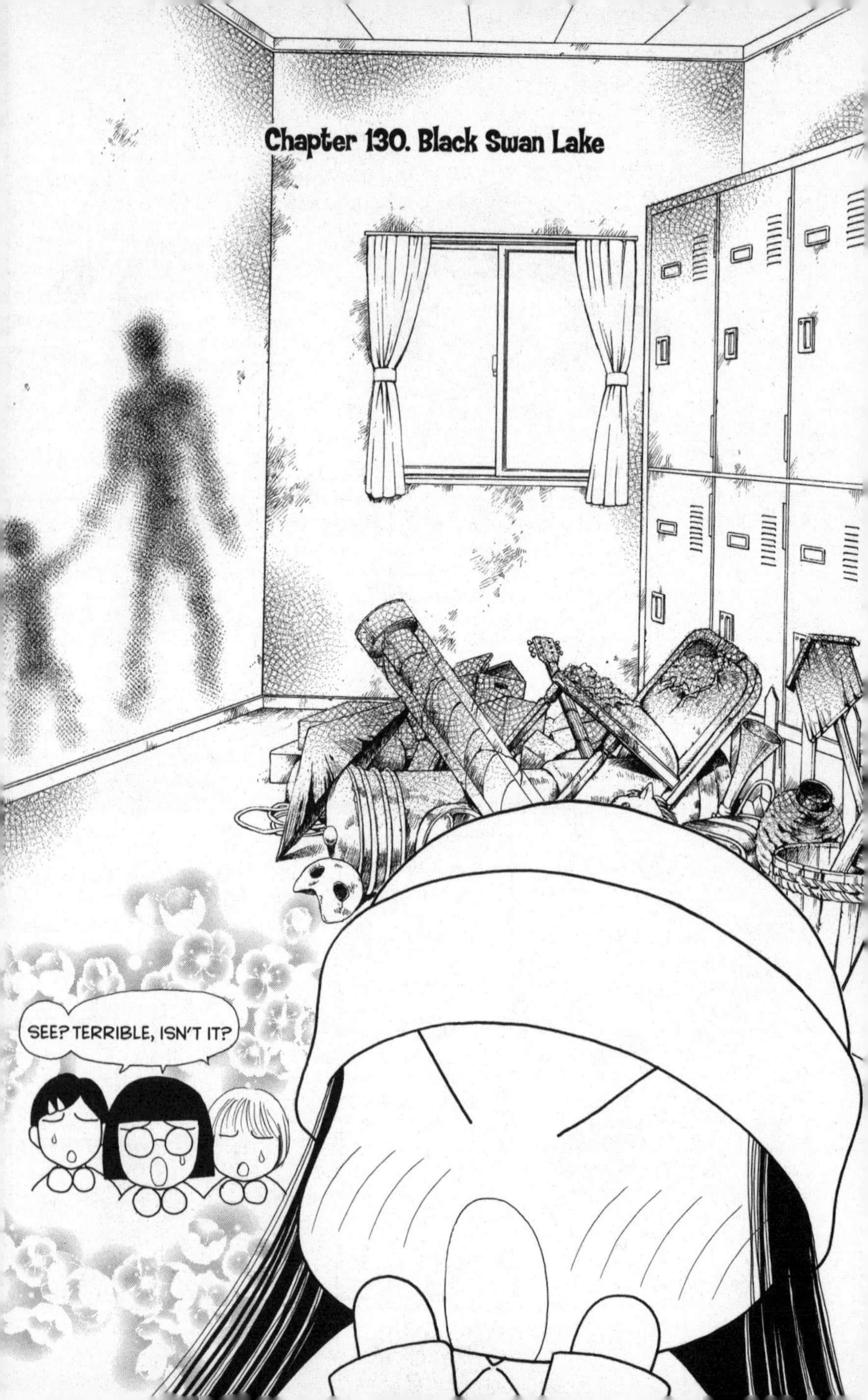
Chapter 130. Black Swan Lake
SEE? TERRIBLE, ISN'T IT?

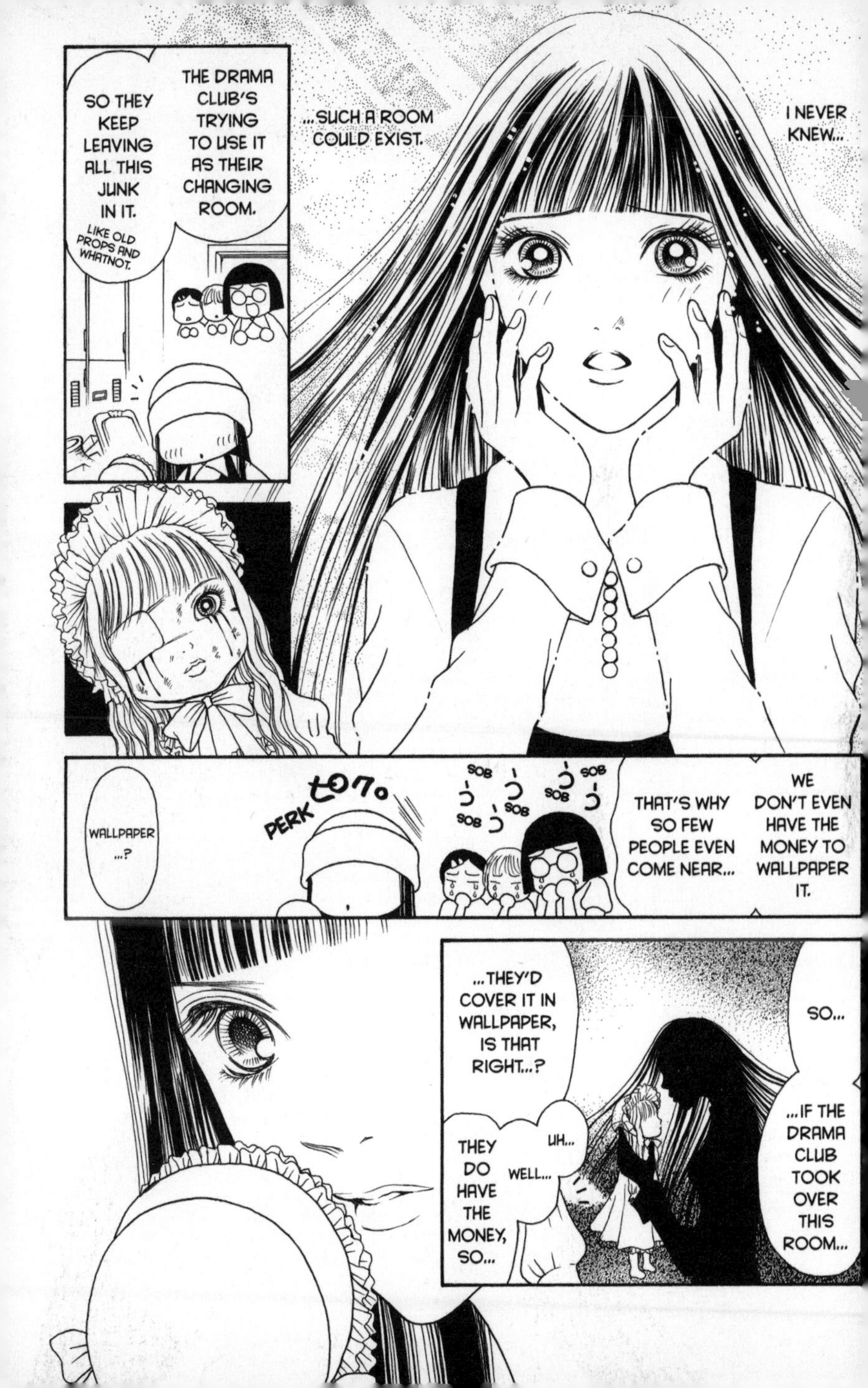
I NEVER KNEW...
...SUCH A ROOM COULD EXIST.
THE DRAMA CLUB'S TRYING TO USE IT AS THEIR CHANGING ROOM.
SO THEY KEEP LEAVING ALL THIS JUNK IN IT.
LIKE OLD PROPS AND WHATNOT.
WE DON'T EVEN HAVE THE MONEY TO WALLPAPER IT.
THAT'S WHY SO FEW PEOPLE EVEN COME NEAR...
SOB SOB SOB SOB SOB SOB
PERK
WALLPAPER ...?
SO...
...IF THE DRAMA CLUB TOOK OVER THIS ROOM...
...THEY'D COVER IT IN WALLPAPER, IS THAT RIGHT...?
UH... WELL...
THEY DO HAVE THE MONEY, SO...

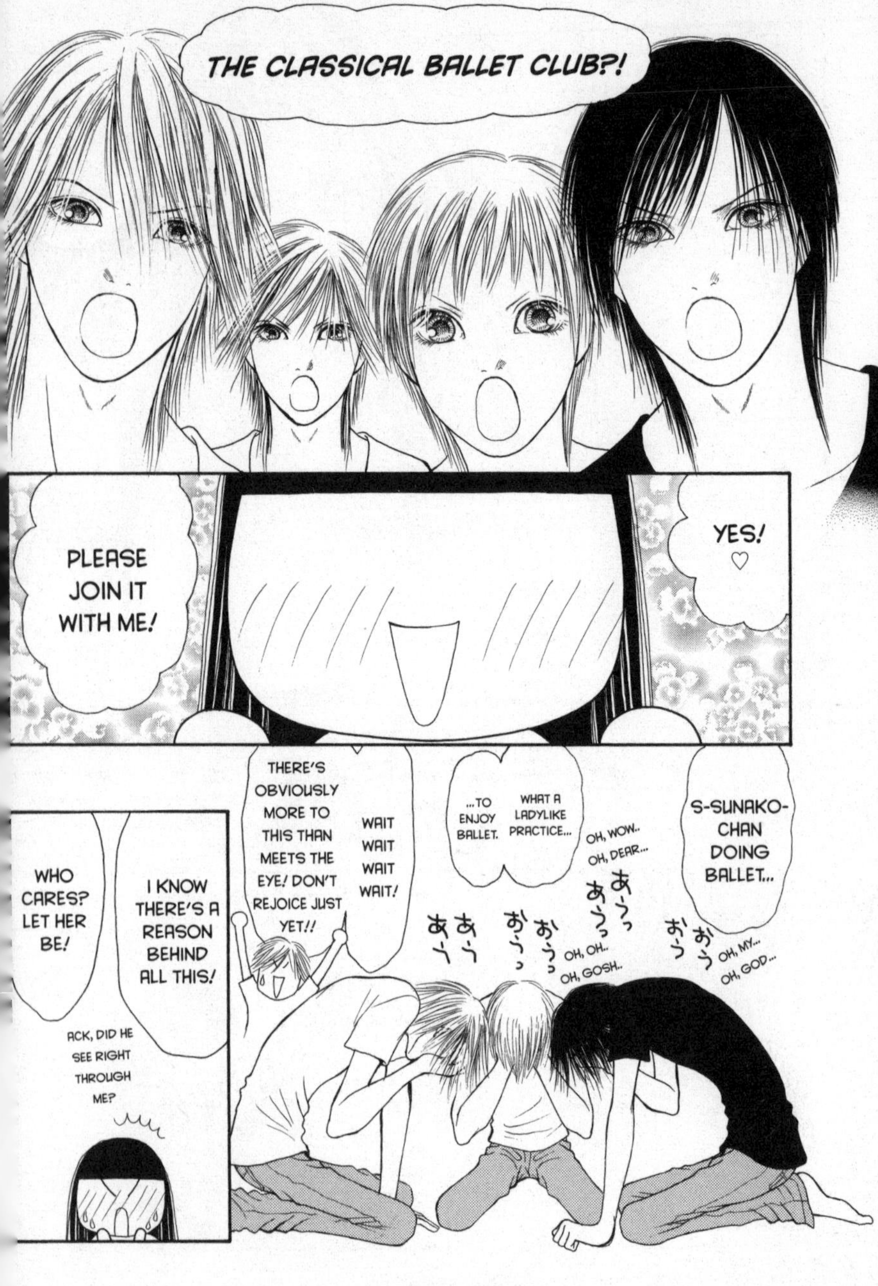

THE CLASSICAL BALLET CLUB?!
YES! ♡
PLEASE JOIN IT WITH ME!
S-SUNAKO-CHAN DOING BALLET...
おうおう
OH, MY... OH, GOD...
WHAT A LADYLIKE PRACTICE...
...TO ENJOY BALLET.
あうっあうっ
OH, WOW.. OH, DEAR...
おうっおうっ
OH, OH.. OH, GOSH..
あうあう
WAIT WAIT WAIT WAIT!
THERE'S OBVIOUSLY MORE TO THIS THAN MEETS THE EYE! DON'T REJOICE JUST YET!!
I KNOW THERE'S A REASON BEHIND ALL THIS!
WHO CARES? LET HER BE!
ACK, DID HE SEE RIGHT THROUGH ME?

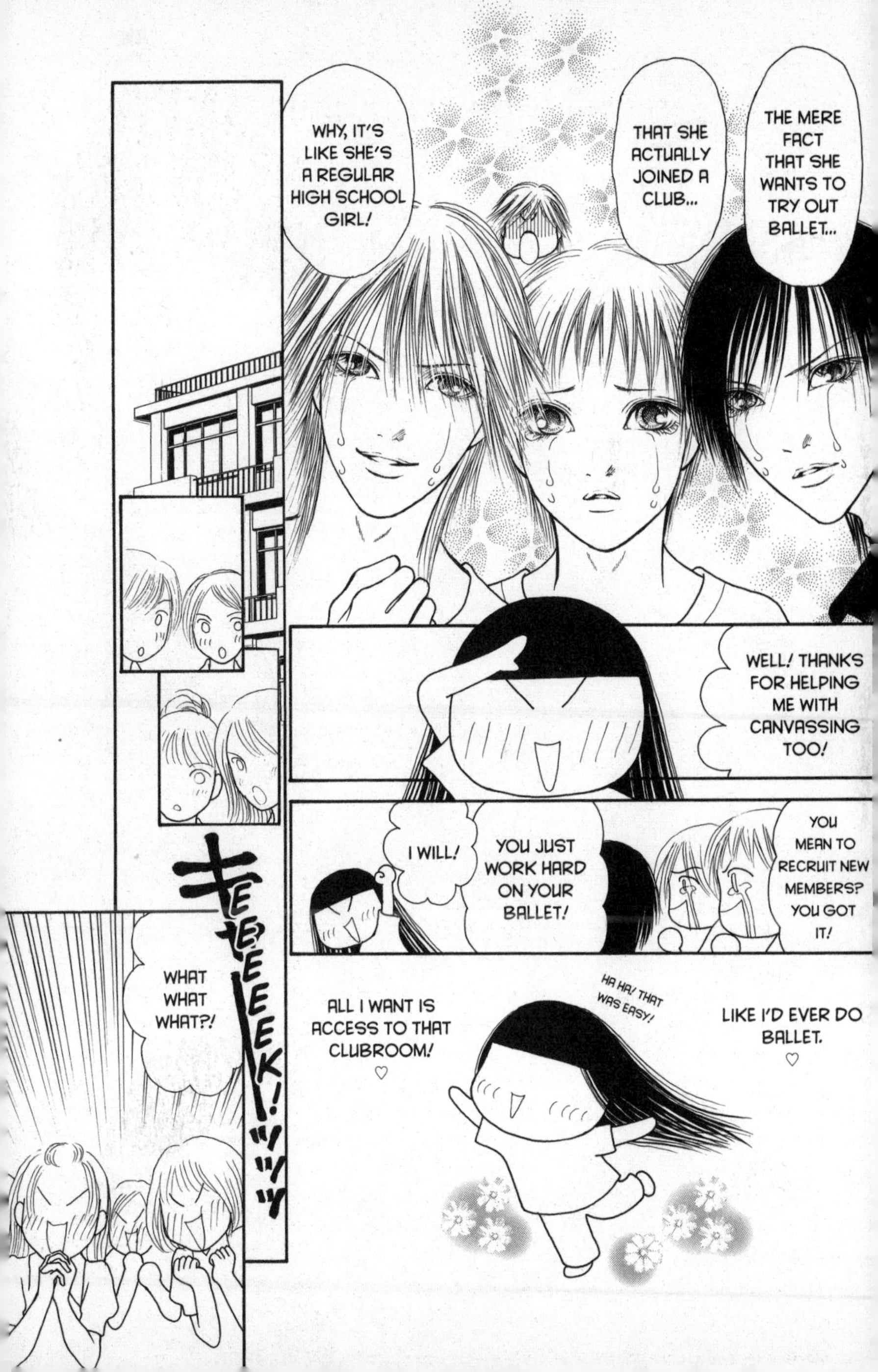
THE MERE FACT THAT SHE WANTS TO TRY OUT BALLET...
THAT SHE ACTUALLY JOINED A CLUB...
WHY, IT'S LIKE SHE'S A REGULAR HIGH SCHOOL GIRL!
WELL! THANKS FOR HELPING ME WITH CANVASSING TOO!
YOU MEAN TO RECRUIT NEW MEMBERS? YOU GOT IT!
YOU JUST WORK HARD ON YOUR BALLET!
I WILL!
LIKE I'D EVER DO BALLET. ♡
HA HA! THAT WAS EASY!
ALL I WANT IS ACCESS TO THAT CLUBROOM! ♡
EEEEEK!
WHAT WHAT WHAT?!

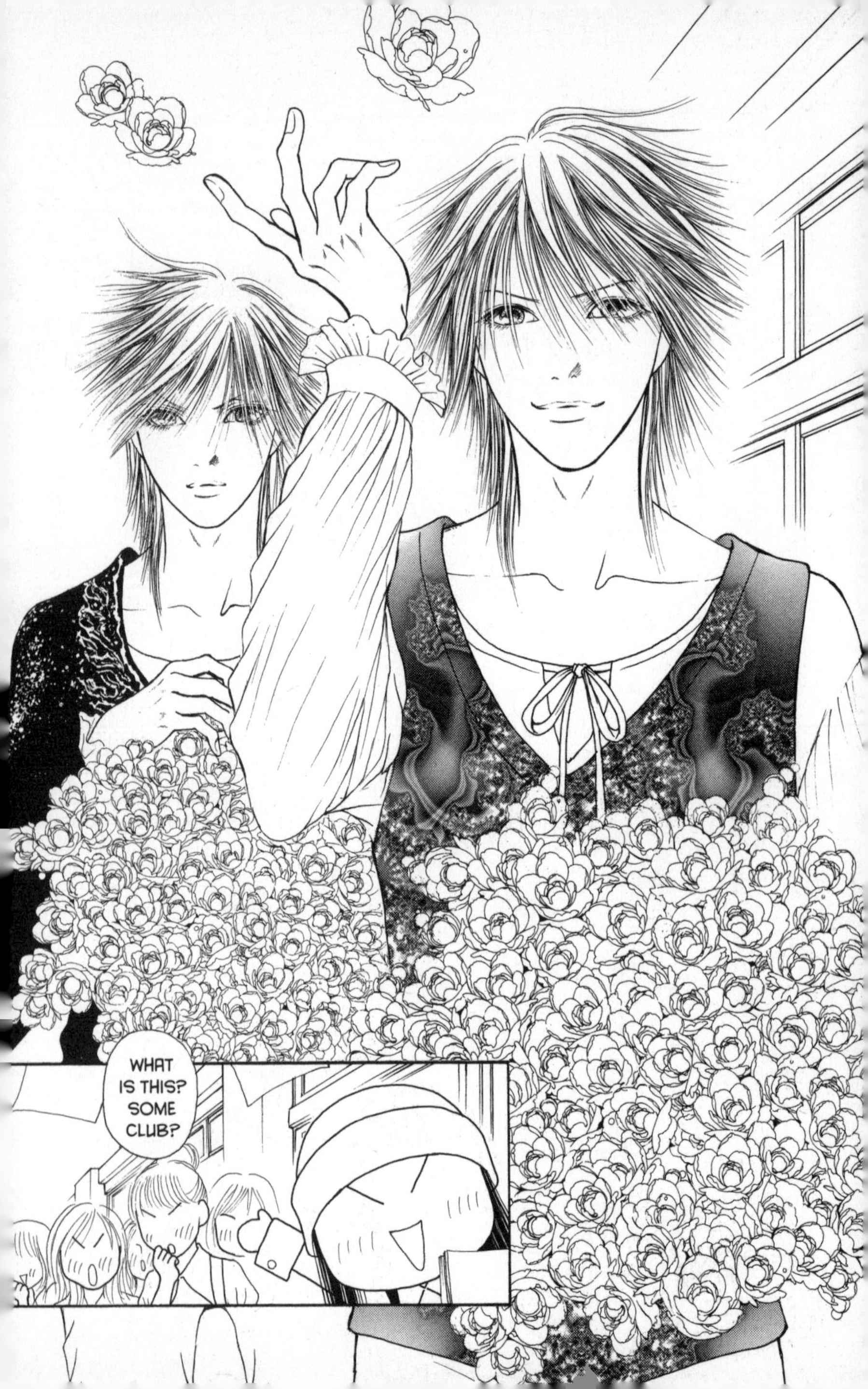
WHAT IS THIS? SOME CLUB?

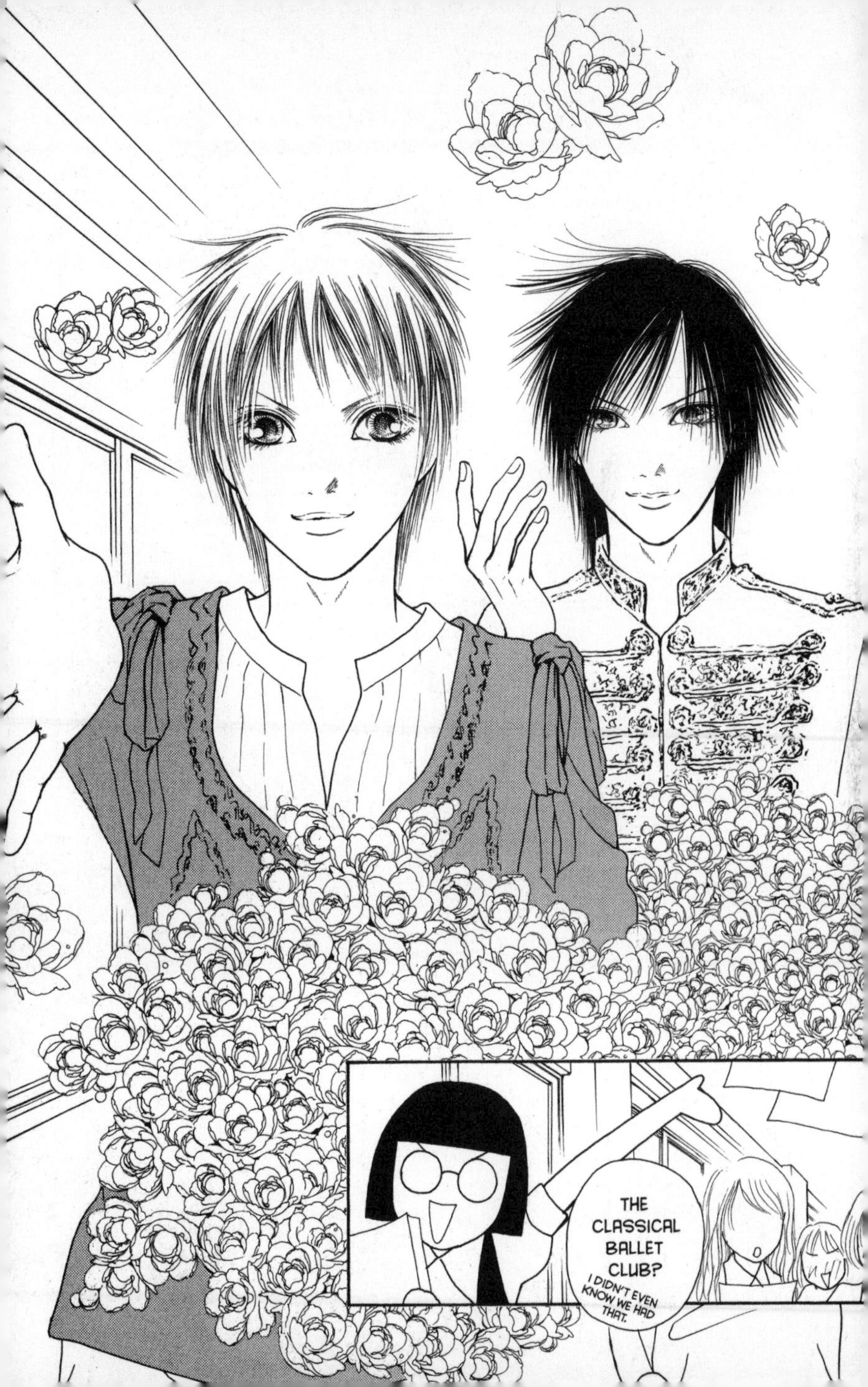
THE CLASSICAL BALLET CLUB?
I DIDN'T EVEN KNOW WE HAD THAT.

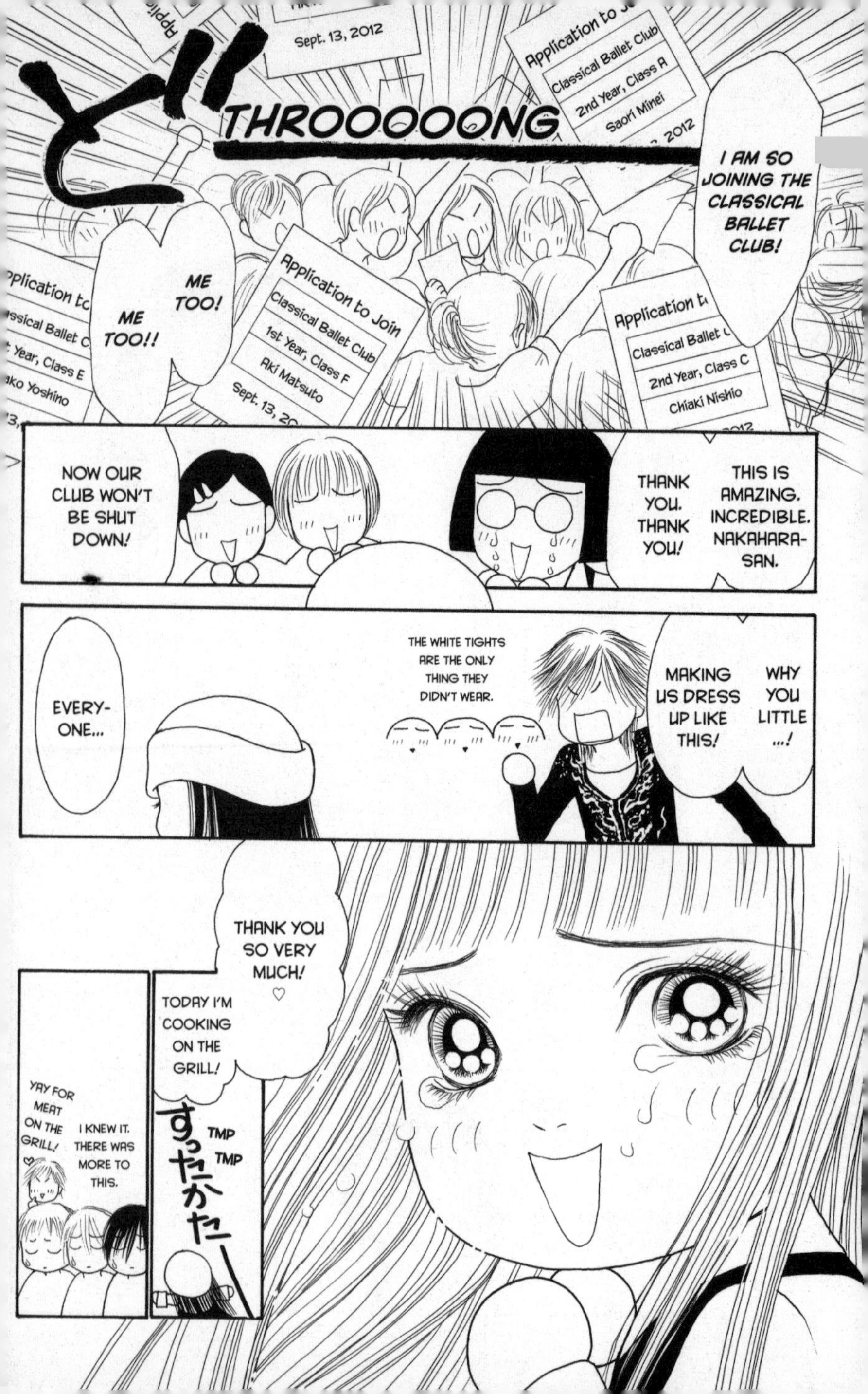
THROOOOONG
Application to Join
Classical Ballet Club
2nd Year, Class A
Saori Minei
Sept. 13, 2012
I AM SO JOINING THE CLASSICAL BALLET CLUB!
Application to Join
Classical Ballet Club
1st Year, Class F
Aki Matsuto
Classical Ballet Club
2nd Year, Class C
Chiaki Nishio
ME TOO!
ME TOO!!
THIS IS AMAZING. INCREDIBLE. NAKAHARA-SAN.
THANK YOU. THANK YOU!
NOW OUR CLUB WON'T BE SHUT DOWN!
WHY YOU LITTLE ...!
MAKING US DRESS UP LIKE THIS!
THE WHITE TIGHTS ARE THE ONLY THING THEY DIDN'T WEAR.
EVERY-ONE...
THANK YOU SO VERY MUCH! ♡
TODAY I'M COOKING ON THE GRILL!
すったかたー
TMP TMP
I KNEW IT. THERE WAS MORE TO THIS.
YAY FOR MEAT ON THE GRILL! ♡

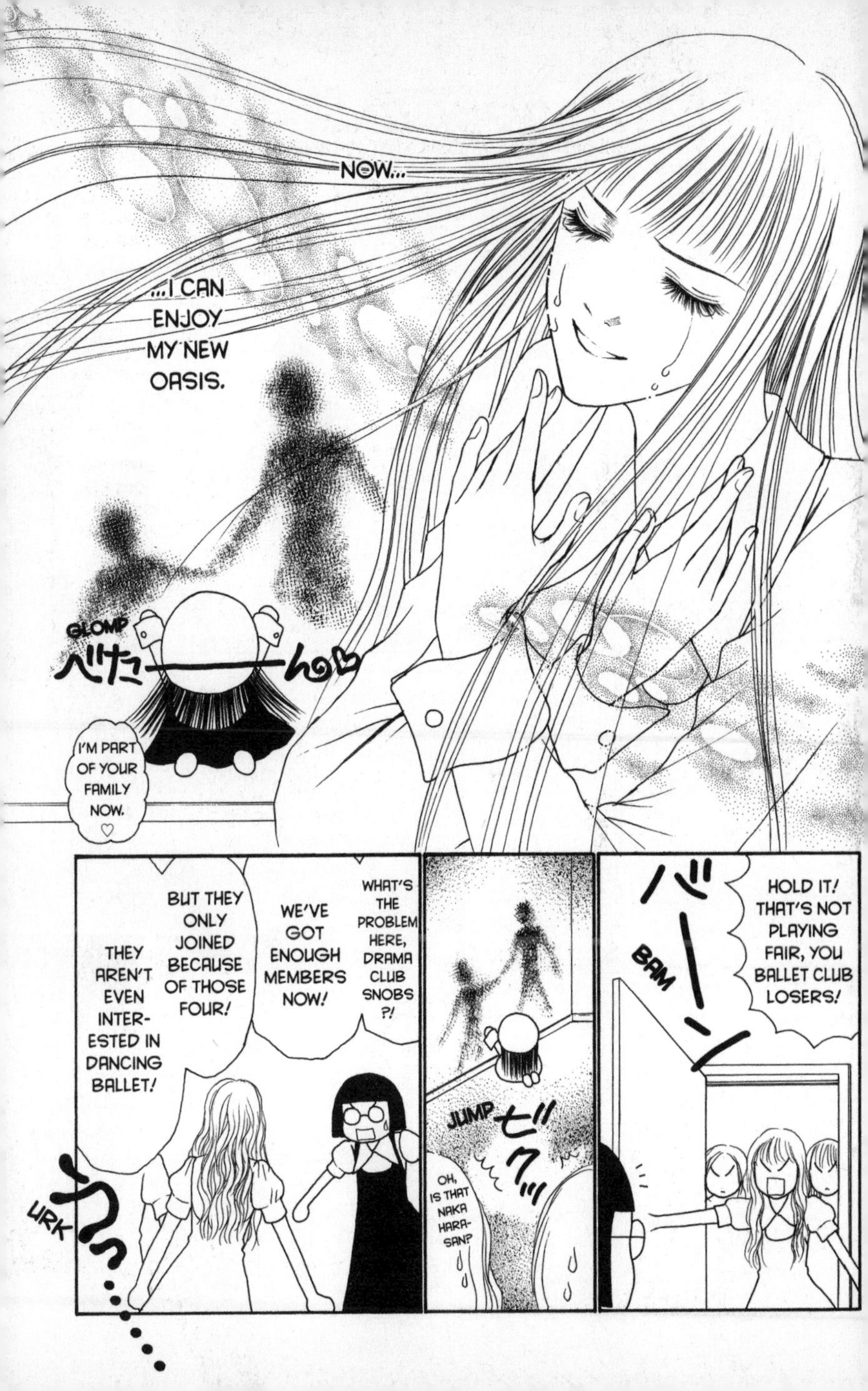
NOW...
...I CAN ENJOY MY NEW OASIS.
GLOMP
べったーーん♡
I'M PART OF YOUR FAMILY NOW. ♡
バーーン
BAM
HOLD IT! THAT'S NOT PLAYING FAIR, YOU BALLET CLUB LOSERS!
JUMP
ビクッ
OH, IS THAT NAKAHARA-SAN?
WHAT'S THE PROBLEM HERE, DRAMA CLUB SNOBS?!
WE'VE GOT ENOUGH MEMBERS NOW!
BUT THEY ONLY JOINED BECAUSE OF THOSE FOUR!
THEY AREN'T EVEN INTERESTED IN DANCING BALLET!
URK
うっ……

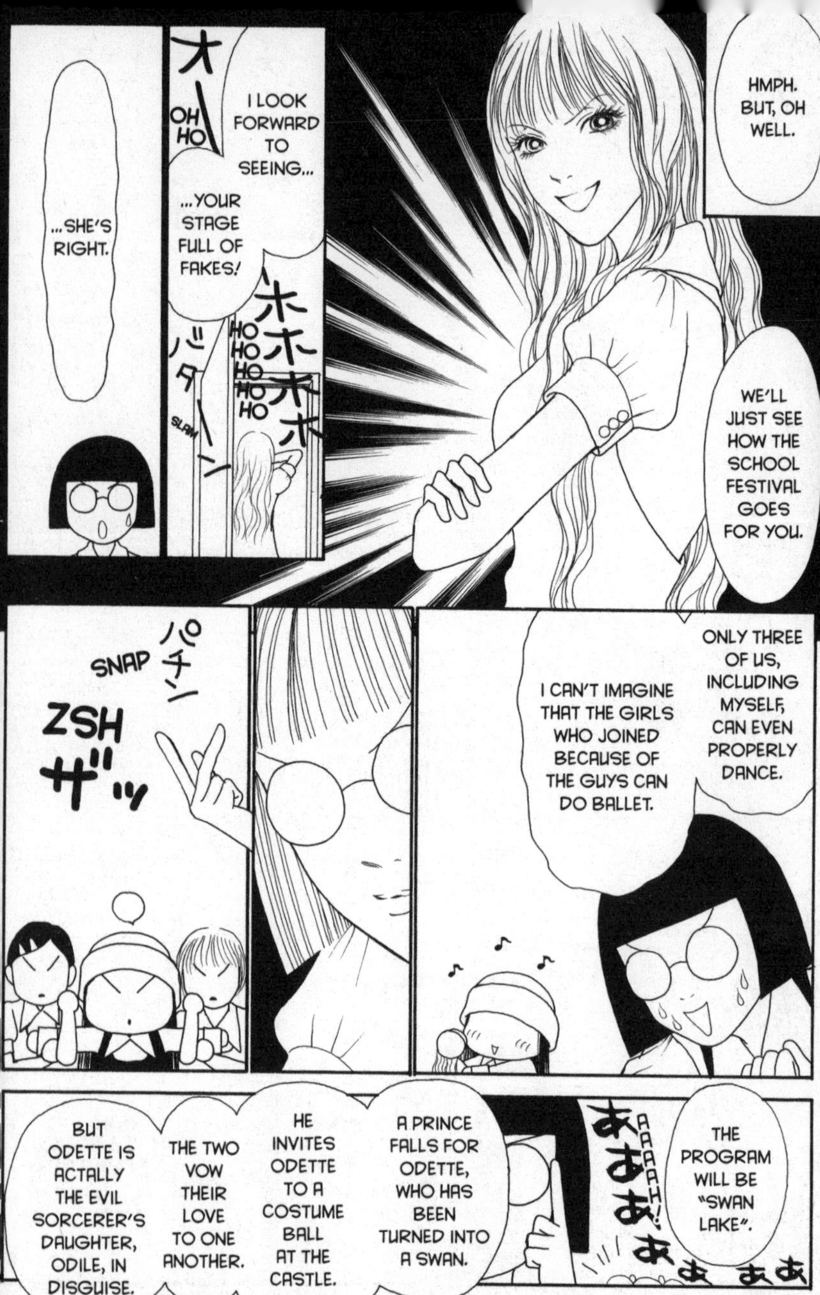
HMPH. BUT, OH WELL.
WE'LL JUST SEE HOW THE SCHOOL FESTIVAL GOES FOR YOU.
I LOOK FORWARD TO SEEING...
オー
OH HO
...YOUR STAGE FULL OF FAKES!
ホホホホ
HO HO HO HO HO
バターン
SLAM
...SHE'S RIGHT.
ONLY THREE OF US, INCLUDING MYSELF, CAN EVEN PROPERLY DANCE.
I CAN'T IMAGINE THAT THE GIRLS WHO JOINED BECAUSE OF THE GUYS CAN DO BALLET.
パチン
SNAP
ZSH
ザッ
THE PROGRAM WILL BE "SWAN LAKE".
あああ
AAAAAH!
ああ ああ
A PRINCE FALLS FOR ODETTE, WHO HAS BEEN TURNED INTO A SWAN.
HE INVITES ODETTE TO A COSTUME BALL AT THE CASTLE.
THE TWO VOW THEIR LOVE TO ONE ANOTHER.
BUT ODETTE IS ACTALLY THE EVIL SORCERER'S DAUGHTER, ODILE, IN DISGUISE.

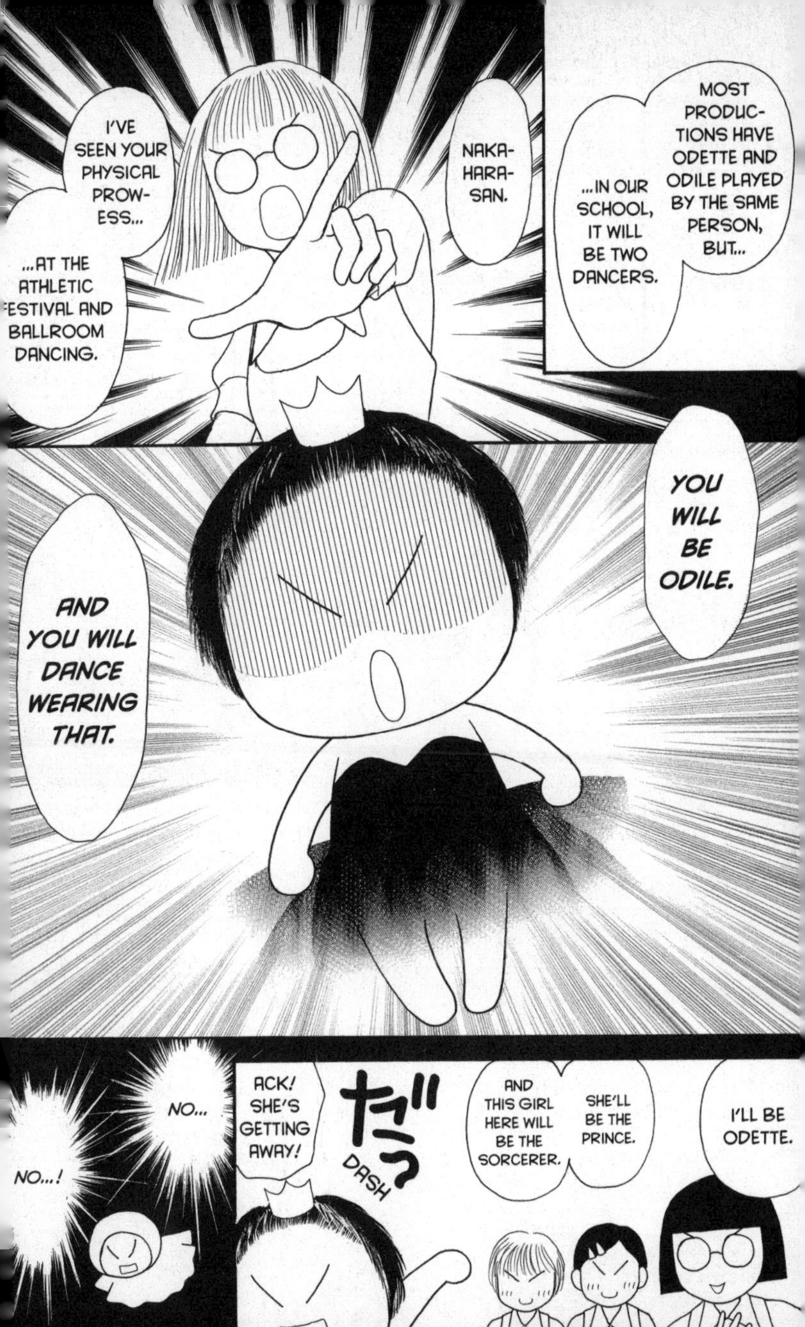
MOST PRODUC-TIONS HAVE ODETTE AND ODILE PLAYED BY THE SAME PERSON, BUT...
...IN OUR SCHOOL, IT WILL BE TWO DANCERS.
NAKA-HARA-SAN.
I'VE SEEN YOUR PHYSICAL PROW-ESS...
...AT THE ATHLETIC FESTIVAL AND BALLROOM DANCING.
YOU WILL BE ODILE.
AND YOU WILL DANCE WEARING THAT.
I'LL BE ODETTE.
SHE'LL BE THE PRINCE.
AND THIS GIRL HERE WILL BE THE SORCERER.
だっ
DASH
ACK! SHE'S GETTING AWAY!
NO...
NO...!

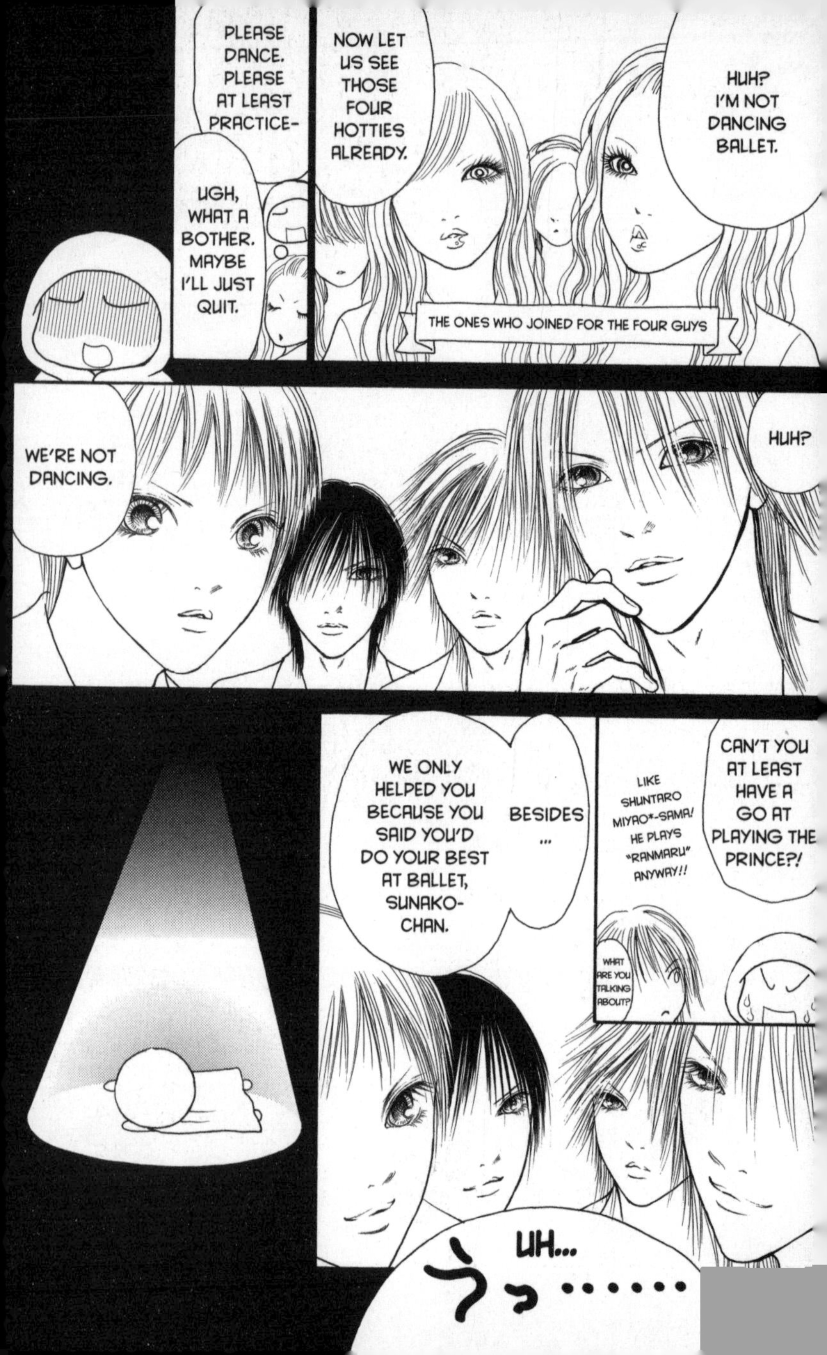
HUH? I'M NOT DANCING BALLET.
NOW LET US SEE THOSE FOUR HOTTIES ALREADY.
THE ONES WHO JOINED FOR THE FOUR GUYS
PLEASE DANCE. PLEASE AT LEAST PRACTICE-
UGH, WHAT A BOTHER. MAYBE I'LL JUST QUIT.
HUH?
WE'RE NOT DANCING.
CAN'T YOU AT LEAST HAVE A GO AT PLAYING THE PRINCE?!
LIKE SHUNTARO MIYAO*-SAMA! HE PLAYS "RANMARU" ANYWAY!!
WHAT ARE YOU TALKING ABOUT?
BESIDES...
WE ONLY HELPED YOU BECAUSE YOU SAID YOU'D DO YOUR BEST AT BALLET, SUNAKO-CHAN.
UH...
うっ......

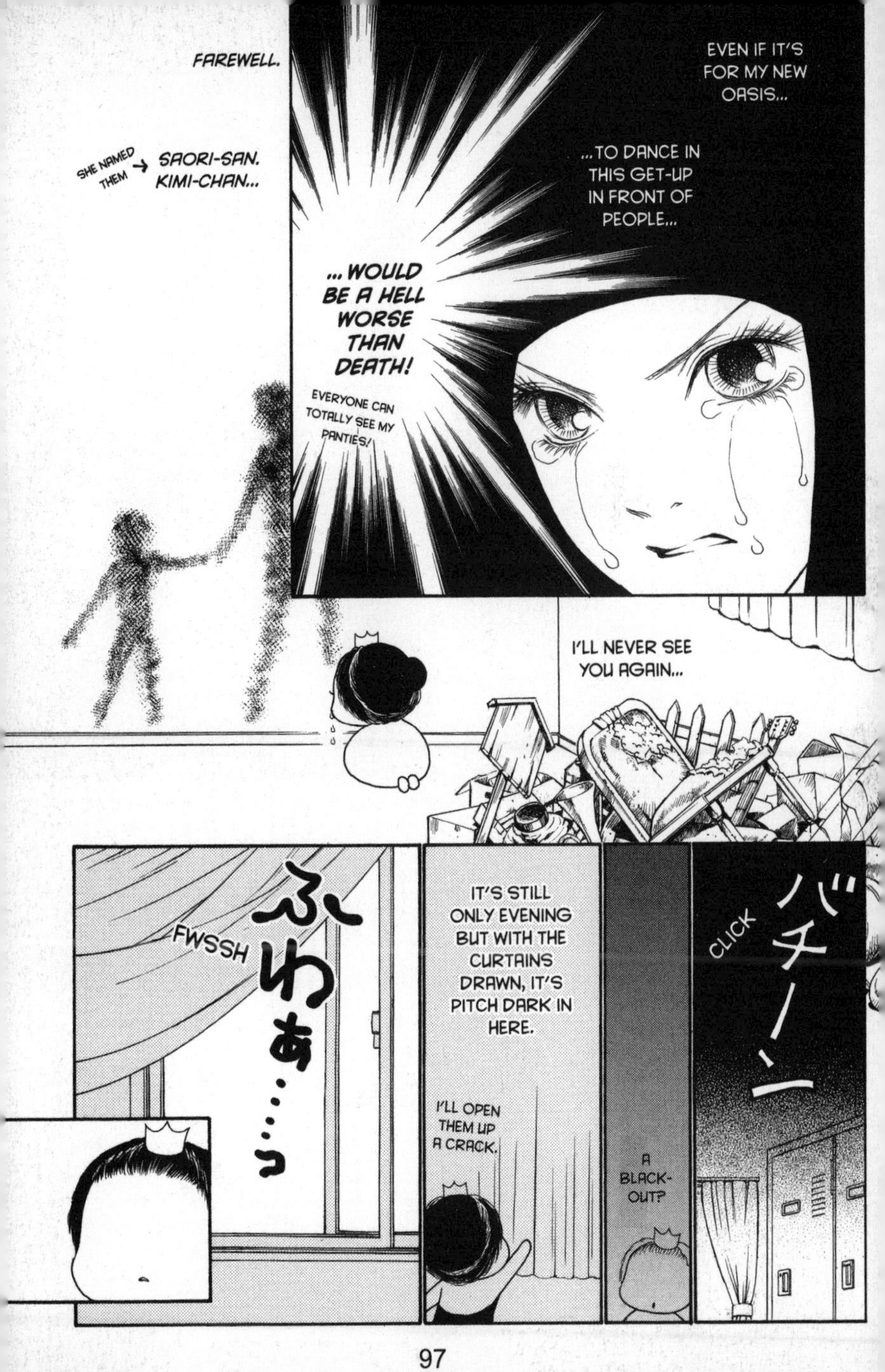

EVEN IF IT'S FOR MY NEW OASIS...
...TO DANCE IN THIS GET-UP IN FRONT OF PEOPLE...
...WOULD BE A HELL WORSE THAN DEATH!
EVERYONE CAN TOTALLY SEE MY PANTIES!
FAREWELL.
SHE NAMED THEM
SAORI-SAN. KIMI-CHAN...
I'LL NEVER SEE YOU AGAIN...
バチーン
CLICK
A BLACK-OUT?
IT'S STILL ONLY EVENING BUT WITH THE CURTAINS DRAWN, IT'S PITCH DARK IN HERE.
I'LL OPEN THEM UP A CRACK.
ふわぁ…っ
FWSSH

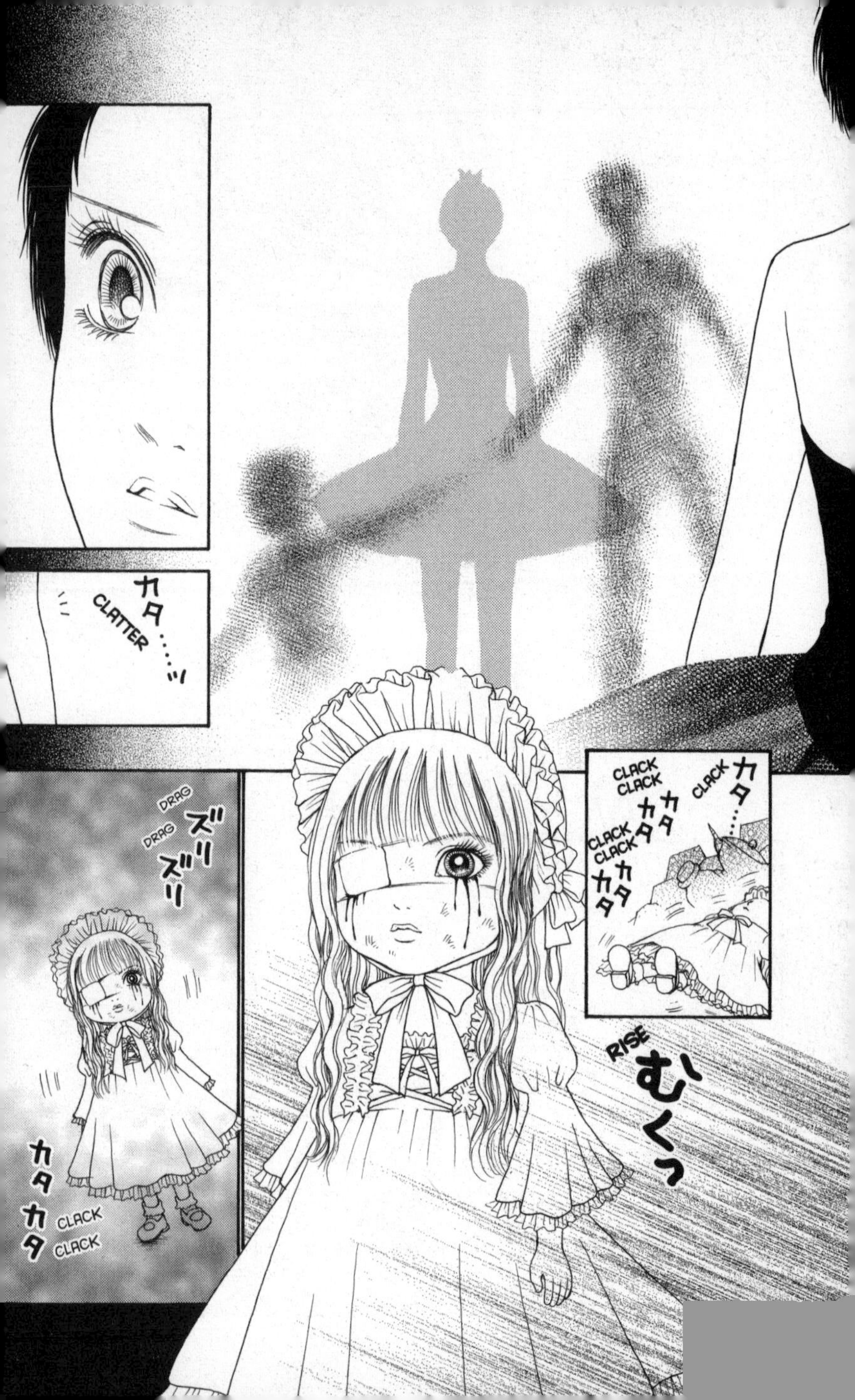
カタ……ッ
CLATTER
カタ……
CLACK
カタカタ
CLACK CLACK
カタカタ
CLACK CLACK
むくっ
RISE
ズリズリ
DRAG DRAG
カタカタ
CLACK CLACK

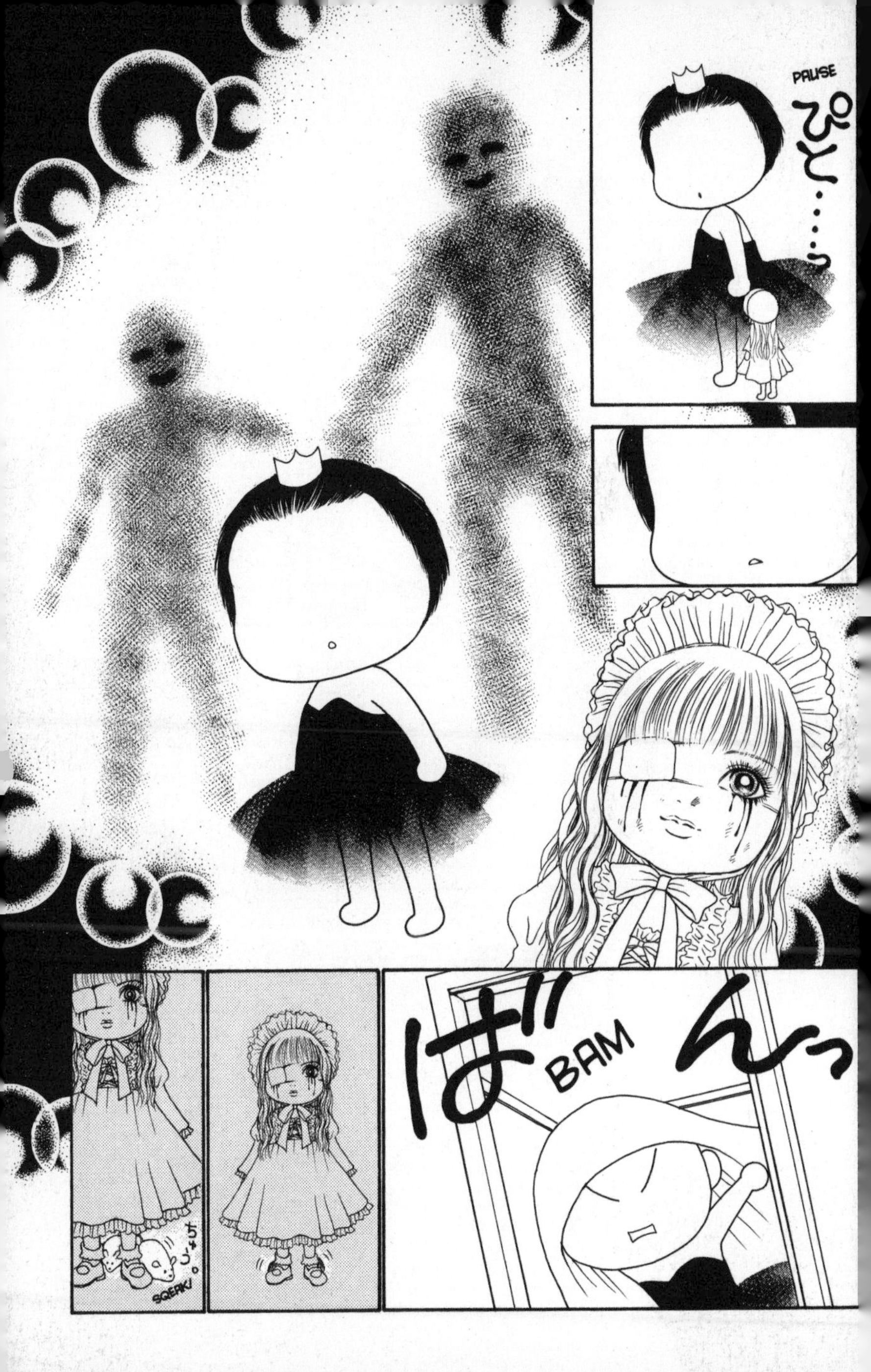
PAUSE
ぴと…っ
ばんっ
BAM
ちゅう。
SQEAK!

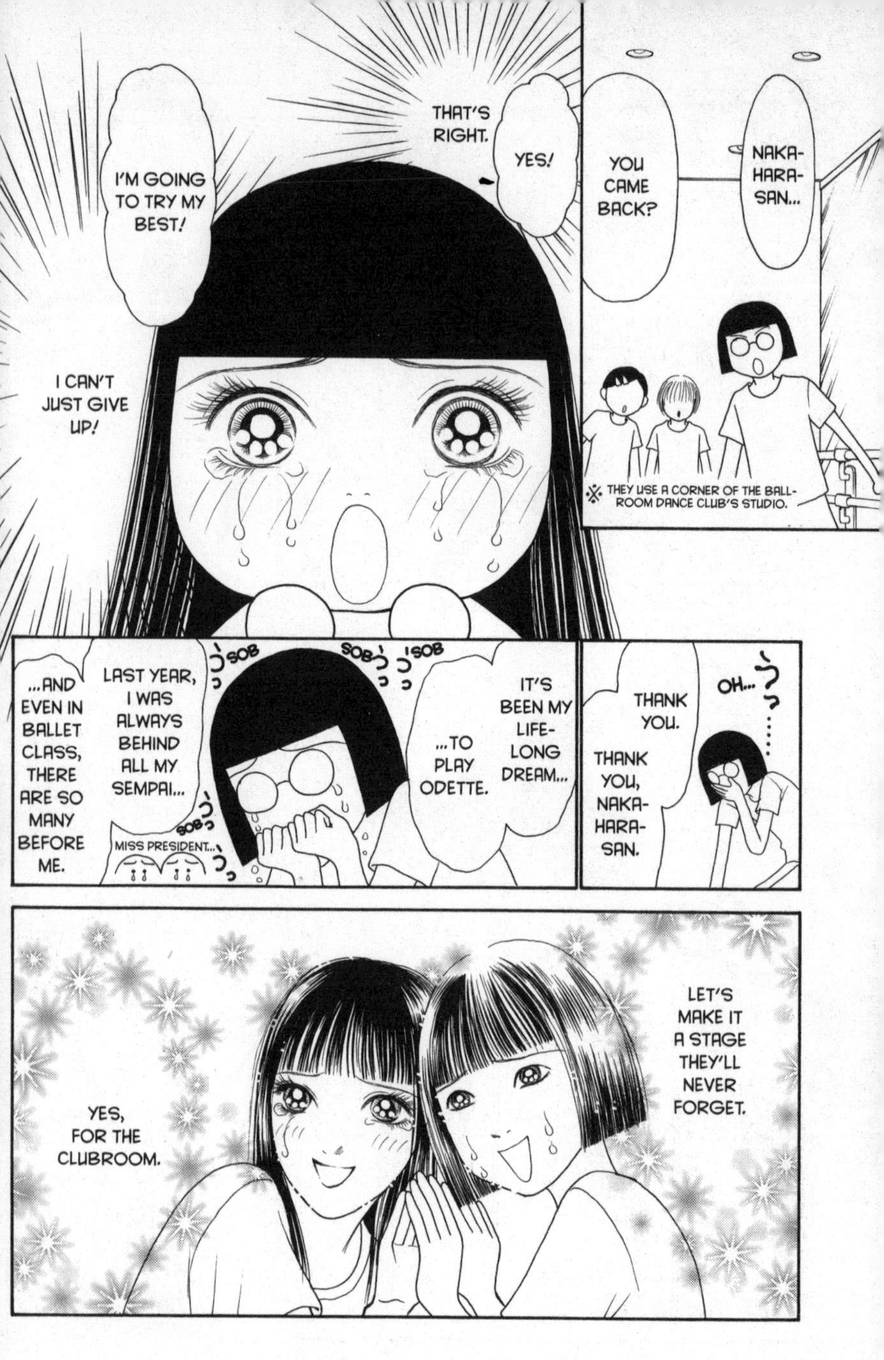
NAKA-HARA-SAN...
YOU CAME BACK?
※ THEY USE A CORNER OF THE BALLROOM DANCE CLUB'S STUDIO.
YES!
THAT'S RIGHT.
I'M GOING TO TRY MY BEST!
I CAN'T JUST GIVE UP!
OH...
THANK YOU.
THANK YOU, NAKA-HARA-SAN.
IT'S BEEN MY LIFE-LONG DREAM...
...TO PLAY ODETTE.
SOB
SOB
SOB
LAST YEAR, I WAS ALWAYS BEHIND ALL MY SEMPAI...
SOB
...AND EVEN IN BALLET CLASS, THERE ARE SO MANY BEFORE ME.
MISS PRESIDENT...
LET'S MAKE IT A STAGE THEY'LL NEVER FORGET.
YES, FOR THE CLUBROOM.

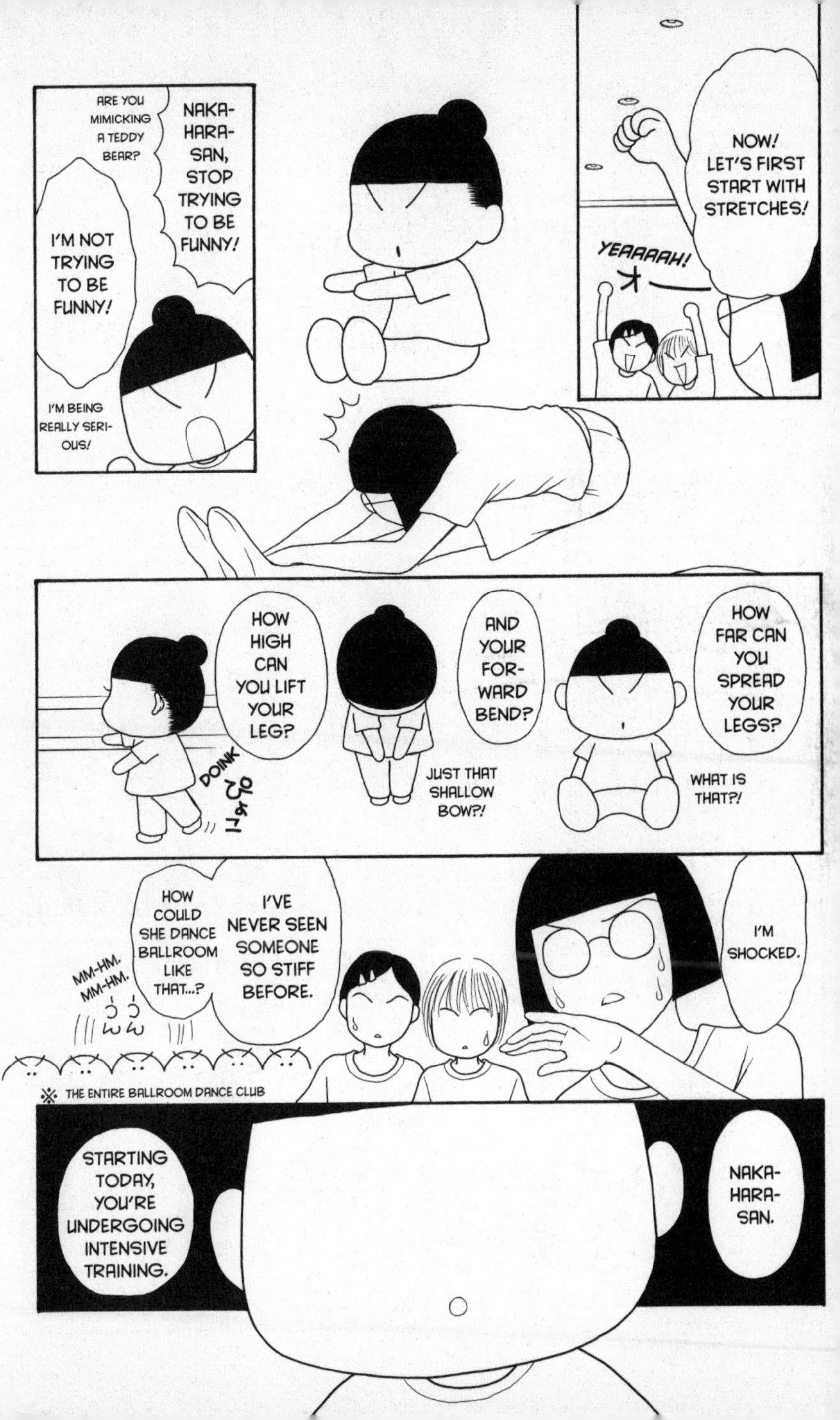
NOW! LET'S FIRST START WITH STRETCHES!
YEAAAAH!
NAKA-HARA-SAN, STOP TRYING TO BE FUNNY!
ARE YOU MIMICKING A TEDDY BEAR?
I'M NOT TRYING TO BE FUNNY!
I'M BEING REALLY SERI-OUS!
HOW FAR CAN YOU SPREAD YOUR LEGS?
WHAT IS THAT?!
AND YOUR FOR-WARD BEND?
JUST THAT SHALLOW BOW?!
HOW HIGH CAN YOU LIFT YOUR LEG?
DOINK
I'M SHOCKED.
I'VE NEVER SEEN SOMEONE SO STIFF BEFORE.
HOW COULD SHE DANCE BALLROOM LIKE THAT...?
MM-HM. MM-HM.
※ THE ENTIRE BALLROOM DANCE CLUB
NAKA-HARA-SAN.
STARTING TODAY, YOU'RE UNDERGOING INTENSIVE TRAINING.

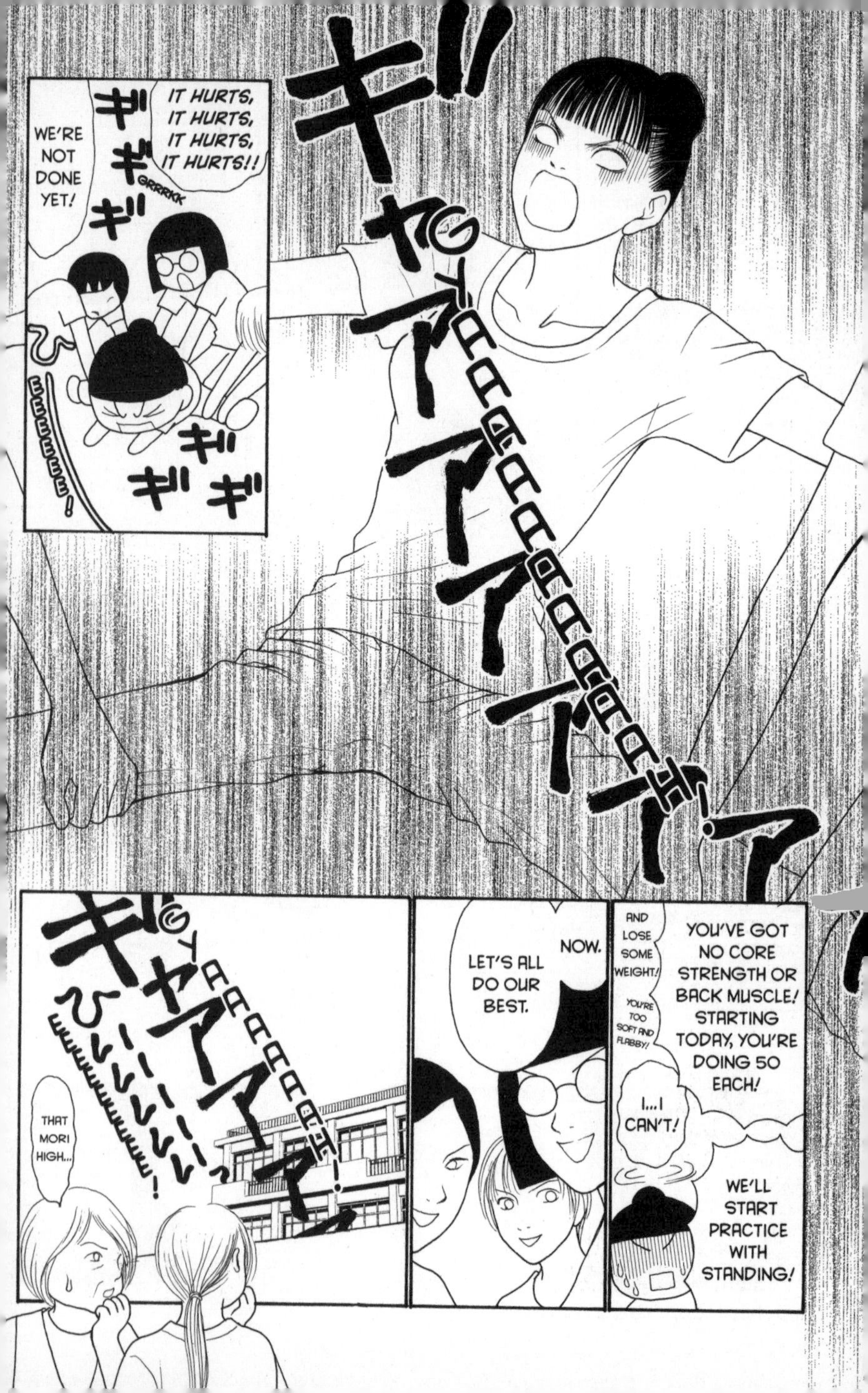
GYAAAAAAAAAAAH!
IT HURTS, IT HURTS, IT HURTS, IT HURTS!!
WE'RE NOT DONE YET!
GRRRKK
EEEEEEEE!
YOU'VE GOT NO CORE STRENGTH OR BACK MUSCLE! STARTING TODAY, YOU'RE DOING 50 EACH!
AND LOSE SOME WEIGHT!
YOU'RE TOO SOFT AND FLABBY!
I...I CAN'T!
WE'LL START PRACTICE WITH STANDING!
NOW.
LET'S ALL DO OUR BEST.
GYAAAAAAAAH!
EEEEEEEEEE!
THAT MORI HIGH...

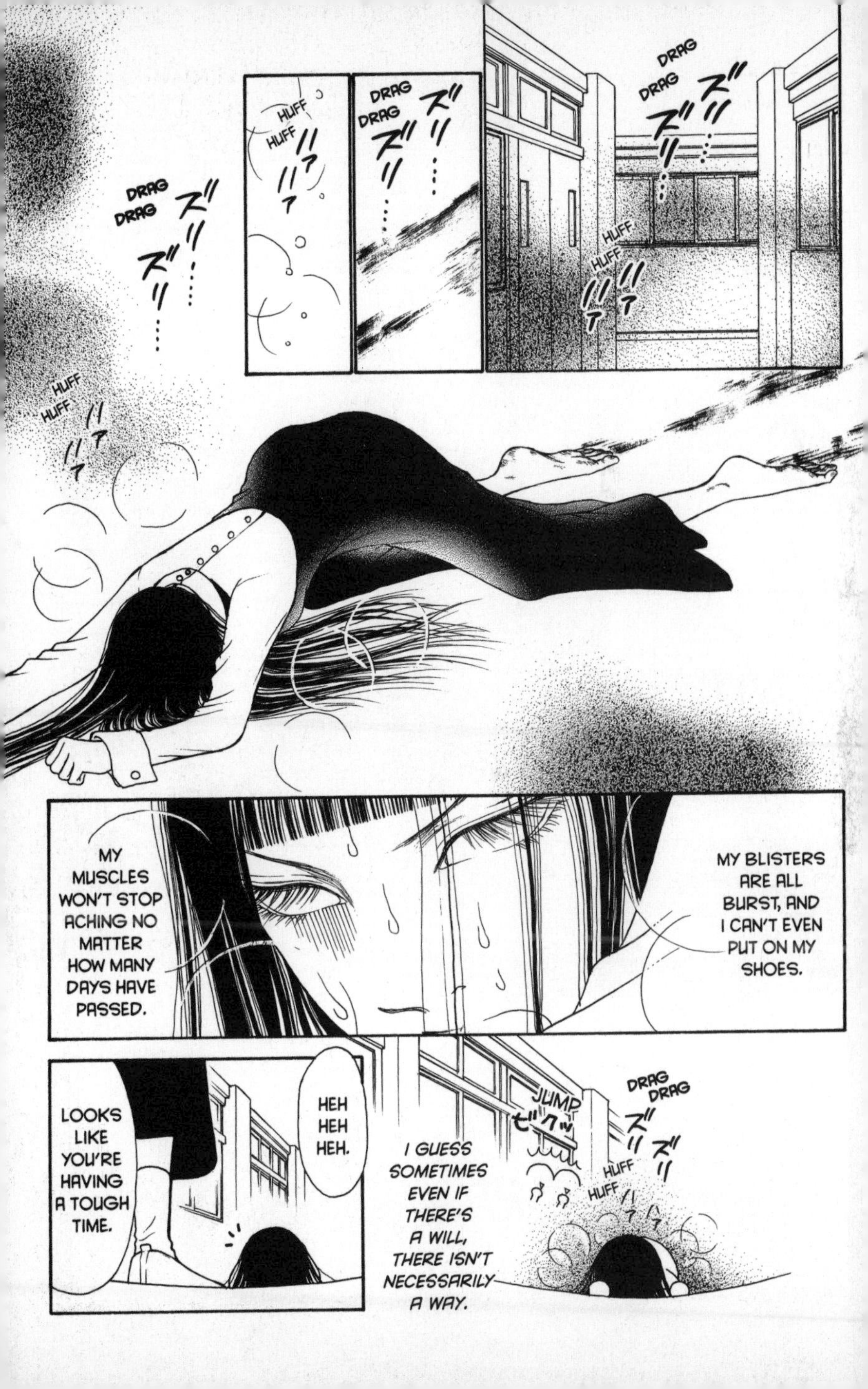
DRAG
DRAG
HUFF
HUFF
DRAG
DRAG
HUFF
HUFF
DRAG
DRAG
HUFF
HUFF
MY BLISTERS ARE ALL BURST, AND I CAN'T EVEN PUT ON MY SHOES.
MY MUSCLES WON'T STOP ACHING NO MATTER HOW MANY DAYS HAVE PASSED.
DRAG
DRAG
HUFF
HUFF
JUMP
I GUESS SOMETIMES EVEN IF THERE'S A WILL, THERE ISN'T NECESSARILY A WAY.
HEH HEH HEH.
LOOKS LIKE YOU'RE HAVING A TOUGH TIME.

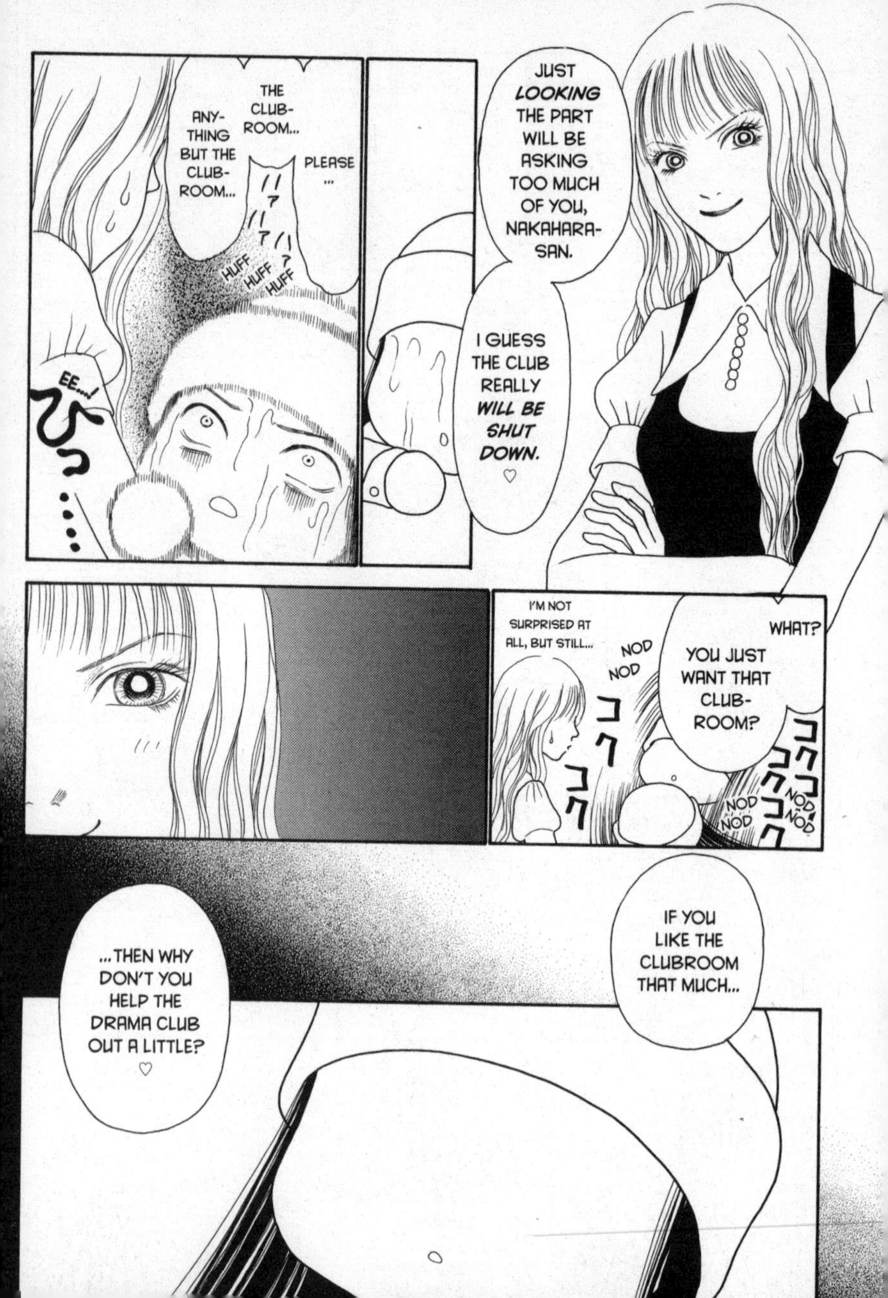
JUST LOOKING THE PART WILL BE ASKING TOO MUCH OF YOU, NAKAHARA-SAN.
I GUESS THE CLUB REALLY WILL BE SHUT DOWN. ♡
PLEASE...
THE CLUB-ROOM...
ANY-THING BUT THE CLUB-ROOM...
ハァハァハァ
HUFF HUFF HUFF
ひっ...
EE...!
WHAT?
YOU JUST WANT THAT CLUB-ROOM?
コクコク
NOD NOD
I'M NOT SURPRISED AT ALL, BUT STILL...
コクコクコクコク
NOD NOD NOD NOD
IF YOU LIKE THE CLUBROOM THAT MUCH...
...THEN WHY DON'T YOU HELP THE DRAMA CLUB OUT A LITTLE? ♡

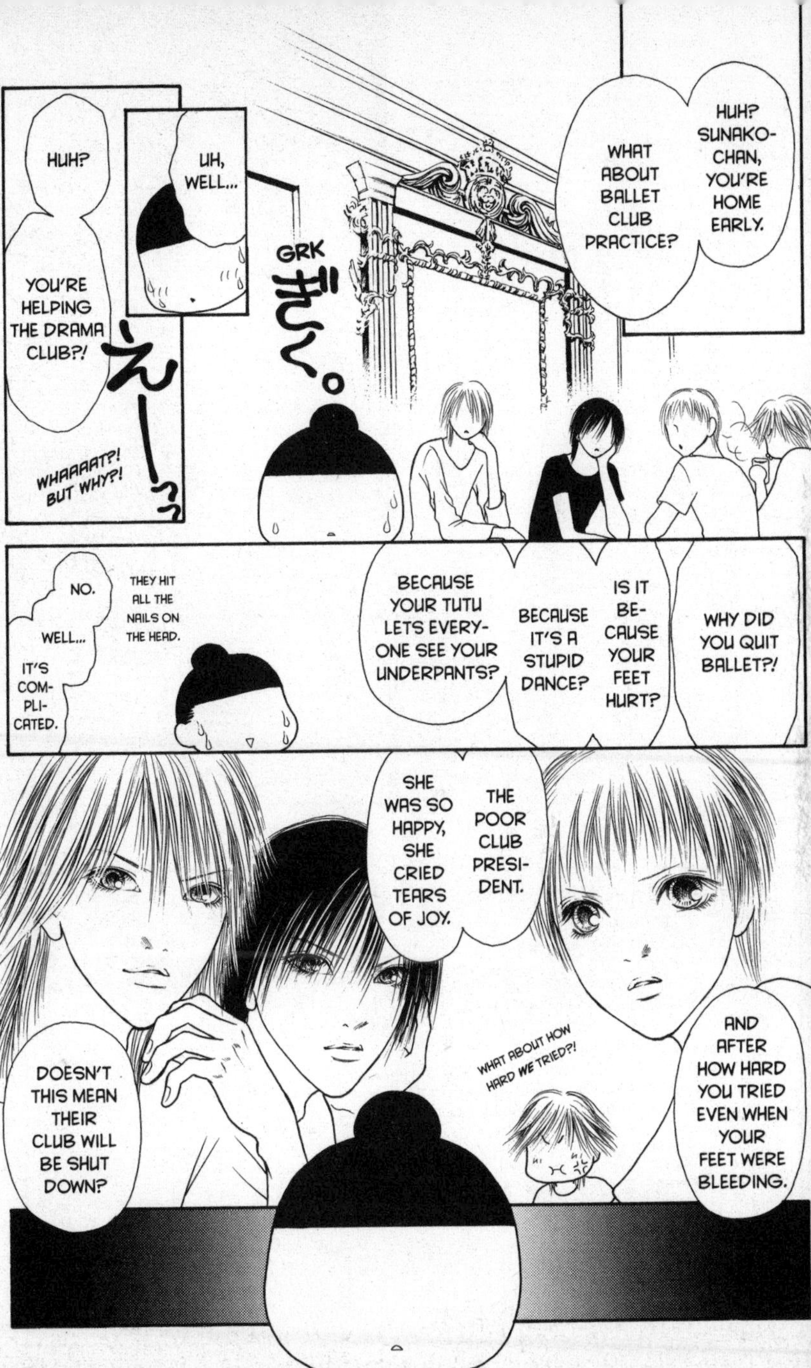
HUH? SUNAKO-CHAN, YOU'RE HOME EARLY.
WHAT ABOUT BALLET CLUB PRACTICE?
GRK
ぎく。
UH, WELL...
HUH?
YOU'RE HELPING THE DRAMA CLUB?!
えーっ
WHAAAAT?! BUT WHY?!
WHY DID YOU QUIT BALLET?!
IS IT BE-CAUSE YOUR FEET HURT?
BECAUSE IT'S A STUPID DANCE?
BECAUSE YOUR TUTU LETS EVERY-ONE SEE YOUR UNDERPANTS?
THEY HIT ALL THE NAILS ON THE HEAD.
NO.
WELL...
IT'S COM-PLI-CATED.
AND AFTER HOW HARD YOU TRIED EVEN WHEN YOUR FEET WERE BLEEDING.
THE POOR CLUB PRESI-DENT.
SHE WAS SO HAPPY, SHE CRIED TEARS OF JOY.
WHAT ABOUT HOW HARD WE TRIED?!
DOESN'T THIS MEAN THEIR CLUB WILL BE SHUT DOWN?

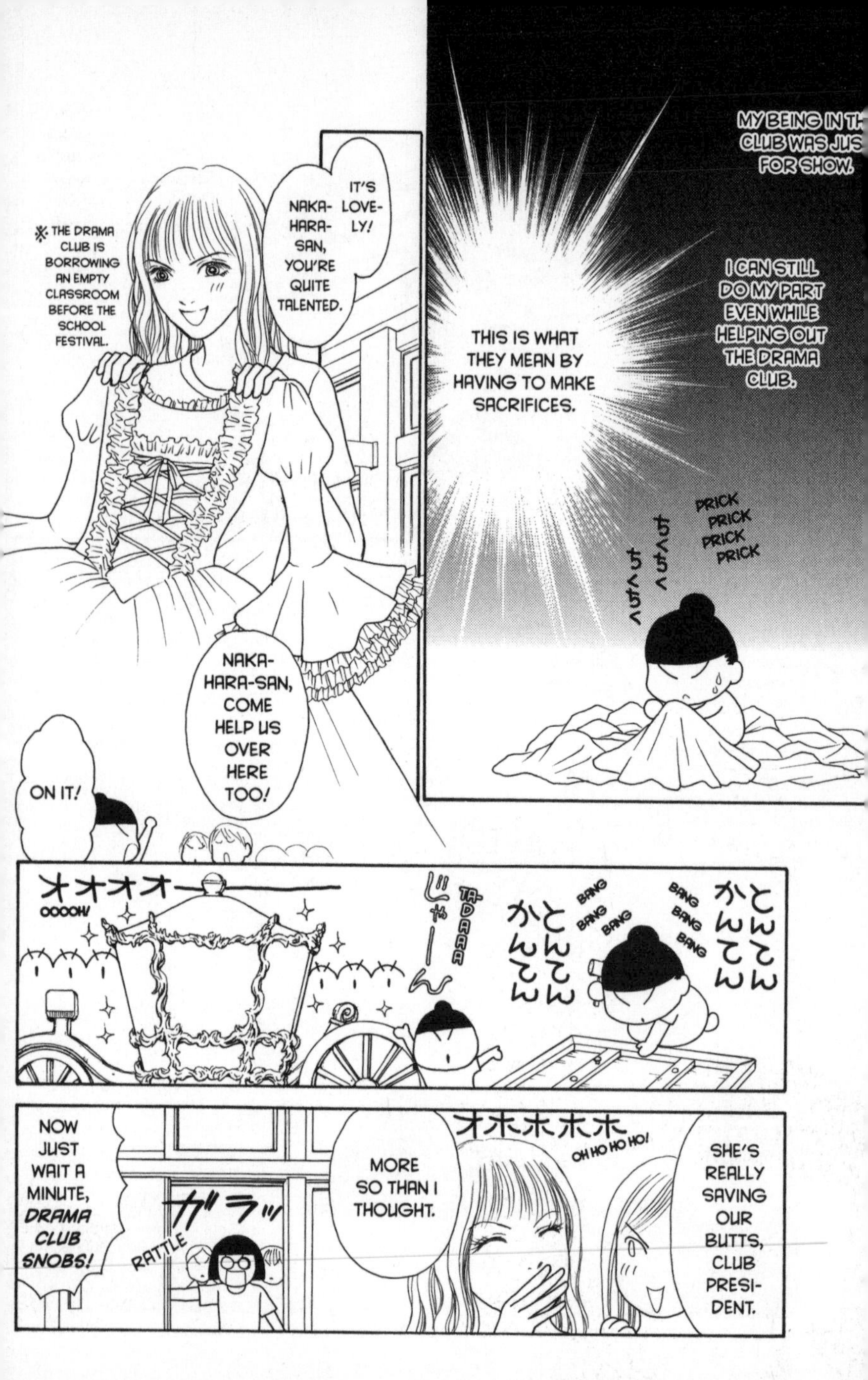
MY BEING IN TH CLUB WAS JUS FOR SHOW.
I CAN STILL DO MY PART EVEN WHILE HELPING OUT THE DRAMA CLUB.
THIS IS WHAT THEY MEAN BY HAVING TO MAKE SACRIFICES.
ちくちく ちくちく
PRICK PRICK PRICK PRICK
IT'S LOVELY!
NAKA-HARA-SAN, YOU'RE QUITE TALENTED.
※THE DRAMA CLUB IS BORROWING AN EMPTY CLASSROOM BEFORE THE SCHOOL FESTIVAL.
NAKA-HARA-SAN, COME HELP US OVER HERE TOO!
ON IT!
とんてんかんてん
BANG BANG BANG
とんてんかんてん
BANG BANG BANG
じゃーん
TA-DAAAA
オオオオー
OOOOH!
SHE'S REALLY SAVING OUR BUTTS, CLUB PRESI-DENT.
オホホホホ
OH HO HO HO!
MORE SO THAN I THOUGHT.
ガラッ
RATTLE
NOW JUST WAIT A MINUTE, DRAMA CLUB SNOBS!

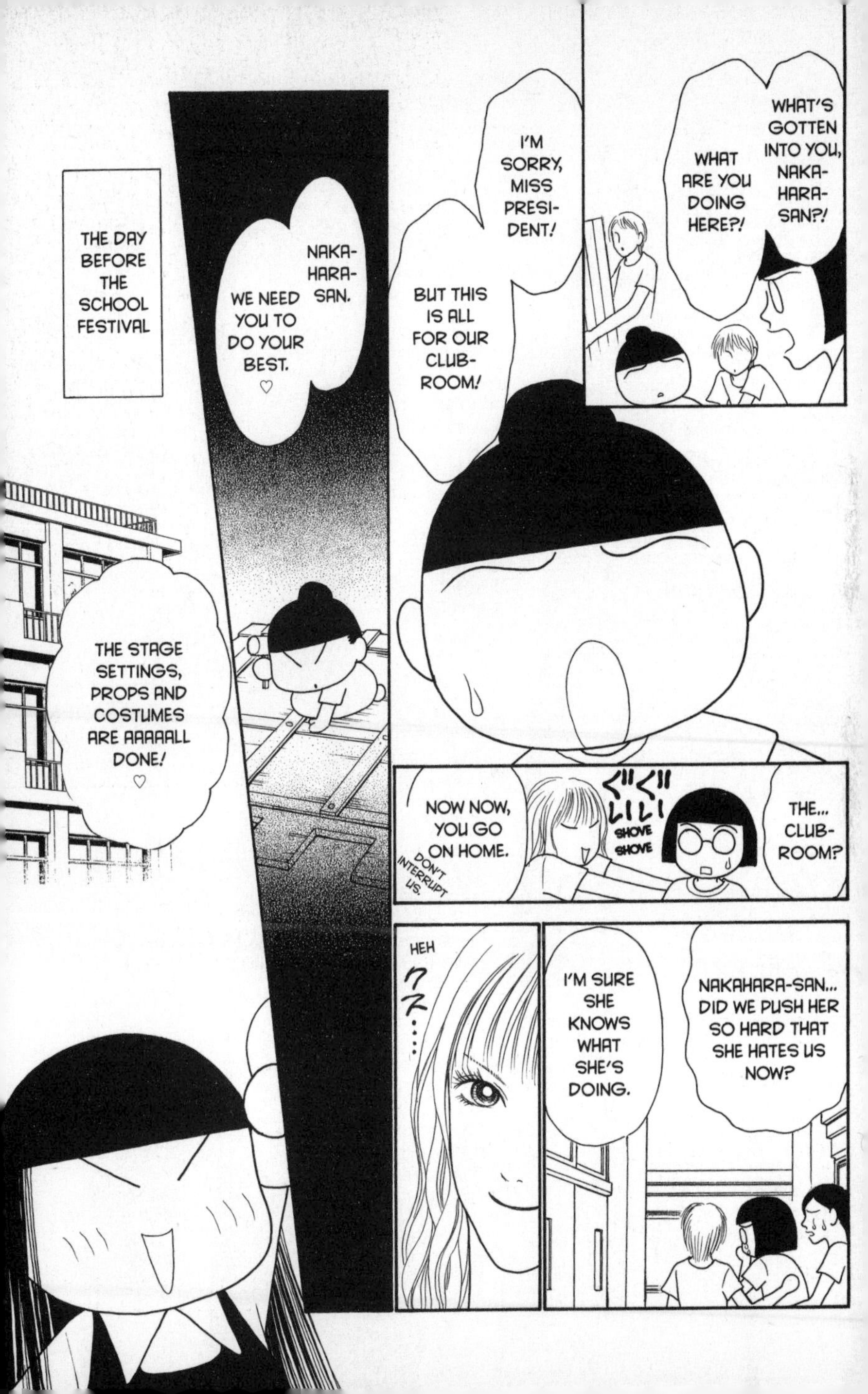

WHAT'S GOTTEN INTO YOU, NAKAHARA-SAN?!
WHAT ARE YOU DOING HERE?!
I'M SORRY, MISS PRESIDENT!
BUT THIS IS ALL FOR OUR CLUBROOM!
THE... CLUBROOM?
SHOVE SHOVE
NOW NOW, YOU GO ON HOME.
DON'T INTERRUPT US.
NAKAHARA-SAN... DID WE PUSH HER SO HARD THAT SHE HATES US NOW?
I'M SURE SHE KNOWS WHAT SHE'S DOING.
HEH
クス……
NAKAHARA-SAN.
WE NEED YOU TO DO YOUR BEST. ♡
THE DAY BEFORE THE SCHOOL FESTIVAL
THE STAGE SETTINGS, PROPS AND COSTUMES ARE AAAAALL DONE! ♡

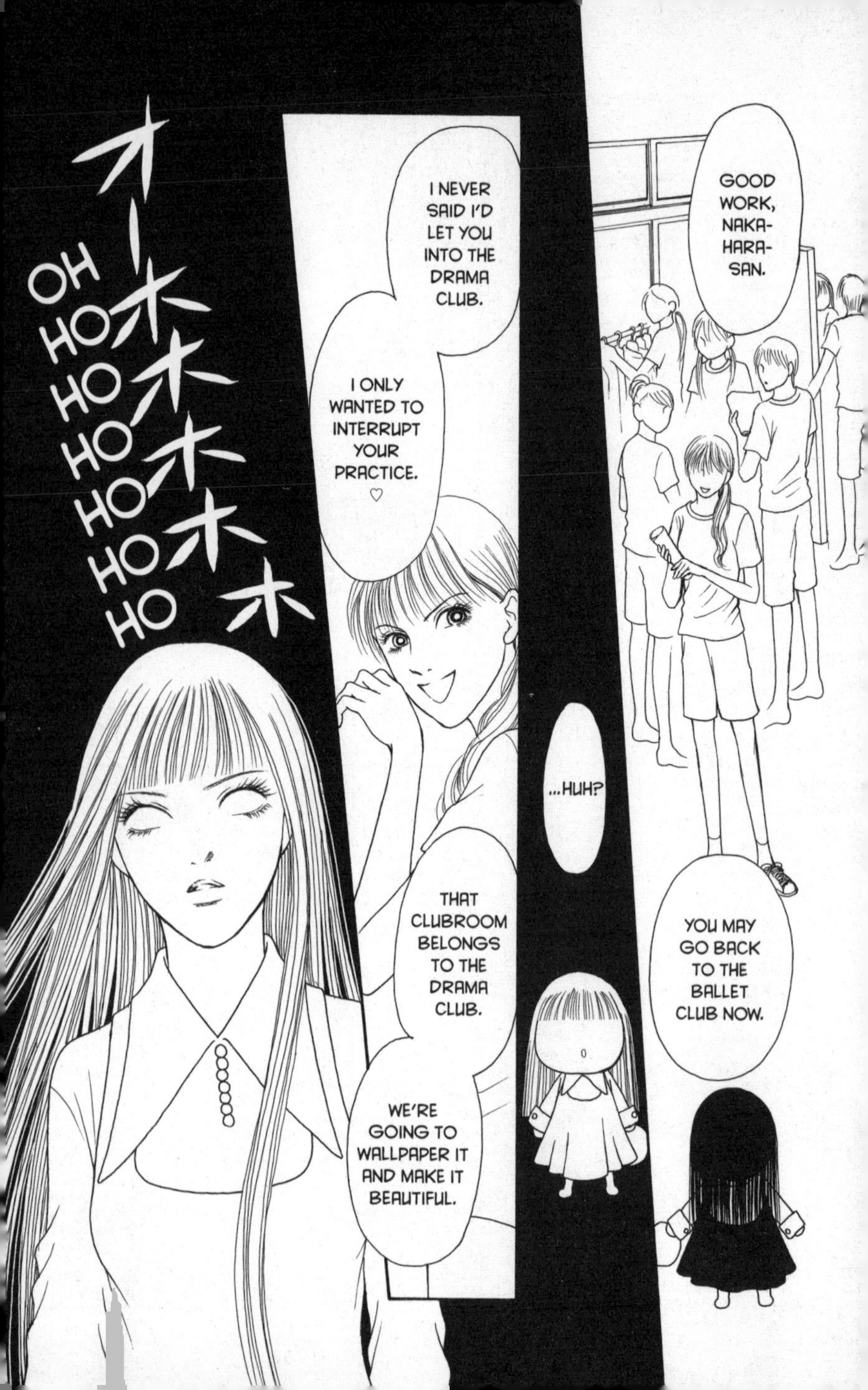
GOOD WORK, NAKA-HARA-SAN.
YOU MAY GO BACK TO THE BALLET CLUB NOW.
...HUH?
I NEVER SAID I'D LET YOU INTO THE DRAMA CLUB.
I ONLY WANTED TO INTERRUPT YOUR PRACTICE. ♡
THAT CLUBROOM BELONGS TO THE DRAMA CLUB.
WE'RE GOING TO WALLPAPER IT AND MAKE IT BEAUTIFUL.
オーホホホホホホ
OH HO HO HO HO HO HO

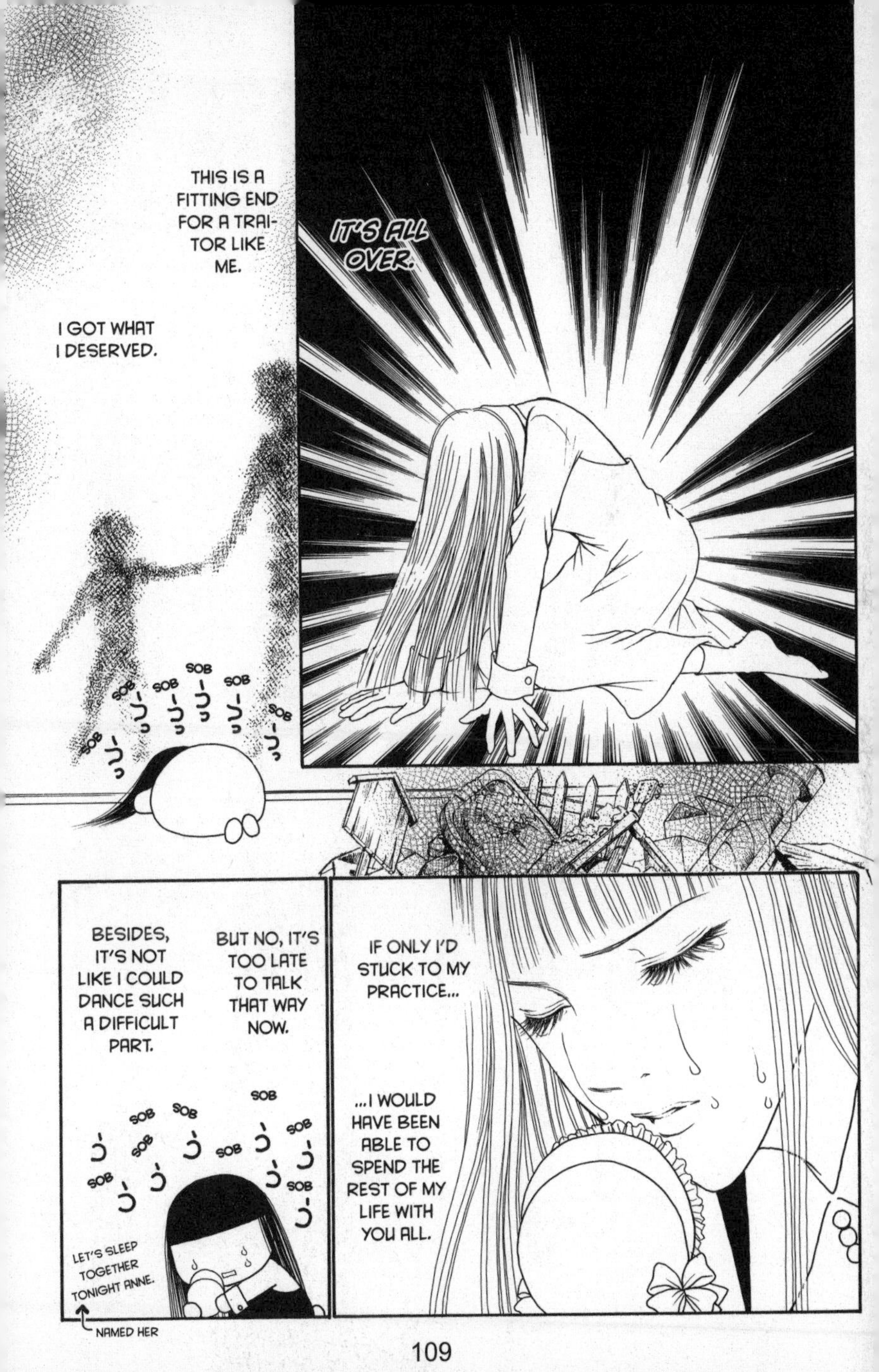
IT'S ALL OVER.
THIS IS A FITTING END FOR A TRAI-TOR LIKE ME.
I GOT WHAT I DESERVED.
SOB SOB SOB SOB SOB SOB
IF ONLY I'D STUCK TO MY PRACTICE...
...I WOULD HAVE BEEN ABLE TO SPEND THE REST OF MY LIFE WITH YOU ALL.
BUT NO, IT'S TOO LATE TO TALK THAT WAY NOW.
BESIDES, IT'S NOT LIKE I COULD DANCE SUCH A DIFFICULT PART.
SOB SOB SOB SOB SOB SOB SOB SOB
LET'S SLEEP TOGETHER TONIGHT ANNE.
NAMED HER

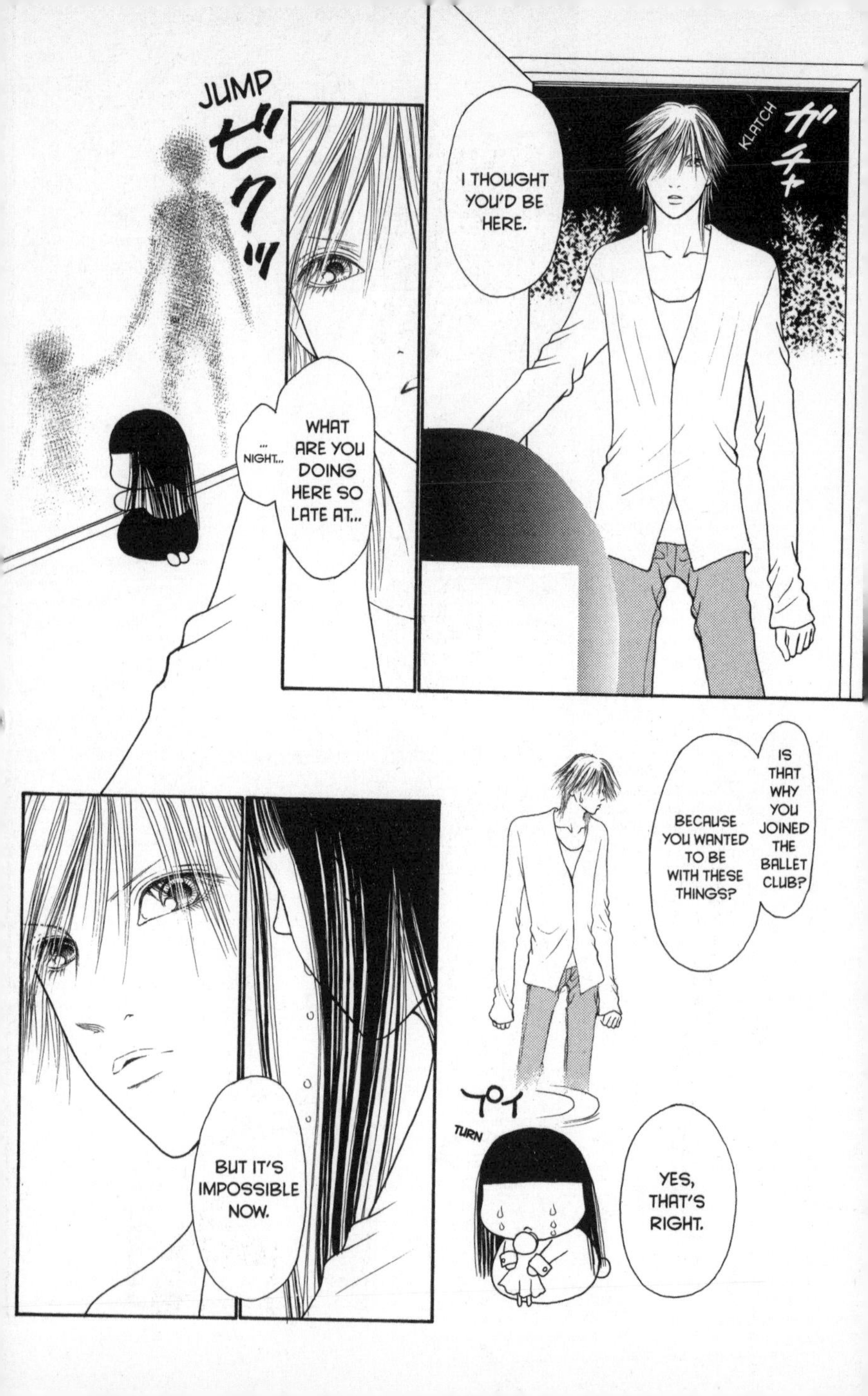
ガチャ
KLATCH
I THOUGHT YOU'D BE HERE.
WHAT ARE YOU DOING HERE SO LATE AT...
... NIGHT...
ビクッ
JUMP
IS THAT WHY YOU JOINED THE BALLET CLUB?
BECAUSE YOU WANTED TO BE WITH THESE THINGS?
プイ
TURN
YES, THAT'S RIGHT.
BUT IT'S IMPOSSIBLE NOW.

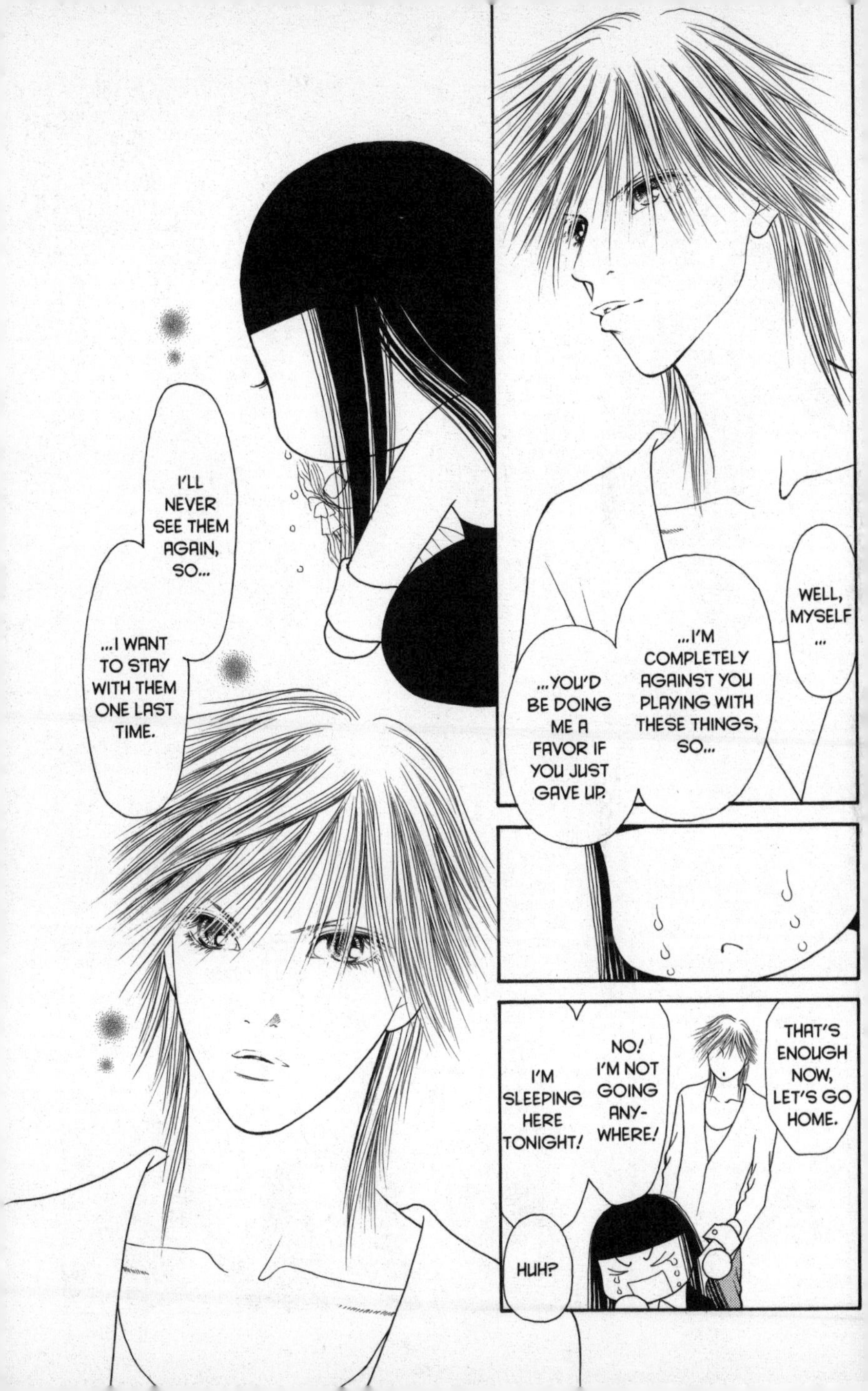
WELL, MYSELF ...
...I'M COMPLETELY AGAINST YOU PLAYING WITH THESE THINGS, SO...
...YOU'D BE DOING ME A FAVOR IF YOU JUST GAVE UP.
THAT'S ENOUGH NOW, LET'S GO HOME.
NO! I'M NOT GOING ANY-WHERE!
I'M SLEEPING HERE TONIGHT!
HUH?
I'LL NEVER SEE THEM AGAIN, SO...
...I WANT TO STAY WITH THEM ONE LAST TIME.

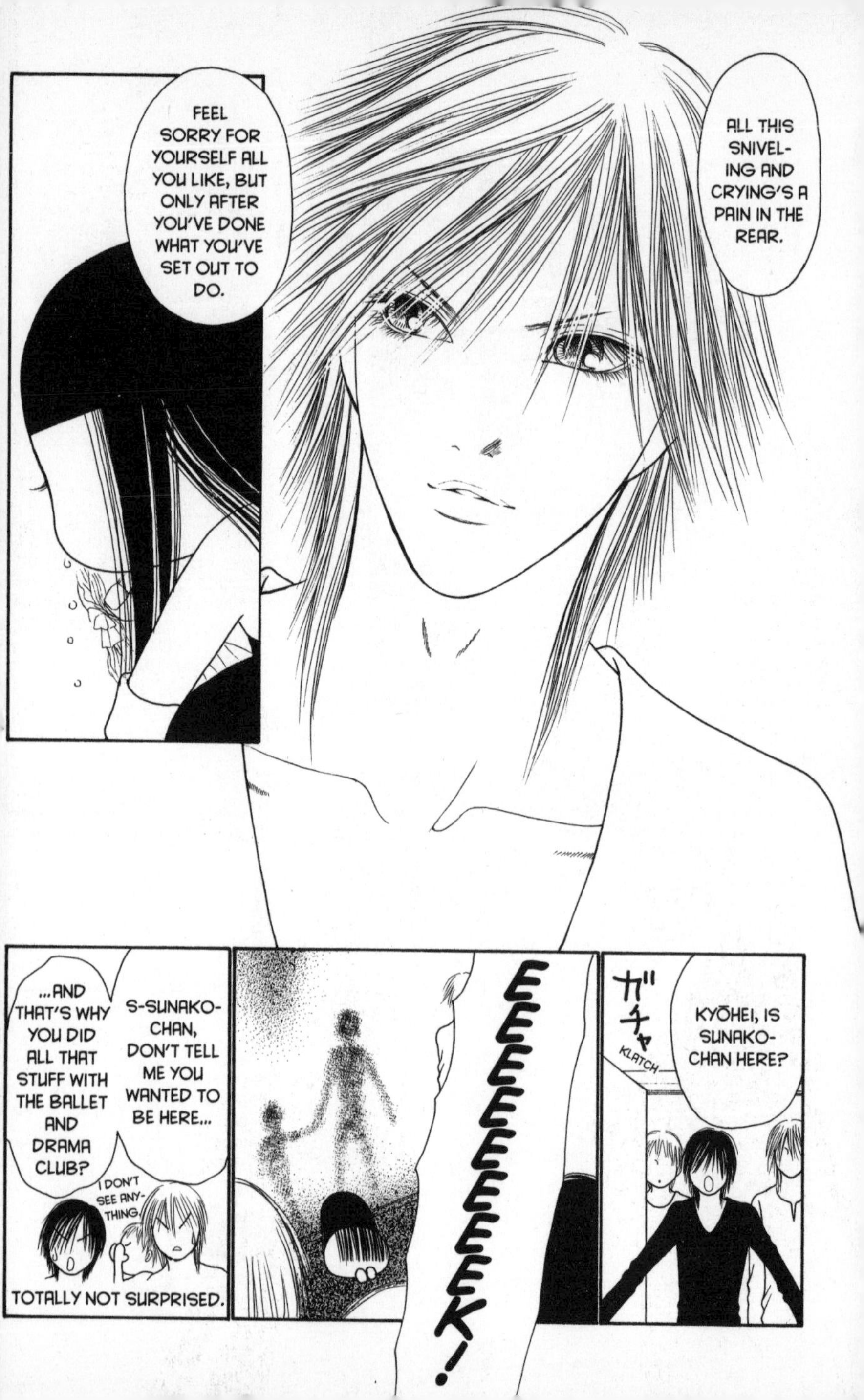
ALL THIS SNIVEL-ING AND CRYING'S A PAIN IN THE REAR.
FEEL SORRY FOR YOURSELF ALL YOU LIKE, BUT ONLY AFTER YOU'VE DONE WHAT YOU'VE SET OUT TO DO.
ガチャ
KLATCH
KYŌHEI, IS SUNAKO-CHAN HERE?
EEEEEEEEEEK!
S-SUNAKO-CHAN, DON'T TELL ME YOU WANTED TO BE HERE...
...AND THAT'S WHY YOU DID ALL THAT STUFF WITH THE BALLET AND DRAMA CLUB?
I DON'T SEE ANY-THING.
TOTALLY NOT SURPRISED.

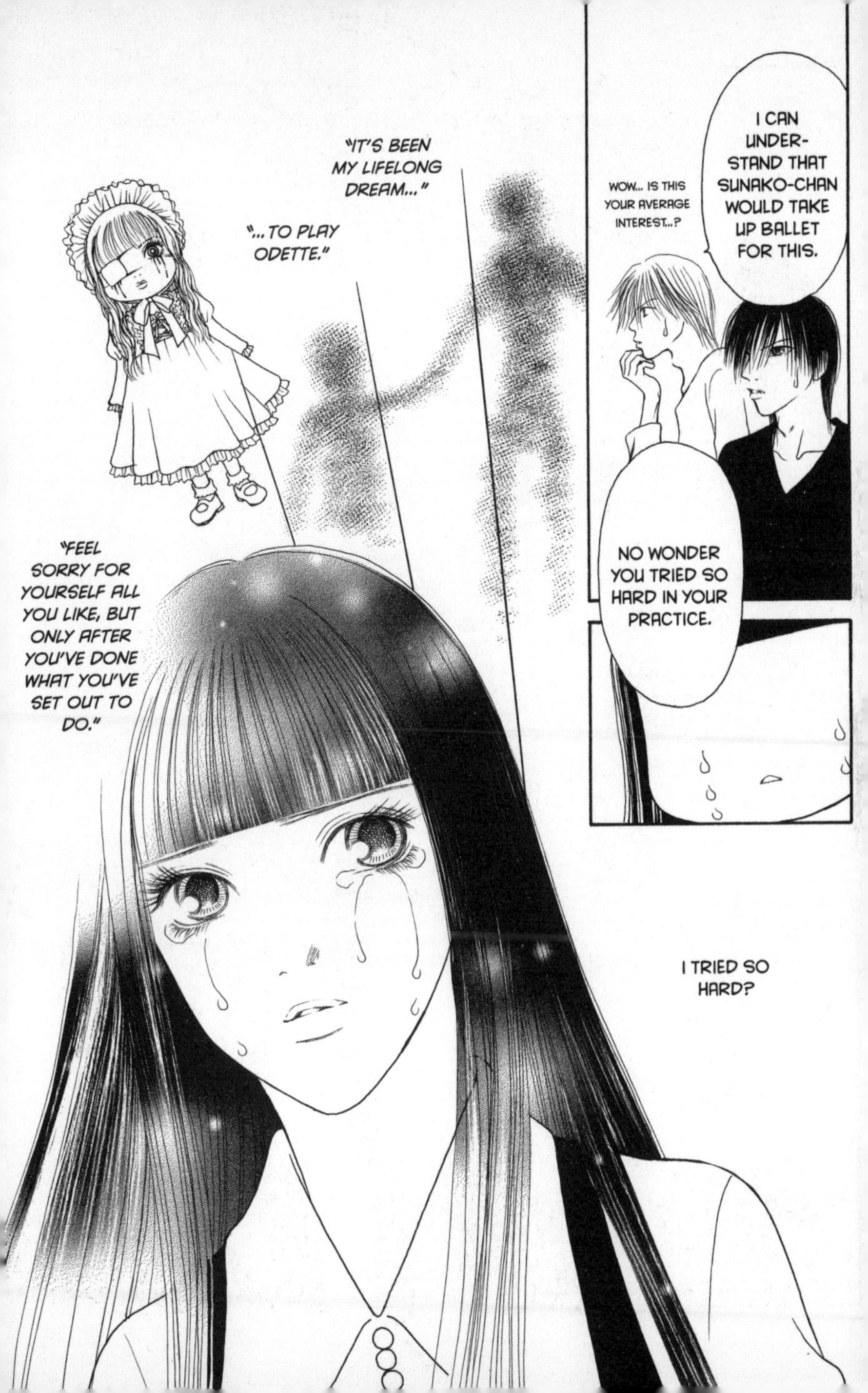
I CAN UNDER-STAND THAT SUNAKO-CHAN WOULD TAKE UP BALLET FOR THIS.
WOW... IS THIS YOUR AVERAGE INTEREST...?
NO WONDER YOU TRIED SO HARD IN YOUR PRACTICE.
"IT'S BEEN MY LIFELONG DREAM..."
"...TO PLAY ODETTE."
"FEEL SORRY FOR YOURSELF ALL YOU LIKE, BUT ONLY AFTER YOU'VE DONE WHAT YOU'VE SET OUT TO DO."
I TRIED SO HARD?

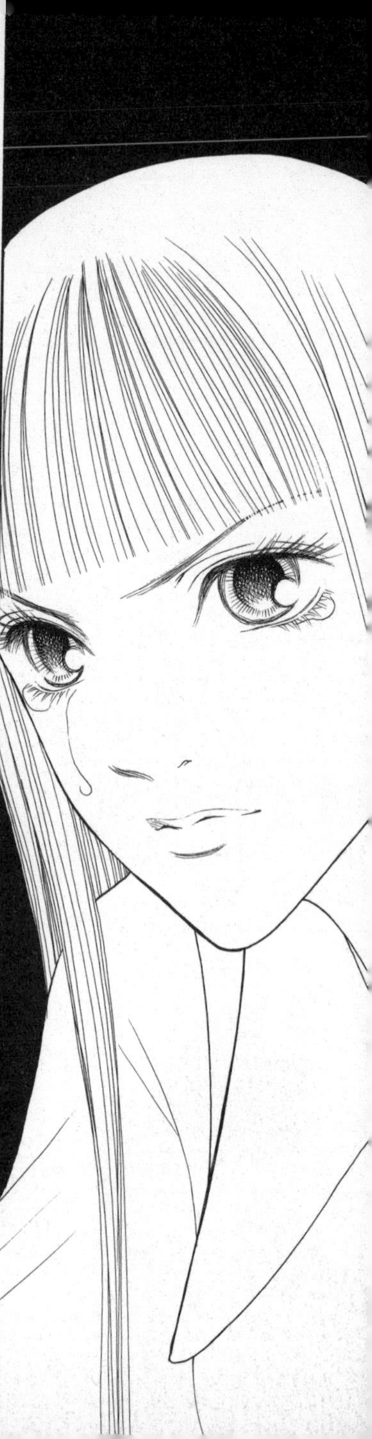

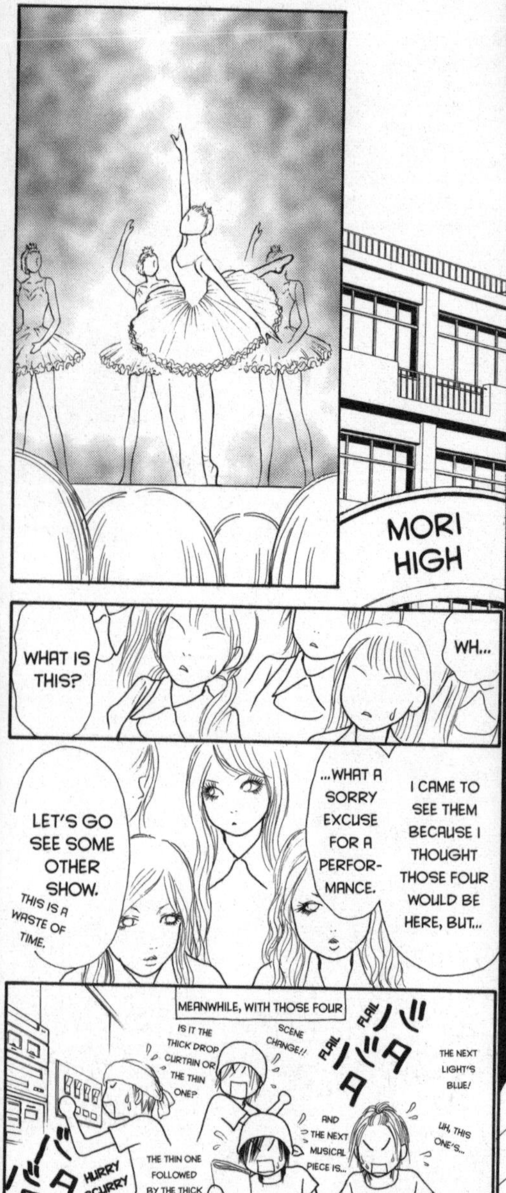

MORI HIGH
WH...
WHAT IS THIS?
I CAME TO SEE THEM BECAUSE I THOUGHT THOSE FOUR WOULD BE HERE, BUT...
...WHAT A SORRY EXCUSE FOR A PERFORMANCE.
LET'S GO SEE SOME OTHER SHOW.
THIS IS A WASTE OF TIME.
MEANWHILE, WITH THOSE FOUR
バタバタ
FLAIL FLAIL
THE NEXT LIGHT'S BLUE!
SCENE CHANGE!!
IS IT THE THICK DROP CURTAIN OR THE THIN ONE?
UH, THIS ONE'S...
AND THE NEXT MUSICAL PIECE IS...
THE THIN ONE FOLLOWED BY THE THICK ONE!
HURRY SCURRY
バタバタ

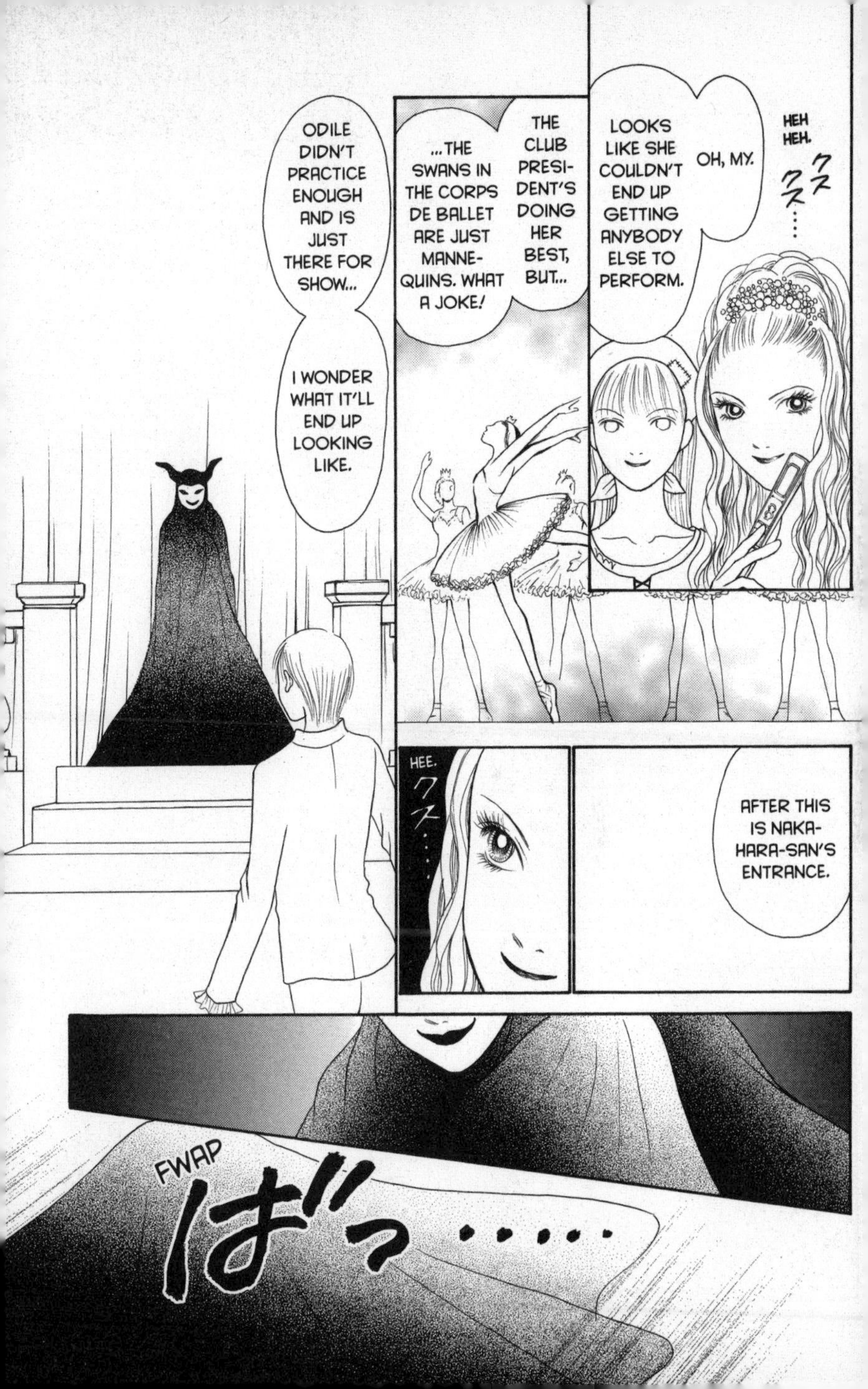
HEH HEH.
クスクス…
OH, MY.
LOOKS LIKE SHE COULDN'T END UP GETTING ANYBODY ELSE TO PERFORM.
THE CLUB PRESI-DENT'S DOING HER BEST, BUT...
...THE SWANS IN THE CORPS DE BALLET ARE JUST MANNE-QUINS. WHAT A JOKE!
AFTER THIS IS NAKA-HARA-SAN'S ENTRANCE.
HEE.
クス……
ODILE DIDN'T PRACTICE ENOUGH AND IS JUST THERE FOR SHOW...
I WONDER WHAT IT'LL END UP LOOKING LIKE.
FWAP
ばっ……

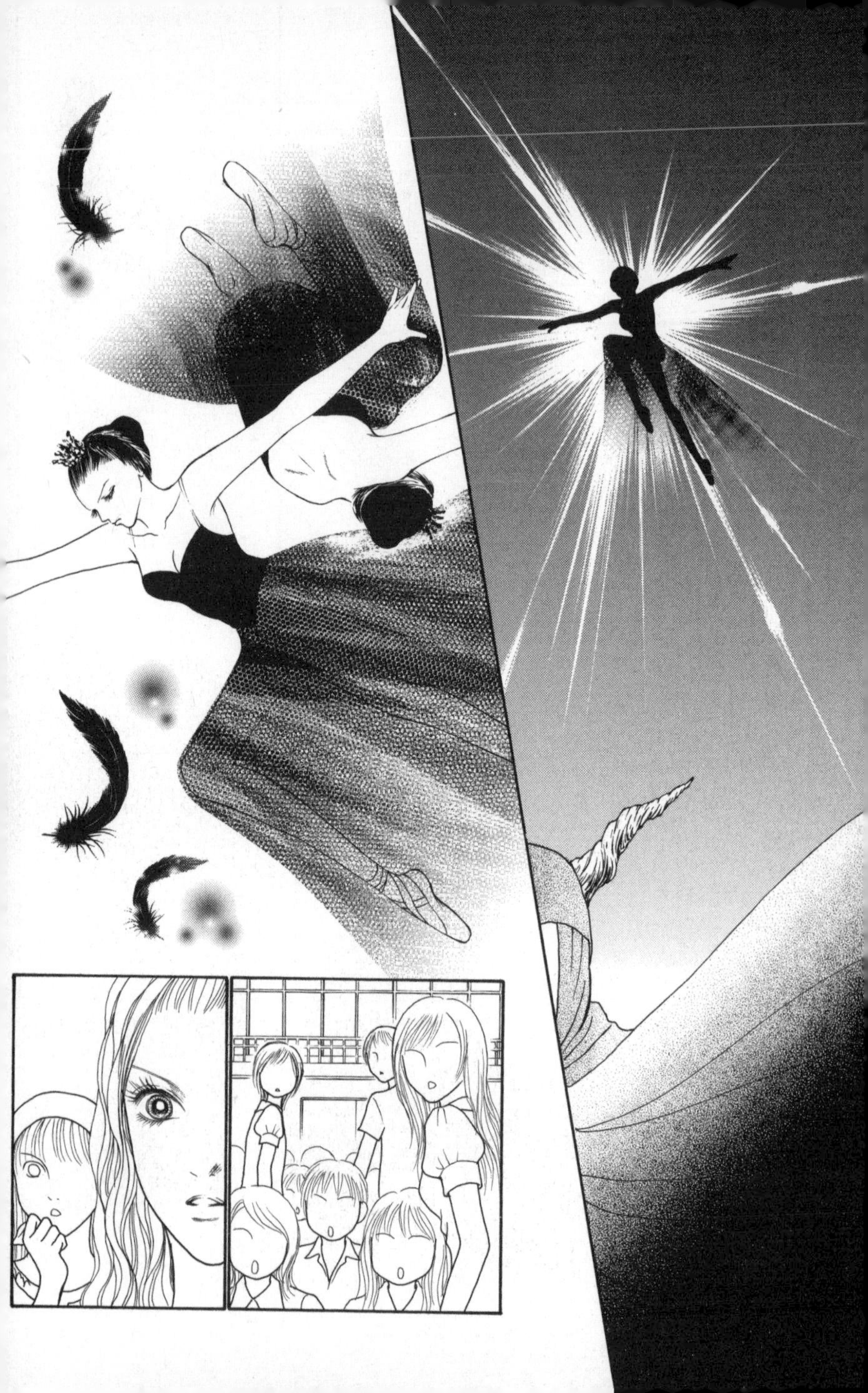

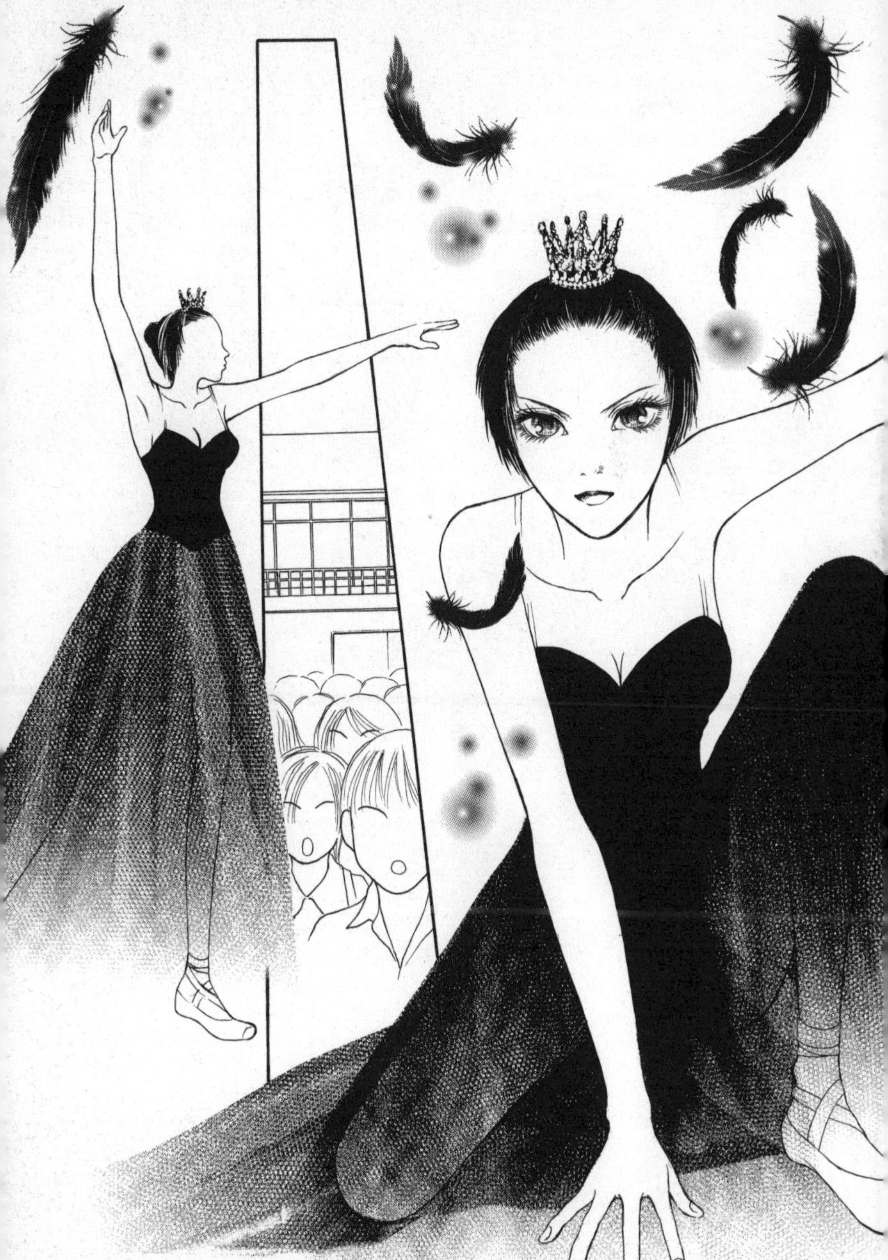

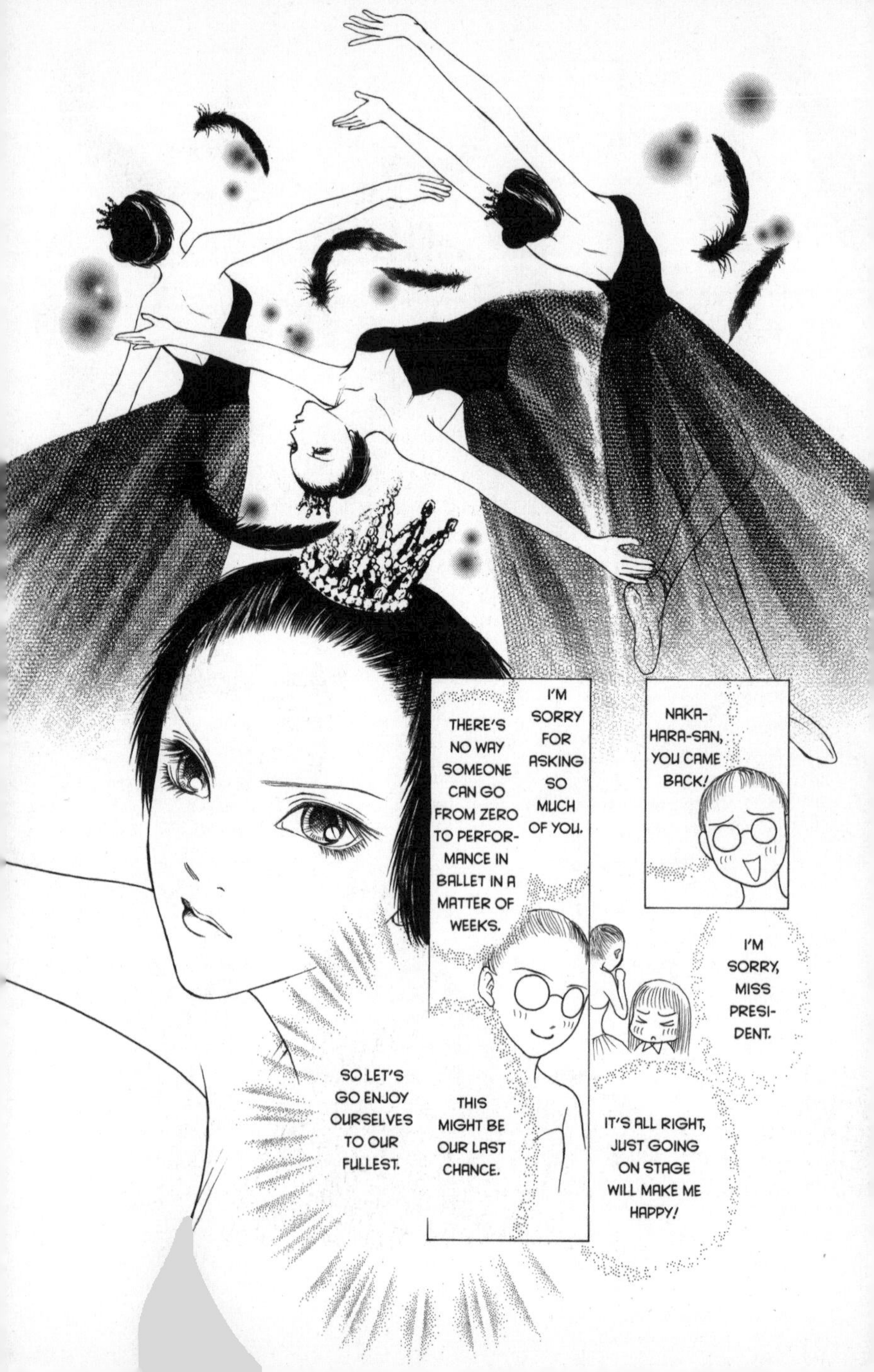
NAKA-HARA-SAN, YOU CAME BACK!
I'M SORRY, MISS PRESI-DENT.
IT'S ALL RIGHT, JUST GOING ON STAGE WILL MAKE ME HAPPY!
I'M SORRY FOR ASKING SO MUCH OF YOU.
THERE'S NO WAY SOMEONE CAN GO FROM ZERO TO PERFOR-MANCE IN BALLET IN A MATTER OF WEEKS.
THIS MIGHT BE OUR LAST CHANCE.
SO LET'S GO ENJOY OURSELVES TO OUR FULLEST.

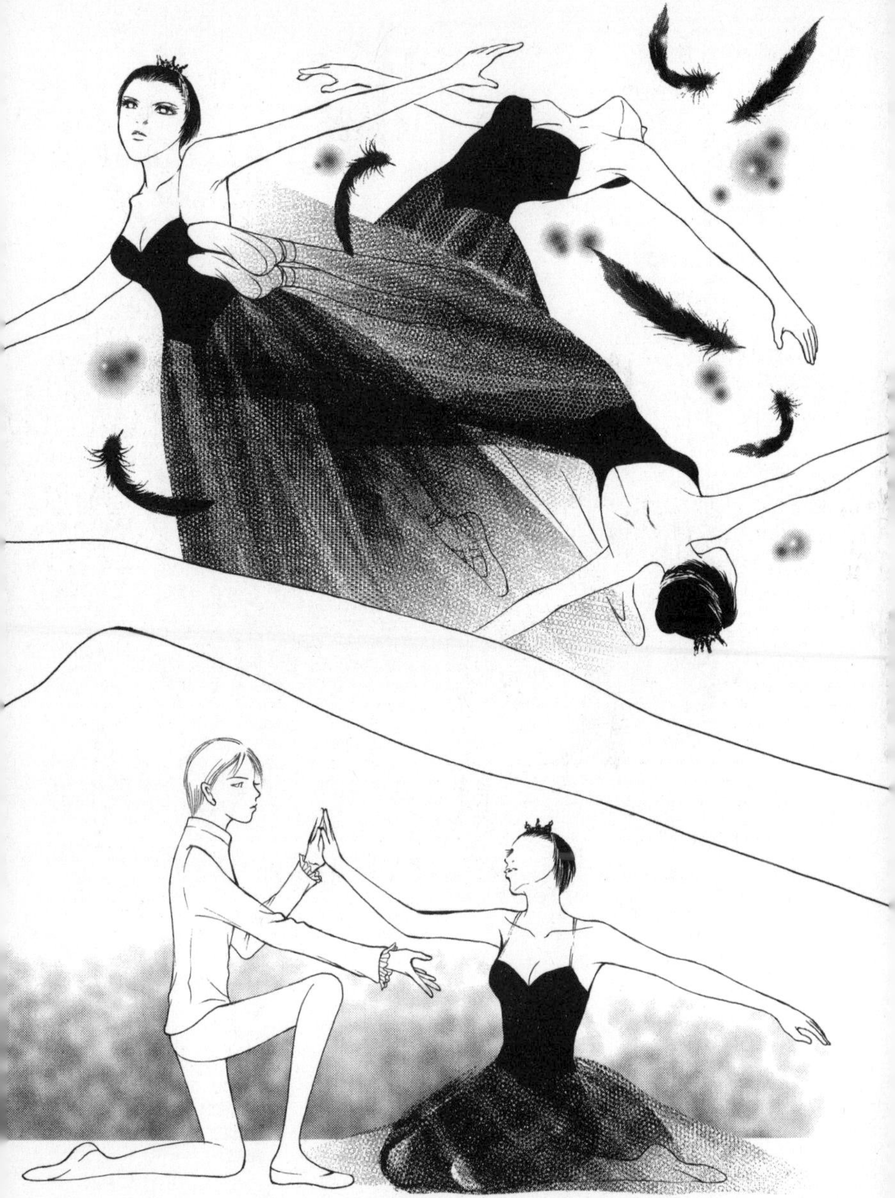

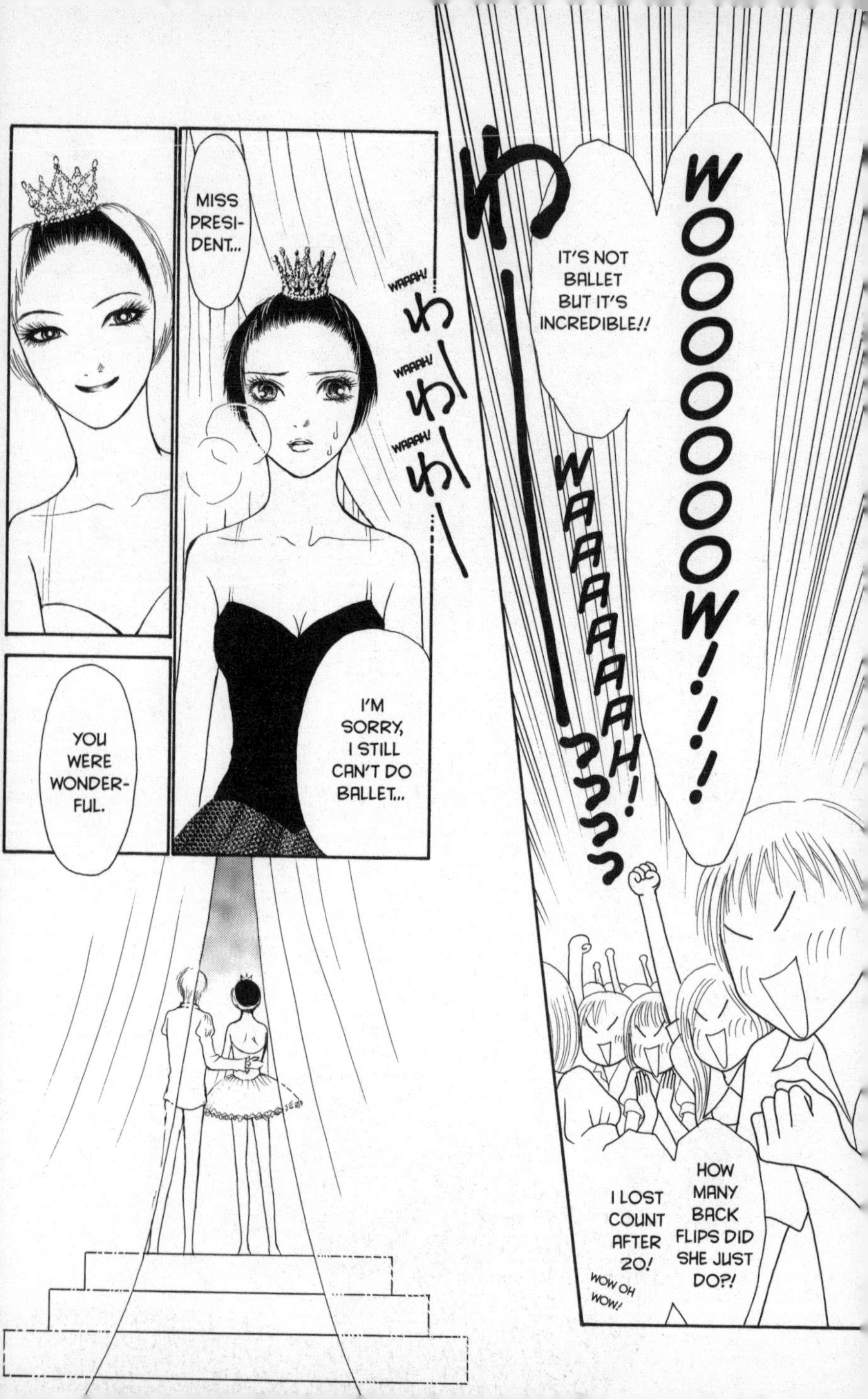
WOOOOOOOW!!!
WAAAAAAAH!
IT'S NOT BALLET BUT IT'S INCREDIBLE!!
HOW MANY BACK FLIPS DID SHE JUST DO?!
I LOST COUNT AFTER 20!
WOW OH WOW!
MISS PRESI-DENT...
WAAAH!
WAAAH!
WAAAH!
I'M SORRY, I STILL CAN'T DO BALLET...
YOU WERE WONDER-FUL.

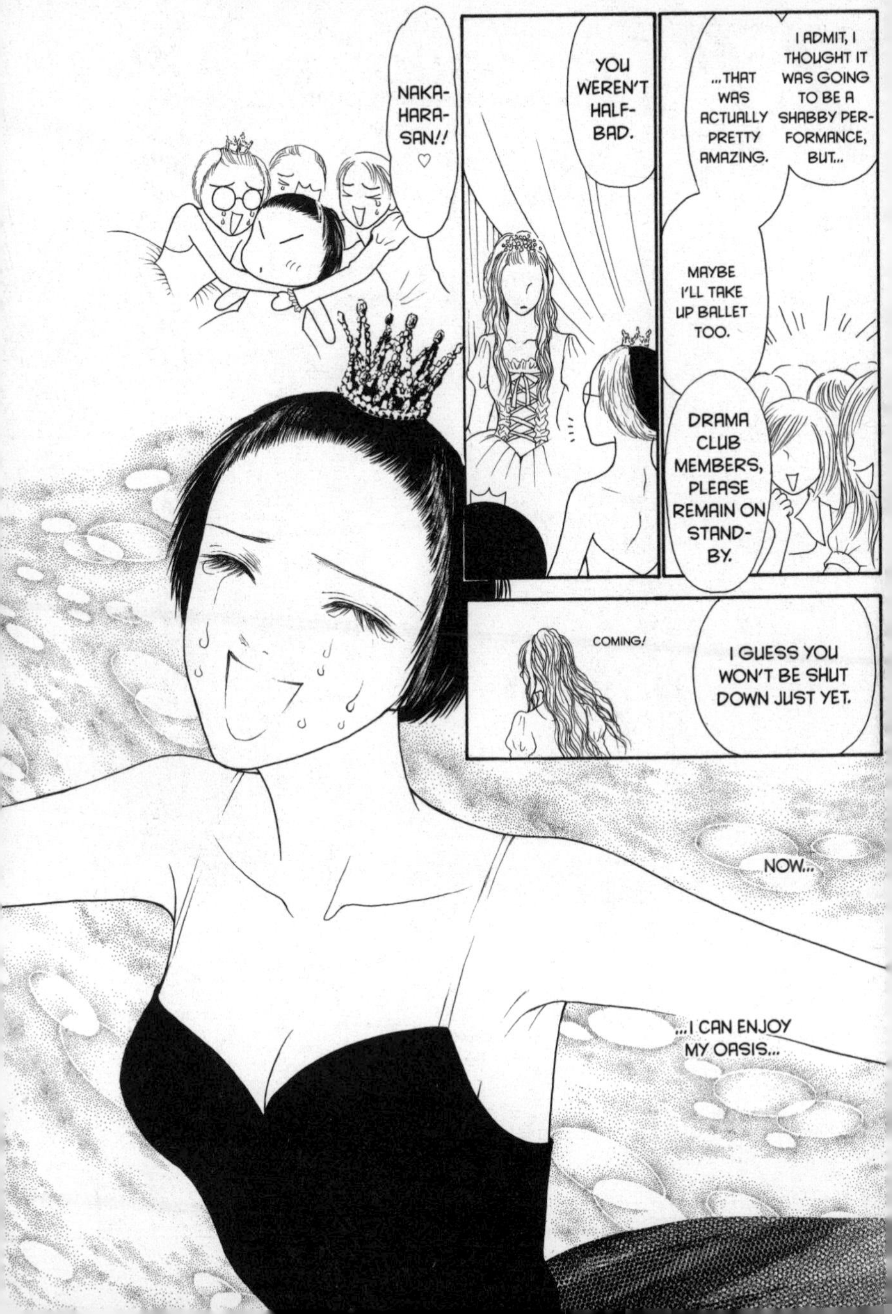
I ADMIT, I THOUGHT IT WAS GOING TO BE A SHABBY PER-FORMANCE, BUT...
...THAT WAS ACTUALLY PRETTY AMAZING.
MAYBE I'LL TAKE UP BALLET TOO.
DRAMA CLUB MEMBERS, PLEASE REMAIN ON STAND-BY.
YOU WEREN'T HALF-BAD.
NAKA-HARA-SAN!! ♡
I GUESS YOU WON'T BE SHUT DOWN JUST YET.
COMING!
NOW...
...I CAN ENJOY MY OASIS...

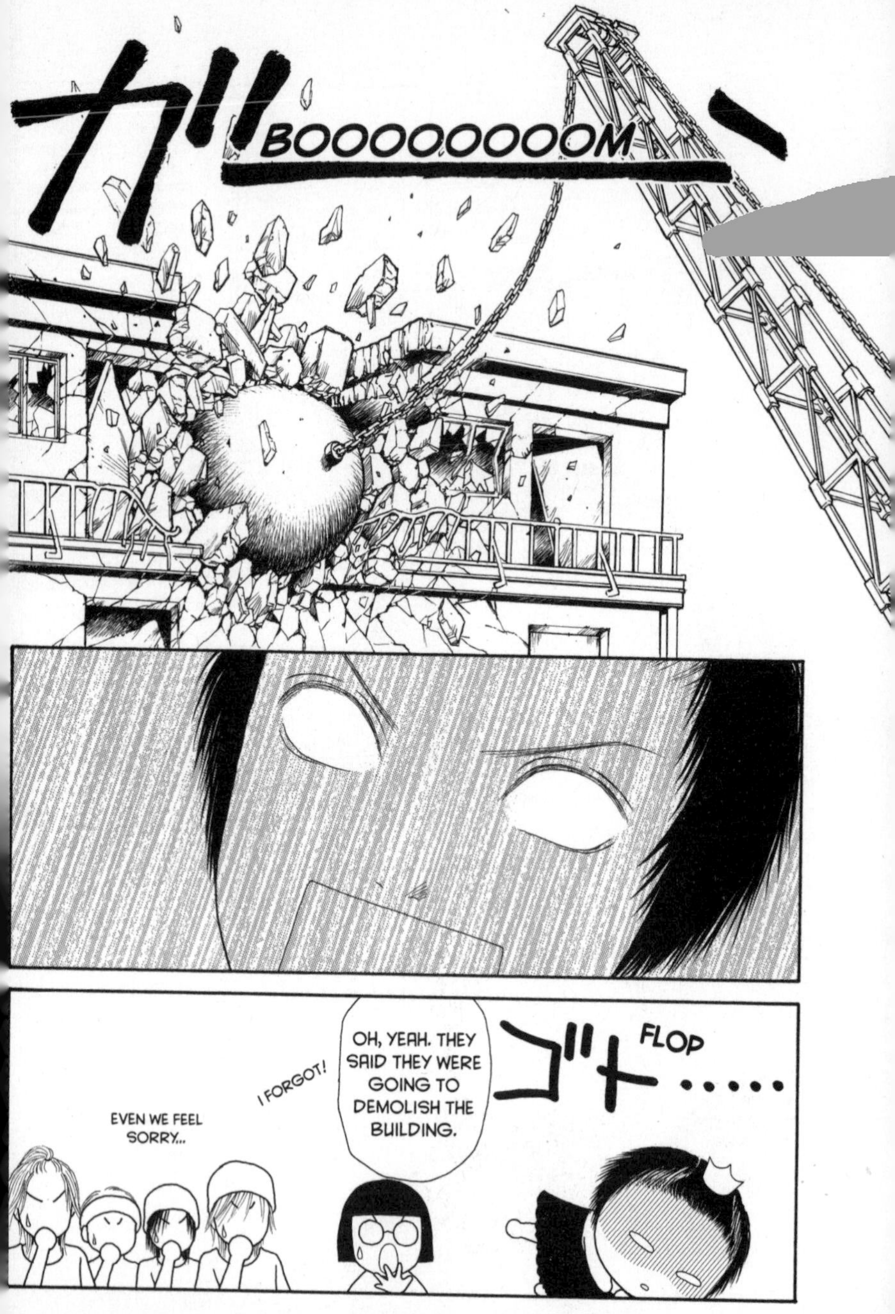
ガー
BOOOOOOOOM
ゴト…..
FLOP
OH, YEAH. THEY SAID THEY WERE GOING TO DEMOLISH THE BUILDING.
I FORGOT!
EVEN WE FEEL SORRY...

THIS LITTLE GAL'S THE ONLY ONE WHO MADE IT OUT SAFELY.

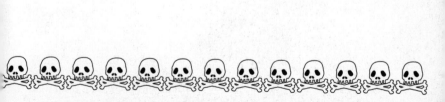

Chapter 131: Sky and Sun! Earth Below!

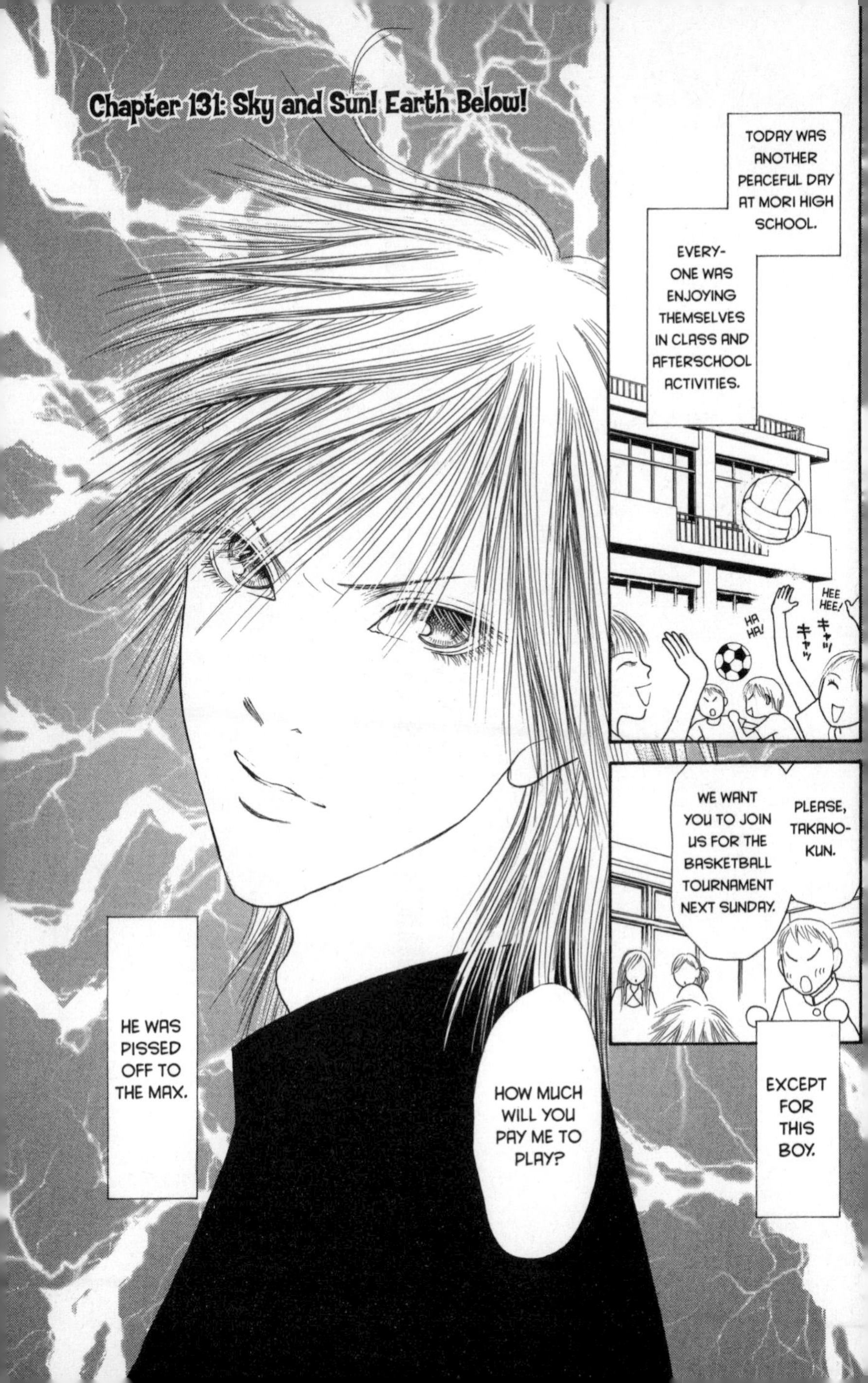
TODAY WAS ANOTHER PEACEFUL DAY AT MORI HIGH SCHOOL.
EVERY-ONE WAS ENJOYING THEMSELVES IN CLASS AND AFTERSCHOOL ACTIVITIES.
HEE HEE!
キャッ キャッ
HA HA!
PLEASE, TAKANO-KUN.
WE WANT YOU TO JOIN US FOR THE BASKETBALL TOURNAMENT NEXT SUNDAY.
EXCEPT FOR THIS BOY.
HOW MUCH WILL YOU PAY ME TO PLAY?
HE WAS PISSED OFF TO THE MAX.

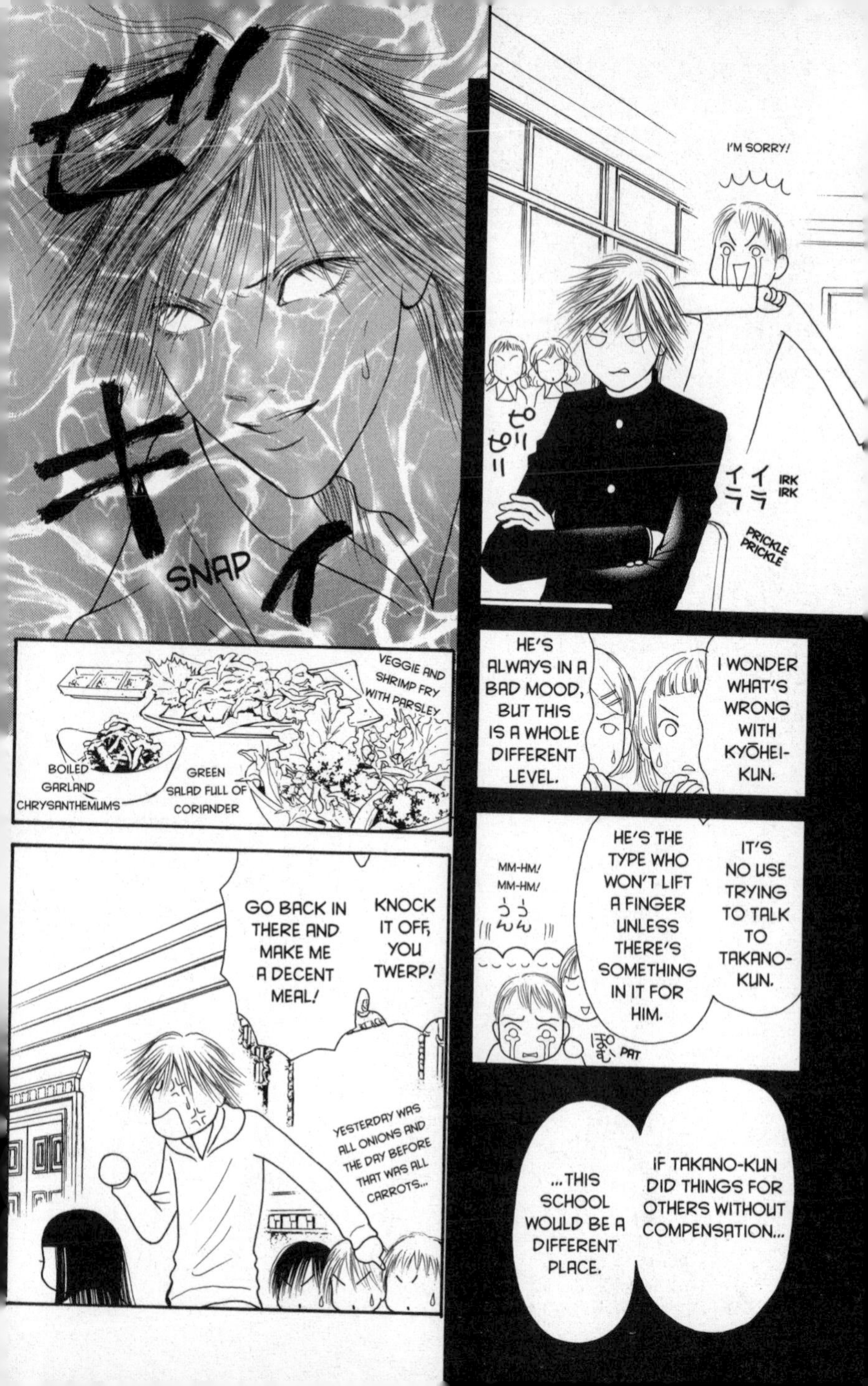
I'M SORRY!
ぴりぴり
イライラ
IRK IRK
PRICKLE PRICKLE
HE'S ALWAYS IN A BAD MOOD, BUT THIS IS A WHOLE DIFFERENT LEVEL.
I WONDER WHAT'S WRONG WITH KYŌHEI-KUN.
IT'S NO USE TRYING TO TALK TO TAKANO-KUN.
HE'S THE TYPE WHO WON'T LIFT A FINGER UNLESS THERE'S SOMETHING IN IT FOR HIM.
MM-HM! MM-HM!
PAT
IF TAKANO-KUN DID THINGS FOR OTHERS WITHOUT COMPENSATION...
...THIS SCHOOL WOULD BE A DIFFERENT PLACE.
SNAP
VEGGIE AND SHRIMP FRY WITH PARSLEY
BOILED GARLAND CHRYSANTHEMUMS
GREEN SALAD FULL OF CORIANDER
KNOCK IT OFF, YOU TWERP!
GO BACK IN THERE AND MAKE ME A DECENT MEAL!
YESTERDAY WAS ALL ONIONS AND THE DAY BEFORE THAT WAS ALL CARROTS...

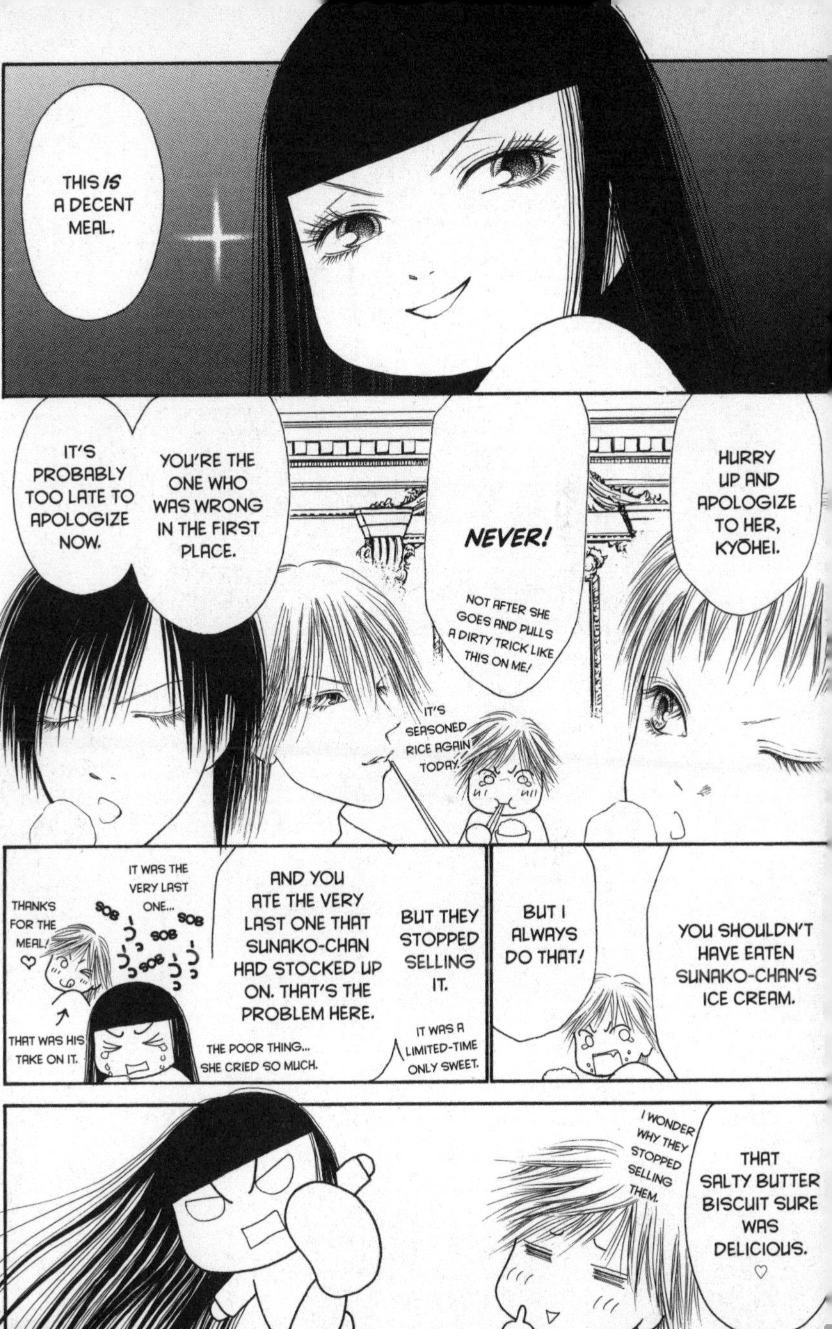
THIS *IS* A DECENT MEAL.
HURRY UP AND APOLOGIZE TO HER, KYŌHEI.
NEVER!
NOT AFTER SHE GOES AND PULLS A DIRTY TRICK LIKE THIS ON ME!
YOU'RE THE ONE WHO WAS WRONG IN THE FIRST PLACE.
IT'S PROBABLY TOO LATE TO APOLOGIZE NOW.
IT'S SEASONED RICE AGAIN TODAY.
YOU SHOULDN'T HAVE EATEN SUNAKO-CHAN'S ICE CREAM.
BUT I ALWAYS DO THAT!
BUT THEY STOPPED SELLING IT.
AND YOU ATE THE VERY LAST ONE THAT SUNAKO-CHAN HAD STOCKED UP ON. THAT'S THE PROBLEM HERE.
IT WAS A LIMITED-TIME ONLY SWEET.
IT WAS THE VERY LAST ONE...
SOB SOB SOB SOB
THANKS FOR THE MEAL! ♡
THAT WAS HIS TAKE ON IT.
THE POOR THING... SHE CRIED SO MUCH.
THAT SALTY BUTTER BISCUIT SURE WAS DELICIOUS. ♡
I WONDER WHY THEY STOPPED SELLING THEM.

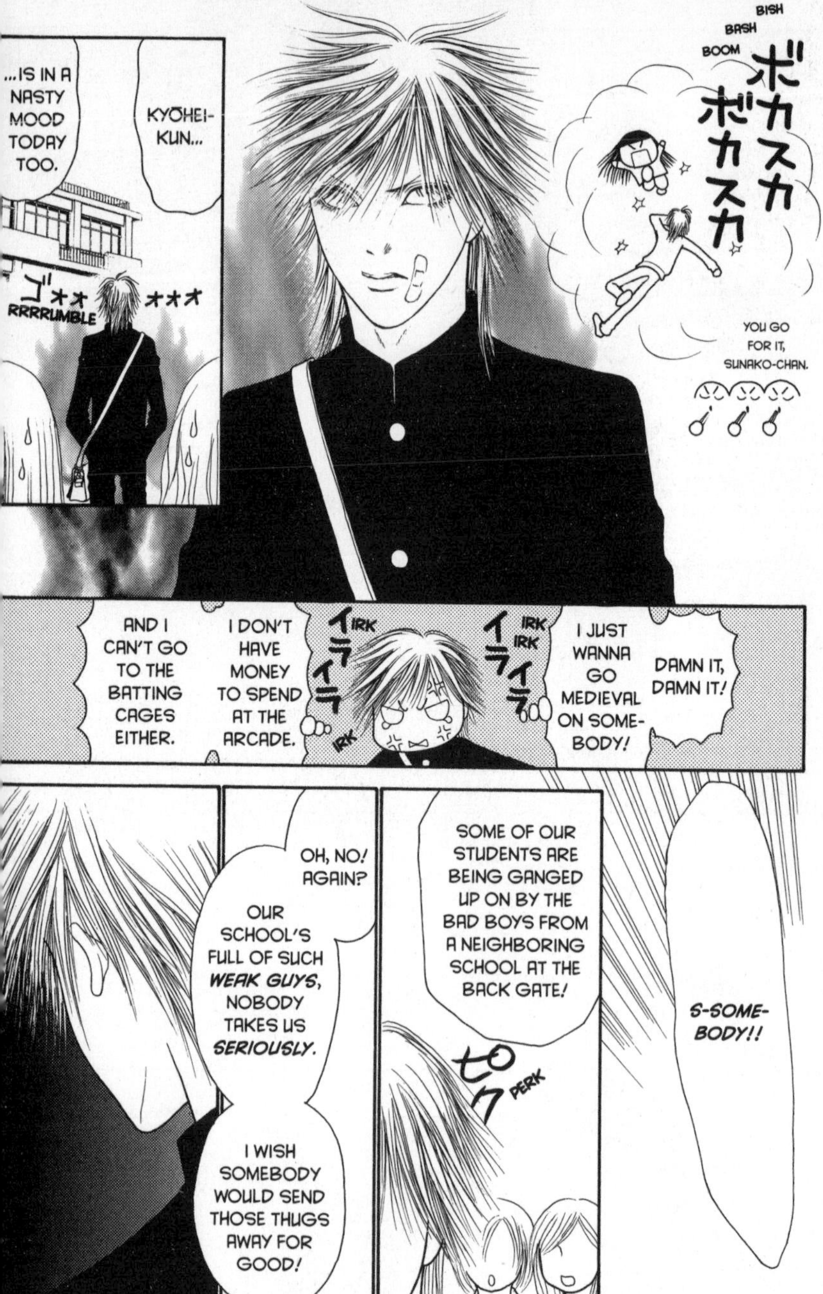

BISH
BASH
BOOM
ボカスカボカスカ
YOU GO FOR IT, SUNAKO-CHAN.
KYŌHEI-KUN...
...IS IN A NASTY MOOD TODAY TOO.
ゴオオオ
RRRRUMBLE
DAMN IT, DAMN IT!
I JUST WANNA GO MEDIEVAL ON SOME-BODY!
イライラ
IRK
IRK
イライラ
IRK
IRK
I DON'T HAVE MONEY TO SPEND AT THE ARCADE.
AND I CAN'T GO TO THE BATTING CAGES EITHER.
S-SOME-BODY!!
SOME OF OUR STUDENTS ARE BEING GANGED UP ON BY THE BAD BOYS FROM A NEIGHBORING SCHOOL AT THE BACK GATE!
ピク
PERK
OH, NO! AGAIN?
OUR SCHOOL'S FULL OF SUCH ***WEAK GUYS***, NOBODY TAKES US ***SERIOUSLY***.
I WISH SOMEBODY WOULD SEND THOSE THUGS AWAY FOR GOOD!

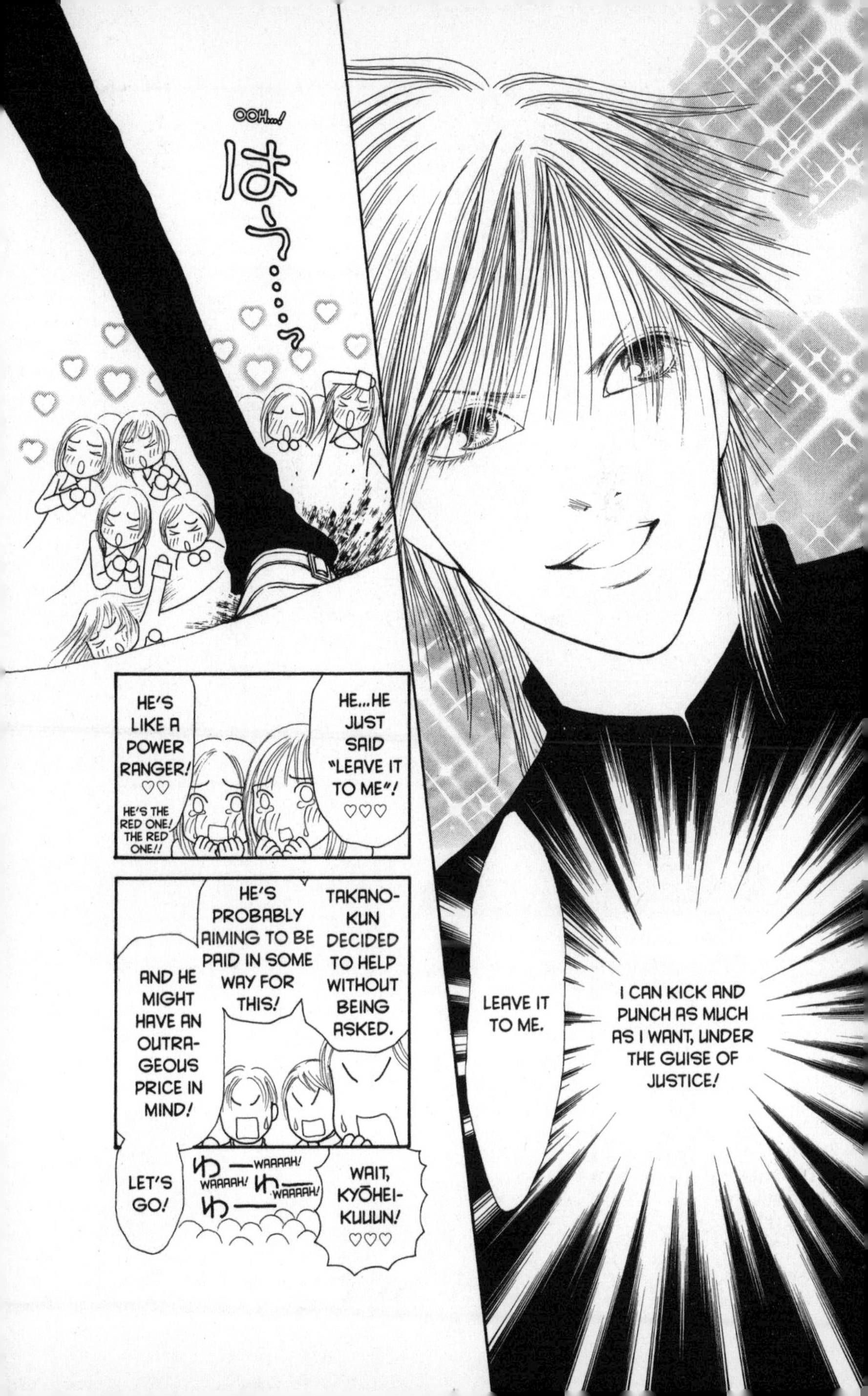
I CAN KICK AND PUNCH AS MUCH AS I WANT, UNDER THE GUISE OF JUSTICE!
LEAVE IT TO ME.
はう〜。。。。
OOH...!
HE...HE JUST SAID "LEAVE IT TO ME"! ♡♡♡
HE'S LIKE A POWER RANGER! ♡♡
HE'S THE RED ONE! THE RED ONE!!
TAKANO-KUN DECIDED TO HELP WITHOUT BEING ASKED.
HE'S PROBABLY AIMING TO BE PAID IN SOME WAY FOR THIS!
AND HE MIGHT HAVE AN OUTRAGEOUS PRICE IN MIND!
WAIT, KYŌHEI-KUUUN! ♡♡♡
わー WAAAAH!
わー WAAAAH!
わー WAAAAH!
LET'S GO!

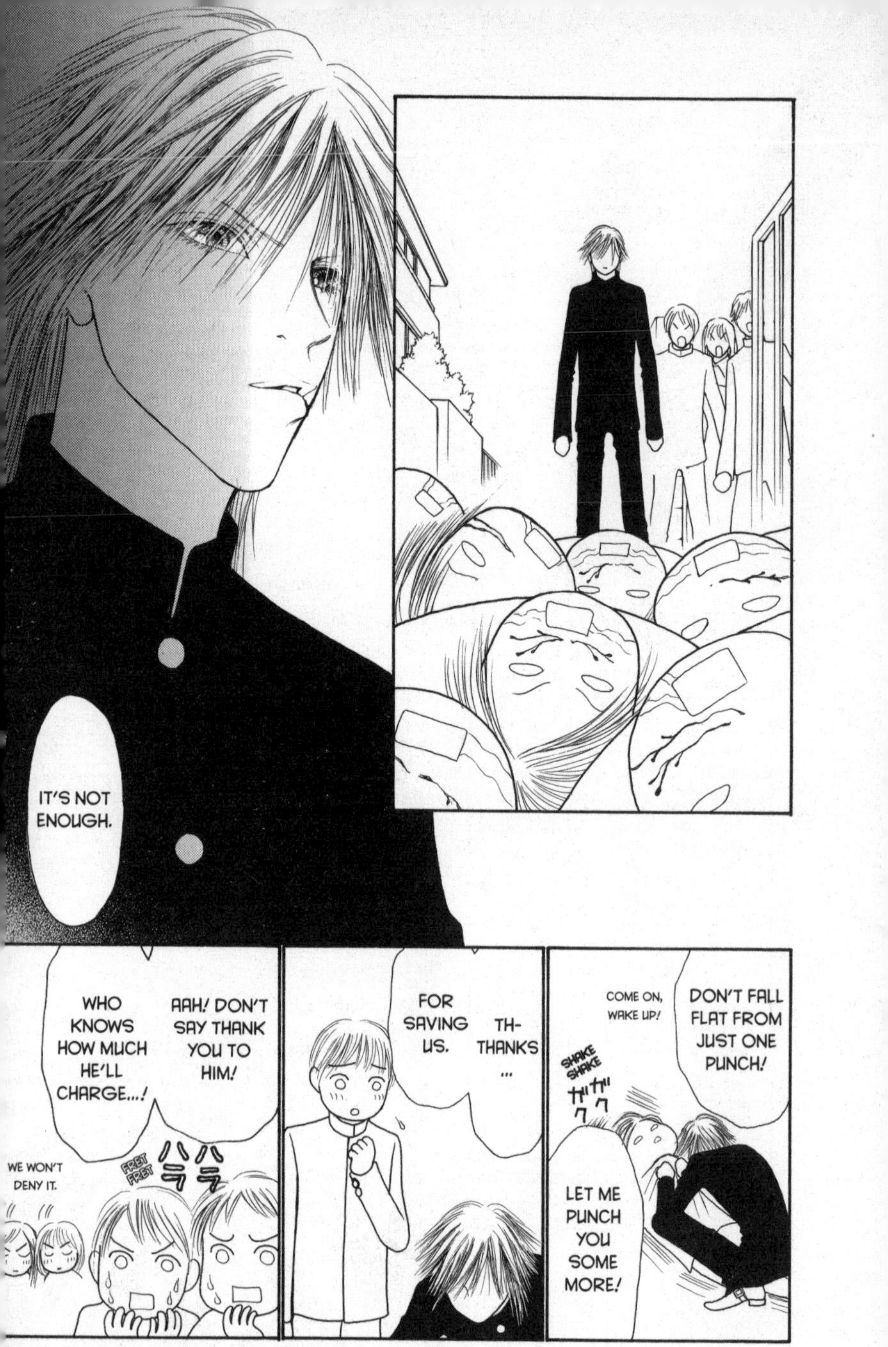
IT'S NOT ENOUGH.
DON'T FALL FLAT FROM JUST ONE PUNCH!
COME ON, WAKE UP!
SHAKE SHAKE
LET ME PUNCH YOU SOME MORE!
TH-THANKS...
FOR SAVING US.
AAH! DON'T SAY THANK YOU TO HIM!
WHO KNOWS HOW MUCH HE'LL CHARGE...!
FRET FRET
WE WON'T DENY IT.

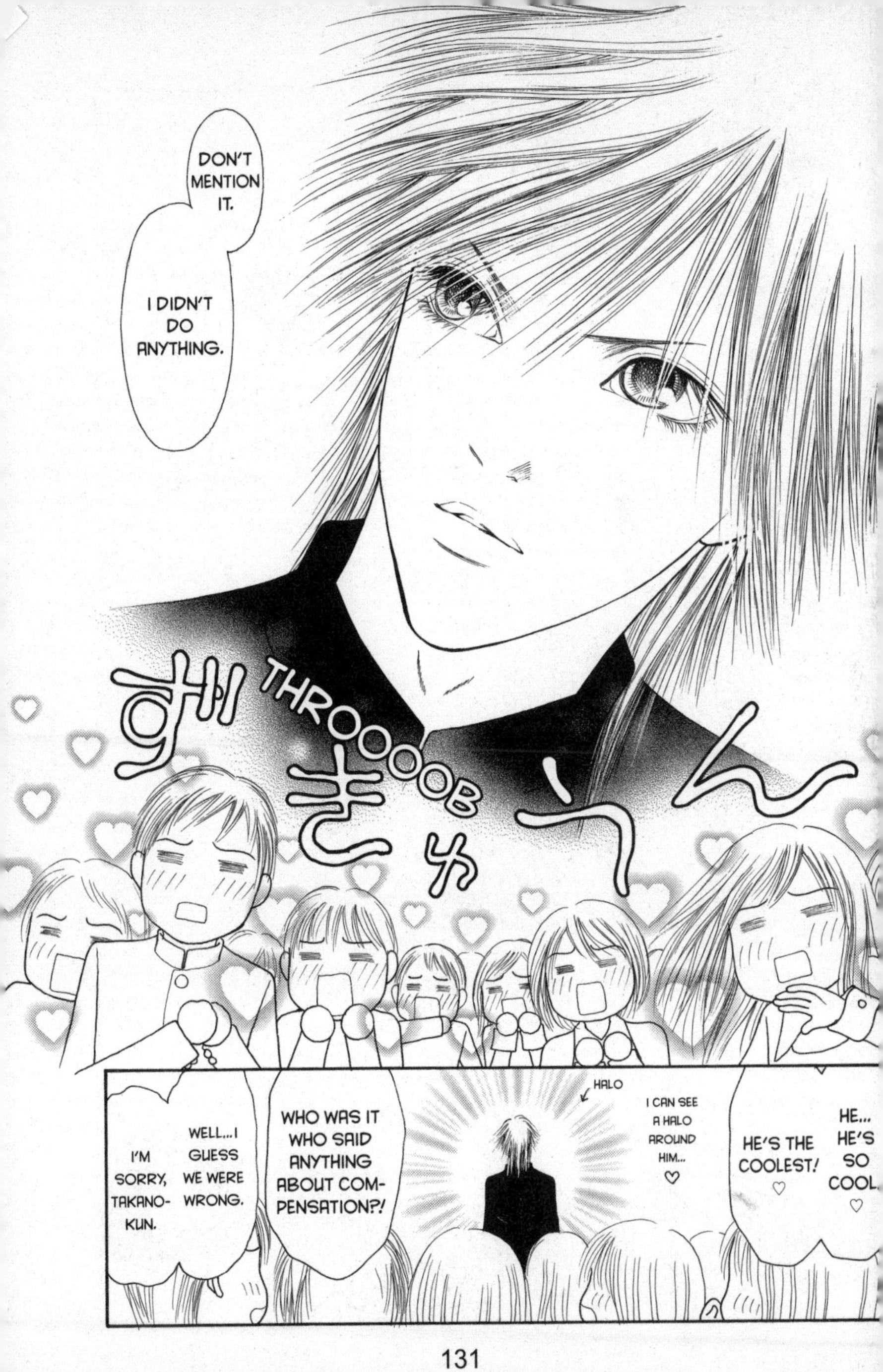
DON'T MENTION IT.
I DIDN'T DO ANYTHING.
THROOOOB
HE... HE'S SO COOL. ♡
HE'S THE COOLEST! ♡
I CAN SEE A HALO AROUND HIM... ♡
HALO
WHO WAS IT WHO SAID ANYTHING ABOUT COM-PENSATION?!
WELL... I GUESS WE WERE WRONG.
I'M SORRY, TAKANO-KUN.

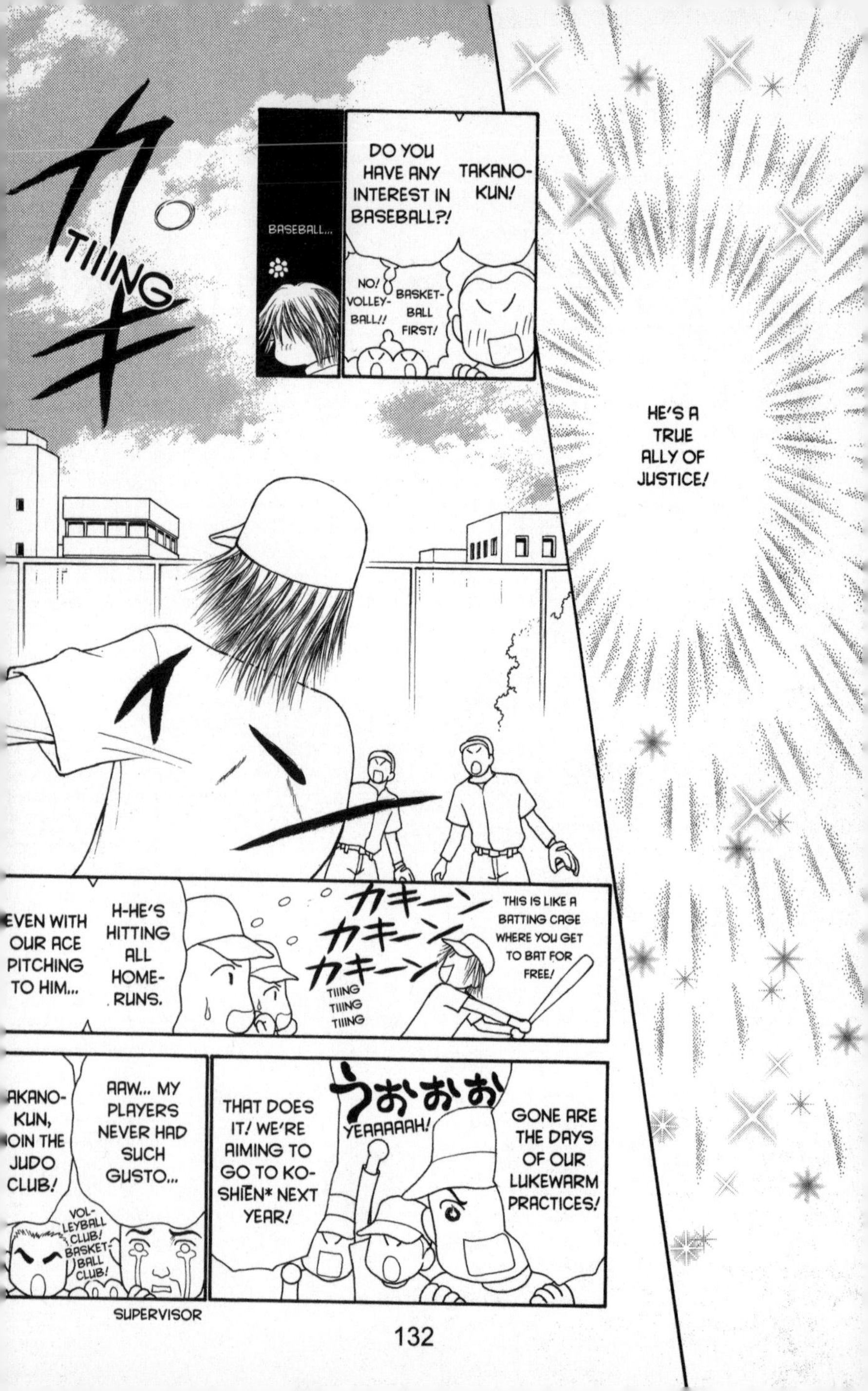

HE'S A TRUE ALLY OF JUSTICE!
TAKANO-KUN!
DO YOU HAVE ANY INTEREST IN BASEBALL?!
BASKET-BALL FIRST!
NO! VOLLEY-BALL!!
BASEBALL...
カキーン
TIIING
THIS IS LIKE A BATTING CAGE WHERE YOU GET TO BAT FOR FREE!
カキーン カキーン カキーン
TIIING TIIING TIIING
H-HE'S HITTING ALL HOME-RUNS.
EVEN WITH OUR ACE PITCHING TO HIM...
GONE ARE THE DAYS OF OUR LUKEWARM PRACTICES!
うおおお
YEAAAAAH!
THAT DOES IT! WE'RE AIMING TO GO TO KO-SHIEN* NEXT YEAR!
AAW... MY PLAYERS NEVER HAD SUCH GUSTO...
AKANO-KUN, OIN THE JUDO CLUB!
VOL-LEYBALL CLUB! BASKET-BALL CLUB!
SUPERVISOR

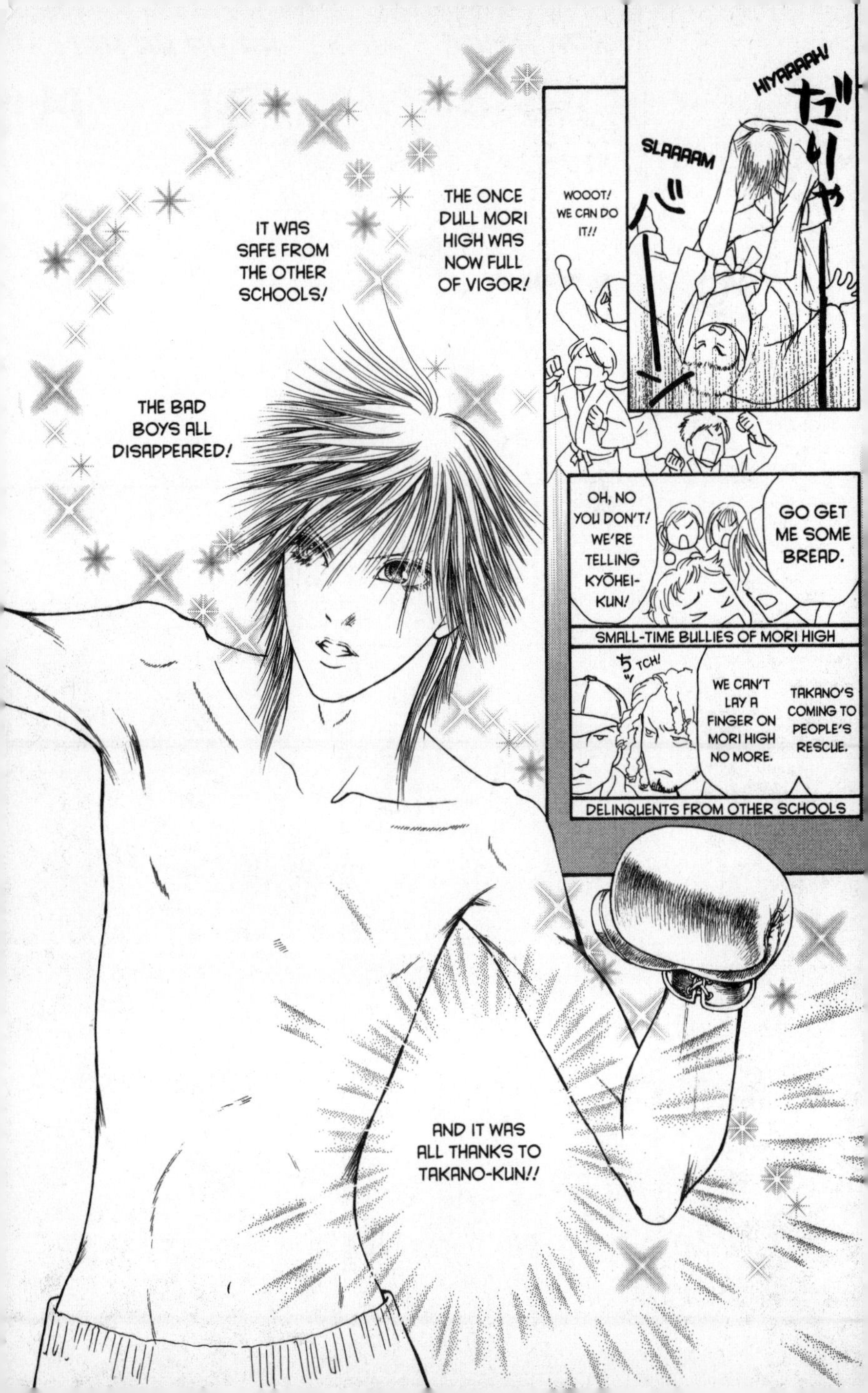
HIYAAAAH!
SLAAAAM
WOOOT! WE CAN DO IT!!
GO GET ME SOME BREAD.
OH, NO YOU DON'T! WE'RE TELLING KYŌHEI-KUN!
SMALL-TIME BULLIES OF MORI HIGH
TAKANO'S COMING TO PEOPLE'S RESCUE.
WE CAN'T LAY A FINGER ON MORI HIGH NO MORE.
TCH!
DELINQUENTS FROM OTHER SCHOOLS
THE ONCE DULL MORI HIGH WAS NOW FULL OF VIGOR!
IT WAS SAFE FROM THE OTHER SCHOOLS!
THE BAD BOYS ALL DISAPPEARED!
AND IT WAS ALL THANKS TO TAKANO-KUN!!

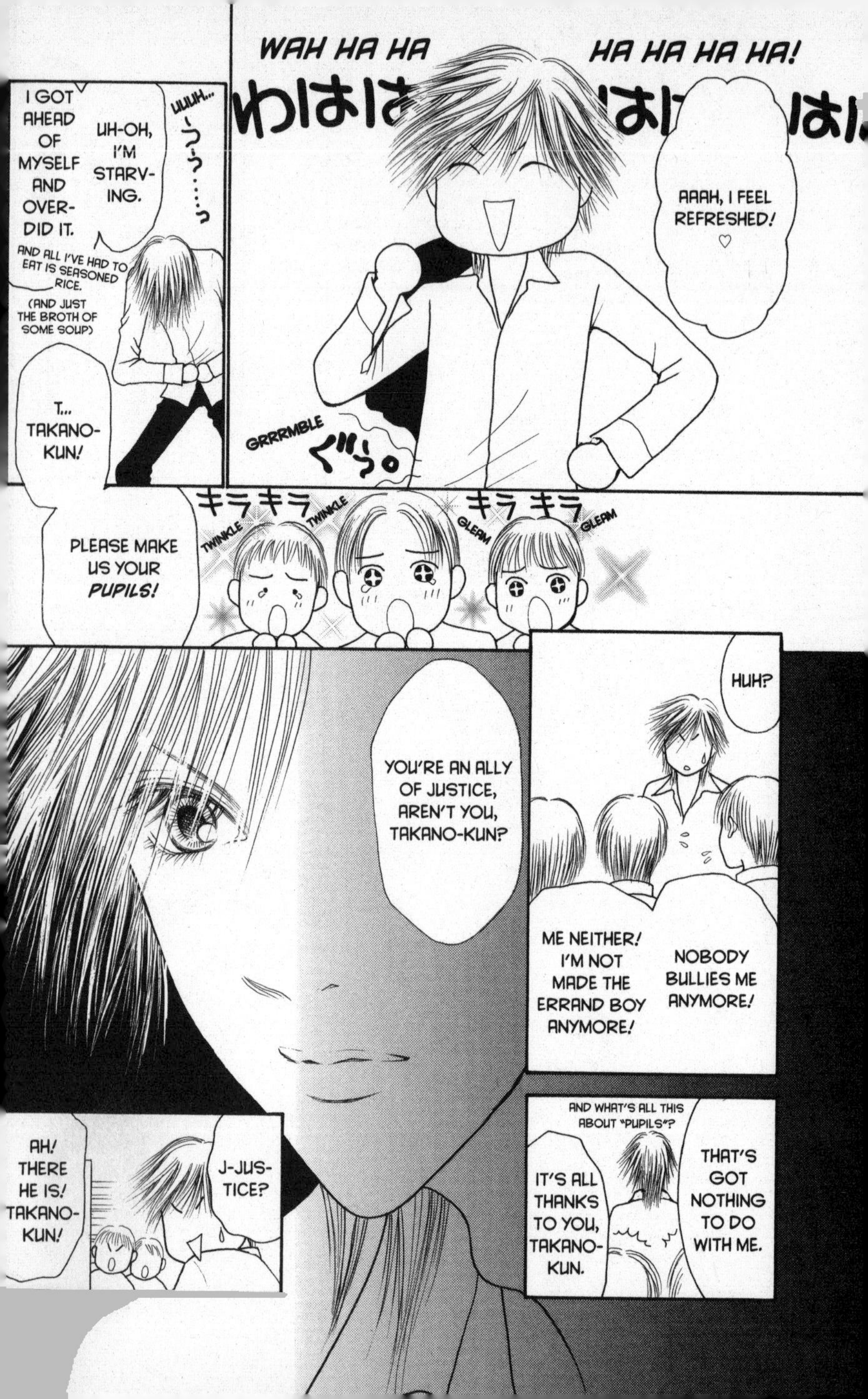
WAH HA HA
HA HA HA HA!
わはは
はは
はは
AAAH, I FEEL REFRESHED! ♡
GRRRMBLE
ぐぅ。
UH-OH, I'M STARV-ING.
I GOT AHEAD OF MYSELF AND OVER-DID IT.
UUUH...
うう…
AND ALL I'VE HAD TO EAT IS SEASONED RICE.
(AND JUST THE BROTH OF SOME SOUP)
T... TAKANO-KUN!
キラ キラ
TWINKLE
TWINKLE
キラ キラ
GLEAM
GLEAM
PLEASE MAKE US YOUR PUPILS!
HUH?
NOBODY BULLIES ME ANYMORE!
ME NEITHER! I'M NOT MADE THE ERRAND BOY ANYMORE!
AND WHAT'S ALL THIS ABOUT "PUPILS"?
THAT'S GOT NOTHING TO DO WITH ME.
IT'S ALL THANKS TO YOU, TAKANO-KUN.
YOU'RE AN ALLY OF JUSTICE, AREN'T YOU, TAKANO-KUN?
J-JUS-TICE?
AH! THERE HE IS! TAKANO-KUN!

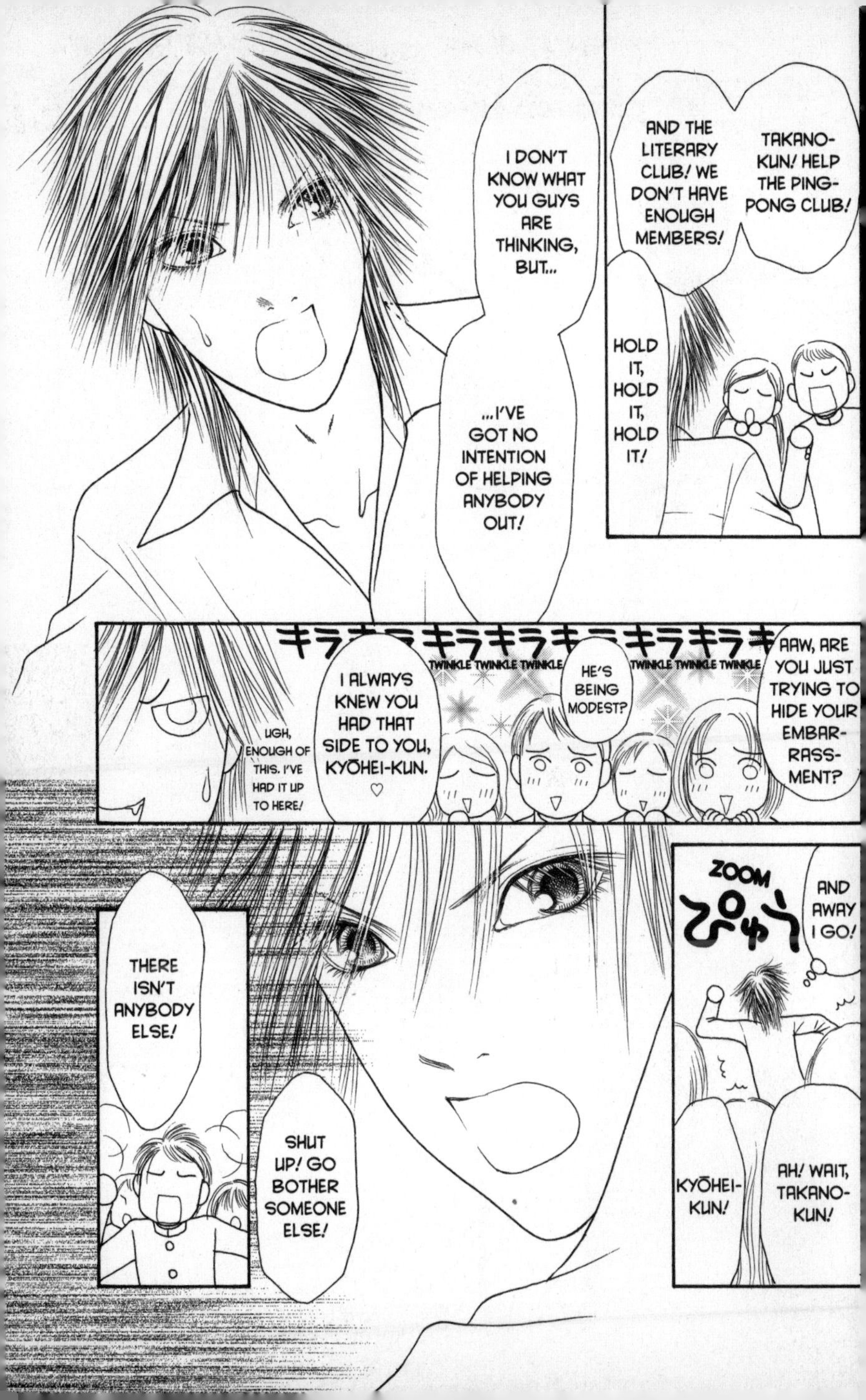
TAKANO-KUN! HELP THE PING-PONG CLUB!
AND THE LITERARY CLUB! WE DON'T HAVE ENOUGH MEMBERS!
HOLD IT, HOLD IT, HOLD IT!
I DON'T KNOW WHAT YOU GUYS ARE THINKING, BUT...
...I'VE GOT NO INTENTION OF HELPING ANYBODY OUT!
AAW, ARE YOU JUST TRYING TO HIDE YOUR EMBARRASSMENT?
キラキラキラキラキラキラキラキ
TWINKLE TWINKLE TWINKLE TWINKLE TWINKLE TWINKLE
HE'S BEING MODEST?
I ALWAYS KNEW YOU HAD THAT SIDE TO YOU, KYŌHEI-KUN. ♡
UGH, ENOUGH OF THIS. I'VE HAD IT UP TO HERE!
AND AWAY I GO!
ぴゅう
ZOOM
AH! WAIT, TAKANO-KUN!
KYŌHEI-KUN!
SHUT UP! GO BOTHER SOMEONE ELSE!
THERE ISN'T ANYBODY ELSE!

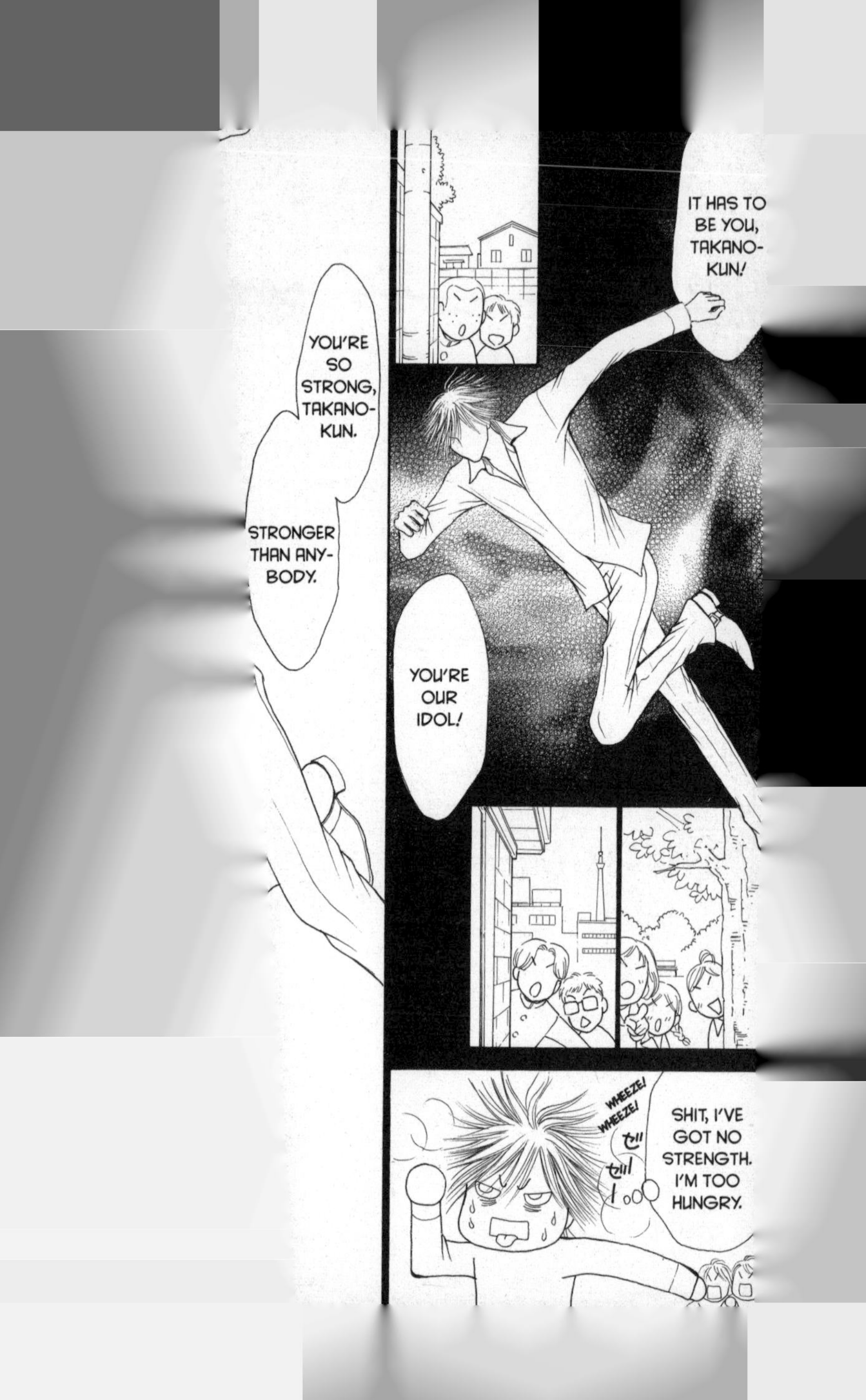
IT HAS TO BE YOU, TAKANO-KUN!
YOU'RE OUR IDOL!
WHEEZE! WHEEZE!
SHIT, I'VE GOT NO STRENGTH. I'M TOO HUNGRY.
YOU'RE SO STRONG, TAKANO-KUN.
STRONGER THAN ANYBODY.

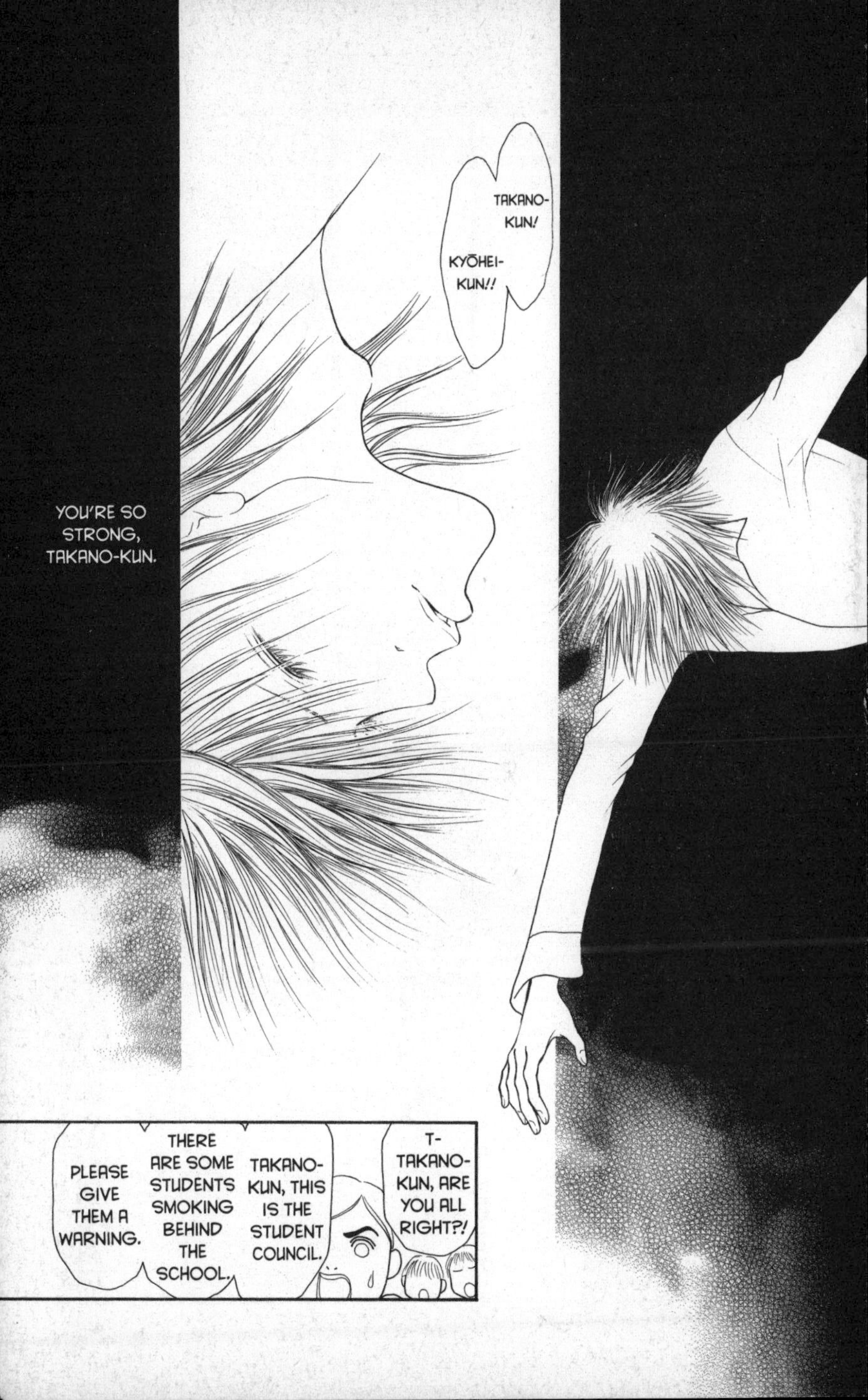
TAKANO-KUN!
KYŌHEI-KUN!!
YOU'RE SO STRONG, TAKANO-KUN.
T-TAKANO-KUN, ARE YOU ALL RIGHT?!
TAKANO-KUN, THIS IS THE STUDENT COUNCIL.
THERE ARE SOME STUDENTS SMOKING BEHIND THE SCHOOL.
PLEASE GIVE THEM A WARNING.

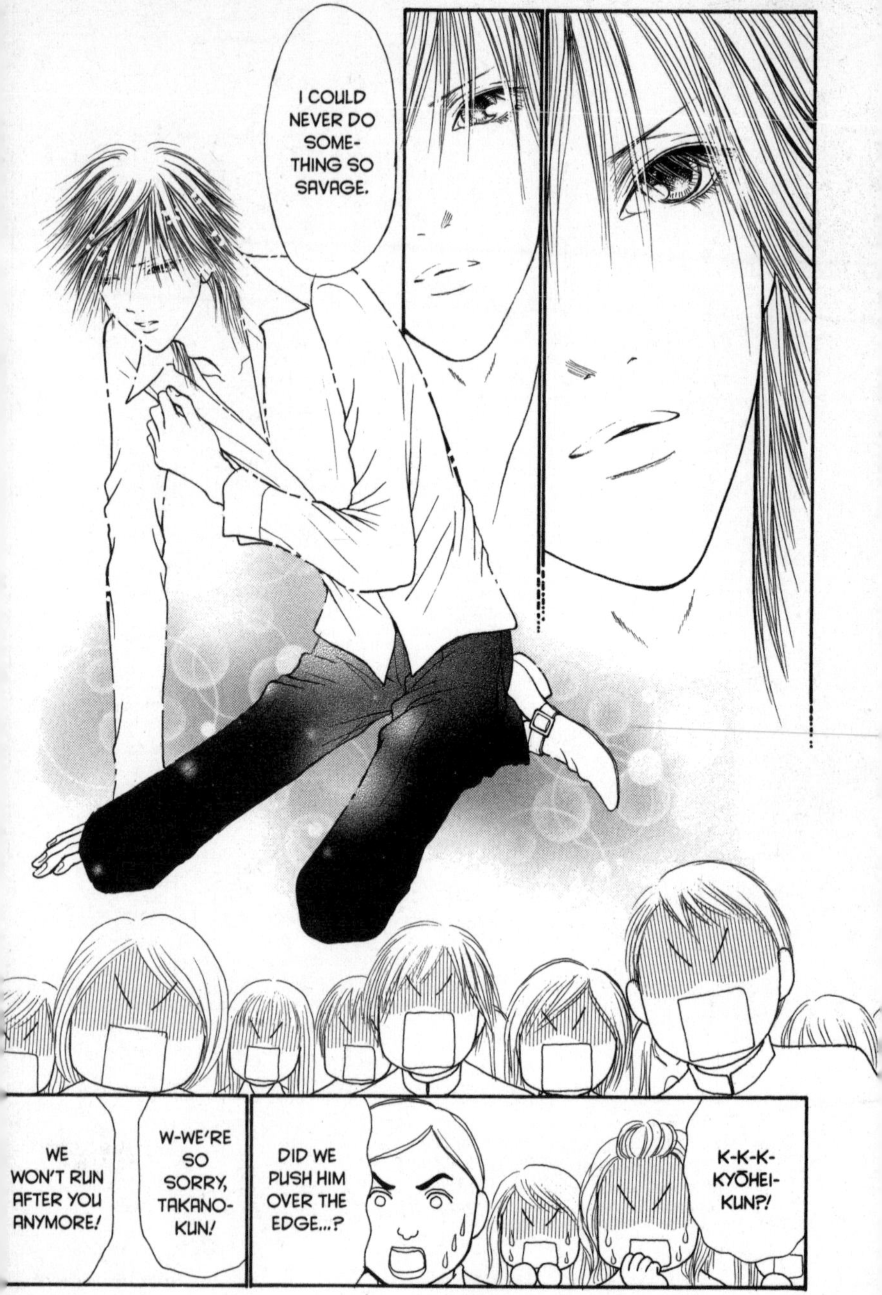
I COULD NEVER DO SOME-THING SO SAVAGE.
K-K-K-KYŌHEI-KUN?!
DID WE PUSH HIM OVER THE EDGE...?
W-WE'RE SO SORRY, TAKANO-KUN!
WE WON'T RUN AFTER YOU ANYMORE!

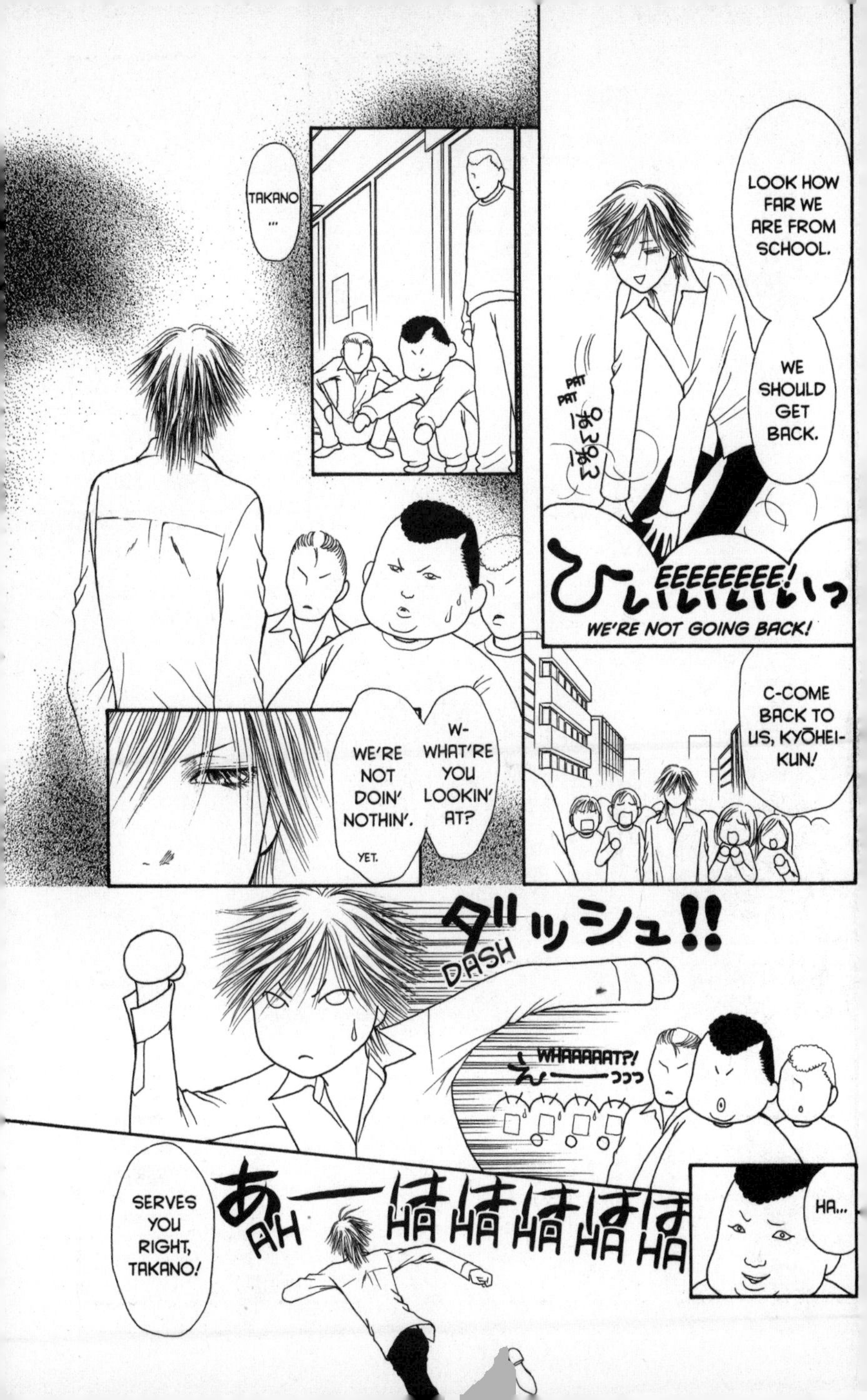
LOOK HOW FAR WE ARE FROM SCHOOL.
WE SHOULD GET BACK.
ぽんぽん
PAT PAT
ひいいいいいっ
EEEEEEEE!
WE'RE NOT GOING BACK!
TAKANO ...
C-COME BACK TO US, KYŌHEI-KUN!
W- WHAT'RE YOU LOOKIN' AT?
WE'RE NOT DOIN' NOTHIN'.
YET.
ダッシュ!!
DASH
えーっっっ
WHAAAAAT?!
HA...
あーはははははは
AH HA HA HA HA HA
SERVES YOU RIGHT, TAKANO!

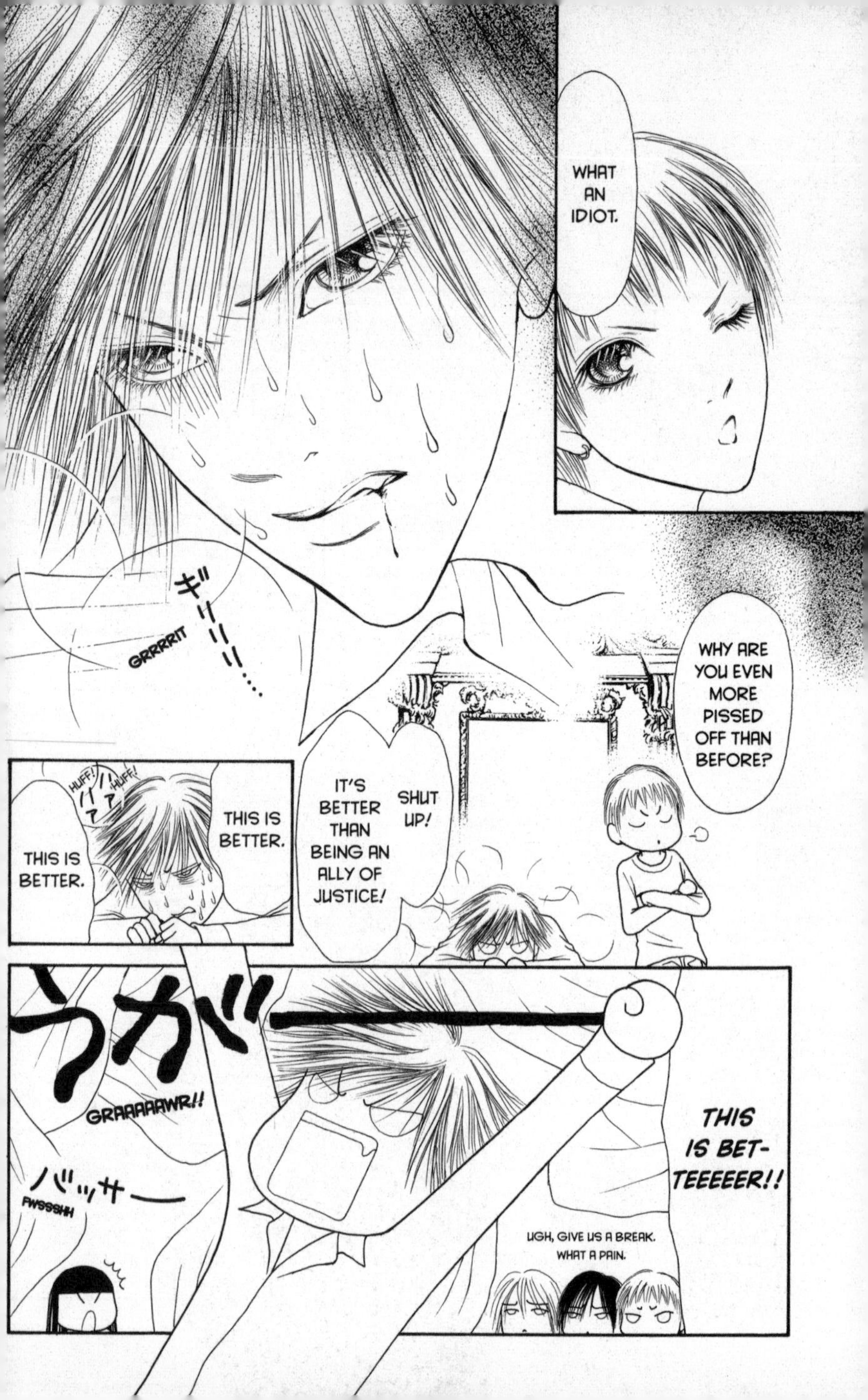
WHAT AN IDIOT.
ギリリリ…
GRRRRIT
WHY ARE YOU EVEN MORE PISSED OFF THAN BEFORE?
SHUT UP!
IT'S BETTER THAN BEING AN ALLY OF JUSTICE!
THIS IS BETTER.
ハァ HUFF!
ハァ HUFF!
THIS IS BETTER.
THIS IS BET-TEEEEER!!
UGH, GIVE US A BREAK. WHAT A PAIN.
うがー
GRAAAAAAWR!!
バッサー
AWSSSHH

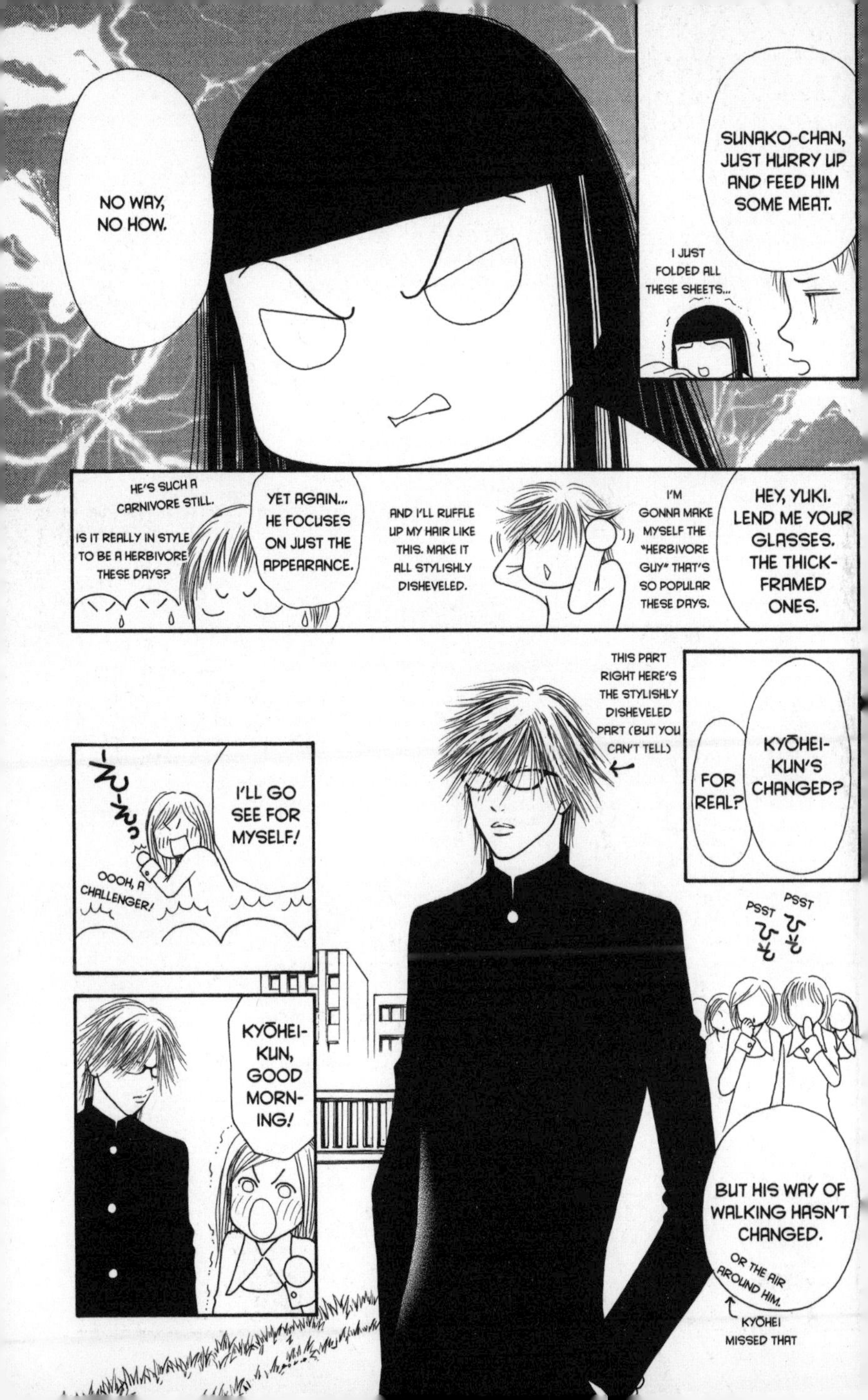
SUNAKO-CHAN, JUST HURRY UP AND FEED HIM SOME MEAT.
I JUST FOLDED ALL THESE SHEETS...
NO WAY, NO HOW.
HEY, YUKI. LEND ME YOUR GLASSES. THE THICK-FRAMED ONES.
I'M GONNA MAKE MYSELF THE "HERBIVORE GUY" THAT'S SO POPULAR THESE DAYS.
AND I'LL RUFFLE UP MY HAIR LIKE THIS. MAKE IT ALL STYLISHLY DISHEVELED.
YET AGAIN... HE FOCUSES ON JUST THE APPEARANCE.
HE'S SUCH A CARNIVORE STILL.
IS IT REALLY IN STYLE TO BE A HERBIVORE THESE DAYS?
KYŌHEI-KUN'S CHANGED?
FOR REAL?
THIS PART RIGHT HERE'S THE STYLISHLY DISHEVELED PART (BUT YOU CAN'T TELL)
PSST
PSST
BUT HIS WAY OF WALKING HASN'T CHANGED.
OR THE AIR AROUND HIM.
KYŌHEI MISSED THAT
I'LL GO SEE FOR MYSELF!
OOOH, A CHALLENGER!
KYŌHEI-KUN, GOOD MORNING!

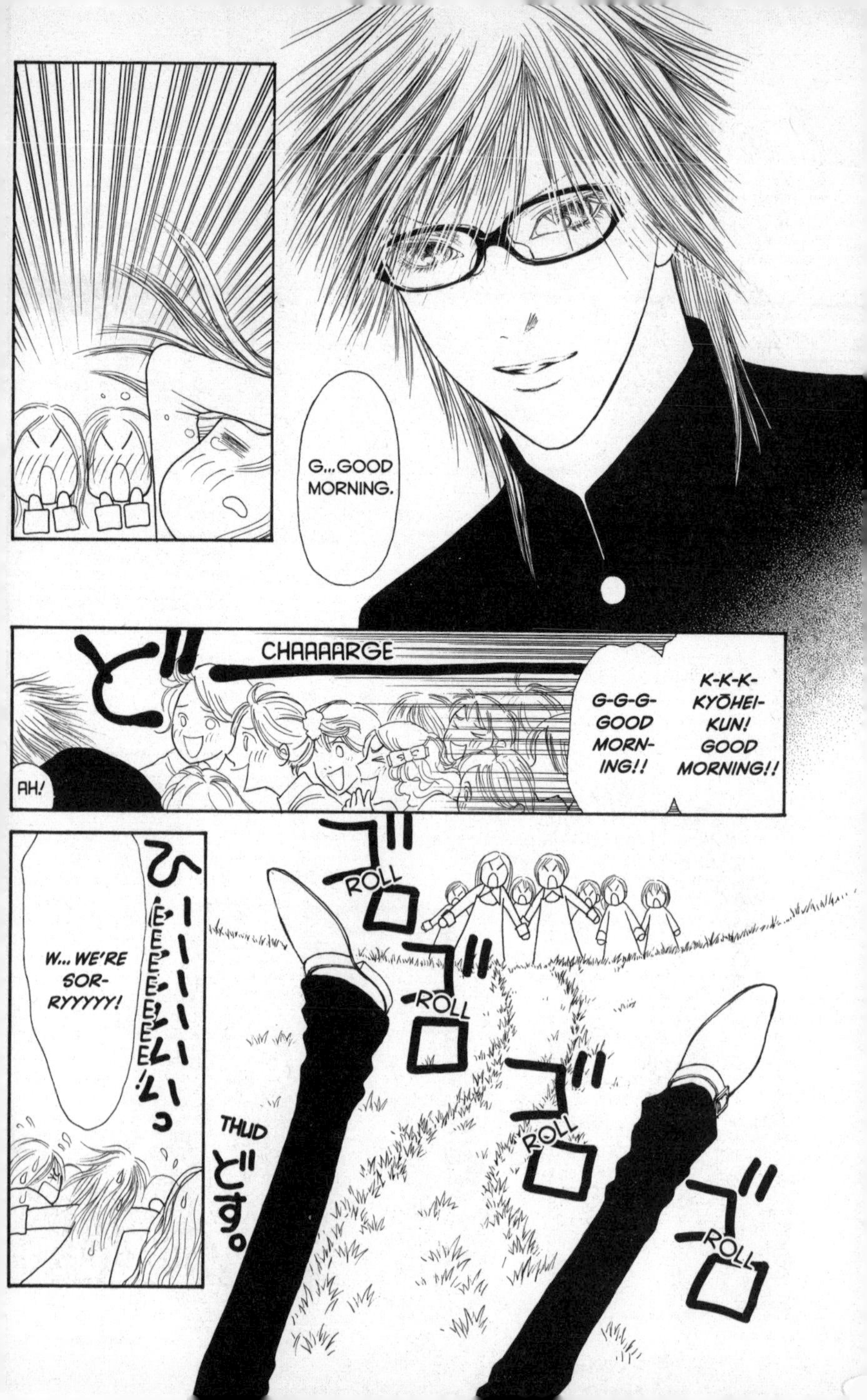
G...GOOD MORNING.
K-K-K-KYŌHEI-KUN! GOOD MORNING!!
G-G-G-GOOD MORN-ING!!
CHAAAARGE
AH!
ROLL
ROLL
ROLL
ROLL
THUD
W... WE'RE SOR-RYYYYY!

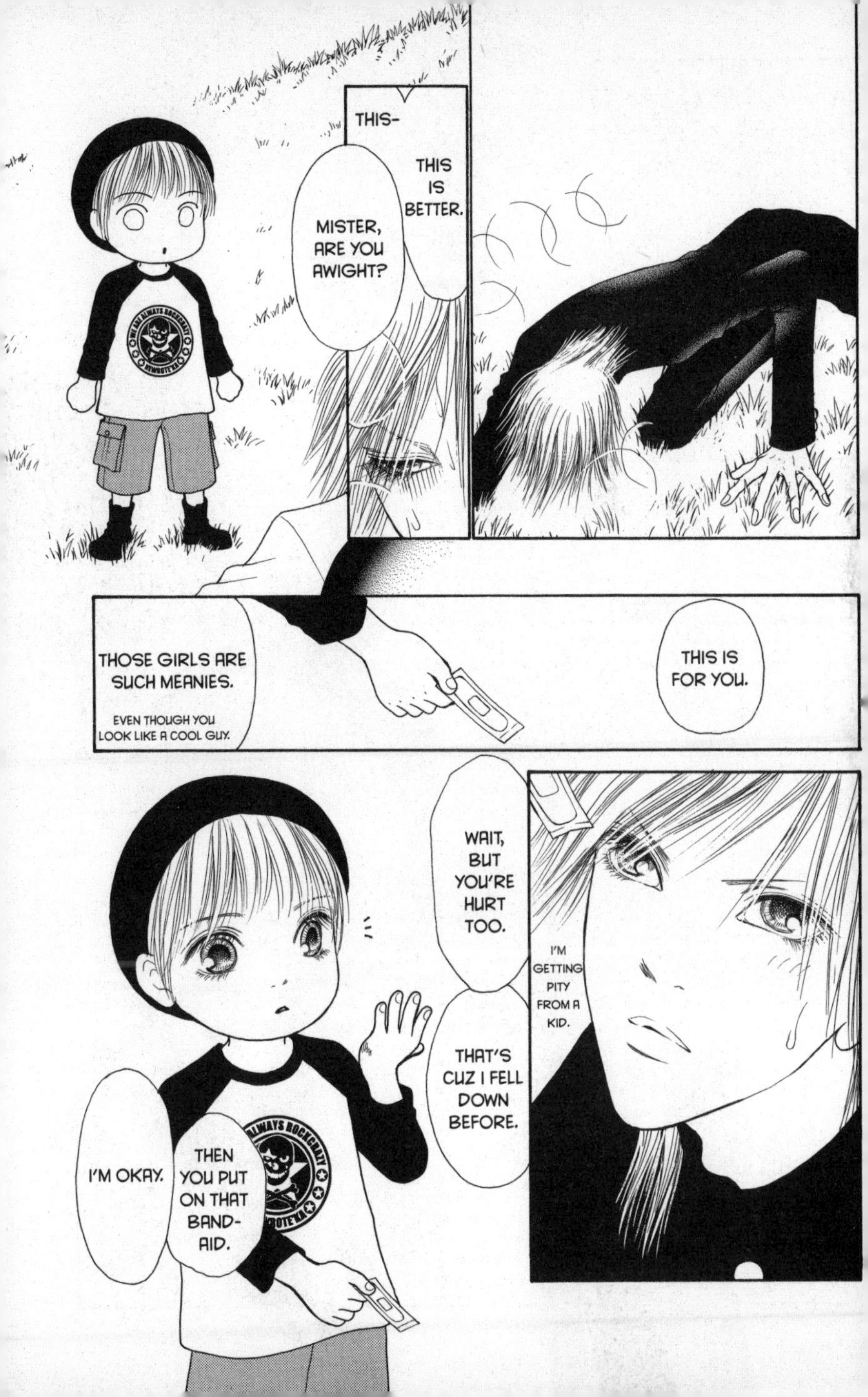

THIS-
THIS IS BETTER.
MISTER, ARE YOU AWIGHT?
THIS IS FOR YOU.
THOSE GIRLS ARE SUCH MEANIES.
EVEN THOUGH YOU LOOK LIKE A COOL GUY.
I'M GETTING PITY FROM A KID.
WAIT, BUT YOU'RE HURT TOO.
THAT'S CUZ I FELL DOWN BEFORE.
THEN YOU PUT ON THAT BAND-AID.
I'M OKAY.

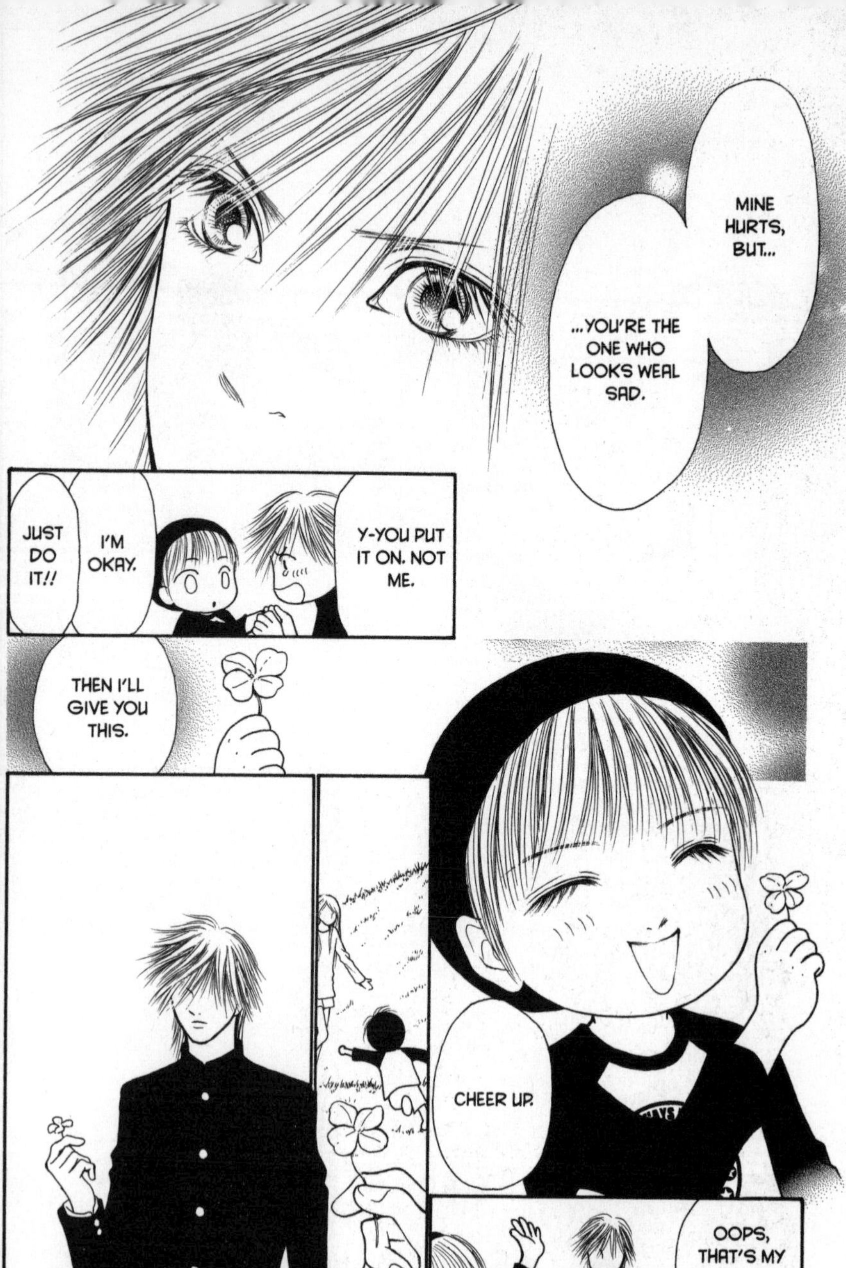
MINE HURTS, BUT...
...YOU'RE THE ONE WHO LOOKS WEAL SAD.
Y-YOU PUT IT ON. NOT ME.
I'M OKAY.
JUST DO IT!!
THEN I'LL GIVE YOU THIS.
CHEER UP.
OOPS, THAT'S MY MOMMY. I GOTTA GO!
BYE-BYE!

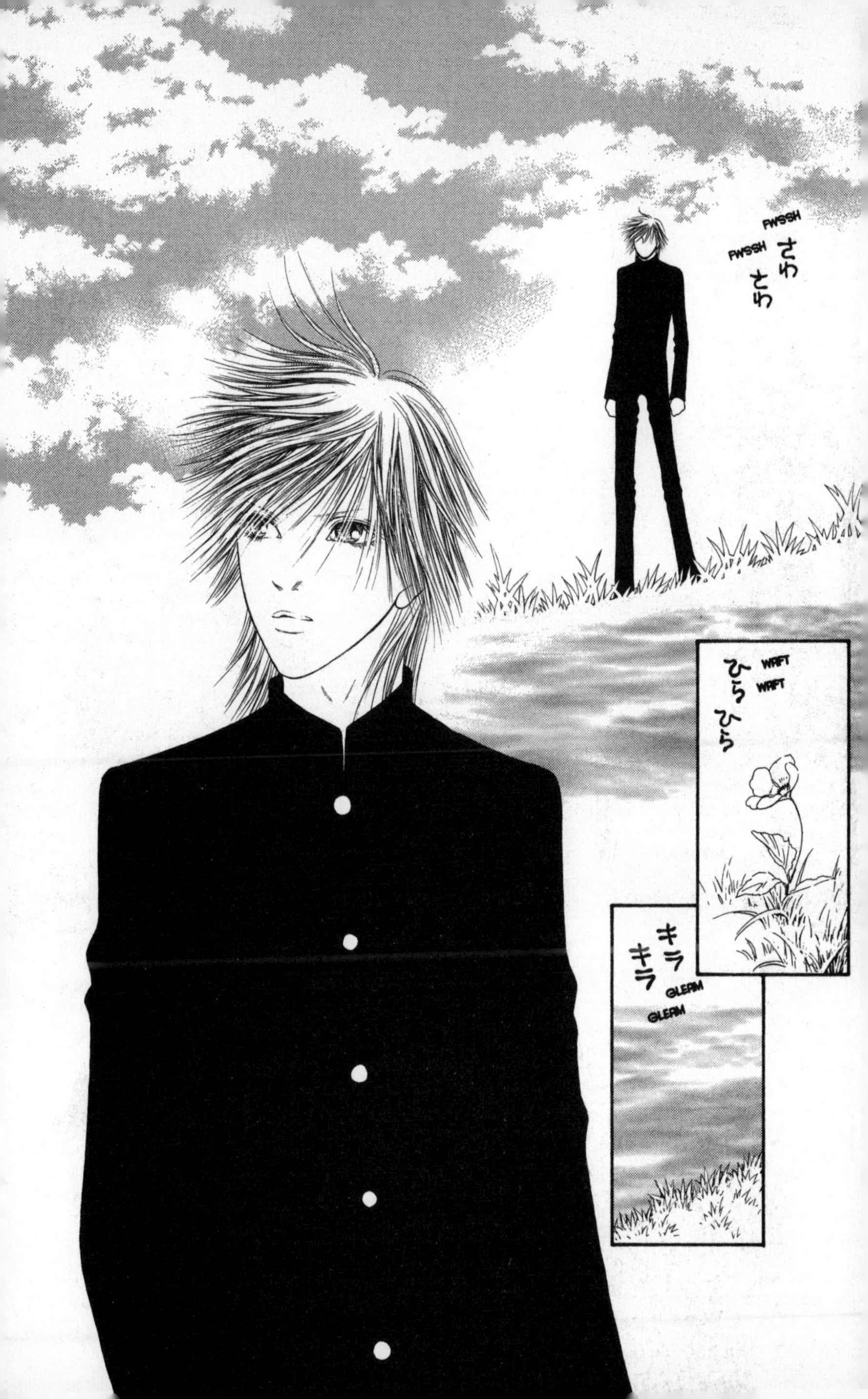
さわさわ
FWSSH
FWSSH
ひらひら
WAFT
WAFT
キラキラ
GLEAM
GLEAM

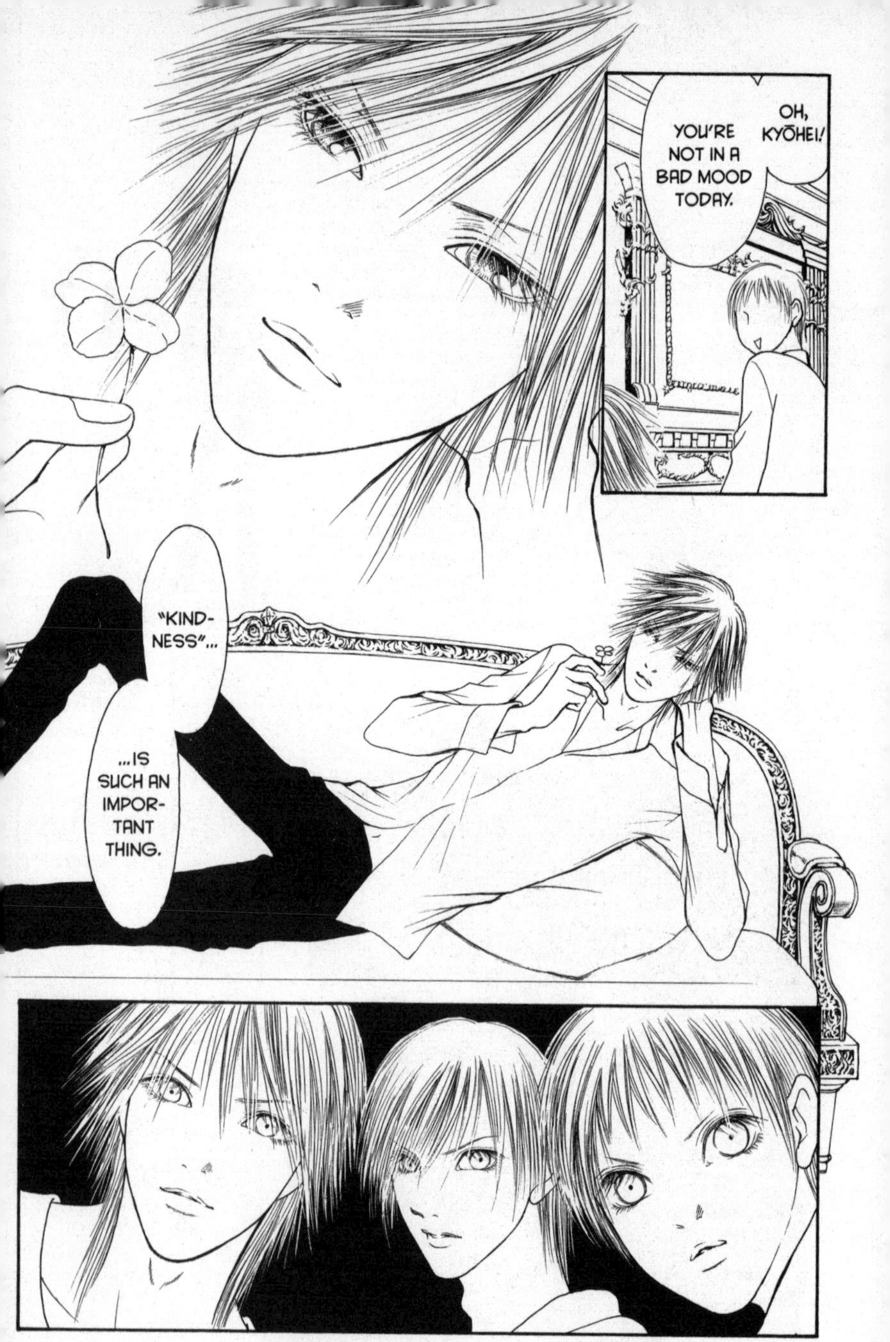
OH, KYŌHEI!
YOU'RE NOT IN A BAD MOOD TODAY.
"KIND-NESS"...
...IS SUCH AN IMPOR-TANT THING.

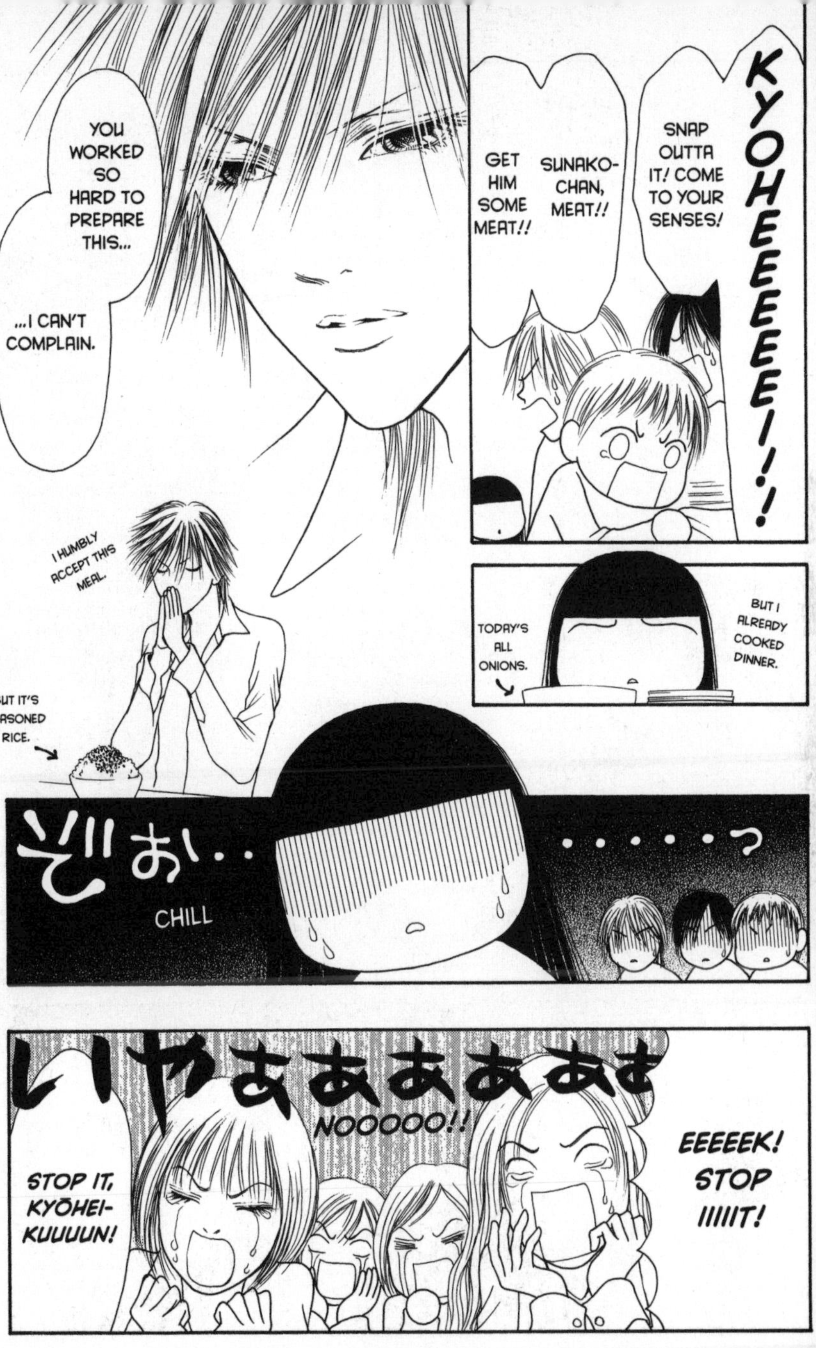
KYOHEEEEEEI!!!
SNAP OUTTA IT! COME TO YOUR SENSES!
SUNAKO-CHAN, MEAT!!
GET HIM SOME MEAT!!
BUT I ALREADY COOKED DINNER.
TODAY'S ALL ONIONS.
YOU WORKED SO HARD TO PREPARE THIS...
...I CAN'T COMPLAIN.
I HUMBLY ACCEPT THIS MEAL.
BUT IT'S SEASONED RICE.
......?
ぞおい..
CHILL
いやああああああ
NOOOOO!!
EEEEEK! STOP IIIIIT!
STOP IT, KYŌHEI-KUUUUN!

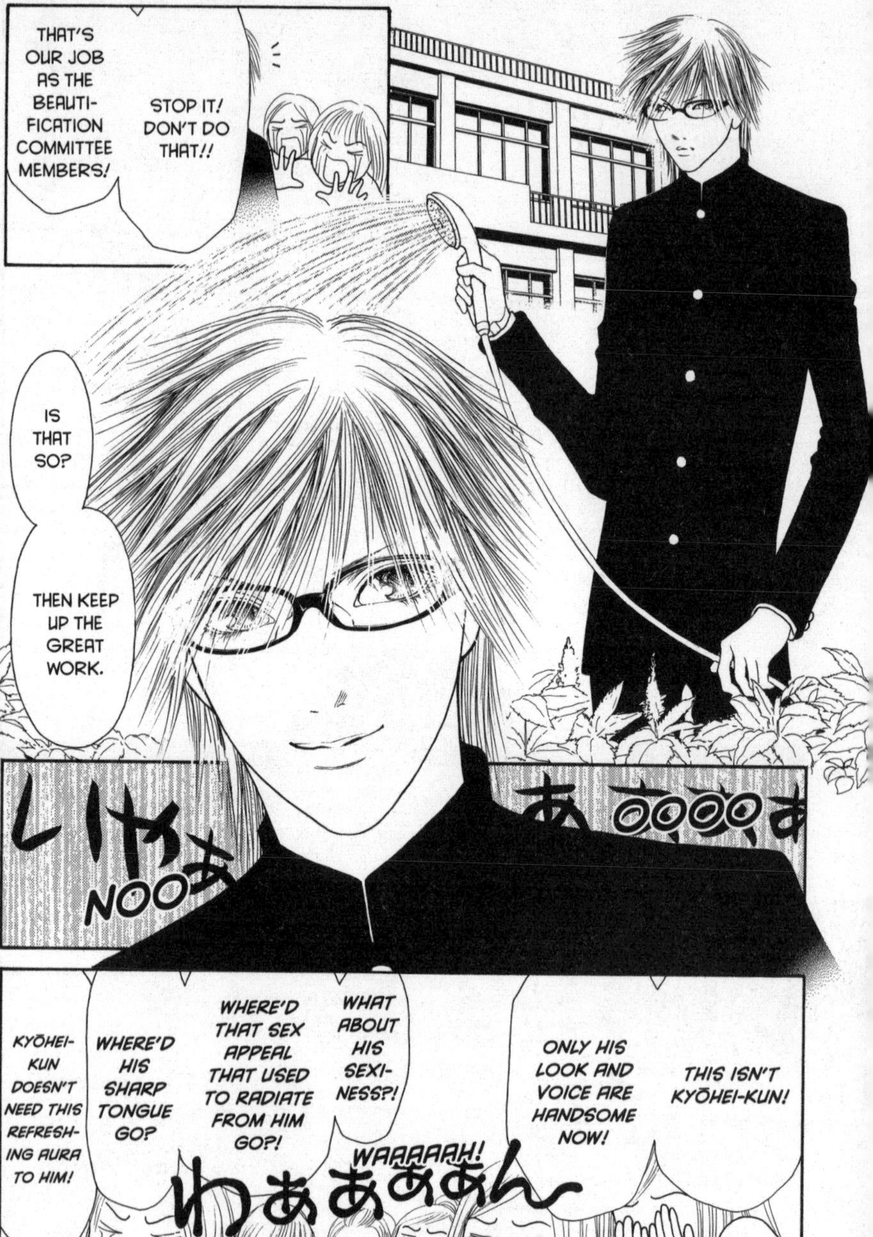
STOP IT! DON'T DO THAT!!
THAT'S OUR JOB AS THE BEAUTI-FICATION COMMITTEE MEMBERS!
IS THAT SO?
THEN KEEP UP THE GREAT WORK.
NOOO
THIS ISN'T KYŌHEI-KUN!
ONLY HIS LOOK AND VOICE ARE HANDSOME NOW!
WHAT ABOUT HIS SEXI-NESS?!
WHERE'D THAT SEX APPEAL THAT USED TO RADIATE FROM HIM GO?!
WHERE'D HIS SHARP TONGUE GO?
KYŌHEI-KUN DOESN'T NEED THIS REFRESH-ING AURA TO HIM!
WAAAAAH!
わぁあぁあん

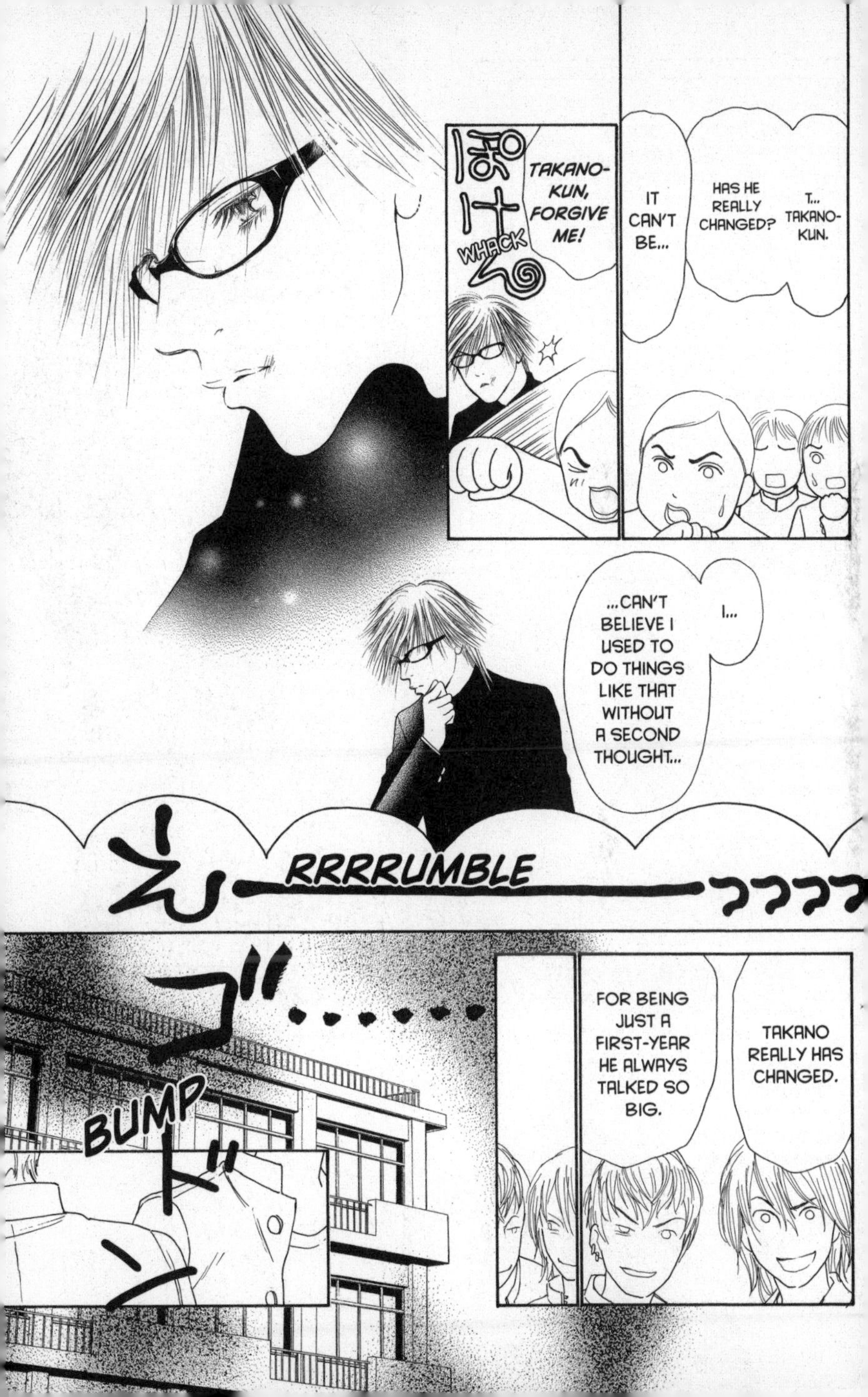
T... TAKANO-KUN.
HAS HE REALLY CHANGED?
IT CAN'T BE...
TAKANO-KUN, FORGIVE ME!
WHACK
I...
...CAN'T BELIEVE I USED TO DO THINGS LIKE THAT WITHOUT A SECOND THOUGHT...
RRRRUMBLE
TAKANO REALLY HAS CHANGED.
FOR BEING JUST A FIRST-YEAR HE ALWAYS TALKED SO BIG.
BUMP

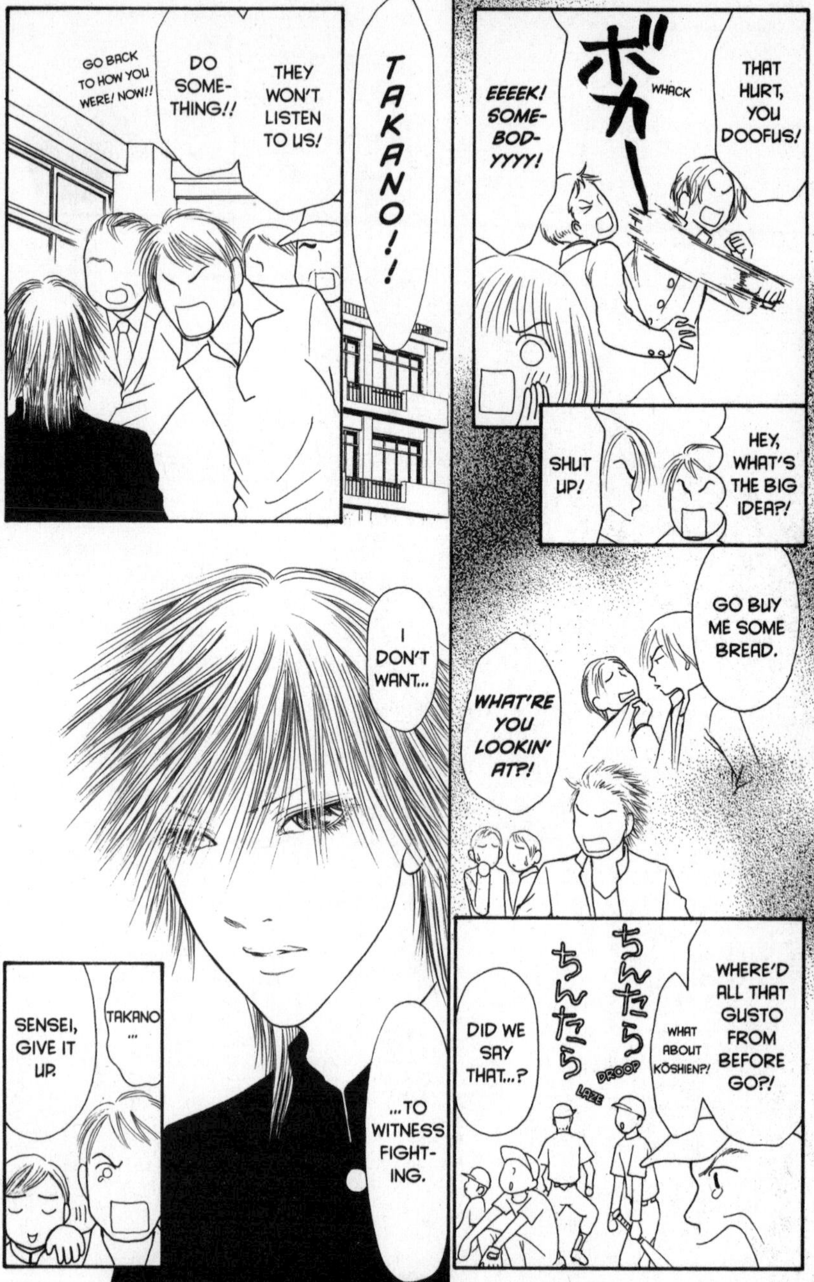
THAT HURT, YOU DOOFUS!
ボカー
WHACK
EEEEK! SOME-BOD-YYYY!
HEY, WHAT'S THE BIG IDEA?!
SHUT UP!
GO BUY ME SOME BREAD.
WHAT'RE YOU LOOKIN' AT?!
WHERE'D ALL THAT GUSTO FROM BEFORE GO?!
WHAT ABOUT KŌSHIEN?!
ちんたらちんたら
DROOP
LAZE
DID WE SAY THAT...?
TAKANO!!
THEY WON'T LISTEN TO US!
DO SOME-THING!!
GO BACK TO HOW YOU WERE! NOW!!
I DON'T WANT...
...TO WITNESS FIGHT-ING.
TAKANO ...
SENSEI, GIVE IT UP.

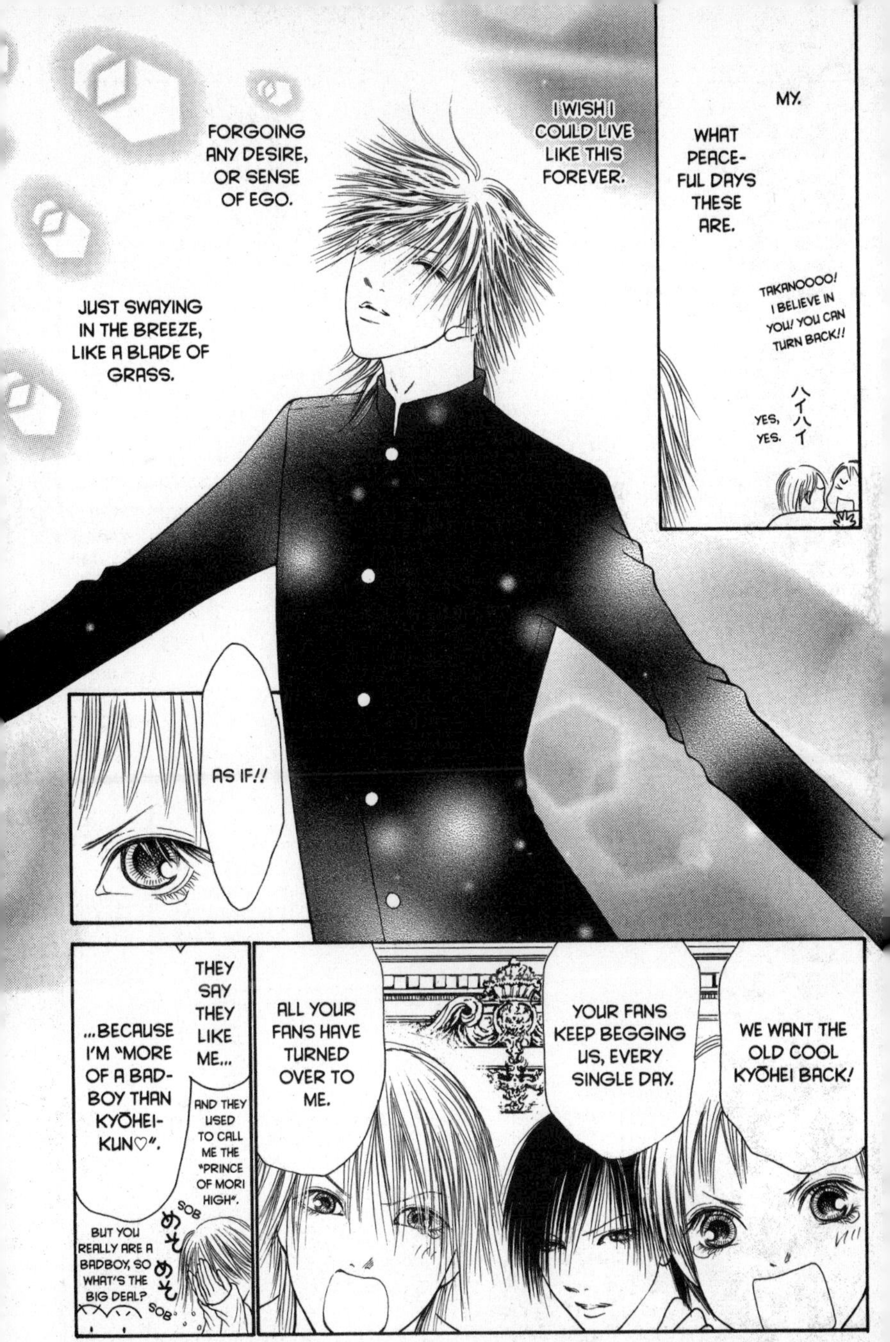
MY.
WHAT PEACE-FUL DAYS THESE ARE.
TAKANOOOO! I BELIEVE IN YOU! YOU CAN TURN BACK!!
ハイハイ
YES, YES.
I WISH I COULD LIVE LIKE THIS FOREVER.
FORGOING ANY DESIRE, OR SENSE OF EGO.
JUST SWAYING IN THE BREEZE, LIKE A BLADE OF GRASS.
AS IF!!
WE WANT THE OLD COOL KYŌHEI BACK!
YOUR FANS KEEP BEGGING US, EVERY SINGLE DAY.
ALL YOUR FANS HAVE TURNED OVER TO ME.
THEY SAY THEY LIKE ME...
...BECAUSE I'M "MORE OF A BAD-BOY THAN KYŌHEI-KUN♡".
AND THEY USED TO CALL ME THE "PRINCE OF MORI HIGH".
めそめそ
SOB SOB
BUT YOU REALLY ARE A BADBOY, SO WHAT'S THE BIG DEAL?

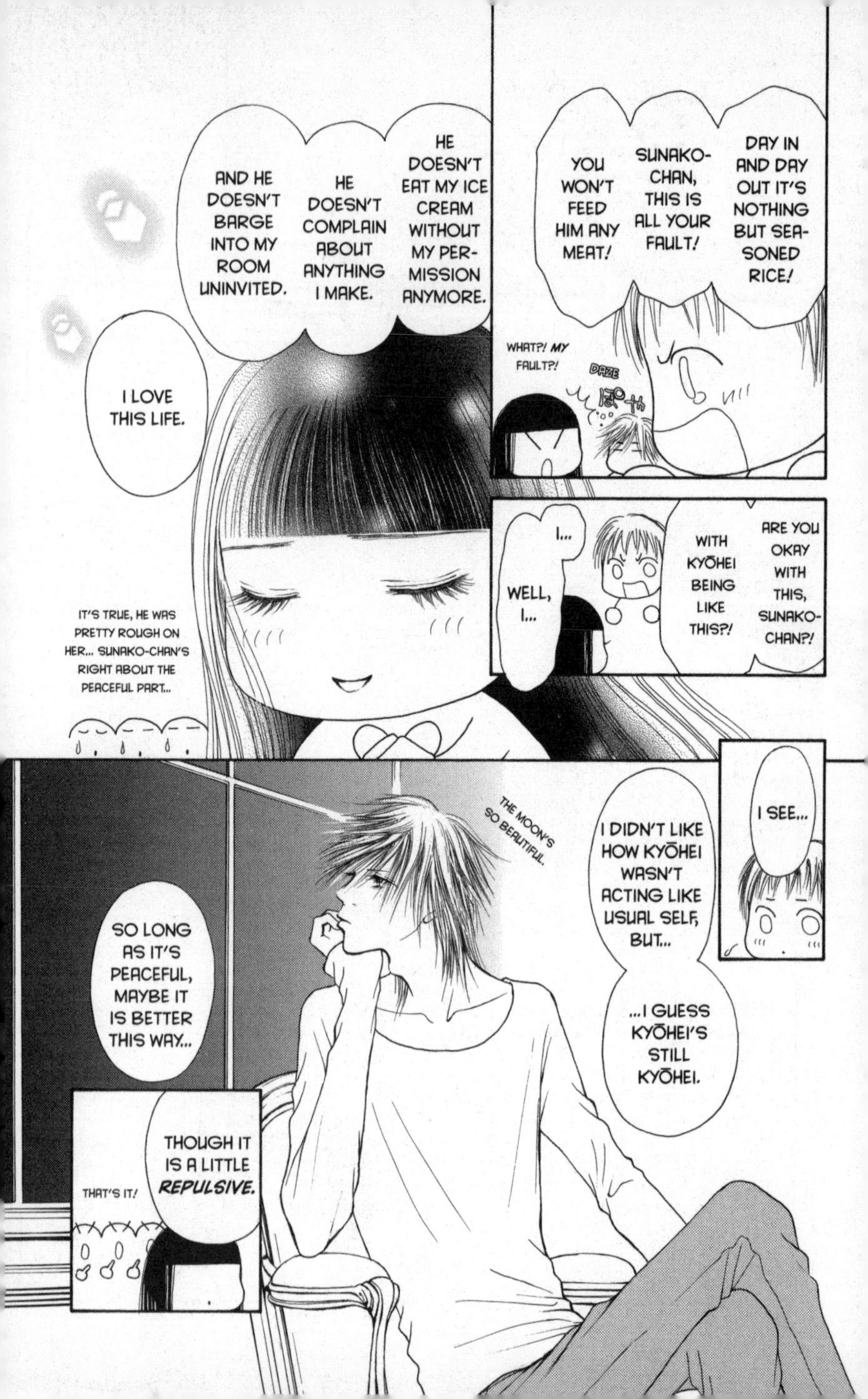
DAY IN AND DAY OUT IT'S NOTHING BUT SEA-SONED RICE!
SUNAKO-CHAN, THIS IS ALL YOUR FAULT!
YOU WON'T FEED HIM ANY MEAT!
WHAT?! *MY* FAULT?!
DAZE
ARE YOU OKAY WITH THIS, SUNAKO-CHAN?!
WITH KYŌHEI BEING LIKE THIS?!
I... WELL, I...
HE DOESN'T EAT MY ICE CREAM WITHOUT MY PER-MISSION ANYMORE.
HE DOESN'T COMPLAIN ABOUT ANYTHING I MAKE.
AND HE DOESN'T BARGE INTO MY ROOM UNINVITED.
I LOVE THIS LIFE.
IT'S TRUE, HE WAS PRETTY ROUGH ON HER... SUNAKO-CHAN'S RIGHT ABOUT THE PEACEFUL PART...
I SEE...
I DIDN'T LIKE HOW KYŌHEI WASN'T ACTING LIKE USUAL SELF, BUT...
...I GUESS KYŌHEI'S STILL KYŌHEI.
THE MOON'S SO BEAUTIFUL.
SO LONG AS IT'S PEACEFUL, MAYBE IT IS BETTER THIS WAY...
THOUGH IT IS A LITTLE ***REPULSIVE.***
THAT'S IT!

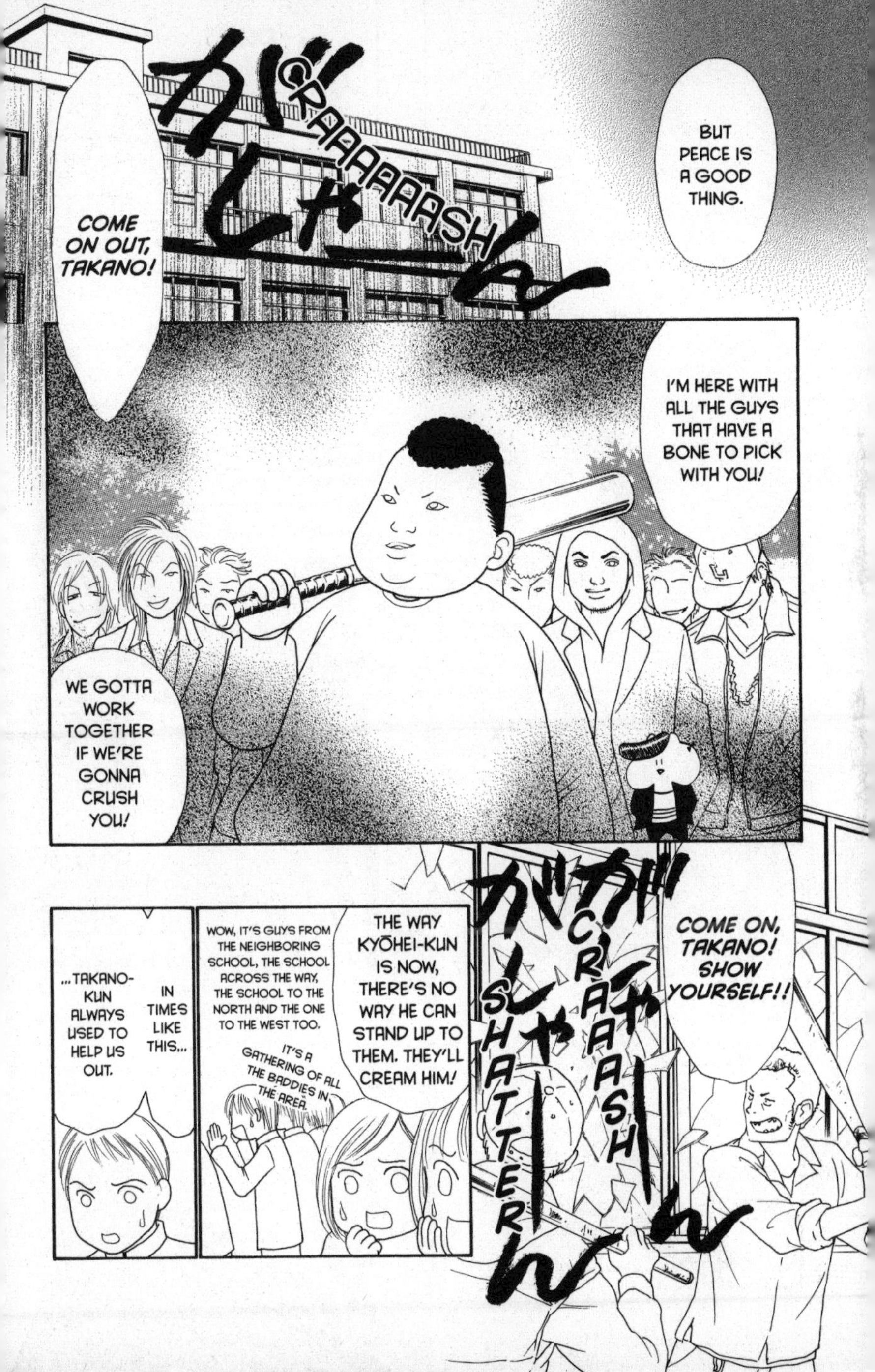

BUT PEACE IS A GOOD THING.
CRAAAAAAASH
COME ON OUT, TAKANO!
I'M HERE WITH ALL THE GUYS THAT HAVE A BONE TO PICK WITH YOU!
WE GOTTA WORK TOGETHER IF WE'RE GONNA CRUSH YOU!
COME ON, TAKANO! SHOW YOURSELF!!
CRAAASH
SHATTER
THE WAY KYŌHEI-KUN IS NOW, THERE'S NO WAY HE CAN STAND UP TO THEM. THEY'LL CREAM HIM!
WOW, IT'S GUYS FROM THE NEIGHBORING SCHOOL, THE SCHOOL ACROSS THE WAY, THE SCHOOL TO THE NORTH AND THE ONE TO THE WEST TOO.
IT'S A GATHERING OF ALL THE BADDIES IN THE AREA.
IN TIMES LIKE THIS...
...TAKANO-KUN ALWAYS USED TO HELP US OUT.

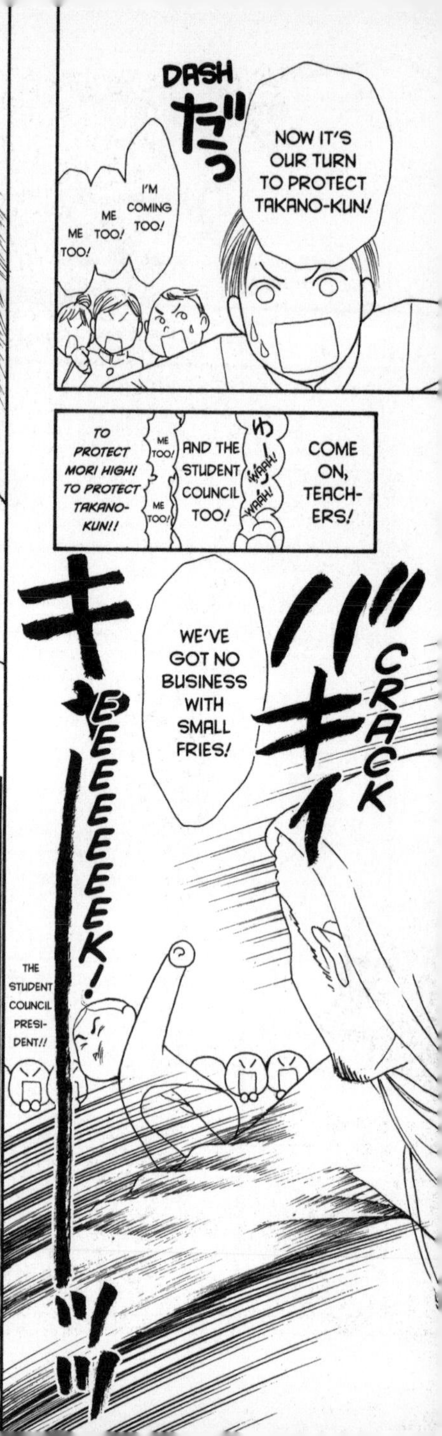
DASH
だっ
NOW IT'S OUR TURN TO PROTECT TAKANO-KUN!
I'M COMING TOO!
ME TOO!
ME TOO!
COME ON, TEACHERS!
わー
WAAH! WAAH!
AND THE STUDENT COUNCIL TOO!
ME TOO!
ME TOO!
TO PROTECT MORI HIGH! TO PROTECT TAKANO-KUN!!
バキィ
CRACK
WE'VE GOT NO BUSINESS WITH SMALL FRIES!
キーッ
EEEEEEEEEK!
THE STUDENT COUNCIL PRESIDENT!!

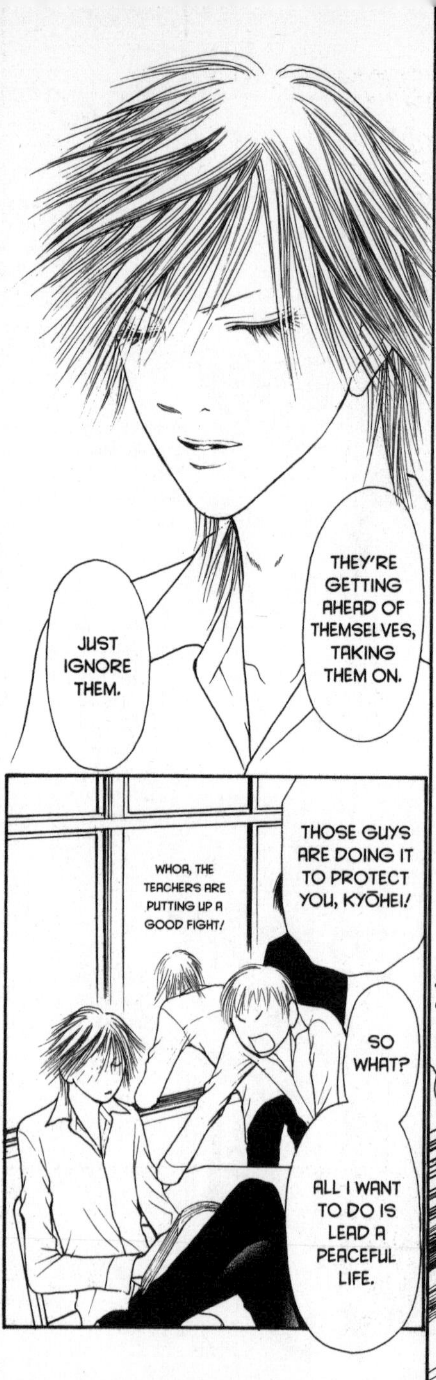
THEY'RE GETTING AHEAD OF THEMSELVES, TAKING THEM ON.
JUST IGNORE THEM.
THOSE GUYS ARE DOING IT TO PROTECT YOU, KYŌHEI!
WHOA, THE TEACHERS ARE PUTTING UP A GOOD FIGHT!
SO WHAT?
ALL I WANT TO DO IS LEAD A PEACEFUL LIFE.

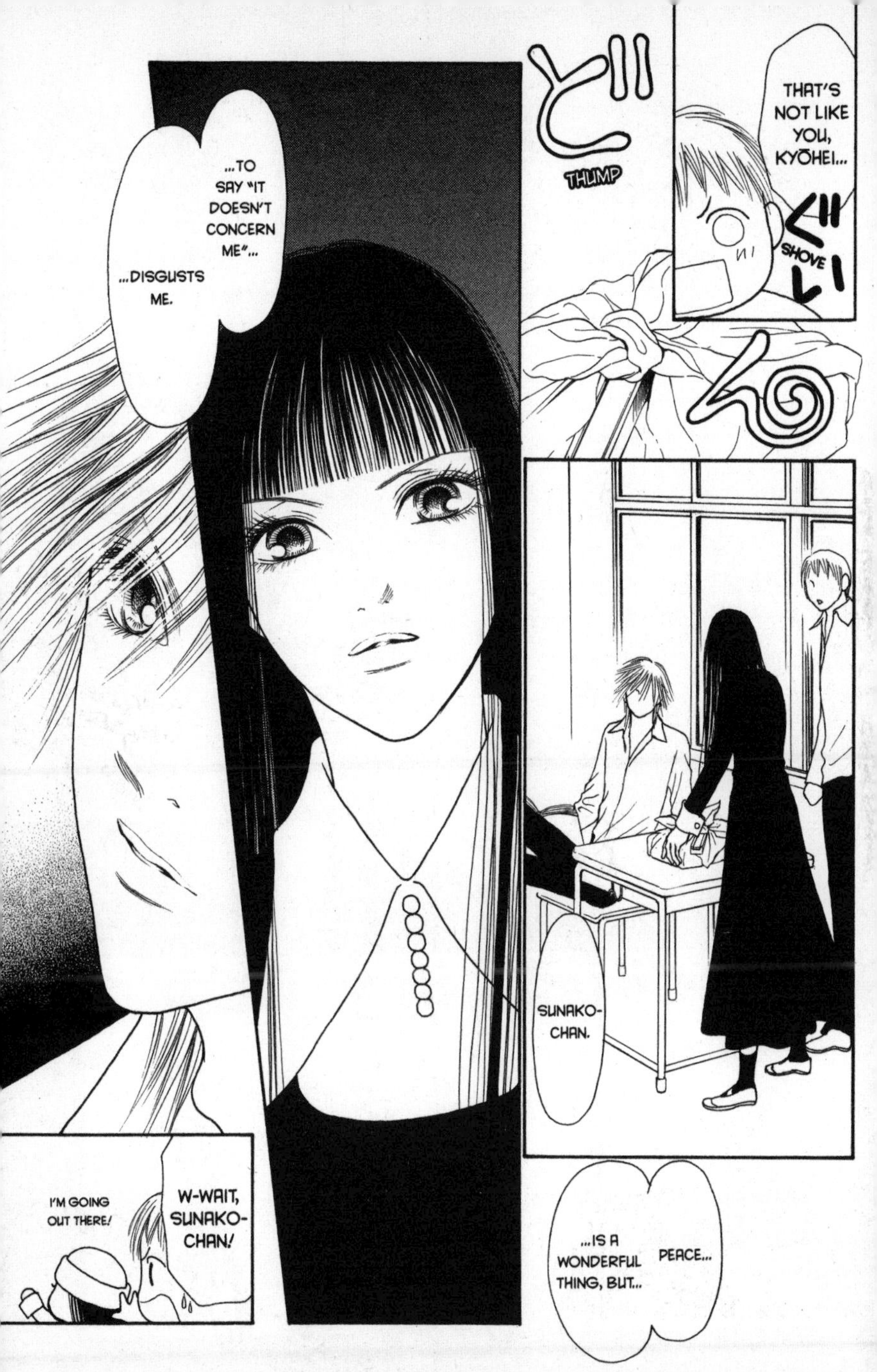
THAT'S NOT LIKE YOU, KYŌHEI...
SHOVE
THUMP
SUNAKO-CHAN.
PEACE...
...IS A WONDERFUL THING, BUT...
...TO SAY "IT DOESN'T CONCERN ME"...
...DISGUSTS ME.
W-WAIT, SUNAKO-CHAN!
I'M GOING OUT THERE!

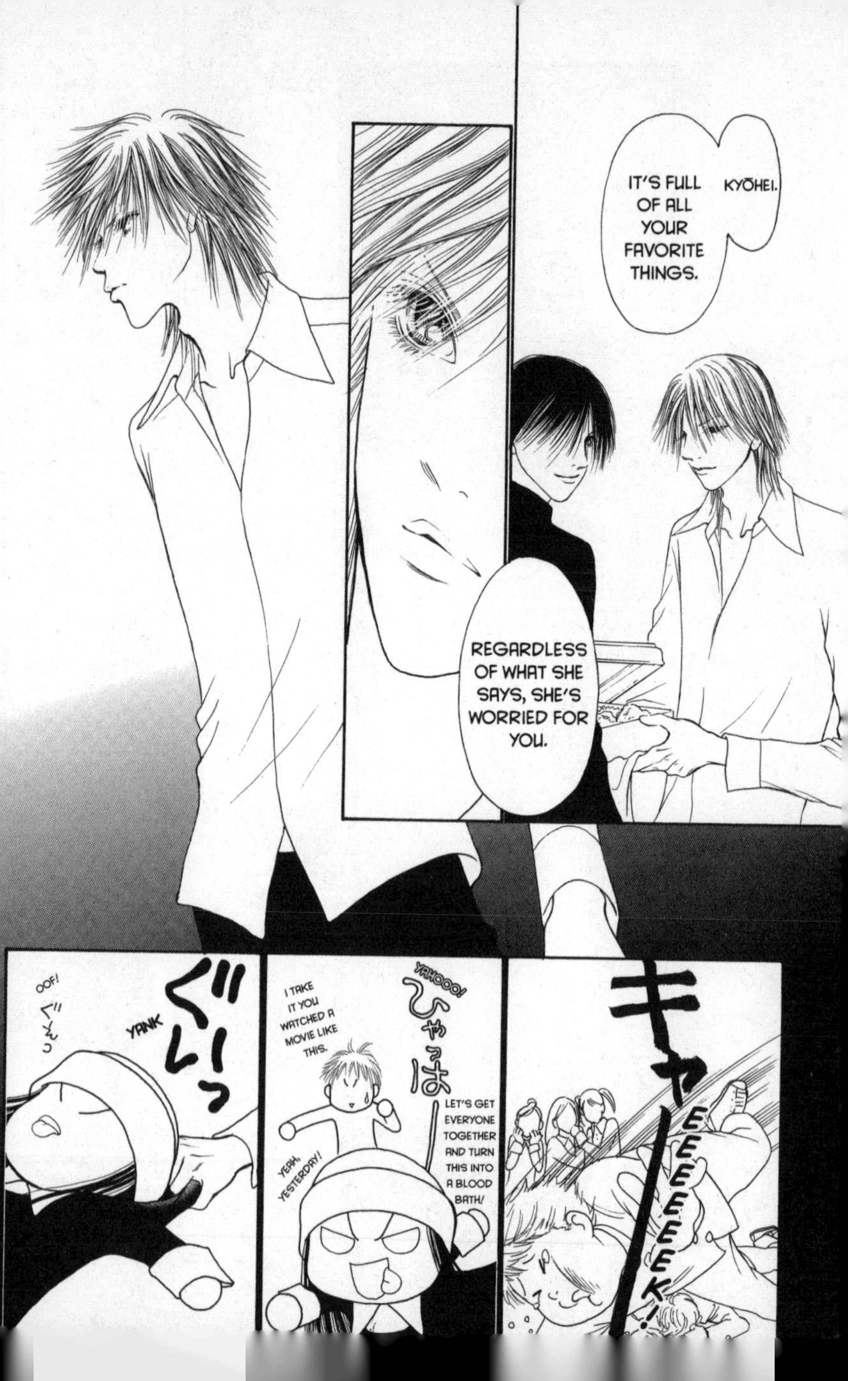
KYŌHEI.
IT'S FULL OF ALL YOUR FAVORITE THINGS.
REGARDLESS OF WHAT SHE SAYS, SHE'S WORRIED FOR YOU.
キャー
EEEEEEEK!
YAHOOO!
ひゃっほー
I TAKE IT YOU WATCHED A MOVIE LIKE THIS.
LET'S GET EVERYONE TOGETHER AND TURN THIS INTO A BLOOD BATH!
YEAH, YESTERDAY!
ぐいっ
YANK
OOF!

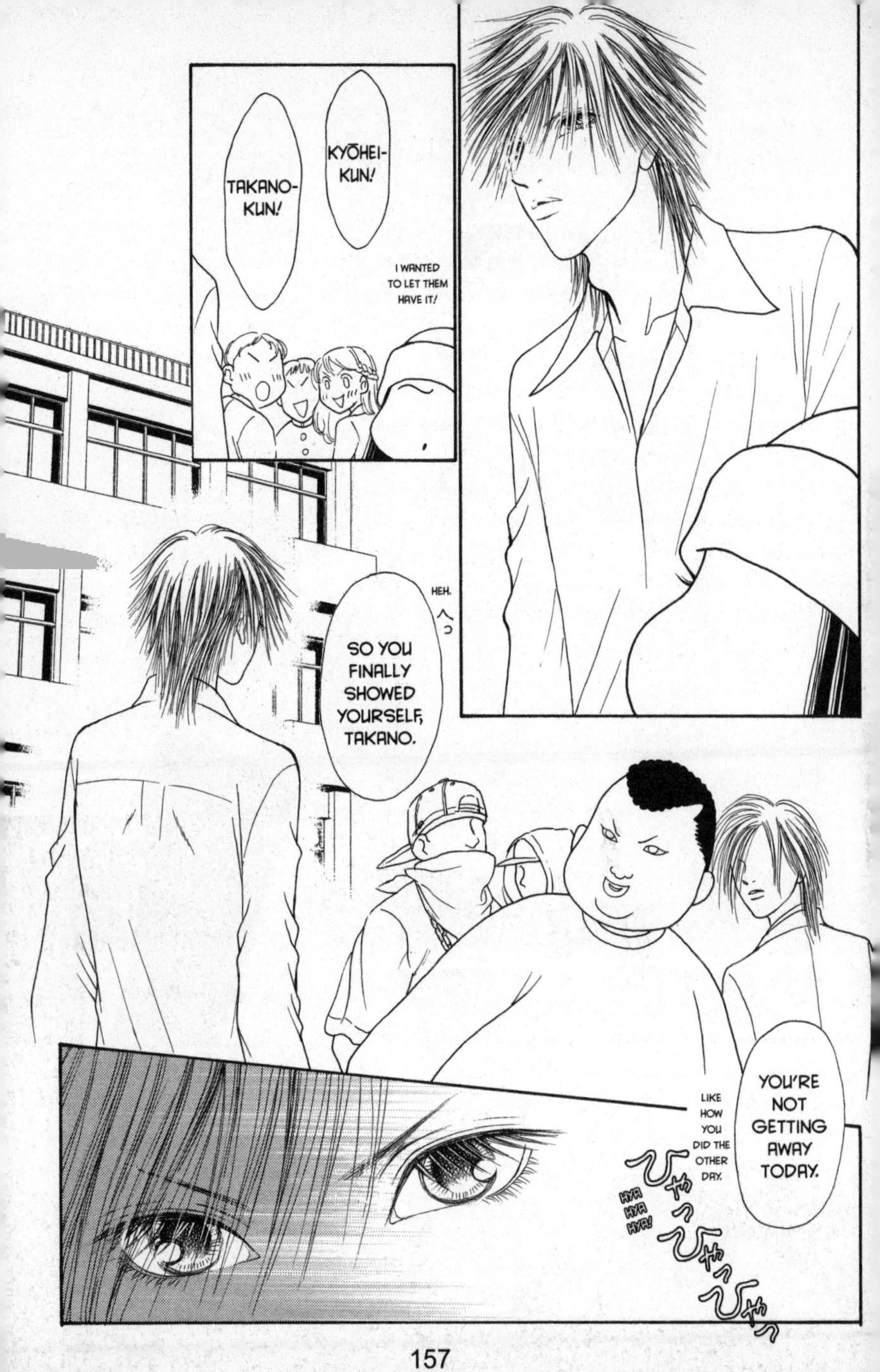
KYŌHEI-KUN!
TAKANO-KUN!
I WANTED TO LET THEM HAVE IT!
HEH.
SO YOU FINALLY SHOWED YOURSELF, TAKANO.
YOU'RE NOT GETTING AWAY TODAY.
LIKE HOW YOU DID THE OTHER DAY.
HYA HYA HYA!

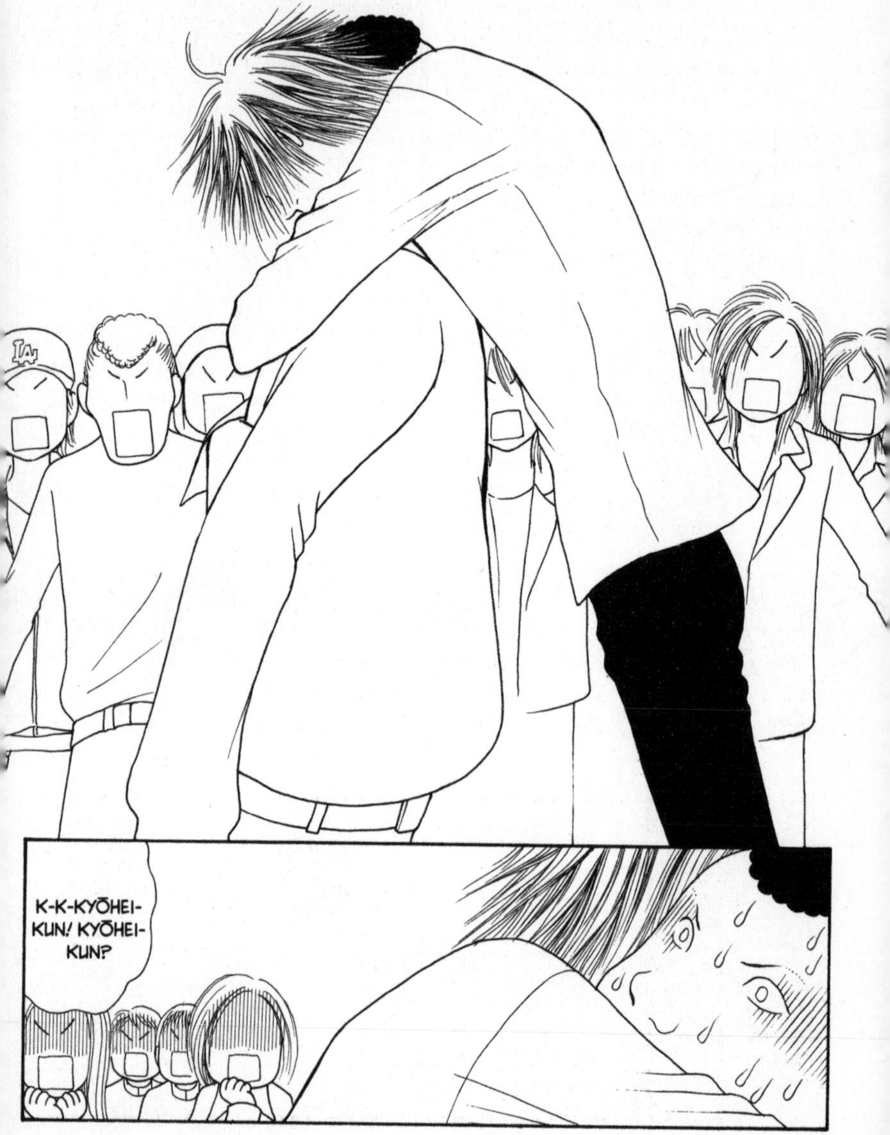
K-K-KYŌHEI-KUN! KYŌHEI-KUN?

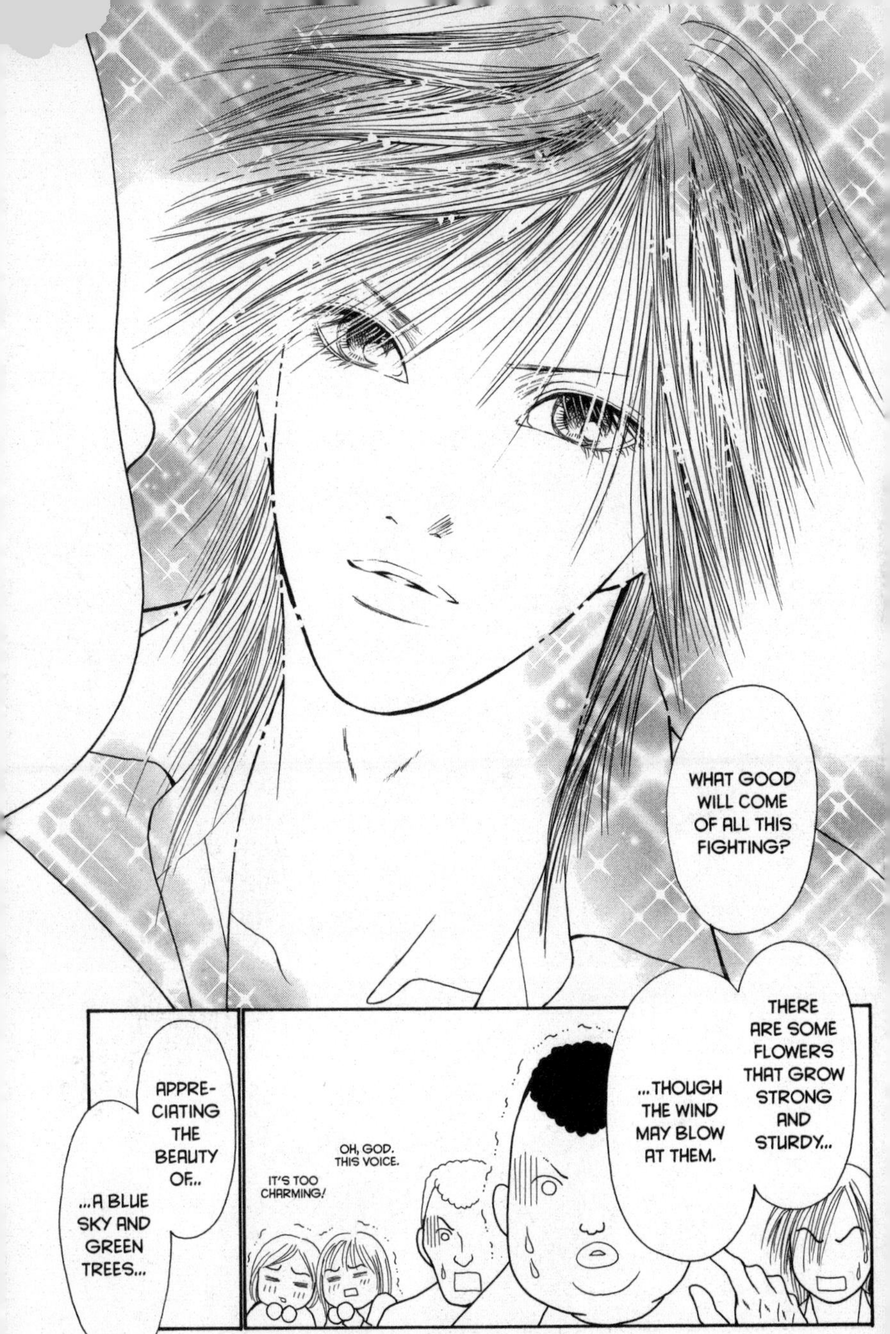
WHAT GOOD WILL COME OF ALL THIS FIGHTING?
THERE ARE SOME FLOWERS THAT GROW STRONG AND STURDY...
...THOUGH THE WIND MAY BLOW AT THEM.
OH, GOD. THIS VOICE.
IT'S TOO CHARMING!
APPRE-CIATING THE BEAUTY OF...
...A BLUE SKY AND GREEN TREES...

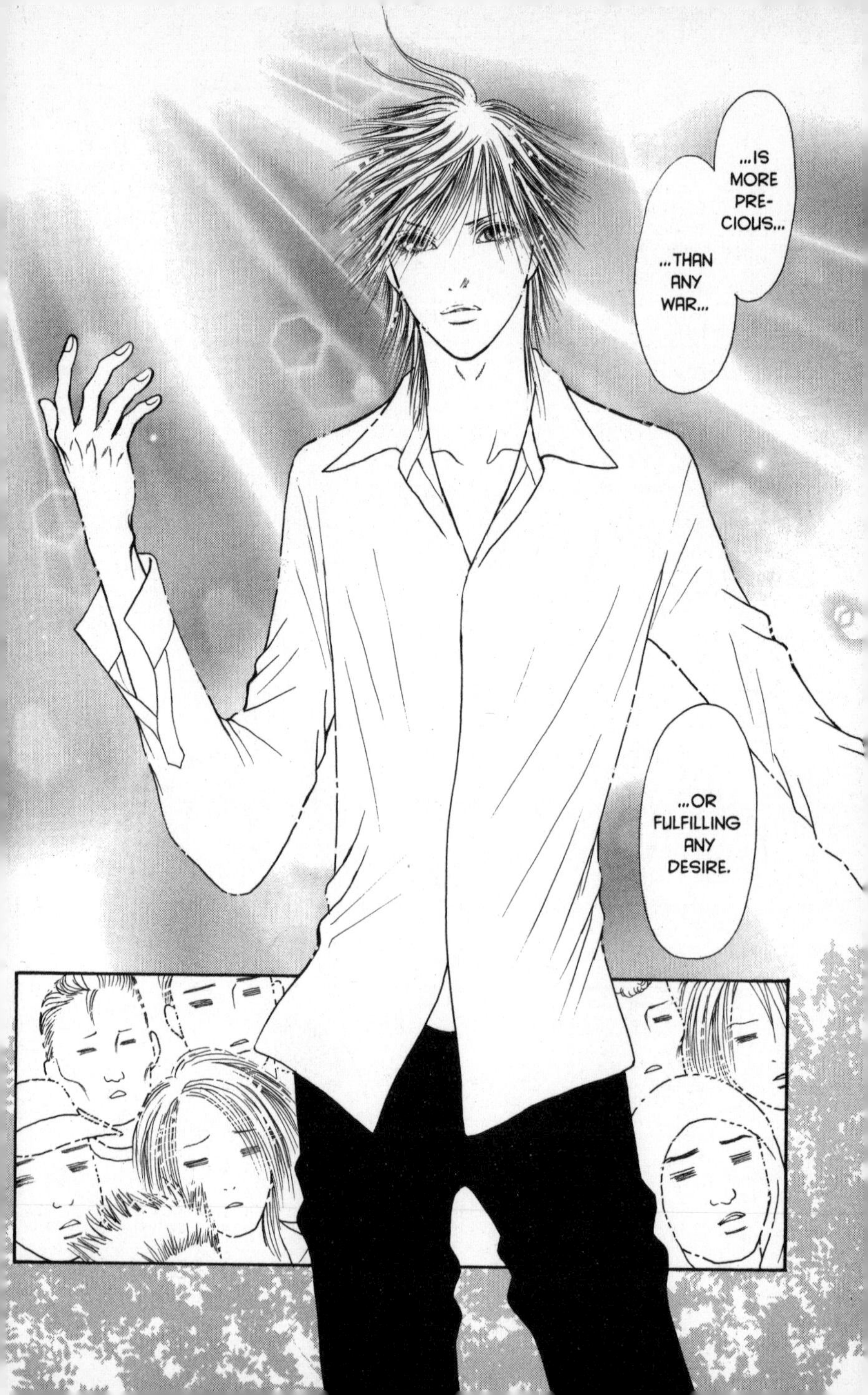
...IS MORE PRECIOUS...
...THAN ANY WAR...
...OR FULFILLING ANY DESIRE.

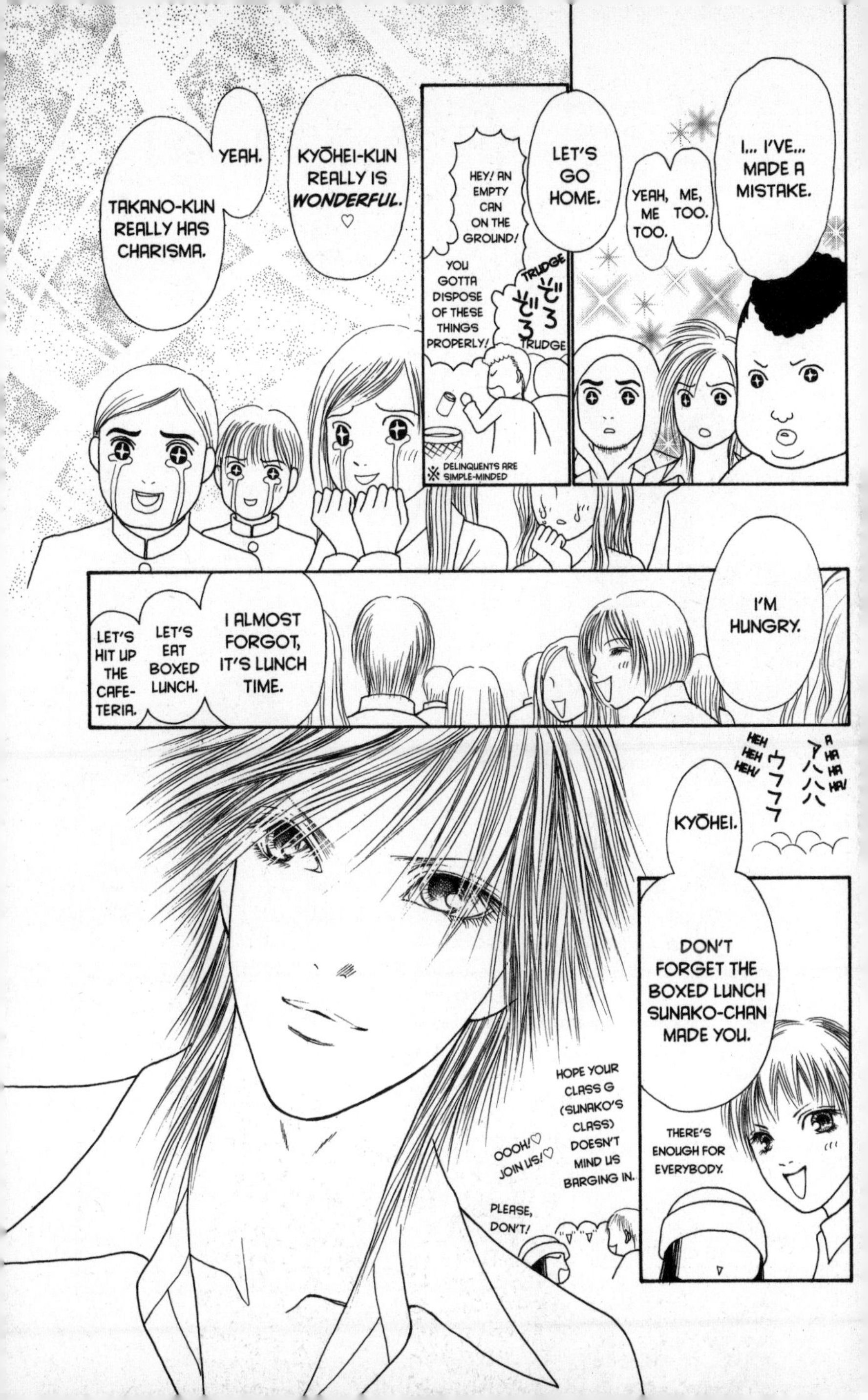
I... I'VE... MADE A MISTAKE.
ME, TOO.
YEAH, ME TOO.
LET'S GO HOME.
HEY! AN EMPTY CAN ON THE GROUND!
YOU GOTTA DISPOSE OF THESE THINGS PROPERLY!
TRUDGE TRUDGE
※ DELINQUENTS ARE SIMPLE-MINDED
KYŌHEI-KUN REALLY IS *WONDERFUL*. ♡
YEAH.
TAKANO-KUN REALLY HAS CHARISMA.
I'M HUNGRY.
I ALMOST FORGOT, IT'S LUNCH TIME.
LET'S EAT BOXED LUNCH.
LET'S HIT UP THE CAFETERIA.
A HA HA HA!
HEH HEH HEH!
KYŌHEI.
DON'T FORGET THE BOXED LUNCH SUNAKO-CHAN MADE YOU.
THERE'S ENOUGH FOR EVERYBODY.
HOPE YOUR CLASS G (SUNAKO'S CLASS) DOESN'T MIND US BARGING IN.
OOOH!♡ JOIN US!♡
PLEASE, DON'T!

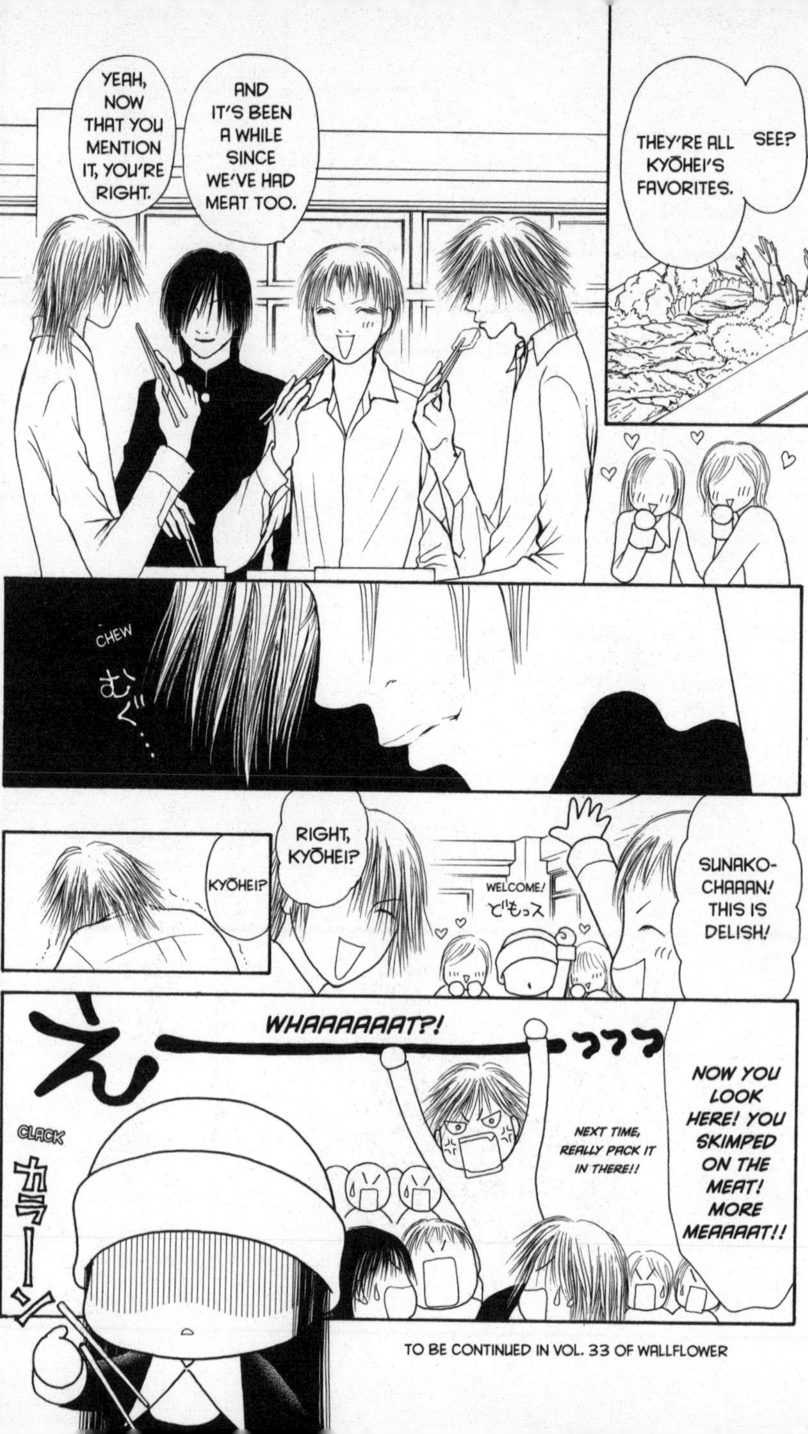
SEE?
THEY'RE ALL KYŌHEI'S FAVORITES.
AND IT'S BEEN A WHILE SINCE WE'VE HAD MEAT TOO.
YEAH, NOW THAT YOU MENTION IT, YOU'RE RIGHT.
CHEW
むぐ…
SUNAKO-CHAAAN! THIS IS DELISH!
WELCOME!
どもっス
RIGHT, KYŌHEI?
KYŌHEI?
NOW YOU LOOK HERE! YOU SKIMPED ON THE MEAT! MORE MEAAAAT!!
NEXT TIME, REALLY PACK IT IN THERE!!
WHAAAAAAT?!
えーーっっっ
CLACK
カラーン

TO BE CONTINUED IN VOL. 33 OF WALLFLOWER

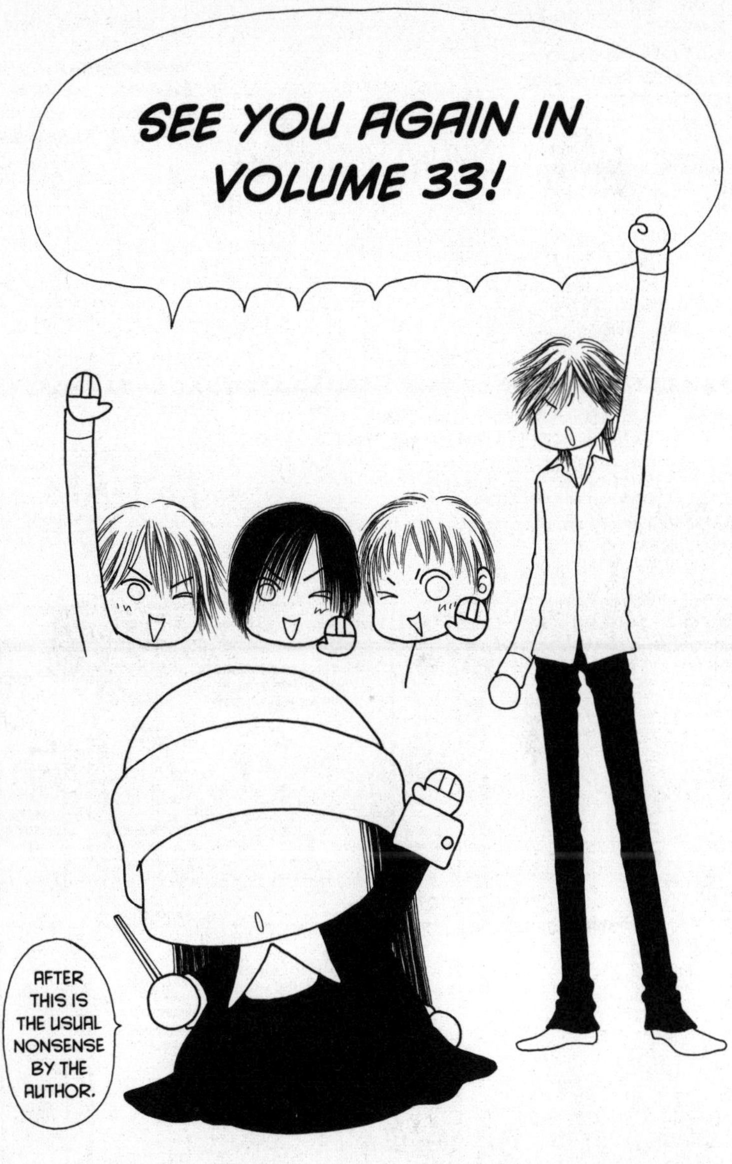
SEE YOU AGAIN IN VOLUME 33!
AFTER THIS IS THE USUAL NONSENSE BY THE AUTHOR.

THANK YOU FOR PURCHASING THIS KODANSHA COMIC♡

THE FACT THAT THE STORY'S GONE ON FOR AS LONG AS IT HAS IS REEEEEALLY ALL THANKS TO YOU GUYS.

I HAVE NOTHING BUT GRATITUDE FOR YOU. ♡

THANK YOU TO ALL OF YOU WHO WRITE ME. ♡♡♡

YOU ARE THE SOURCE OF MY POWER.

I'M AS DOTING A PARENT AS EVER AND LOVE MORE THAN ANYTHING THE TIME I SPEND SNUGGLING WITH TEN. ♡

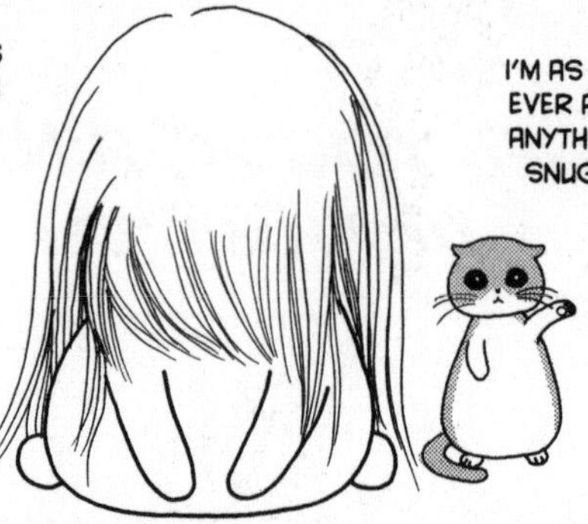
SOMETIMES TEN REALLY DOES TAKE THIS POSE. ♡ SO CUTE! ♡

I WENT TO SEE DREAM BOYS 2012

SEPTEMBER!! I TOOK AN ACTUAL VACATION IN SEPTEMBER ♡
SO I COULD GO SEE DREAM BOYS ON STAGE ANY TIME I WANTED! ♡

I CAN GO AT THE END OF THE MONTH TOO ♡♡♡
EVEN FOR THE CLOSING PERFORMANCE. ♡
(THOUGH I ENDED UP NOT BEING ABLE TO GO)

KAMENASHI-KUN WAS SO SERIOUSLY SUPER DUPER COOL THAT IT WAS JUST *CRAZY* ♡♡♡

REALLY "COOL" IS ALL I CAN DESCRIBE HIM WITH. ♡♡♡

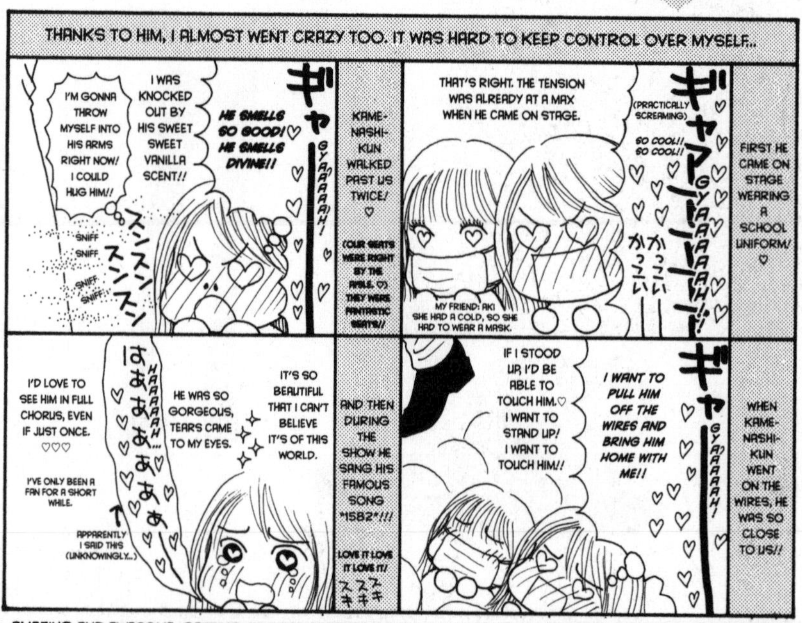
THANKS TO HIM, I ALMOST WENT CRAZY TOO. IT WAS HARD TO KEEP CONTROL OVER MYSELF...
FIRST HE CAME ON STAGE WEARING A SCHOOL UNIFORM! ♡
ギャアーーー!! GYAAAAAAAH!!
(PRACTICALLY SCREAMING)
SO COOL!! SO COOL!!
かっこいい かっこいい
THAT'S RIGHT. THE TENSION WAS ALREADY AT A MAX WHEN HE CAME ON STAGE.
MY FRIEND: AKI SHE HAD A COLD, SO SHE HAD TO WEAR A MASK.
KAME-NASHI-KUN WALKED PAST US TWICE! ♡
(OUR SEATS WERE RIGHT BY THE AISLE. ♡) THEY WERE FANTASTIC SEATS!!
ギャ GYAAAAAH!
HE SMELLS SO GOOD! ♡ HE SMELLS DIVINE!!
I WAS KNOCKED OUT BY HIS SWEET SWEET VANILLA SCENT!!
I'M GONNA THROW MYSELF INTO HIS ARMS RIGHT NOW! I COULD HUG HIM!!
スンスン スンスン
SNIFF SNIFF SNIFF SNIFF
WHEN KAME-NASHI-KUN WENT ON THE WIRES, HE WAS SO CLOSE TO US!!
ギャ GYAAAAAH!
I WANT TO PULL HIM OFF THE WIRES AND BRING HIM HOME WITH ME!!
IF I STOOD UP, I'D BE ABLE TO TOUCH HIM. ♡ I WANT TO STAND UP! I WANT TO TOUCH HIM!!
AND THEN DURING THE SHOW HE SANG HIS FAMOUS SONG "1582"!!!
LOVE IT LOVE IT LOVE IT!
ステキ ステキ ステキ
IT'S SO BEAUTIFUL THAT I CAN'T BELIEVE IT'S OF THIS WORLD.
HE WAS SO GORGEOUS, TEARS CAME TO MY EYES.
はあああああ HAAAAAH...
I'D LOVE TO SEE HIM IN FULL CHORUS, EVEN IF JUST ONCE. ♡♡♡
I'VE ONLY BEEN A FAN FOR A SHORT WHILE.
APPARENTLY I SAID THIS (UNKNOWINGLY...)

AMAZING AND AWESOME. GETTING TO WATCH FROM A GREAT SEAT MADE ME SO HAPPY. ♡♡♡ THOUGH I'D HAVE BEEN ABLE TO ENJOY IT FROM THE VERY BACK SEAT TOO!! THEY WERE GREAT SEATS! ♡

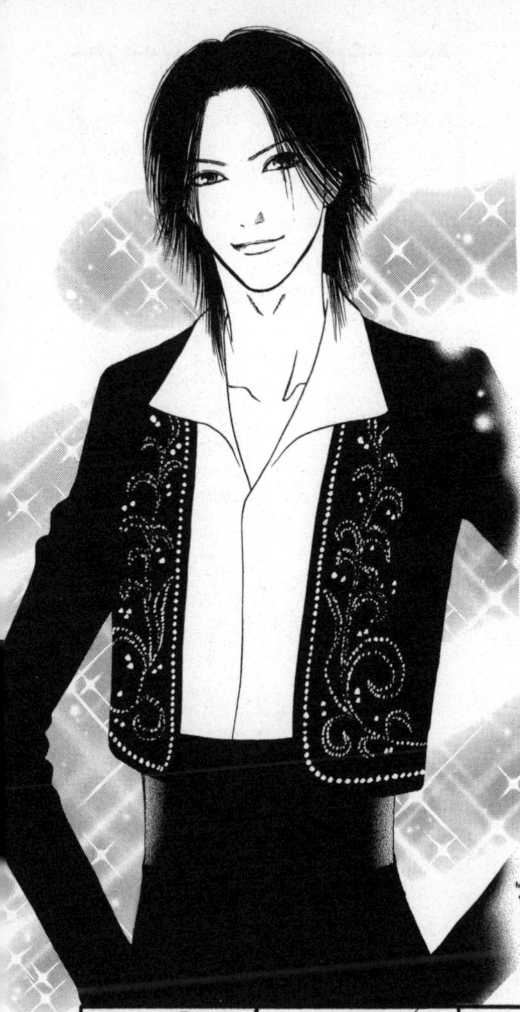

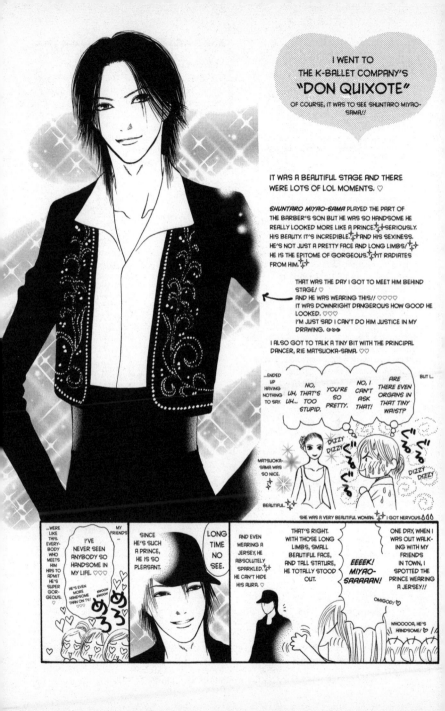

I WENT TO THE K-BALLET COMPANY'S "DON QUIXOTE"

OF COURSE, IT WAS TO SEE SHUNTARO MIYAO-SAMA!!

IT WAS A BEAUTIFUL STAGE AND THERE WERE LOTS OF LOL MOMENTS. ♡

SHUNTARO MIYAO-SAMA PLAYED THE PART OF THE BARBER'S SON BUT HE WAS SO HANDSOME HE REALLY LOOKED MORE LIKE A PRINCE. SERIOUSLY. HIS BEAUTY. IT'S INCREDIBLE. AND HIS SEXINESS. HE'S NOT JUST A PRETTY FACE AND LONG LIMBS! HE IS THE EPITOME OF GORGEOUS. IT RADIATES FROM HIM.

THAT WAS THE DAY I GOT TO MEET HIM BEHIND STAGE! ♡
AND HE WAS WEARING THIS!! ♡♡♡♡
IT WAS DOWNRIGHT DANGEROUS HOW GOOD HE LOOKED. ♡♡♡
I'M JUST SAD I CAN'T DO HIM JUSTICE IN MY DRAWING.

I ALSO GOT TO TALK A TINY BIT WITH THE PRINCIPAL DANCER, RIE MATSUOKA-SAMA. ♡♡

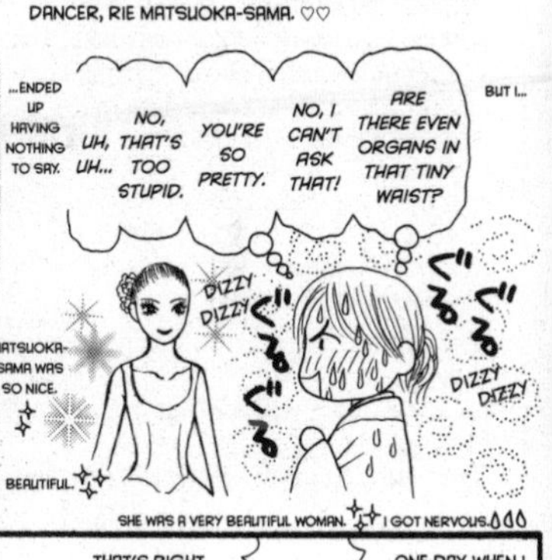
BUT I...
ARE THERE EVEN ORGANS IN THAT TINY WAIST?
NO, I CAN'T ASK THAT!
YOU'RE SO PRETTY.
NO, THAT'S TOO STUPID.
UH, UH...
...ENDED UP HAVING NOTHING TO SAY.
ぐるぐる
ぐるぐる
DIZZY DIZZY
DIZZY DIZZY
MATSUOKA-SAMA WAS SO NICE.
BEAUTIFUL.
SHE WAS A VERY BEAUTIFUL WOMAN. I GOT NERVOUS.

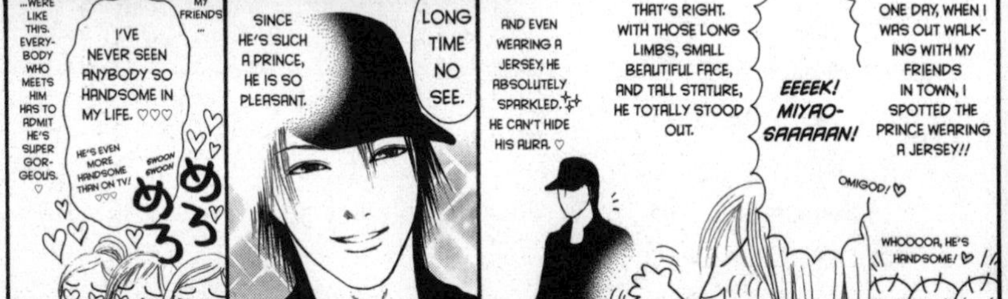
ONE DAY, WHEN I WAS OUT WALKING WITH MY FRIENDS IN TOWN, I SPOTTED THE PRINCE WEARING A JERSEY!!
EEEEK! MIYAO-SAAAAAN!
OMIGOD! ♡
WHOOOOA, HE'S HANDSOME!
THAT'S RIGHT. WITH THOSE LONG LIMBS, SMALL BEAUTIFUL FACE, AND TALL STATURE, HE TOTALLY STOOD OUT.
AND EVEN WEARING A JERSEY, HE ABSOLUTELY SPARKLED. HE CAN'T HIDE HIS AURA. ♡
LONG TIME NO SEE.
SINCE HE'S SUCH A PRINCE, HE IS SO PLEASANT.
MY FRIENDS...
I'VE NEVER SEEN ANYBODY SO HANDSOME IN MY LIFE. ♡♡♡
SWOON SWOON
HE'S EVEN MORE HANDSOME THAN ON TV! ♡♡♡
めろめろ
...WERE LIKE THIS. EVERYBODY WHO MEETS HIM HAS TO ADMIT HE'S SUPER GORGEOUS. ♡

A COUPLE OF YEARS AGO, I WANDERED INTO A SALON AND ENCOUNTERED AN EXTREMELY TALENTED HAIRDRESSER. (AND SHE'S SUPER CUTE TO BOOT) ♡
I LEAVE MY HAIR DYING, CUT AND LENGTH AAAAAALL TO HER. ♡
THAT'S WHY MY MAKE-OVER WAS SO SUCCESSFUL. ♡
THANKS, AI-CHAN. ♡
I LOVE MY NEW LOOK SO MUCH! ♡♡
AND I GET COMPLIMENTS FROM EVERYONE I MEET. ♡

❀❀❀❀❀❀❀❀❀❀❀❀❀

MY FAVORITE FORTUNETELLER
MIKHAIL-SAN ALSO SAID IT WAS A GOOD MOVE!!
I WONDER IF IT'LL GIVE ME MORE LUCK IN LOVE... ♡
HOW THINGS STAND NOW, THERE'S NOTHING IN THE WORKS!!
MIKHAIL-SAN IS INCREDIBLE. ♡
NATURALLY, SHE HITS THE MARK. WHEN I TALK WITH HER, I FEEL LIKE MY HEART IS BEING RESET.
SO I HAVEN'T BEEN WORRYING AT ALL THESE DAYS.

❀❀❀❀❀❀❀❀❀❀❀❀❀

MY VOICE TRAINER RYONRYON ALSO COMPLIMENTED ME. ♡
SHE KEPT TELLING ME, "BLACK HIDES THE COLOR OF YOUR FACE SO WEAR MORE ATTRACTIVE CLOTHES."
AND I GUESS I FINALLY HEARD HER. ⊙⊙
RYONRYON ALWAYS TELLS ME THINGS FOR MY OWN GOOD. ♡
I READ HER "TRAINING BOOK". IT HELPED OUT EVEN SOMEONE LIKE ME WHO CAN'T SING. ✧
RYONRYON REALLY IS AMAZING. ✧ AND THE BOOK COMES WITH A DVD. ✧

RECENTLY, WOULDN'T YOU BELIEVE IT?! I'VE UNDERGONE A MAKE-OVER!!

WHO CARES?
NOBODY, BUT HERE IT GOES ANYWAY:

ALL IN BLACK
CAN'T SEE ANKLES
SKIRTS
OR PANTS

FROM THIS...

BLACK SEAL

I WEAR PINK OR FLORAL PRINT DRESSES AND EVEN JEANS. I SOMETIMES EVEN SHOW MY LEGS. EVEN THOUGH I SWORE I NEVER WOULD. THANKS, TATTOO STOCKINGS! MY WARDROBE'S DONE A COMPLETE TURNAROUND.

AFTER MY MAKE-OVER, MY FRIENDS DIDN'T EVEN RECOGNIZE ME.
I GUESS I'D GOTTEN USED TO IT ALREADY.
BUT REALLY, MY SHOES, BAG, AND EVERYTHING IS DIFFERENT NOW.
THEY USED TO CALL ME "AN OFFICE LADY ON HOLIDAY".
AS USUAL, I STILL CHOOSE CLOTHES THAT HIDE THE CONTOURS OF MY BODY.
OTHERWISE, IT'D *SHOW HOW FAT I AM.*

IF I DON'T GET SERIOUS ABOUT MY DIET, I'LL BE IN REAL TROUBLE!!
HOW MANY YEARS HAVE I BEEN TELLING MYSELF THAT...?
BUT THIS TIME, I'M REALLY GOING TO WORK AT IT!!
HOW MANY TIMES HAVE I SAID THAT BEFORE...?

❀❀❀❀❀❀❀❀❀❀❀❀❀❀❀❀❀❀❀❀❀❀❀❀❀❀❀

AND WITH THAT... THANK YOU FOR STAYING WITH ME FOR THIS WHOLE LONG TIME.

SEE YOU AGAIN IN VOLUME 33! ♡

FOR SURE! ♡

SPECIAL THANKS

TOMMY   AKI-CHAN   ALL MY EDITORS

CHIAKI-CHAN   AND THANKS TO YOU FOR READING ♡

YOSSHII

A Note from the Author

♡♡♡ My pet cat, Ten ♡♡♡

She's a prim girl, but...

...when she drinks water, this is the other awful face she makes.
She looks like an owl, but she's still the world's cutest kitty. ♡

(I'm a doting mama)

Translation Notes

Japanese is a tricky language for most Westerners, and translation is often more art than science. For your edification and reading pleasure, here are notes on some of the places where we could have gone in a different direction in our tranlsation of the work, or where a Japanese cultural reference is used.

Page 41
Visual Kei

A genre of musician in Japan featuring really elaborate make-up and hairstyles, that can have a somewhat dark edginess to them. Hence the relation to Sunako's spooky room.

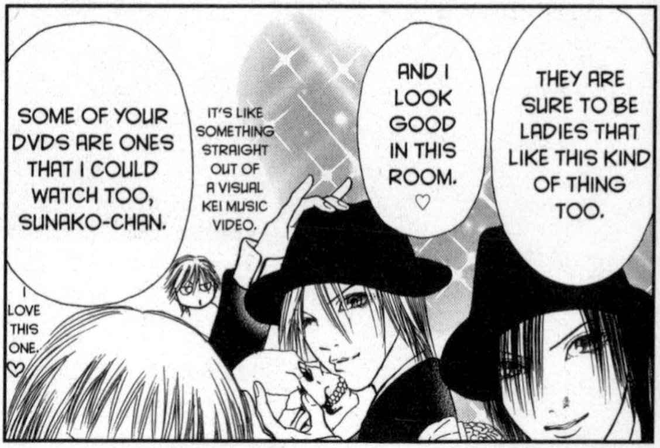
THEY ARE SURE TO BE LADIES THAT LIKE THIS KIND OF THING TOO.
AND I LOOK GOOD IN THIS ROOM. ♡
IT'S LIKE SOMETHING STRAIGHT OUT OF A VISUAL KEI MUSIC VIDEO.
SOME OF YOUR DVDS ARE ONES THAT I COULD WATCH TOO, SUNAKO-CHAN.
I LOVE THIS ONE. ♡

Page 45
nagashi-somen

A style of enjoying thin wheat noodles (somen) by way of flowing them down a bamboo flume with running water and having to catch them with your chopsticks as they pass by. This is particularly popular in the summer time.

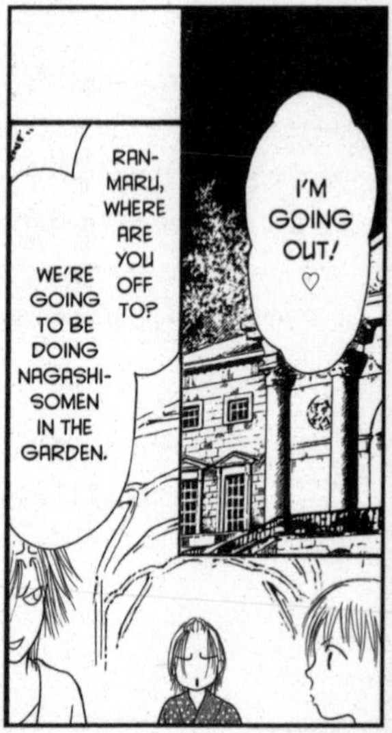
I'M GOING OUT! ♡
RAN-MARU, WHERE ARE YOU OFF TO?
WE'RE GOING TO BE DOING NAGASHI-SOMEN IN THE GARDEN.

Page 45

kinshi tamago

Thinly sliced fried eggs that are used as toppings and garnish for dishes such as noodles, or in this case, nagashi-somen.

yukata

A light version of the kimono, typically worn in the summer for festivals and the like.

NO CUCUMBERS FOR ME.
IGNORING
I WANT A LOT OF KINSHI TAMAGO. ♡
AND GINGER AND PERILLA TOO. ♡
I AM A BUTTERFLY OF THE NIGHT.
TODAY IS THE ONE AND ONLY YUKATA DAY OF THE YEAR!
SEE YOU LATER! ♡
HE'S GOING TO A HOSTESS BAR.
UH... UM...!

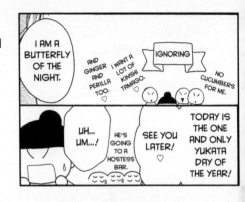

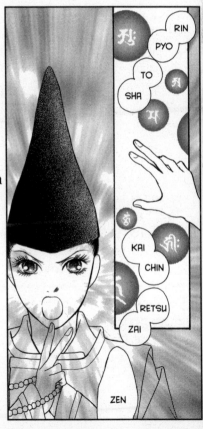

Page 66

RinPyoToShaKaiChinRetsuZaiZen

Meaning "celestial soldiers descend and arrange yourselves in front of me, these nine syllables are a mantra from Buddhist tradition that are supposed to invoke power to the speaker.

RIN
PYO
TO
SHA
KAI
CHIN
RETSU
ZAI
ZEN

Page 96
Shuntaro Miyao

A Japanese actor who plays the part of Ranmaru in the drama version of The Wallflower.

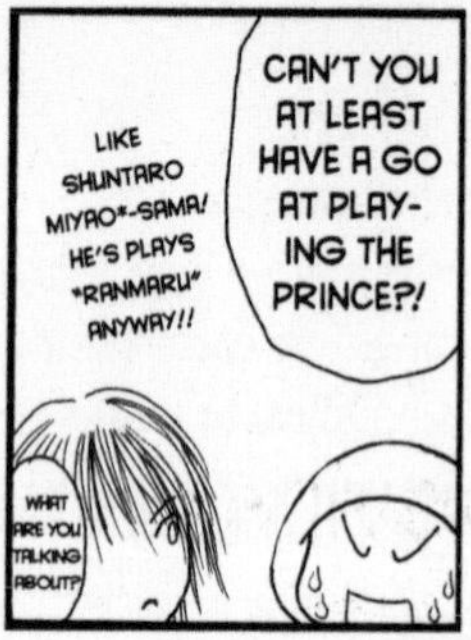
CAN'T YOU AT LEAST HAVE A GO AT PLAY-ING THE PRINCE?!
LIKE SHUNTARO MIYAO*-SAMA! HE'S PLAYS "RANMARU" ANYWAY!!
WHAT ARE YOU TALKING ABOUT?

Page 132
Koushien

A famous baseball stadium that hosts the national high school baseball tournaments.

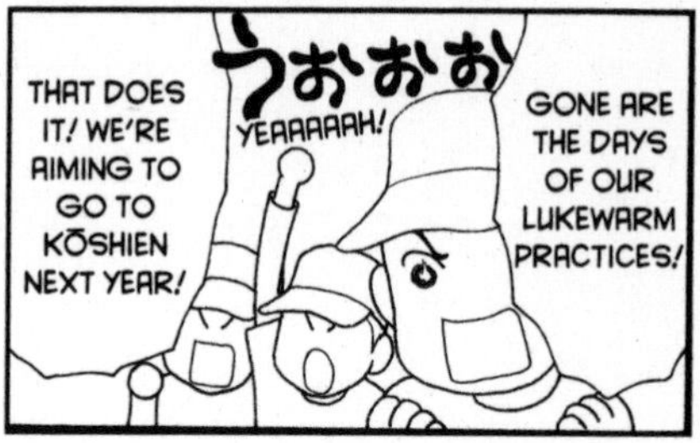
GONE ARE THE DAYS OF OUR LUKEWARM PRACTICES!
うおおお
YEAAAAAH!
THAT DOES IT! WE'RE AIMING TO GO TO KŌSHIEN NEXT YEAR!

Page 141
"herbivore guy"

A fad, of sorts, for men to be meeker, gentle, and not the type to take advantage of women. The "herbivore" part referring to how herbivorous animals tend to be more docile than, say, carnivores.

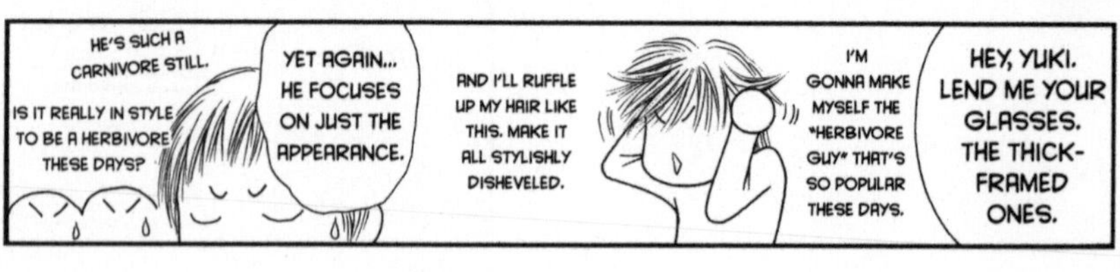
HEY, YUKI. LEND ME YOUR GLASSES. THE THICK-FRAMED ONES.
I'M GONNA MAKE MYSELF THE "HERBIVORE GUY" THAT'S SO POPULAR THESE DAYS.
AND I'LL RUFFLE UP MY HAIR LIKE THIS. MAKE IT ALL STYLISHLY DISHEVELED.
YET AGAIN... HE FOCUSES ON JUST THE APPEARANCE.
HE'S SUCH A CARNIVORE STILL.
IS IT REALLY IN STYLE TO BE A HERBIVORE THESE DAYS?

PREVIEW OF THE WALLFLOWER, VOLUME 33

WE'RE PLEASED TO PRESENT YOU A PREVIEW FROM THE WALLFLOWER, VOLUME 33. PLEASE CHECK OUR WEBSITE (KODANSHACOMICS.COM) TO SEE WHEN THIS VOLUME WILL BE AVAILABLE IN ENGLISH.

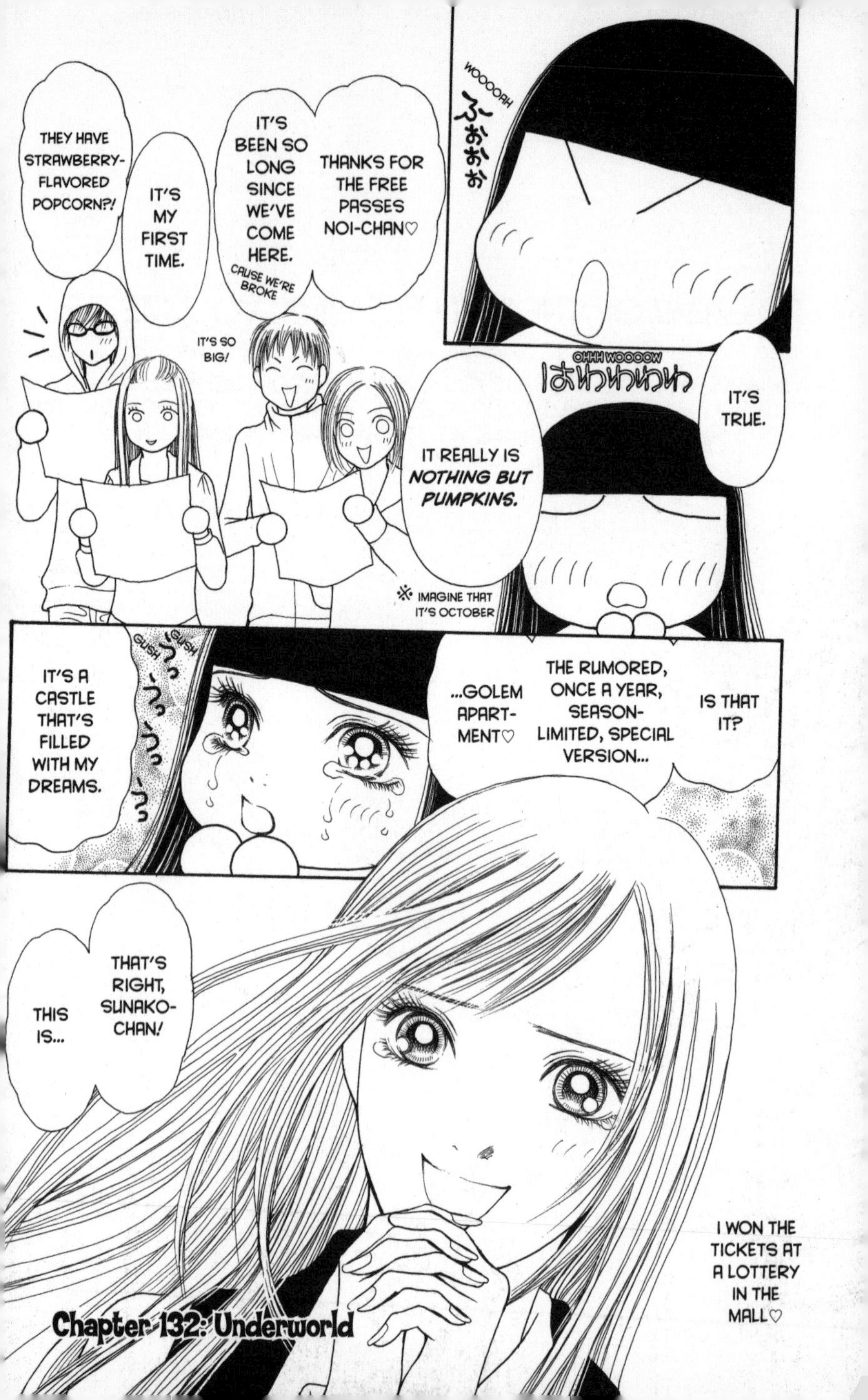
WOOOOAH
ふぉおお
OHHH WOOOOW
はわわわわ
IT'S TRUE.
THANKS FOR THE FREE PASSES NOI-CHAN♡
IT'S BEEN SO LONG SINCE WE'VE COME HERE.
CAUSE WE'RE BROKE
IT'S MY FIRST TIME.
THEY HAVE STRAWBERRY-FLAVORED POPCORN?!
IT'S SO BIG!
IT REALLY IS *NOTHING BUT PUMPKINS.*
※ IMAGINE THAT IT'S OCTOBER
IS THAT IT?
THE RUMORED, ONCE A YEAR, SEASON-LIMITED, SPECIAL VERSION...
...GOLEM APARTMENT♡
GUSH GUSH
うっうっうっうっ
IT'S A CASTLE THAT'S FILLED WITH MY DREAMS.
I WON THE TICKETS AT A LOTTERY IN THE MALL♡
THAT'S RIGHT, SUNAKO-CHAN!
THIS IS...
Chapter 132: Underworld

Chapter 132: Underworld

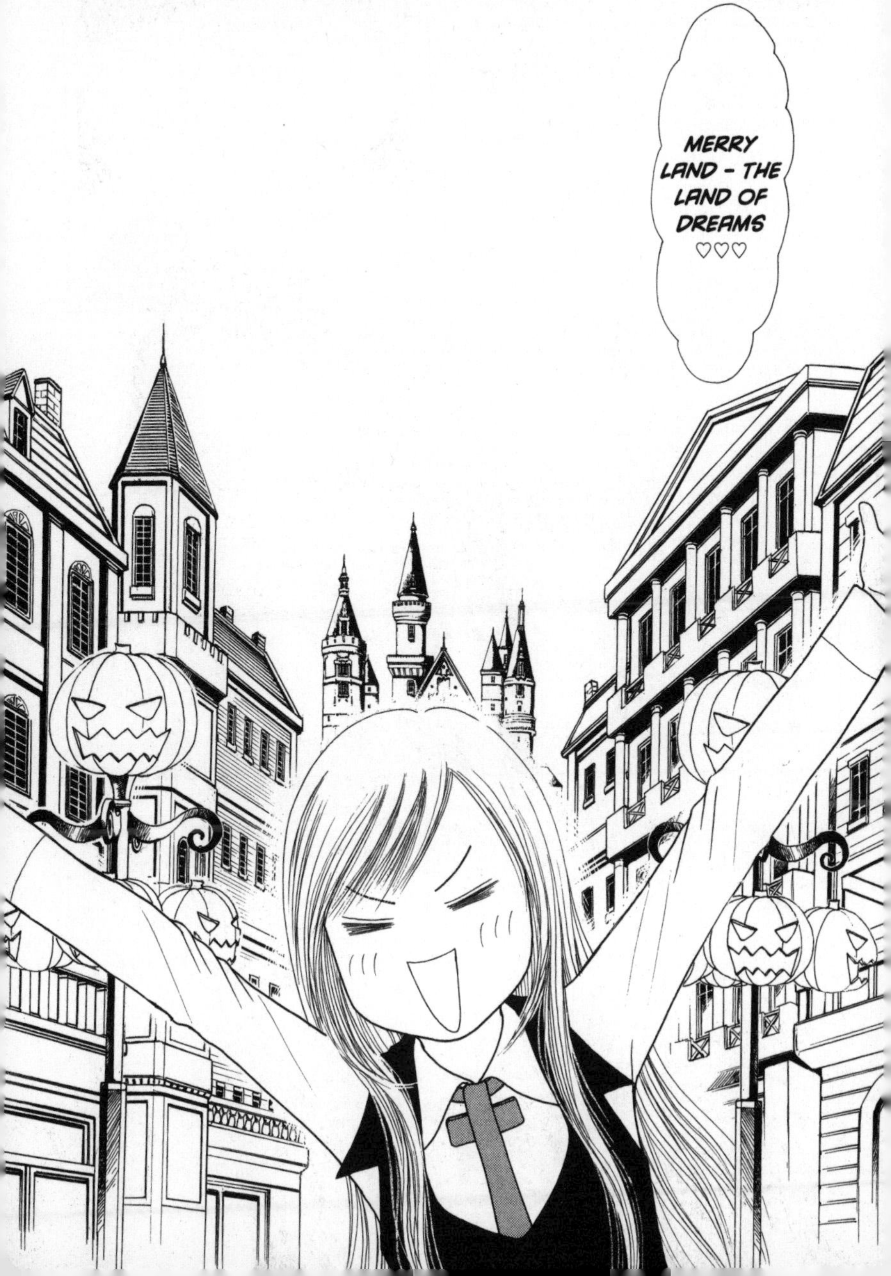
MERRY LAND - THE LAND OF DREAMS ♡♡♡

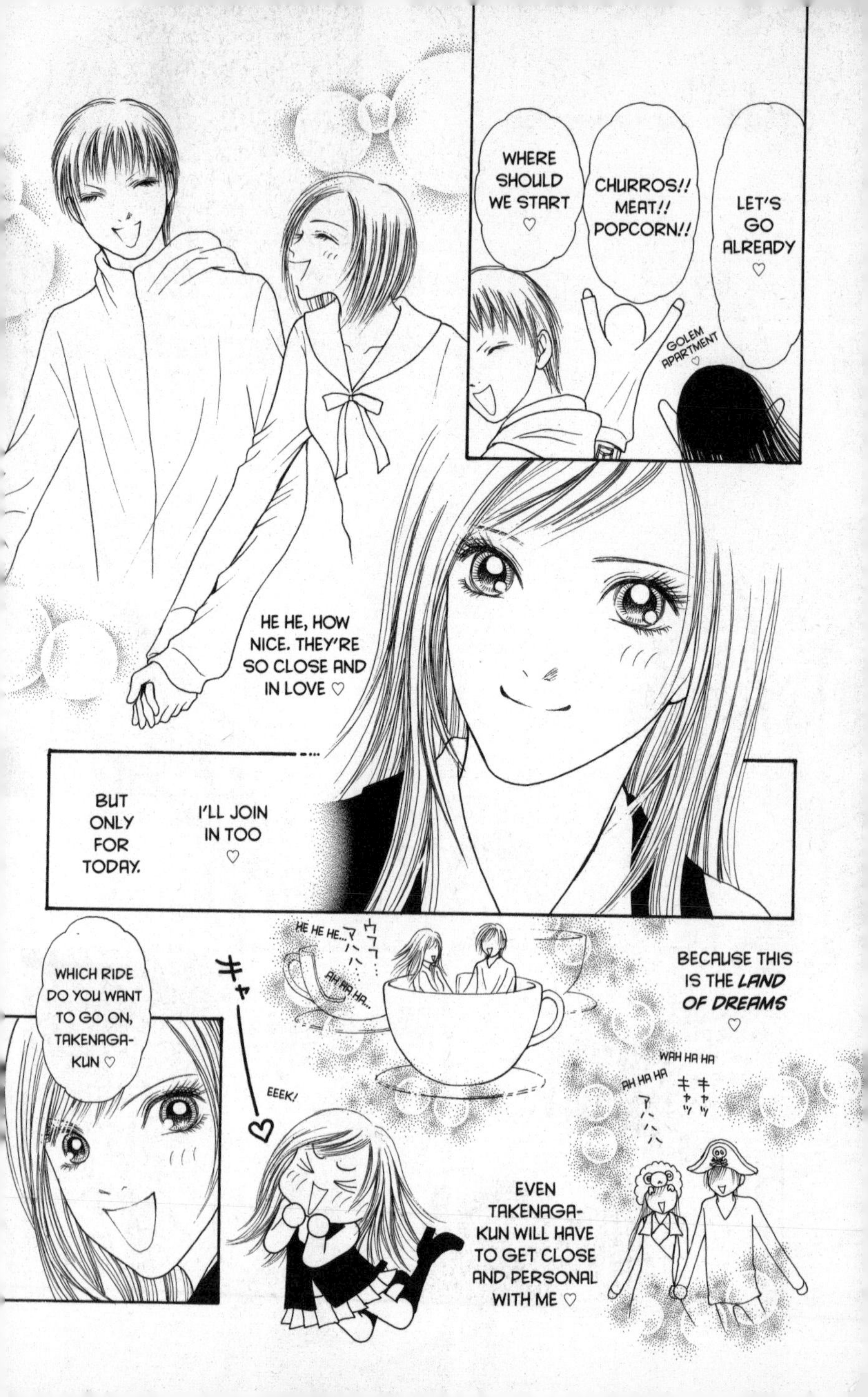
LET'S GO ALREADY ♡
CHURROS!! MEAT!! POPCORN!!
WHERE SHOULD WE START ♡
GOLEM APARTMENT ♡
HE HE, HOW NICE. THEY'RE SO CLOSE AND IN LOVE ♡
I'LL JOIN IN TOO ♡
BUT ONLY FOR TODAY.
BECAUSE THIS IS THE *LAND OF DREAMS* ♡
ウフフ
HE HE HE...
アハハ
AH HA HA...
WAH HA HA
キャッ キャッ
AH HA HA
アハハ
EVEN TAKENAGA-KUN WILL HAVE TO GET CLOSE AND PERSONAL WITH ME ♡
キャー ♡
EEEK!
WHICH RIDE DO YOU WANT TO GO ON, TAKENAGA-KUN ♡

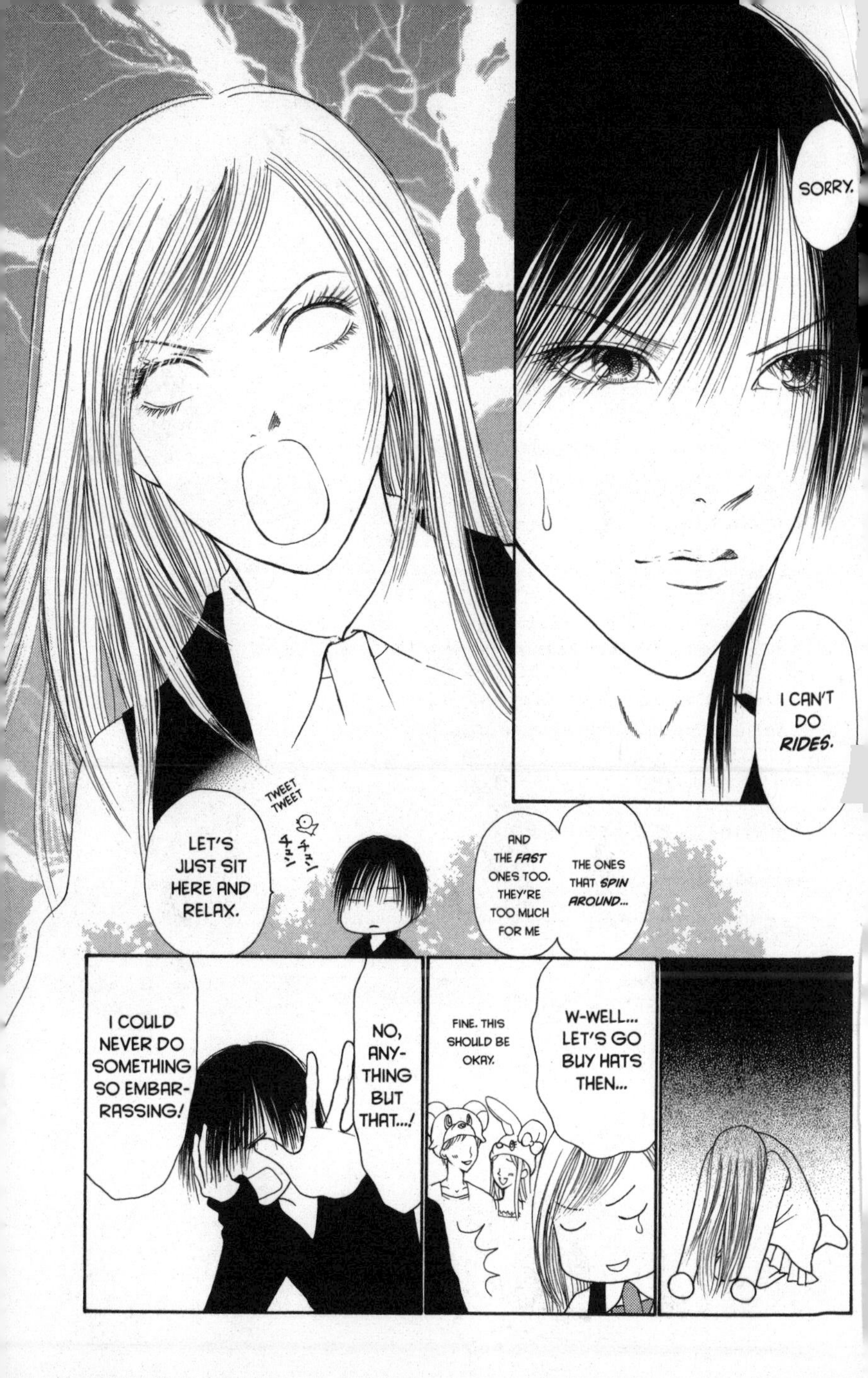
SORRY.
I CAN'T DO *RIDES.*
THE ONES THAT *SPIN AROUND...*
AND THE *FAST* ONES TOO. THEY'RE TOO MUCH FOR ME
TWEET TWEET
チュン チュン
LET'S JUST SIT HERE AND RELAX.
W-WELL... LET'S GO BUY HATS THEN...
FINE. THIS SHOULD BE OKAY.
NO, ANY-THING BUT THAT...!
I COULD NEVER DO SOMETHING SO EMBAR-RASSING!

The Wallflower volume 32 is a work of fiction. Names, characters, places, and incidents are the products of the author's imagination or are used fictitiously. Any resemblance to actual events, locales, or persons, living or dead, is entirely coincidental.

A Kodansha Comics Trade Paperback Original.

Published in the United States by Kodansha Comics, an imprint of Kodansha USA Publishing, LLC, New York.

Publication rights for this English edition arranged through Kodansha Ltd., Tokyo.

First published in Japan in 2012 by Kodansha Ltd., Tokyo
as *Yamatonadeshiko Shichihenge* volume 32

ISBN 978-1-61262-443-3

Printed in the United States of America.

www.kodanshacomics.com

9 8 7 6 5 4 3 2 1

Translator: Christine Dashiell
Lettering: Sara Linsley